Testing the Theory of the
Military-Industrial Complex

Testing the Theory of the Military-Industrial Complex

Steven Rosen
Brandeis University
Editor

Lexington Books
D.C. Heath and Company
Lexington, Massachusetts
Toronto   London

Library of Congress Cataloging in Publication Data

Rosen, Steven, comp.
    Testing the theory of the military-industrial complex.

    CONTENTS: Rosen, S. Testing the theory of the military-industrial
complex.—Slater, J. and Nardin, T. The concept of a military-industrial
complex.—Lieberson, S. An empirical study of military-industrial linkages.
[etc.]
    1. Defense   contracts—United   States—Addresses,   essays,   lectures.
2. Disarmament—Economic aspects—United States—Addresses, essays, lec-
tures.
I. Title.
HC110.D4R64   338.4'7'35562   72-13003
ISBN 0-669-84871-9

Published simultaneously in Canada.

Printed in the United States of America.

International Standard Book Number: 0-669-84871-9

Library of Congress Catalog Card Number: 72-13003

Contents

List of Tables

List of Figures

Testing the Theory of the Military-Industrial Complex

1

Testing the Theory of the Military-Industrial Complex

Steven Rosen

The theory of the military-industrial complex is now one of the most familiar ideas in political thought. It surprises younger students to learn that the modern version of the concept was formulated as recently as 1956 by C. Wright Mills in his classic, *The Power Elite*, and that the idea did not enter the vernacular of popular discourse until 1961, when President Eisenhower gave his famous warning in the Farewell Address:

(The) conjunction of an immense military establishment and a large arms industry is new in the American experience. The total influence—economic, political, even spiritual—is felt in every city, every State House, every office of the Federal Government. . . . We must guard against the acquisition of unwarranted influence, whether sought or unsought, by the military-industrial complex. The potential for the disastrous rise of misplaced power exists and will persist.

In a mere fifteen years, Mills' theory, legitimized by Eisenhower, has come from relative obscurity to being one of the foremost analytical tools employed by laymen to explain events and tendencies, particularly unhappy ones, in American foreign and strategic policy. The theory is employed to explain the high cost of defense, the longevity of the Cold War, the persistence of anticommunist mythology, the "perverted priorities" of the Federal budget, the interventionist proclivities of American foreign policy, and even the generation of cultural values giving rise to riots and assassinations. The theory is part of the consciousness of every attentive student of politics and society.

Yet during this meteoric intellectual rise, very little *scientific* effort has been given to the systematic *testing* of the key propositions in the theory. One can search the pages of the scholarly journals for the years 1956 to 1970 and find only a few attempts to validate or invalidate the theory by rigorous examination of carefully-delineated hypotheses. For example, a recent literature search employing several computerized information bibliographies failed to yield a single reference to "military-industrial complex" in the American Political Science Review for these years (though there were references to several related and tangential topics). To a very large extent, the discussion has been left to polemics by both adherents and opponents of the theory.

This is not to suggest any shortage of data. A vast literature has developed on both sides of the issue. However, scientific use of this data is often limited by the ideological selectivity that guided its compilation. Even the most quantitative polemical studies tend to be collections of sympathetic statistical anecdotes to illustrate truths already arrived at, rather than honest efforts at objectivity. A truly scientific approach to research on the military-industrial complex cannot rely on secondary analysis of this data.

In recent years, a new stream of empirical research has turned to this subject, perhaps stimulated by widespread demands for a relevant but scientific social science. Across the social disciplines, serious efforts are underway to identify pivotal propositions in the theory, formulate them as researchable hypotheses, and subject them to methodologically rigorous efforts at falsification. Broad ideological differences are being reformulated as carefully-defined empirical and analytical issues. The result is not always to reduce the zone of disagreement, but some success is being achieved in developing a cumulative body of confirmed findings which must be explained by theorists regardless of their ideological predispositions. In other words, the goal is to raise the level of discourse and to narrow wide divergences to precise issues.

This book brings together a broad representation of the most pertinent research on the question of testing the theory of the military-industrial complex. Some of the papers derive from meetings at the 1972 International Studies Association convention in Dallas. To these, we have added several new studies and a few previously published pieces which are presented here for their especially close relation to our topic. Taken together, these essays comprise a systematic examination of many of the key empirical and analytical issues in the debate over the military-industrial complex. The authors represent a diversity of academic disciplines and a broad range of ideological positions. What they share is a common commitment to a scientific understanding of this difficult issue.

Summary of the Theory

It may be useful to provide a working summary of the theory under examination, before discussing the papers. The following are the key propositions in the theory as argued by the leading proponents.

The prolonged state of international tensions that has existed since 1945 has been characterized by high levels of military expenditure by the major powers, especially the United States and the Soviet Union. These high levels of expenditure have given rise to powerful domestic groups within the major states who have vested interests in the continuance of military spending and international conflict. These domestic groups who comprise the military-industrial complex include (1) the professional soldiers, (2) managers and (in the capitalist states) owners of industries heavily engaged in military supply, (3) high governmental officials whose careers and interests are tied to military expenditure, and (4) legislators whose districts benefit from defense procurement. These core members of the military-industrial complex are supported by associated and lesser groups like the veterans and military service associations, labor unions tied to the defense industry, and scientists and engineers engaged in defense-related research. These various segments of the complex occupy powerful positions within the internal political structures of the major states, and they exercise their influence in a coordinated and mutually-supportive way to achieve and maintain optimal levels of military expenditure and war preparation, and to direct national security policy. On defense-related matters, their influence exceeds that of any countervailing coalitions or interests that may exist.

The military-industrial complex rationalizes high levels of military spending with an ideology of international conflict, mainly the ideology of the Cold War. Theorists disagree as to whether this ideology is a deliberately manufactured deception to mislead the public or whether it is a militaristic "false consciousness" that arises automatically as an unanticipated consequence of high military spending. Under the former version, the complex is a self-conscious conspiracy acting mainly in its own interest. Under the latter version, it is a coalition of special interests who wrongly believe themselves to be acting in the broader public or national interest. Either way, the complex requires an ideology of international conflict to guarantee its position within the political and economic structure of the society. Most theorists regard this conflict ideology as largely false and exaggerated in its description of supposed external dangers to the respective state.

To the conventional theorist, arms races are caused by international conflict and a cycle of mutual fear between opposing states. To the military-industrial complex theorist, the external strategic threat is merely a rationalization for arms policies that are in fact rooted in the self-aggrandizing activities of the internal military-industrial complexes. In the extreme version, this theory holds that wars are due to arms profiteering, military careerism, and the militarism that is produced by standing armies. Some of these analysts feel that the stock market averages respond favorably to war and unfavorably to peace; "war scares" are said to drive the Dow Jones up, while "peace scares" are bearish.

As argued by C. Wright Mills, the theory of the military-industrial complex applies to both capitalist and socialist states. In the latter, the professional military combine with the managers of state defense industries and with related functionaries within the Communist party apparatus and the ministries and bureaucracies. Despite the ideology of conflict between capitalism and communism, there is a considerable degree of harmony of interest between the complexes on the opposing sides, as both desire to maintain a state of conflict. The "hawks" on both sides want to keep the Cold War going.

The Papers

The eleven contributions in this volume reflect on various aspects of this theory. Several of the papers disconfirm propositions in the theory; others support key statements; and some are equivocal in their findings. It may be useful to review the eleven studies briefly and to survey the results of our testing of the theory of the military-industrial complex.

Slater and Nardin

Jerome Slater and Terry Nardin focus on "The Concept of a Military-Industrial Complex." They argue that the phrase has been taken from the polemical to the scientific literature without a critical evaluation of its terms. In particular, four weaknesses debilitate the theory as a foundation for a program of scientific research: (1) reliance on a theory of conspiracy as the basis of causal inference, (2) simplistic economic determinism, (3) inconsistent specification of the supposed membership of the military-industrial complex, and (4) implausible assumptions about the nature, scope, and type of power ascribed to the complex.

Conspiracy. Proponents of the theory dismiss the orthodox strategic rationale as an official mythology based on a misportrayal of the nature of Soviet intentions and capabilities. To explain high levels of military spending, these theorists look instead to the interests and actions of powerful groups. Those who do not dismiss the official strategic rationale, i.e., analysts who see realistic conflict between U.S. and Soviet policies, do not need to resort to exotic conspiracy theories. In principle, acceptance or rejection of the idea that a military-industrial complex exists and is important should not depend on one's international outlook, but in fact the theory is linked to a global ideology of its adherents. Hence, the ideological origin of the theory prevents its use as a set of scientific statements to guide research. In any case, it is dangerous to trace policy to conspiracies when equally plausible and perhaps more parsimonious nonconspiratorial explanations are available.

Crude Economic Determinism. The theory assumes that self-interests, defined in terms of economic or political gain, predominate in determining behavior. This assumption is only one of three possibilities: (1) the complex could act in the public interest; (2) it could believe itself to be acting in the public interest, but incorrectly define national needs because of distorted perceptions induced by an interest in high defense spending; (3) it could act in its own interest while consciously disguising the national interest. Demonstrating that some segment of the complex will benefit from a given policy is not tantamount to a proof that the policy was in fact initiated for this purpose. Inevitably, private interests will be served by a $30 billion annual procurement, but it does not follow that these interests determine policy.

Composition of the Complex. Is the complex an entity composed of a tight network of small interlocking business, military, and political groups wedded by special interest? Or does it also include veterans associations, labor unions, stockholders, universities, engineers, and other large groups in our society? The literature on this subject is quite inconsistent in specifying whether the complex consists of a tiny elite or a broad part of society. If the latter assumption is made, the "theory loses much of its force, which rests on the premise that high policy in the U.S. is the work of a small, largely nonofficial, and unrepresentative group or coalition."

How Powerful is the Complex? The complex theorists employ dubious measures to assess the power of the complex. One device is to select only favorable cases in which policy decisions help the complex, and to infer from these the power of the special interests in getting the policies they want. This is the fallacy of assuming that Y is caused by X merely because X preceded it. Also, this procedure avoids explaining difficult counterexamples of cases in which the special interests lost out; for example, the decline of military spending, the cutback of weapons systems, and the serious troubles of the aerospace industry, which is suffering a collapse of profits. A theory of defense spending must explain nonprocurement as well as procurement. Finally, if the complex does have power, is this based on positive and negative sanctions that it can impose on those who cooperate or resist, or is it due to correspondence between its interests and widely perceived realities?

On the basis of these objections, Slater and Nardin recommend that the concept of the military-industrial complex be discarded as imprecise and colored by ideology. Perhaps their most telling point is the inseparable connection between the theory as it has developed and prior assumptions about the weakness of the Soviet threat. However, from another point of view, this is the major contribution of the theory: it explains anticommunist "false consciousness" and the persistence of Cold War misperception. If one accepts the reality of the Soviet threat (or from the other side, the American threat), then the theory is superfluous to explain high defense spending, just as it would be to explain wartime mobilization against the Nazis in 1943. But if one believes that the external threat is in fact being exaggerated, the theory of the military-industrial complex is both more plausible and more useful as a concept. One must then ask if the imprecisions and inconsistencies identified by Slater and Nardin inhere in the theory or can it be reformulated with greater scientific rigor and exactness?

Lieberson

Stanley Lieberson's "Empirical Study of Military-Industrial Linkages" in the United States tests the theory against an array of original and secondary data.

His results confirm the existence of a complex dependent on high defense spending, but he argues that neither elitist nor pluralist theory satisfactorily explains the results.

Lieberson focuses on three empirical issues: (1) the relationship between major corporations and high defense spending; (2) the effects of defense dependence on the economy as a whole; and (3) the political power of the defense sector as indicated by positions on Congressional committees.

Corporations. The evidence supports the view that there are extensive linkages among defense corporations and between the corporations and the uniformed services. Over 2000 retired officers at or above the grades of colonel or naval captain now serve as executives of major suppliers to the military. This represents an average of twenty-two former officers per major contractor. In addition, interlocking corporate directorships indicate linkages among the corporations. The corporate members of this defense complex tend to be among the largest industrial firms, and the largest firms tend to be active in the complex. However, "the majority of the largest industrial corporations derive only a small portion of their total business from primary military contracts," though there may be substantial indirect benefits to them. A regression analysis of corporate income after taxes in relation to governmental expenditures between 1916 and 1965 shows that "corporate income is more closely linked to nonmilitary expenditures than to military spending." Thus, while a complex of corporations with an interest in high defense expenditures does exist, military procurement is not the main business of the largest corporations.

The Economy. How important is military spending to the American economy as a whole? Lieberson reviews studies by Kokal (1967) and Leontief and associates (1966) which apply input/output analysis to assess the direct and indirect consequences of possible reductions in military expenditures for various sectors of the economy. In general, gains would balance or exceed losses, except for the most highly dependent industrial sectors, provided that compensating increases were made in nonmilitary expenditures. However, the transitional costs might be very high for some industries. Studies of attempted "conversion" by individual companies suggest that this strategy has not been very successful in the past.

Lieberson also shows that the complex is not as large a portion of the economy as is sometimes suggested. Military expenditure has *not* increased as a proportion of the federal budget over time; levels today compare to the 1830s and 1840s. However, the federal budget has increased as a percentage of GNP, carrying both military and nonmilitary expenditures with it.

Congress. The political power of the complex is tested by a study of the composition of Senate committee membership. Lieberson shows that there is a close association between the concentration of defense industries in a state and the probability of that state being represented on the Armed Services Committee. However, the representation of special interests tends to be the case on all Congressional committees. What is true for Armed Services is also true for Agriculture and Forestry, Minerals, Indian Affairs, etc.

Essentially, Lieberson confirms that the military-industrial complex exists as a coherent interest group, but he places it among a collection of special interests rather than giving it principal position in the American politico-economic structure. Each special interest has exceptional power in its sphere of operation, in Lieberson's theory of "compensating strategies." An interest group spends political capital to balance an array of potential gains and losses for the greatest net gain. As a result, different interest groups are not "countervailing powers" as the pluralist would argue, but rather each is dominant in the policy area in which it concentrates its political resources. Each tolerates the gains of the others because resistance would be too costly, relative to the proportional share of losses that it would suffer. The result is that this type of complex is able to exercise considerable influence over governmental spending.

Lieberson's findings support the view that there is a military-industrial complex in the United States with an interest in high levels of military spending, and that this complex is influential in the determination of national policy. However, his study does not support the view that large corporations and the economy as a whole need defense spending to maintain present levels of profit and prosperity, nor is he sympathetic to a portrayal of the complex as the pinnacle of a ruling class. America is not a "Warfare State" with an "Economy of Death" ruled by "Pentagon Capitalism." The military-industrial complex shares power with the transportation complex, the education complex, the black/urban complex, the agriculture complex, and other segments of a plural economy, though it has special influence in its sphere.

Reich

Michael Reich also asks, "Does the U.S. Economy Require Military Spending?", but reaches a rather different conclusion. Reich argues that the military-industrial complex is a function of capitalism, and that high military spending is likely to continue regardless of changes in the external strategic environment. The military-industrial complex has a special position in the American economic and political structure.

Orthodox and radical economists agree that modern capitalism requires high levels of governmental expenditure to maintain an adequate level of aggregate demand. The issue, according to Reich, is whether military spending is necessary, or whether "social" (nonmilitary) expenditure could not be an acceptable substitute in the event that strategic considerations permitted a reduction in arsenals. "Liberal" economists like Leontief see an essential equality of military and nonmilitary budgetary dollars in macroeconomic perspective, while radicals argue that military spending could not be terminated without altering the basic structure of the capitalist economy and deposing the most powerful interests in the political system.

Reich sees several key differences between social and military expenditures. Military purchases are characterized by rapid built-in obsolescence and must be constantly replenished, while social demands are eventually satisfied. Technological developments and "gold-plating" encourage continuous and extensive retooling in defense plants, while production for social needs utilizes a relatively stable infrastructure of capital equipment. Military spending is especially beneficial for the capital goods industry, which is the traditional flywheel of the capitalist economy. Thus, military spending hits the most strategic sectors of the economy, while social expenditures affect mainly the periphery.

Military spending is more conducive to high corporate profits than social expenditure. In the social field, there are familiar "common sense" criteria by which to assess reasonable costs, while the exotic technology of military hardware restricts knowledge of appropriate cost standards to a relative handful of specialists subject to influence by the contractors. As a result, Reich argues that defense work is more profitable—a conclusion disputed later in this volume by Robert Art.

Military expenditures are more consistent with the social and class composition of capitalist society. High social expenditures tend to compete with the private sector, while military spending complements private demand. High social expenditure is inconsistent with the class system, as it upsets the labor market and violates the key tenets of capitalist ideology. In general, social expenditures benefit a broad spectrum of society and drive up labor costs, while military expenditures have more focused benefits for the major corporations.

Proponents of the social expenditures argument say that defense is going down as a percentage of GNP, while social spending is going up. This is not true. Defense is down slightly, but nonmilitary federal expenditures are 2.3 percent of GNP today, compared with 4.6 percent in 1938 and 1.9 percent in 1954. Thus, the case cannot be made that social spending is replacing defense *de facto*.

Proponents of the social argument also point to the supposed counterexamples of Germany and Japan, which are capitalist countries with high GNP and relatively low defense sectors. However, the prosperity of these countries depends largely on exports to the U.S. and other markets where defense spending maintains adequate levels of demand. Thus, they are not truly counterexamples and would suffer a decline if the U.S. disarmed.

In general, Reich argues that capitalism *could*, despite all these objections, go to social expenditures in lieu of defense. But such a transition would reduce profits and other interests for the largest corporations, and hence would be resisted by the most powerful segments in the national economy. Does the U.S. economy, then, "need" military spending? Harry Magdoff has argued that the "necessity" question is a sterile framework for analysis. Capitalism may not "need" military spending or foreign investments, in the sense that the economy could survive without them. But neither does the U.S. economy "need" Texas and New Mexico, which in principle could be returned to Mexico to redress past injustices, without bringing about economic collapse.[1] What is more useful than a "necessity" framework is to study the interests that are in fact served by high military spending and to identify the political and economic structures which would be radically altered by a reduction. From this point of view, the corporate economy does need defense and could not convert to social expenditures at acceptable cost, according to Reich.

Aspaturian

The Soviet side of the military-industrial complex argument is sometimes forgotten in the polemical literature. Vernon Aspaturian's paper is a careful analysis of "The Soviet Military-Industrial Complex: Does it Exist?" Aspaturian finds that a network of interlocking interests with a stake in high defense spending does indeed exist, consisting of (1) defense industries and related research and development, (2) heavy industry in general, (3) the armed forces, and (4) the conservative wing of the party apparatus. "What ties the major components of the Soviet complex together is their understanding of the interdependency that exists between security, heavy industry, and ideological orthodoxy." The highest councils of the Soviet state are the battleground for a resource competition between two diverse alliances: a security-producer-ideological grouping (of which the military-industrial complex is the pinnacle) versus a consumer-agricultural-public services coalition. The relative strength of the first is manifest in the fact that "During the past decade, the Soviet regime has devoted 50 percent of its durable output to defense, leaving 40 percent for investment and the remaining 10 percent for the consumer sector." Heavy industry has priority over consumer demands, and defense has priority within heavy industry.

Heavy industry "is not absolutely dependent upon military orders," but without arms expenditures "both the share of resources assigned to heavy industry and the prestige it now enjoys would decline." This would cause "considerable reorganization, disorientation, and dislocation among personnel who are among the best paid in the country." Several branches of heavy industry "would cease to exist in their present form if the military were substantially reduced."

The Soviet military-industrial complex is well represented in the highest party and state organs. The core components of the complex represent 13 percent of the membership of the Central Committee. However, it is interesting to note that the uniformed services are deliberately excluded from leadership of the top councils (Politburo, Presidium of the Party, Party Secretariat, Presidium of Supreme Soviet, Presidium of Council of Ministers), with few exceptions. But the professional military do have a high degree of access and representation in lower political organs. There is an interpenetration of the party and the services to assure party supremacy.

The political influence of the Soviet military-industrial complex depends on a widespread perception of external dangers and international tensions. Aspaturian does not believe that there is a conscious process of misrepresentation of a nonexistent external threat. But he does argue that reliance on heavy defense expenditures gives rise to a conflicting perception of objective reality. In particular, the needs of the complex depend on attributing aggressive and imperialist motives to the U.S., despite arms control and tension-reducing agreements. Aspaturian takes the persistence of this ideological position as an indicator of the continued strength of the complex.

Essentially, Aspaturian's findings are consistent with the key propositions in the Millsian theory of the military-industrial complex: at the pinnacle of power in the USSR are factions with vested interests in high defense spending, and these needs are furthered by the maintenance of a state of conflict in the Cold War. There are some differences from the U.S. case. The circulation of personnel is negligible—high-ranking officers do not retire to industry—and buyer corruption is minimal due to state monopoly. But Aspaturian's paper can be seen as a confirmation of the essential likeness of the position of the complex within both superpowers.

The first four papers that we have reviewed are discussions of the military-industrial complex in the U.S. and the USSR. The next six focus more intensively on selected aspects of the theory.

Kurth

James Kurth's "Aerospace Production Lines and American Defense Spending" is an analysis of competing theories of the logic of weapons procurement. Why do we spend so much on defense? Kurth identifies four theories: (1) the (official) strategic rationale, (2) economic explanations; (3) bureaucratic theories; and (4) democratic explanations. Strategic explanations argue that weapons procurement "results from rational calculations about foreign threats or from the reciprocal dynamics of arms races." The other three explain military spending by reference to internal influences rather than the external environment. Economic theories see procurement as the result of aggregate economic imperatives or corporate needs. Bureaucratic explanations emphasize bureaucratic politics and competition between bureaucracies, especially the military services. Democratic/ electoral theories see weapons procurement as a function of electoral politics. The theory of the military-industrial complex is in effect a combination of

Kurth's economic (corporate), bureaucratic (military), and democratic (political) explanations, as against the official strategic rationale. Are high levels of military expenditure a response to perceived external threats, or is procurement the result of special economic, bureaucratic, and electoral interests within the internal political structure?

Kurth examines the recent history (1960-1971) of major aerospace procurement decisions in some detail. He finds that the key decisions can be explained primarily by the economic, bureaucratic, and democratic theories; that is, procurement can be explained without the official strategic rationale. Major aircraft procurement was determined by the needs of eight major industrial production lines. The timing and awarding of aircraft contracts was keyed to maintaining profits and employment for these firms. Major missile procurement (Minuteman, Polaris, MIRV) is best explained by bureaucratic politics and bargaining among different segments within the executive branch, the armed forces, and Congressional interests. Major antimissile procurement (ABM) is best explained by "the efforts of Presidents to satisfy the electorate and win the next election." In all three groups of cases, the official strategic rationale is secondary or superfluous in understanding the logic of procurement decisions, with some lesser exceptions. These findings may be taken as a substantiation of the theory of the military-industrial complex.

Kurth infers two principles guiding aerospace procurement that are of special interest in relation to the present theory: the "follow-on" imperative and the "bail-out" imperative. Kurth finds that the timing and awarding of major aerospace contracts coincide nicely with the corporate requirements of the large defense contractors. There are eight major aerospace "production lines" in the U.S., and according to the official theory these lines compete with each other for procurement contracts that are dictated by national strategic needs. But when Kurth charts the major contracts against the production lines, he finds that contracts tend to be let at such times and to such bidders that all production lines are kept active at all times.

About the time that a production line phases out production of one major government contract, it phases in production of a new one, usually within a year. . . . Further, in most cases, the new contract is for a system which is structurally similar while technologically superior to the system being phased out, i.e., the new contract is a follow-on contract.

This observation leads Kurth to contrast the official procurement rationale with the "follow-on imperative":

The official imperative for weapons procurement might be phrased as follows: If a military service needs a new weapons system, it will solicit bids from several competing companies; ordinarily, the service will award the contract to the company with the most cost-effective design. The follow-on imperative is rather different: If one of the . . . production lines is opening up, it will receive a new major contract from a military service (or from NASA); ordinarily, the new contract will be structurally similar to the old, i.e., a follow-on contract. Relatedly, the design competition between production lines is only a peripheral factor in the award.

Kurth argues in effect that the procurement of aerospace weapons is supply— rather than demand—induced.

The "follow-on imperative" is supplemented by a "bail-out imperative": "the government comes to the aid of corporations in deep financial trouble" by offering them lucrative rescue contracts. Kurth identifies twelve major new military contracts whose timing was immediately preceded by a significant decline in corporate sales, income, or employment for the company which got the award. It is plausible that these were "bail-out" contracts, motivated more by corporate than by strategic needs, to restore health and profitability to private firms.

Kanter and Thorson

In "The Weapons Procurement Process: Choosing Among Competing Theories," Arnold Kanter and Stuart Thorson develop an alternative "theory of weapons procurement" from an earlier paper by Kurth, and contrast this theory with the follow-on and bail-out imperatives. The weapons procurement theory empha- sizes the critical decision point at which a prospective weapons system moves from the research and development stage to the production and deployment stage. New systems at the R&D stage have low visibility and tend to "proceed unhampered by competition or opposition." But when they reach the point of production and deployment decisions they become more visible, and encounter resistance by newly alerted policy opponents and competitors for scarce budgetary resources. At this stage,

The probability of a system being produced and deployed is a function of (1) the strategic environment; (2) the distribution of influence within the military services; and (3) the support available from and opposition generated by coalitions of defense contractors and Congressmen.

The more heavily a project can be committed in the early periods of research and development, the greater the probability of its subsequent production and deployment.

Kanter and Thorson argue that the weapons procurement theory should be preferred to the follow-on and bail-out because it permits "policy predictions" while they are limited to "point-in-time" predictions. They argue that point predictions can make quantitative projections but provide no guidelines for intervention to modify the future. Policy predictions associate changes in the structure of the system with changes in behavioral outcomes. Thus, policy theories allow intervention and manipulation choices, though they may be less precise from a quantitative point of view.

The theory of weapons procurement is a policy theory because, unlike the follow-on, it includes "variables which seem potentially susceptible to manipulation." The follow-on is "helpless in the face of an open production line." It predicts what will happen but is silent regarding how this may be changed. The weapons procurement theory, on the other hand, suggests several possible lines of intervention to reduce the probability that a major system will be procured: (1) Early budgetary monitoring can make projects more visible before they are heavily committed through research and development. (2) Deliberate balancing of power between competing military organizations and coalitions may affect the relative influence of a program's advocates and opponents. And (3), actions which alter perceptions of the strategic environment, such as SALT agreements, may change the probability of a future weapons system going into production. Kanter and Thorson argue that, if change is the objective, a policy theory should be preferred to a point theory. The weapons procurement theory provides policy options, while the follow-on leaves us with cold predictions.

We may comment that Kanter and Thorson do not dispute Kurth's discovery of a substantial coincidence of timing and awarding of major procurement contracts with the development of corporate needs in the private economy. The follow-on and bail-out principles are fully compatible with the weapons procurement theory and in fact could easily be integrated into Kanter and Thorson's statement of it. If a "policy" format is preferred to a "point" format, the propositions of Kurth may be recast in policy terms: "The higher the probability that the contract, if awarded, will go to an open production line, the higher the probability of an affirmative decision." If this sentence were added to Kanter and Thorson's enumeration of policy predictions in the weapons procurement theory, another policy option could be added to their "variables which are manipulable": timing the production and deployment decision on a major weapons system during a period when all production lines are heavily committed will reduce the probability of that system being adopted. Thus, the criticism of Kanter and Thorson would lose much of its force if such policy implications were carefully derived from the follow-on and bail-out principles. We may also comment that the influence of special interests will likely persist despite the best prescriptive innovations of the policy theorist, and that a scientific finding cannot be faulted for its implied pessimism.

Cobb

Stephen Cobb is concerned with "The United States Senate and the Impact of Defense Spending Concentrations." The theory of the military-industrial complex suggests that Congressmen are brought into alliance with the corporations and the military because of the reliance of their districts on large defense contracts. If this is so, then legislators from districts or states with heavy concentrations of defense spending should be more sympathetic to the interests of the complex than those whose constituencies have other concerns. In particular, the published voting behavior of Congressmen from defense-dependent areas should be more "hawkish."

There have been several efforts to test this theory, and the results have been somewhat inconsistent. Cobb, in two earlier papers on the House of Representatives, found "almost no evidence that concentrations of defense spending had an influence on how members of the House voted on a series of foreign policy issues he labeled the jingoism scales." Studies by Gray and Gregory and by Russett, on the other hand, have found small but statistically significant correlations between defense spending concentrations and voting in the Senate on some but not other clusters of complex-related issues. Russett concluded that "expenditures for military installations go to support and reinforce if not to promote a set of hawkish and strongly anticommunist postures in American political life," though he did admit that his correlations "are not . . . astonishingly high." The earlier studies of Gray and Gregory and Russett, then, take a limited pattern of significant correlations as support for the basic military-industrial-complex hypothesis, while the earlier studies of Cobb conclude that the evidence does not support the hypothesis. The present paper tries to resolve the discrepancies between the previous studies on the basis of a new study of the Senate.

Cobb employs for the dependent (voting) variable two "jingoism scales" based on Senate roll-call votes. Ideally, a test of the hypothesis would employ votes on defense appropriation bills. But this is not possible because of the lack of variance in voting on defense appropriation measures; until recently there was little opposition in roll-calls. So the jingoism scales comprise votes on civil defense, the Arms Control and Disarmament Agency, selective service, foreign aid, and other tangential issues. Similar votes are used in the previous studies.

For the independent variable, defense dependence of the Senator's state, Cobb uses six measures of defense spending concentrations. He compares prime contract values, defense generated jobs, and payroll figures with aggregate economic indicators by state, to develop indices of the relative weight of defense in each state's economy. He then correlates these indices against the jingoism scales.

Cobb finds that most of his correlations are below the level of statistical significance. Of the four correlations that *are* significant, three are counterintuitive and point in the opposite direction of the hypothesis (the more defense spending the less hawkish). In general, the pattern of correlations is so inconsistent as to defy meaningful interpretation. Cobb concludes that "The findings reported in this paper do not support the contention that defense spending concentrations have a significant influence on the manner in which

Senators vote in the area of foreign policy." Cobb goes on to assess the apparent contradiction between this finding and the results of Russett, and concludes that the differences in findings are in fact very narrow and that none of the studies provide significant support for the hypothesis.

It appears, then, that the proposition linking military spending and Congressional hawkishness is not supported by the evidence. Cobb suggests the possibility that significant correlations will develop in future voting on defense appropriations as these measures move from unanimity to controversy. But for the present, it is not the case that Congressmen from defense-dependent districts are significantly more hawkish than their colleagues from other districts. Region of the country explains some variance, as does party affiliation. But defense spending concentrations are not a significant factor in producing hawkishness, as measured here.

Evaluation of these results depends on a larger framework of analysis concerning the logic of the military-industrial complex. If the theory is taken to predict a direct association between interests and behavior, then it is disconfirmed because "it does not appear that votes are being crudely traded for defense spending. . . ." Rather, "the Senator appears to be free to vote . . . convictions . . . in broad ideological terms." But it may be argued that the theory predicts a more subtle relationship between interests and behavior, with ideology as the intervening variable. Mills himself said that defense dependence gives rise to a rationale of Cold War ideology, and that perceptions rather than crude interests are the immediate determinants of behavior. As Aspaturian argues in his analysis of the Soviet case, "perception itself is frequently a reflection of self-interest rather than objective reality," possibly because of "unconscious distortion of the objective situation through the prism of individual or group self-interest." If indeed perceptual distortion is the intervening variable between interests and behavior, conscience cannot be so neatly opposed to crude interests in explaining Congressional voting. Also, it may be argued that the need for Cold War ideology is not confined by district and state boundaries, but rather pervades the entire society. "False consciousness" may be national in scope, not just confined to districts with high defense dependence. If this is the case, it is not surprising that Cobb will find little variance explained by the geographic distribution of defense spending concentrations. Still, it must be conceded that Cobb has the theory on the retreat, and that at least some crude versions of the theory must be discarded in the light of his findings.

Hanson and Russett

Another easy assumption of polemical theorists is given careful scrutiny by Betty Hanson and Bruce Russett in "Testing Some Economic Interpretations of American Intervention." In the hard-core ideological literature, it is often asserted that war is good for business, and that the roots of American military interventionism can be traced to Wall Street and the interests of finance capital. In the business community, on the other hand, it is a commonplace that the efficient conduct of international exchange requires domestic and international economic stability, making capital inherently an ally of peace rather than war. Hanson and Russett offer an empirical study of the stock market's reactions to escalation and de-escalation events in Indochina and Korea, on the basis of which some conclusions may be reached concerning the real attitudes of investors toward foreign wars.

Hanson and Russett identify four theories of investor attitudes toward war. The "simple Marxist" theory holds that war is good for a capitalist economy, as it stimulates aggregate demand and primes the pump of profits, especially in defense industries. Consequently, Marxists expect the stock market to respond favorably to war and conflict and unfavorably to reconciliation and the restoration of peace.

The "inverse Marxist" theory, favored in some business circles, holds that the side effects of war are harmful to a modern economy: inflation, large budgetary deficits, adverse balance of payments effects, the possibility of wage and price controls, and potentially the subordination of business to the higher national interest. The simple inverse Marxist theory expects the stock market to respond unfavorably to escalatory news, and favorably to news of peaceful settlement and de-escalation.

The "modified Marxist/inverse Marxist" theory is a mixture of favorable and unfavorable reactions to war signals. A small "brushfire" flare-up is said by these theorists to be good for business, as it stimulates defense spending. But large wars entail adverse side effects which cancel these small gains. Thus, a little war is a stimulant, but beyond a certain limit war news is bad news for Wall Street. The modified Marxist/inverse Marxist theorist expects the Dow Jones average to respond favorably to conflict escalation at first, but subsequently to respond unfavorably as a critical threshold is passed.

Finally, the "neo-imperialism" theory is identified as an important and distinct variant of the Marxist position. Here, it is not war but the Open Door that capital seeks. An end to war is welcomed if it represents concession by the other side. Hanson and Russett distinguish this from the Marxist position, in that the Marxist would have Wall Street respond unfavorably to conciliatory statements by the communists, while the neo-imperialist expects these to be welcomed. The Marxist sees war itself as beneficial, while the neo-imperialist emphasizes only the maintenance of empire.

To subject these four alternative theories to empirical testing, the authors examine the reaction of the prices of selected securities traded on the New York Stock Exchange to key escalation and de-escalation events in Indochina from August 1964 to December 1970 and in Korea from June 1950 to July 1953. Key events were selected for each month, and the net change in the Dow Jones

Index at the close of trading on the selected days was taken to represent the Wall Street reaction. In addition, ten stocks with especially heavy investments in less developed countries (LDCs) were studied individually.

The general results for both wars and both groups of stocks did not support the simplified Marxist (nor the simplified military-industrial-complex)thesis. On the whole, the stock market responded favorably to peace news. "The American financial community in general clearly wanted to see the Indochina War de-escalated by the beginning of 1967." Before this date, the multiple regression analysis did not yield significant correlations between escalation and stock prices in either direction. These results are not completely consistent with any of the four theories, but they are least consistent with the simple Marxist and probably most consistent with the inverse Marxist. Essentially, we may say that Wall Street attitudes, as reflected in stock market prices, either opposed foreign wars or were not affected by them.

It is by now quite obvious to everyone that Vietnam was not good for the stock market. It is interesting that this was equally true for Hanson and Russett's LDC stocks. Even companies with special interest in "third world" holdings stood to benefit from an end to the war, as indicated by investor expectations reflected in stock prices. The Marxist/military-industrial-complex theory is wrong even when restricted to "neo-imperialist" companies.

Hanson and Russett do not develop a separate assessment of the performance of *defense* industry stocks in relation to Vietnam and Korea escalation and de-escalation events. It might be expected that at least these stocks would benefit from military conflict. If this were true, it would lend limited but significant support to the Marxist/military-industrial-complex view. However, it is probably the case that a replication of the Hanson and Russett study for defense issues would find the same pattern that is reported here. Even the stocks of major defense contractors declined during the Vietnam war years, largely as a result of the war itself. The defense budget was not substantially increased during the war years, in constant dollars, compared to the overall Federal budget. Instead, there was a reallocation of resources from major weapons systems to expenditure on ordnance and manpower. The effect of Vietnam was to divert funds from major aerospace contractors to smaller firms or to large firms less dependent on military orders. Also, the defense sector moved from capital-intensive (aerospace) to labor-intensive (infantry) expenditure. The result was that defense profits after 1965 ran at a substantially depressed rate compared to the early 1960s (before Vietnam). After four years of escalated war, several of the largest aircraft and missile contractors faced serious financial decay. Lockheed escaped bankruptcy only through a special Congressional dispensation. Overall, the war did little good for the defense industry. The continuing arms race with the Soviet Union provides a relatively stable level of military orders. The war resulted in diversion of funding to less profitable channels, devastating inflation, Congressional hostility to defense spending, and a general atmosphere of gloom in military supply firms. One is led to the paradoxical conclusion that the war was on the whole antithetical to the interests of the largest defense contractors, and that their renewal awaited the restoration of peace and the Cold War. For defense stocks as for other securities, defense spending may be good for the market but war is not.

Art

Robert Art is concerned with "Why We Overspend and Underaccomplish: Major Weapons Procurement and the Military-Industrial Complex." What are the causes of billion dollar cost overruns in the production of weapons systems? Why was the final cost of the average major order during the 1960s over 200 percent of the original budget? What is the relationship between cost-overruns and the military-industrial complex?

It is often argued that massive overruns are due to huge profit windfalls and reflect the power of the corporations in controlling public policy without regard for the public interest. Some theorists argue that defense profits exceed those in the commercial economy, and that overruns are one of the reasons (compare Michael Reich in this volume). However, careful studies of defense profits do not support this contention. Defense profits were higher during the early sixties, but *lower* than commercial profits after 1965, in studies by Weidenbaum, Baldwin, and the General Accounting Office. Weidenbaum found a profit-to-net-worth ratio of 17.5 percent for defense firms compared to 10.6 percent for comparable nondefense firms from 1962-65. But a GAO study of profits compared to total capital investment for 1966-69, found a rate of 11.2 percent for defense compared to 14.0 percent for nondefense. In all the studies, the profits-to-sales ratio ranged from 3 to no more than 6 percent for defense. In general, these findings do not support the widespread impression of unusual profits in defense.

Art contends that profits account for only a small portion of overruns. While profits are 6 percent at best, overruns are often 100 percent and more. Art identifies five other factors which "reward waste and penalize efficiency," all deriving from the special functional problems of advance contracting for innovative high-technology systems under time constraints. The five factors producing cost overruns are: (1) goldplating; (2) bidding and lying; (3) profits for inefficiency; (4) managers without power; and (5) concurrency.

1. "Goldplating" is the tendency to build into new systems needless levels of technological sophistication. The purchase of exotic features is encouraged by competition between the military services and among the corporations, and is relatively uncontrolled because of military self-regulation in the definition of tactical needs.
2. "Bidding and lying" is the process of making performance and cost

promises during contract negotiations which will not be fulfilled after development begins and the government is "locked-in" to the developer. The contractor knows that no penalty will be exacted later for any failure to fulfill performance or price commitments. An added element of confusion is the frequent use of "contract change orders" which change the stipulations of the original contract while the program is in progress, on a cost-reimbursable basis. The effect is to hamper monitoring of contract promise fulfillment. "The weapons acquisition environment has been conducive, not to realistic price competition, but to extravagant performance promises and overoptimistic (low) bids."

3. "Profits for inefficiency" result from the way that profits are calculated. On defense contracts, "profits are negotiated as a percentage of sales." The firm is actually rewarded for inefficiency, as profits go up with costs. Conversely, efficiency is punished. Capital investments to increase productivity actually tend to reduce profits. "Once again, the system rewards waste and penalizes economy."

4. "Managers without power" cannot effectively oversee contracts. Weapons programs tend to be overseen by middle-ranking military officers who must carry every decision to superiors and who are prevented from developing expertise by frequent job rotation.

5. "Concurrency" is the practice of beginning weapons production before development is complete, to speed deployment and cut lead time. Problems discovered later must be corrected on already produced units, driving up costs.

Art reviews recent reforms to cut overruns and suggests other possibilities. In general, though, he sees severe limits to a simple cost-control point of view. More realistic contracting will have the effect of inflating original estimates. This will prevent "overruns" but result in the same high costs. In addition, it is realistic to assume that some overruns will continue under the best circumstances, given the inherent inefficiencies and difficulties of forecasting costs for unique systems (Art sets a conservative figure at 20 percent). Also, weapons systems are and will be expensive even if overruns are reduced. The significant question, more important than cost controls, will be which systems we in fact need to procure at all. "Improving the procedures through which we develop and produce major weapons systems should be no substitute for intelligent decisions on which systems to procure."

Art's purpose is not to test the theory of the military-industrial complex, but his analysis does have implications for an assessment of the theory. Perhaps most interesting is his rejection of the excess profits explanation of cost overruns. If cost inflation is in fact a function of the inherent inefficiency of military contracting, overruns cannot be attributed to special political influence of the military-industrial complex. This does not mean that there are not extensive linkages between industry and the military. Indeed, Art compares the contract negotiation relationship to labor-management collective bargaining.

Some interests are opposed, but many are shared. Too often, the shared interests have predominated. The services have stressed promised performance; the contractors have given it to them. The contractors have taken advantage of contractual loopholes; the services have encouraged them to do so.

But the frequency of overruns is not mainly an indicator of super-profits in the defense sector, and the possibility of overruns cannot be taken as a substantial advantage of defense spending as against social alternatives in discussing the disadvantages of economic conversion (see Reich).

Galloway

Jonathan Galloway's study of "Multinational Corporations and Military-Industrial Linkages" examines the overlap between U.S. based multinational firms and the largest defense contractors. Galloway identifies four types of firms: (1) those dependent on both sales abroad and military contracts (e.g., GE and ITT); (2) those dependent on sales abroad but not military contracts (e.g., Exxon, Ford); (3) those dependent on military contracts but not sales abroad (e.g., Lockheed, McDonnell Douglas); and (4) those dependent on neither market, though they may be large defense contractors (e.g., AT&T). Thus, "there is no one-to-one relationship between dependence on the governmental market and the international market." But it does tend to be the case that "the top defense contractors have significant assets in foreign countries" and that "the top U.S. based multinational corporations are also among the top defense contractors." In general, "the giant firms of the economy are apt to be both major defense contractors and worldwide companies." Of the top 100 DOD contractors in 1971, 39 were multinationals; of the top 25, multinationals were more than half (13). Also, many of the major European defense contractors are substantially owned by the U.S. multinationals. Thus, while there is considerable variation across industries, there is a tendency to the multinationalization of the major military suppliers. "There is enough overlap between multinationals and defense contractors in the aircraft, oil, electronics, rubber, and automobile industries to make the question of multinational corporate involvement in the military-industrial complex interesting. . . ."

What are the consequences of this overlap? A new "dynamic equilibrium" is created between defense, foreign trade, and foreign investment, with effects on the military-industrial complex, the conduct of arms races, the frequency of wars, and the granting of foreign military aid.

The complex itself is multinationalized, with potentially profound consequences: "It may be postulated that to the extent that multinational corporations, which are either under the influence of foreign nations or are not under the control of nations at all, are supplying some of the defense needs of a state, then military defense in that state is being multinationalized." Galloway sees a movement toward the creation of a common North Atlantic defense market.

Arms races may be exacerbated by the multinationalization of the complex. "While war itself is antithetical to the interests of multinational enterprise . . . the perpetuation of arms races seems quite functional." And since "there is a close relationship between these sectors of the American economy and the ruling elite in many less developed states," the multinationalized complex has political influence to stimulate arms sales. "To the extent that one market declines or is saturated, these firms and industries have an interest in expanding into the other markets." Even the outbreak of local wars may serve the interests of multinational defense firms. "There have been at least eleven nonmajor armed conflicts which have been associated with the activities of multinational firms," and other incidents which "cannot be thoroughly documented" because of the covert means used to exercise influence. In general, the multinational defense firm has an interest in the maintenance of a condition of international tension.

The multinational defense firms may be especially active in lobbying for optimal levels of foreign military aid by the U.S. and other developed states. In the U.S. in 1971, 20 of the 25 largest DOD contractors were also involved in arms sales abroad, much of it financed by the military assistance program. Eleven of these 20 were multinationals, as are 8 of the 16 largest arms exporters. Edward Levine derives from this the following hypothesis in his commentary: "If the continuation of military aid is threatened, multinational corporations interested in preserving their foreign interests will combine with U.S. arms manufacturers to oppose such threats to arms aid programs." Thus, a new ally is brought into the military-industrial complex.

Acceptance of these conclusions depends on one's general position regarding the theories of economic imperialism and the military-industrial complex. But Galloway does demonstrate a fairly impressive set of linkages between the multinational corporation and military contractors and these findings must be part of any larger framework of analysis. If manufacturers of war supplies multinationalize their operations, the consequences for relations between nations may be considerable, and the theory of the military-industrial complex will have to be revised accordingly.

Levine

Edward Levine discusses "Methodological Problems in Research on the Military-Industrial Complex," including in his analysis commentaries on many of the papers in this volume. Levine concentrates on the problems of research orientation, research design, and measurement. He concludes that the theory of the military-industrial complex is a poor guide to research. It does "not tell us how to conduct our research, but rather how to interpret whatever results we obtain." In particular, it does not lead to the optimal strategy for research on defense policy formation:

We probably know less about . . . the military-industrial-complex subsystem . . . than we do about the larger defense policy system in which it is embedded. The result of emphasizing military-industrial-complex theories is therefore that we concentrate upon a portion of the defense policy system which we least understand . . . We might be well advised to investigate (the) larger system, rather than trying to fathom an ill-defined subsystem whose relevance is not yet conclusively established.

One solution to this problem is a form of research design known as "black-boxing": "The investigation of an unknown system should be based upon a definition of the system in terms of its external quantities (i.e., inputs and outputs) and their level of resolution (the precision and frequency of measurement). Only when we have specified and analyzed these 'observables' can we realistically attempt to understand the structure and behavior of the system." Another step is to "determine the range of values that each observed quantity can exhibit. . . . We need to know the activity of a system because it forms our data base for determining the system's behavior (its set of time-invariant relationships between the various measurable quantities.)" Black-boxing is a classic behaviorist device based on "stimulating a system and recording the stimulus-response pairs that result." Levine admits that

Our call for black-boxing is basically negativistic; it is a call for greater caution, for a retreat from heady hypotheses of particular military-industrial-complex structures to an emphasis upon defense policy formation in general, and especially upon input and output variables in the latter system.

Levine also criticizes a tendency of researchers to employ single-case studies and ex post facto experiments. He recommends several quasiexperimental research designs applicable to the military-industrial complex, and especially recommends greater use of longitudinal studies.

Levine concludes that, with some exceptions, the most recent studies of the complex have met the minimal criteria of proper research design, in terms of the formulation of hypotheses so that they are empirical, conditional, and testable. However, he sees serious problems of measurement and selection of indicators. ". . . It is time that we devoted some concentrated effort to the development of new information sources, more valid indicators, and means of manipulating indicators that are already available to us."

Levine applies these propositions in his commentary on the various papers in this volume.

The Findings Condensed

What, then, are the results of our testing of the theory of the military-industrial complex? Different readers of this diverse collection of studies will arrive at different conclusions. However, the following propositions are a reasonable condensation of the findings.

1. The U.S. and the Soviet Union have developed extensive industrial sectors oriented to military orders for their output. A byproduct of this development is the creation of a class of individuals whose interests are served by defense spending. The careers of related managers and (on the U.S. side) the profits of owners and shareholders are tied to high levels of military preparation.
2. These industries are in critical sectors of the economy. On the U.S. side, they include the largest industrial corporations and the crucial capital goods industry. On the Soviet side, they involve the core sectors of heavy industry, and the favorable share of resources allocated to all of heavy industry is due to defense needs. On both sides, the most powerful interests in the economy are substantially tied to continued high levels of military production.
3. However, neither economy *needs* military spending in the sense that the aggregate level of wealth is dependent on manufacture for defense. The majority of U.S. corporations derive only the smaller part of their sales from military contracts, and defense profits are *not* a disproportionate share of corporate earnings (i.e., profits are not higher in defense). On both sides, conversion from defense to social expenditures would hurt some sectors but help others. While such a transformation would be resisted by some of the most powerful sectors and would have very high transitional costs, it would not, in principle, be harmful to the economy as a whole in the long run. It would, however, entail substantial turnover in the composition of political elites and a wholesale revision of the priorities guiding resource allocation.
4. While military spending is good for business, war itself is not, at least not in the case of Vietnam. The response of the stock market averages to Vietnam de-escalation events indicates that the business community expected an end to the war to stimulate profits.
5. Industrial interests reliant on high military expenditures are associated with each other and allied with the armed forces bureaucracies in both the U.S. and the USSR. The political influence of the military and the industries is coordinated. However, the professional military elite are subordinated to political control by civilian leadership in both states.
6. The interests of the complex depend on the prevalence of fear of an external threat, which supplies the strategic rationale for the priority of

military expenditures. This, in turn, depends on exaggerated Cold War thinking to perpetuate the arms race.

7. This ideology of conflict is promoted by the existence of the complex. However, "false consciousness" is not a fabricated deception deliberately engineered by the complex, but rather it is a product of the unconscious distortion of perceptions through "the prism of . . . self-interest."

8. Public policy is influenced more by the ideology of the complex than by direct expression of the complex's self-interest through crude lobbying and the direct exercise of influence. Thus, the immediate determinant of arms spending and hawkish behavior is unwarranted perception of external threat. Perception is an intervening variable between the complex's interests and state behavior. In the U.S., Congressmen from defense-dependent districts are not significantly more hawkish.

9. In general, the military-industrial complex is not best understood as a conspiracy, but as a subtle interplay of interests and perceptions.

10. This is not the only complex of political and economic special interests in the U.S. or the USSR. It competes with other groupings, such as the agricultural, urban, and educational complexes. It does not win every conflict over resource allocation, and it is weakened when confronted with hostile alliances of other interests. However, it generally exceeds the influence of any opposing interests within its issue-area, and tends to prevail unless the opposing political forces are fully alerted and mobilized.

11. These relationships are illustrated by the logic of weapons procurement in the U.S. The critical decision point in the adoption of a new weapons system is the determination to move from research and development to production and deployment. Projects tend to pass this threshold without resistance, especially if major industrial production lines are idle and the regeneration of corporate profits, sales, and employment requires a major new contract. Thus, the inner logic of the complex is sufficient to determine the commitment of resources to major arms procurement, provided that some construction of strategic needs is available as an official rationale.

12. Arresting this process of automatic procurement depends on the imposition of deliberate checks and balances: monitoring research and development at early stages to identify incipient commitments before they are highly advanced; carefully balancing the power of opposing bureaucratic and corporate alliances; and timing major production decisions so that they are taken when production lines are already occupied and corporate demands are relaxed. Without such delicate opposition of forces, new systems tend to generate spontaneously from the military-industrial sectors, and many of them will be adopted.

13. The most important long-run countermeasure to the complex is an alteration of threat perceptions to weaken the strategic rationale.

14. Cost-overruns are caused by deficiencies in the contracting process, not mainly by excess profits.
15. The defense industry is increasingly penetrated by international corporations whose ownership is based in the U.S. but whose operations and interests span the globe. The result is a trend to the multinationalization of the military-industrial complex.
16. The multinationalized complex may exercise new kinds of influence over arms races, the outbreak of war, and the magnitude and allocation of foreign military aid.

Overall, we may say that C. Wright Mills has been sustained in the essential propositions of his theory, though some of the more simplified conspiratorial versions developed by his most ardent followers must be rejected. Reviewing our summary of the theory at the outset, it is remarkable how well it has withstood critical evaluation, some of it from an obviously skeptical perspective. Contrary to some of our contributors (e.g., Slater and Nardin, Levine), we conclude that the theory of the military-industrial complex is a most useful analytical construct for both research and policy evaluation purposes.

Note

1. See Harry Magdoff, "The Logic of Imperialism," SOCIAL POLICY 1, No. 3 (September-October 1970), pp. 13-19.

2

The Concept of a Military-Industrial Complex

Jerome Slater and Terry Nardin[1]

The phrase "military-industrial complex" is now common in political debate, journalism, and, increasingly, academic scholarship in the United States. It is employed both in substantive controversy concerning questions of public policy and in scholarly controversy concerning the definition, explanation, and evaluation of phenomena which the phrase is thought to describe. While there is no doubt that its widespread use indicates the existence of problems or conflicts of great political significance, the concept to which it refers is more often than not associated with a highly misleading analysis of these problems and conflicts. In particular, we will argue, the concept of a military-industrial complex as it is actually employed presupposes an implicit theory of politics that is notably confused and simplistic both in its analysis of political power and motivation, and in its assumptions about causation and scientific explanation.

Because our interest is in a theory rather than a phrase, our discussion of the military-industrial complex literature will deal not only with the work of those writers who use the phrase, but also with the work of those who speak of the "warfare state," the "new state-management," the "national security managers," the "Pentagon partners," and the like.[2] It is our contention, which we will attempt to demonstrate throughout the paper, that these labels identify analyses that in method, style, and substance are sufficiently similar to those referred to by the "military-industrial complex" label to be treated as variants of a single theory. We hold to this contention even though several of the writers whose ideas we discuss seek to differentiate their concepts from those of writers making explicit reference to a "military-industrial complex." As we interpret this literature, the differences of labeling are of secondary theoretical importance in comparison with the substantial agreement within it, recognized or not, with respect to the nature of power, motivation, causation, and explanation. We begin by examining a number of alternative concepts of a military-industrial complex, attempting to identify the characteristics that differentiate them as well as those they share, and then consider a number of important problems raised by these conceptions.

Concepts of the Military-Industrial Complex

The popularity of the phrase "military-industrial complex" and the kinds of analyses associated with that and related phrases have arisen in the context of

27

the following facts and trends in recent American history: (1) a large military establishment supported by vast military budgets; (2) the consequent creation of substantial economic, political, bureaucratic, and psychological interests in the continuation of high levels of military expenditures; (3) the rise of military participation in the making of American foreign policy, largely free from public examination of many aspects of its operation, and the concomitant decline in the influence of the Department of State, the Congress, and of public opinion. In addition to these incontrovertible facts, the military-industrial complex literature stresses the existence of other, more problematic trends, notably (1) the coordination and integration of groups interested in continuing high military expenditures, through extensive formal and informal relationships, particularly between the military and the government bureaucracy, Congress, corporations, industrial associations, veterans groups, and military-oriented scientists and academicians; and (2) massive and largely successful efforts by these groups and organizations that benefit from this state of affairs to militarize attitudes throughout American society—through propaganda, deceit, and manipulation of public opinion—in order to forestall opposition and preserve their privileged positions. The overall result of these developments is seen to be pathology in both policy substance and process: militarist foreign policies in both cold and hot war, and the erosion of democracy and political accountability, as crucial decisions have come to be increasingly dominated by military and industrial elites able to evade public scrutiny and capable of working their will free from effective political opposition or the normal regulation of the constitutional order.[3]

In most of the literature, the concept of a military-industrial complex functions as both a description and an explanation (or theory) of what is being described. Sometimes, though, the military-industrial complex notion is intended as an atheoretical description: simply as a name or label for an area of concern focusing on some or all of the actual or presumed phenomena listed above. In a few instances, especially in the more recent literature, the phrase is used in a low-key, relatively neutral way merely as a fashionable synonym for what formerly would have been called "the military establishment."[4] On rare occasions the term is accepted, even embraced, by those who wish to "thank God" for the military-industrial complex and defend it against its detractors.[5] Overwhelmingly, though, those who make use of the notion of a military-industrial complex use it as a political symbol for institutions and policies that they wish to condemn. Some are primarily concerned with waste, inefficiency, or corruption in the weapons procurement process, alleged to arise out of excessively close ties between the defense industry and the Pentagon.[6] Others have more fundamental concerns, directing their attention to the larger purpose and direction of American policy and the processes by which it is made.[7]

Thus, while the phrase appears in a number of contexts and types of discourse, its most comfortable home remains political debate, where it functions as a dramatic metaphor closely associated with the criticism of American institutions. It is scarcely coincidental that the popularity of the term has occurred at a time when disapproval of American foreign and military policies has become so widespread.[8] The underlying purpose of most analyses of the military-industrial complex is first to identify, and then to mobilize opposition to, the individuals, groups, or institutions thought to be politically and morally responsible for disapproved policies and events. The phrase—and the idea for which it stands—is clearly better suited to the rhetoric of politics than the requirements of analysis. Indeed, it is likely that some of the deficiencies in the more academic analyses of a military-industrial complex arise from the inherent difficulties of adapting a concept derived from partisan controversy to the descriptive and explanatory purposes of political science.

One of these difficulties is that controversy about public affairs tends to be characterized by the search for pragmatic explanations aimed at identifying factors which can and should be manipulated to bring about change, rather than by a search for complete explanations which take account of factors which, while important, are beyond the reach of practical influence. Furthermore, such controversy often focuses on the identification of individuals or groups that seem to be responsible for the occurrence or persistence of disapproved events, policies, or situations, and against whom pressure can be mobilized to effect reform. The phrase "military-industrial complex" strongly suggests—and the concept to which it refers typically embodies—an implicit causal theory, or selective set of assumptions, of this kind. In particular, it suggests that the cause of militarism in the United States today lies in the existence and actions of some entity (an agent, i.e., actor, or group of actors) with an interest in militarism as well as the power to bring it about. To speak, as participants in this particular controversy so frequently do, of "*the* military-industrial complex" as if it were an *entity*, motivated by *interest*, and possessing *power* by reference to which a *causal explanation* of certain features of American society and politics can be framed, is thus to make certain questionable assumptions about power, motivation, causation, and explanation. These assumptions, far from being defended in the literature, are seldom explicitly stated, and are in all probability largely unrecognized. Thus, even those writers who are apparently engaged only in what they intend as nonexplanatory and atheoretical description are in fact likely to be operating within a framework of assumptions that is subject to considerable dispute. It is this framework of assumptions, which in fact constitutes a theory of the military-industrial complex, that we wish to examine.

We will begin by outlining the characteristic features of the four main variants of the concept of a military-industrial complex: the military-industrial complex as a ruling class, as a power elite, as a bureaucracy, and as a loose coalition. In interpreting the literature in this way, we are well aware that we are to some extent imposing our own models or categories on a diverse and frequently vague and ambiguous literature. The views of some of the writers that we discuss can probably be appropriately located in more than one category; others may not quite fit any of our categories. Despite these qualifications (which we will later discuss more specifically), it is our assessment that the main lines of argumentation in the literature are reasonably well encompassed by the suggested models.

The ruling class concept has perhaps the longest history, having its probable origins in the work of Marx and much subsequent socialist political theory, as well as in this century in liberal thought influenced by Marxist and socialist ideas. Many of the central themes of the military-industrial complex literature—the importance of economic interests, the dependence of political upon economic power, the concept of false consciousness—reveal the extent to which contemporary writers are indebted to this earlier literature.[9] What principally distinguishes this concept is the identification of the rich both as a class and as the moving force behind contemporary American policy and institutions. There is, as one writer in this vein has put it,

a national upper class of rich businessmen and their descendants whose members control corporations, foundations, the largest mass media, major opinion-forming associations, and, through campaign financing and their presence in key cabinet and advisory positions, the executive branch of the federal government.[10]

The military itself plays only a subordinate role in the military-industrial complex. On the contrary, it is the case that

civilians—in particular the corporate rich—have dominated the defense department, and the number of military men in important roles in the business world has been greatly exaggerated.[11]

Yet, because "the corporate rich can see no other way out of their problem than military ones," the military definition of reality has become widely accepted. For it is the corporate rich who, while not themselves filling every position of national leadership, do set the standards by which men move into positions of prominence in government and the military services.[12]

A second concept of the military industrial complex is that it constitutes a power elite. As conceived by C. Wright Mills, who popularized the phrase, the "power elite" comprises those whose positions in the principal institutional orders of contemporary American society—the corporate economy, the federal government, and the military hierarchy—give them the capacity to decide the affairs of the nation in the absence of significant constraint or countervailing power by other institutions or groups in American society.[13] As another writer economically puts it,

a power elite may be thought of as a fairly well-defined and organized group of men performing central roles in determining public policy. . . . and whose decisions are regularly imposed on the rest of society, which has no effective means of exercising any degree of control over the decisions.[14]

Much of the military-industrial-complex literature falls into the power elite category, so defined. Mills' book remains the best statement of this model, however, for it anticipates nearly all the major arguments found in more recent versions, and usually states them in a more sophisticated and coherent way.

The current literature tends to portray the military-industrial complex as a small, relatively unified, and frequently conspiratorial group whose members, linked by ties of class, vocation, economic interest, education, and personal friendship, are drawn primarily from the military leadership, industrial firms engaged in military production, nonelected bureaucrats in key positions in the executive branch, and a few key members of Congress. This power elite concept of the military-industrial complex differs from the ruling class concept chiefly in giving governmental and military institutions equal importance with the corporate economy, and thus de-emphasizing the role of wealth and economic class in determining the direction of national policy. It is not wealth that is the dominant tie binding the elite, but power—particularly the power to make the crucial decisions concerning war and peace. Nor, within the elite itself, are big businessmen necessarily the dominant figures: some may so argue (for example, Swomley), while others point to the military leaders themselves (Cook, Lens) or the executive bureaucracy (Barnet).[15] Although the latter emphasizes the central role of "the national security bureaucracy," he too treats the leaders of this bureaucracy ("the national security managers") in power elite terms. For example, he argues that the national security managers—the dominant figures in the White House, the staff of the National Security Council, the Pentagon, the CIA, and the State Department—are a tightly knit social and political community of lawyers, bankers, administrators, and public figures, all graduates of the best private schools and universities, all moving in the same social circles. The "homogeneous backgrounds and virtually identical careers" of these managers, he asserts, ensure that they will share "a standard way of looking at the world."[16] In a more recent work, Barnet concludes that U.S. foreign policy today is "an elite preserve . . . made for the benefit of that elite."[17]

In a third variant, the core of the military-industrial complex is portrayed as a bureaucracy. The most important figures in the complex are nonelected bureaucrats or managers in the executive branch, with the military and its industrial allies playing a supporting but distinctly secondary role. The unprecedented power of these new "state-managers" derives from the importance of their positions in the organization of both government and the economy, both of which have themselves become highly centralized because of the dynamics of modern industrial society and the permanent international crisis of our times.[18] One of the central ideas of this model is that of bureaucratic momentum:

The war establishment . . . originates in the social needs of organized states, but once set up, it lives a life of its own. It follows the law of bureaucracy. Each bureaucracy has a tendency to proliferate, to extend its influence, to augment its power, to create a continuing need for its services, to make itself indispensable as the administrator of the state's business.[19]

The result is not only the militarization of other social and political institutions, but the creation of a situation in which the complex performs functions which would not be needed if it did not exist. As Joseph Schumpeter once put it most succinctly: "Created by the wars that required it, the machine now created the wars it required."[20] Besides the idea of bureaucratic momentum, this model thus displays a concept of the complex as an interest-motivated agent or entity, as well as the assumption that the explanation of militarism is to be found in the actions and power of this entity.

The final model of the military-industrial complex is based on a concept of the complex as comprising a loose coalition of powerful groups linked by common interests in militarized policies: the industrial sector is interested mainly in profits, the political, military and bureaucratic sectors mainly in power. There is no one ruling class or power elite, no internal organization or integrated structure, no conscious coordination or planned action within the complex—or, to the extent that there is, it is limited and local.[21] The shared perceptions of reality and the common actions and policies that emerge from these perceptions—the pursuit of high military budgets and bellicose cold-war policies—are simply a function of the "coincidences of interest" or "symbiotic ties" that link otherwise noncentrally coordinated institutions and groups.[22] President Eisenhower, who coined the phrase "military-industrial complex," clearly thought of it in these terms:

The congressman who sees a new defense establishment in his district; the company in Los Angeles, Denver, or Baltimore that wants an order for more airplanes; the services which want them, the armies of scientists who want so terribly to test their newest views; put all of these together and you have a lobby. This lobby has not necessarily been formed out of a community of interests. . . .[23]

Other writers who share this basic concept include Galbraith, Yarmolinsky, and, to a considerable extent, Pilisuk and Hayden.[24] The latter oscillate between a concept of the military-industrial complex as an actor or entity (a loose coalition of groups) and as an integrated pattern of rules, values, beliefs, and institutions that comprise the American economic, social, and political system. It is this systemic concept that Pilisuk and Hayden appear to have in mind in their well-known remark that "it is not that American society contains a ruling military-industrial complex. . . . American society *is* a military-industrial complex."[25] But they also employ an entity conception of the complex, as when they write:

What we have been calling the military-industrial complex is an informal and changing coalition of groups with vested psychological, moral, and material interests in the continuous development and maintenance of high levels of weaponry, in preservation of colonial markets and in military-strategic conceptions of international affairs.[26]

The Pilisuk and Hayden essay is one of the few explicit attempts to get away from some of the assumptions of the concept of a military-industrial complex as an entity. But here, as in the case of the bureaucratic variant, the result is inconsistency and the continued subterranean existence of the framework of assumptions which constitute the entity conception.

These are the four major variants of the concept of a military-industrial complex as it appears in the literature. Despite the considerable differences among them, they all share a number of significant substantive commonalities: (1) The military-industrial complex is an entity, a specifiable group of people; (2) This group is relatively small and unrepresentative of American society as a whole;[27] (3) Yet it has great political power and is opposed by little or no countervailing power, especially in the area of foreign and military policy; (4) Mostly, this power is exercised covertly, in activities and organizations other than (or at least in substantial addition to) the formal and constitutional institutions of government—the military-industrial complex, that is, constitutes a "state within a state";[28] (5) The exercise of power by the military-industrial complex is motivated by and exerted on behalf of its private interests, defined in economic or power terms; (6) This leads to militarist policies which serve these interests rather than the public interest; (7) The result is a political *process* that is to a great extent undemocratic and which produces *policies* that are irrational and dangerous. In short the military-industrial complex, consisting of groups with economic and institutional interests in cold-war policies and high military expenditures and linked by shared values and beliefs as well as by overlapping or symbiotic positions in the economic, social, and political structure of American society, is America's dominant institution, exercising power over a broad range of military, foreign, and domestic policies in ways which have consequences for even seemingly remote aspects of American life. This concept, shared not only by almost all writers who use the phrase "military-industrial complex" but by others—such as Melman, Barnet, and Kolko—who eschew it, presupposes certain problematic ideas about power, motivation, causation, and explanation that we must now examine.

Causation, Conspiracy, and the Complex

One of the more notable of these ideas is the assumption that the proper way to explain the occurrence or persistence of events, policies, or situations is by reference to the actions and power of individuals or groups with an interest in those outcomes. To hold this view is to accept what years ago Karl Popper labeled "the conspiracy theory of society":

the view that an explanation of a social phenomenon consists in the discovery of the men or groups who are interested in the occurrence of this phenomenon (sometimes it is a hidden interest which has first to be revealed), and who have planned and conspired to bring it about. This view arises, of course, from the mistaken theory that, whatever happens in society . . . which people as a rule dislike . . . is the result of direct design by some powerful individuals and groups.[29]

When writers on the military-industrial complex discuss conspiracies, they appear to get Popper's notion confused with the idea of a conspiracy as a very small and unified group of men, known to each other, who secretly plot some activity which they know to be evil. They have in mind the kind of conspiracy revealed by the *Protocols of the Elders of Zion*, or embodied in the theories of the John Birch Society. Barnet, for example, argues that his is not a conspiracy theory because conspiracy "implies some consciousness of guilt."[30] But this is to make insincerity, rather than interest and design, the defining attribute of conspiracy. Galbraith, Lens, and others also deny that they have a conspiracy in mind, but the main thrust of their argument is also a search for "the men or groups who are interested in the occurrence of this phenomenon."[31]

What is wrong with conspiracy theories (understood in Popper's sense) is that they radically oversimplify the explanation of social and political events. For one thing, they underestimate the level of mere accident and drift in human life, particularly the unintended and unforeseen consequence of actions taken with quite different ends in mind. As conspiracy theories are invented to explain disapproved events, their main concern is to attach some rational purpose to an historical progression of events which would otherwise be meaningless to condemn as *policy*, and for which identifiable men or groups could be blamed.[32] Conspiracy theories also restrict the range of potentially valid types of explanation to those which refer to agents, motives, actions, and powers.[33] They particularly miss the possibilities for explanation which refer to social wholes of various kinds (such as beliefs, rules, practices, and institutions), and in general overlook a wide range of factors which must be considered in any reasonably complete explanation of social and political events. The point is not that such explanatory factors or perspectives never enter into theories of the military-industrial complex—they sometimes do—but rather that the framework of assumptions embodied in such theories hinders them from moving very far or very consistently away from the style of analysis characteristic of conspiracy theories.

It would be beyond the scope of this paper to develop an analysis of militarism (or, more neutrally, of the increased role of military factors in

American domestic and foreign policy) based on different substantive and methodological premises from those presupposed by the theory of the military-industrial complex. But it might help to clarify the foundations of our criticism of that theory to suggest briefly some elements, other than the interests and actions of powerful groups, which would enter into a more complete theory of the military dimensions of American politics, and which are ignored or slighted by the military-industrial complex theory.

Some years ago, a well-known scholarly book on the weapons procurement process began with this statement: "Although it is undoubtedly unfortunate that this country must expend billions of dollars a year on weaponry, few would deny the need for these expenditures."[34] The premise on which this rather quaint-sounding assertion rested, of course, was that the existence of a Soviet military challenge *requiring* an American military response was an obvious fact. It is evident from this and other contexts that one's view of the nature of the political process is likely to be powerfully affected by one's views of policy substance. Thus, it would seem to be a reasonable guess that severe disenchantment with American foreign policy usually precedes the postulation of a military-industrial complex. Something is wrong here, the reasoning goes, and an explanation which goes behind the official mythology is required. For example, Lens argues that the expansion of the complex's role in society is not attributable to external threats or, by implication, to genuine though mistaken beliefs in such threats, and concludes: "There must be an explanation for the rise of the military-industrial complex, therefore, that goes beyond the issue of security."[35] Similarly, Melman writes that "There seemed to be no militarily rational explanation for certain major policies: the persistent pile-up of strategic overkill power and the continuation and expansion of the war in Vietnam," which, he goes on to argue, can be explained only by the "institutionalized power lust" of the "state-management."[36]

On the other hand, those who approve of American policies seldom worry about the existence of a military-industrial complex, or make use of that concept in their explanation of those policies; instead, they typically emphasize the pluralistic (open, competitive, diversified, nonhierarchical—and thus, for them, *legitimate*) nature of the policy process. While it is not logically necessary or inevitable that there be such a nearly perfect correlation between views on policy process and policy substance, it is easy to understand the powerful psychological connection: if one accepts the basic premises of American foreign and military policies in recent decades then no further explanation for the large military budgets or the increased role of the military in government, economy, and society is required—they are seen simply as rational responses to the international situation. We would not wish to enter here into a discussion on the extent to which such perceptions of external military threats were or are accurate; perhaps it is sufficient to observe that to the extent it can be shown that political elites genuinely *believed* (or still believe) in the existence of such threats for reasons not plausibly attributable simply to their "interests," regardless of the extent to which that belief was or is founded on reality, then to that extent a long step has been taken in accounting for the phenomena that some critics attribute solely to the power of a military-industrial complex.

Again, one might point simply to the nature of the international political system, the near anarchic structure of which creates genuine, deep-rooted security dilemmas, action-reaction patterns of conflict, and cycling arms races. It was this security anxiety, rather than "interests," that the late Senator Richard Russell appeared to have in mind when he observed that:

There is something about preparing for destruction that causes men to be more careless in spending money than they would be if they were building for constructive purposes. . . . I have observed over a period of about thirty years in the Senate that there is something about buying arms which causes men not to reckon the dollar cost as closely as they do when they think about proper housing and the care of human beings.[37]

That this structural factor has similar effects on nations with very different institutions, ideologies, and political practices is suggested by the recent literature on the Soviet "military-industrial complex."[38] The same is true of transnational historical developments such as the growth of modern industrialism with its uncontrolled, exploding technological "advances" which, when linked to "worst possible contingency" styles of military planning that have their roots in global insecurities, seriously exacerbates arms races and political tensions.[39]

Besides these factors, there are certain characteristics of American political beliefs or mythologies and political institutions that play a role in explaining American foreign and military policies. For example, there is the strain of what has been called "liberal messianism" in foreign policy, not associated with or plausibly attributable to any specific group, which, because of its expansive conception of America's mission in the world, implies an assertive foreign policy and a military establishment going beyond that required for "security." And at the institutional level there is the well-known conservative structural bias of the political system, which not only overweights in Congress the more militaristic forces within American society but, more broadly, fragments power and thus creates a series of veto-points making change from established policies particularly difficult. The conservative impact of these forces on policy may also be strengthened by a more general human reluctance to re-examine fundamental premises or to alter established practices and institutions even long after their validity or sense has increasingly come to be regarded as dubious.

To take account of these kinds of factors is not only to go beyond an explanation of the military dimensions of American society in terms of the interests and actions of powerful groups, but to reveal those interests and actions as themselves products of an historically changing context of technologies, beliefs, institutions, and situations. From this perspective, the pattern of interests and actions which has been personified in the concept of a military-industrial complex, and regarded as a cause of recent changes in American society, begins to look more like an effect of those changes. Possibly the reason that the concept of a military-industrial complex as a causal entity has such widespread popularity is that American institutions appear more accessible to criticism and reform than other more intangible or complex factors contributing to militarism. And, as we have already noted, the emphasis in debates about American militarism has been on the identification of factors which might be manipulated in order to effect social and political change, and particularly on the identification of men who seem to be responsible and whose power must be curtailed. To the extent that pragmatic, action-oriented theories are subject to this kind of selectivity, their usefulness in helping us to understand the phenomena they purport to explain is limited.

Motivation and the Complex

Another kind of selectivity in the theory of the military-industrial complex is that it rests on a set of oversimplified assumptions about political motivation. It assumes, first of all, that men are invariably motivated by "interests" defined in terms of their immediate economic or political gain. Second, it assumes that in politics men act to maximize their interests, so defined. And finally, it assumes that these interests can be easily and directly inferred from class, social, or institutional position. Given these assumptions, a good deal of human experience must appear anomalous.[40] The point is not that "interests" never determine political action, only that, contrary to the implicit premise of so much of the military-industrial complex literature, they do not invariably do so. That it makes much sense to conceive the military-industrial complex as an interest group sufficiently united, organized, and conscious of itself as a group to act as an entity in politics is doubtful,[41] but even if it did we would still be obliged to discover, rather than presume, in whose interests and to what ends it acts.

There are a number of possibilities, of varying degrees of plausibility, and not necessarily mutually exclusive. One is that the complex genuinely seeks to exercise its power in the public interest, and because it correctly understands reality (it is rational to pursue activist anticommunist policies and high military budgets), it does in fact serve the public interest. Insofar as these policies also further its own economic and political interests, this is a coincidental and unavoidable byproduct. This view, which was implicit in the broad anticommunist consensus in the United States of the late 1940s and 1950s, rarely makes an appearance in the literature on the military-industrial complex. More common is the view that the complex genuinely seeks to act in the public interest, but it misperceives reality—in good part because its own interests unconsciously distort its perceptions—and ends by acting in its own interests but against the public interest. This view would seem to be implicit in Barnet's argument that since the "national security managers" profit so well from the existing structure of American society, they sincerely equate the national interest with the status quo: "When Wilson said . . . 'What is good for the country is good for General Motors and vice-versa,' he was merely restating the basic national security premise."[42] The complex, self-deceived but with a good will, pursues a self-serving conception of the public interest.

A third possibility is that the complex deliberately misrepresents reality in order to legitimate its own power and further its own particular interests; there is no genuine need for large military budgets and anticommunist policies, and those who comprise the military-industrial complex know it. The complex deceives not itself, but others. This is the main theme of the military-industrial complex literature. Its most explicit statements are found in Lens (the defense program is based on "a gigantic hoax" consciously perpetrated by the complex to obscure its economic imperialism: "Convincing the American people that they ought to spend nine times as much on guns as on human welfare was an act of mesmerism by the military establishment without parallel"[43]); Cook (who argues that the military establishment deliberately created "war scares" in the postwar period so that its "naked grasps for power" could be "rationalized on the loftiest plane"[44]); Melman ("the state-management represents an institutionalized power-lust. A normal thirst for more managerial power . . . gives [it] . . . an unprecedented ability and opportunity for building a military-industry empire at home and for using this as an instrument for building an empire abroad."[45]); and, at times, Barnet ("They [the national security managers] used the code word 'national interest' to sanctify policies they perceived to be in their own class interests, i.e. the ever-increasing capitalist system from which they, their friends and employers had amassed great wealth."[46]).

The complexities in the relationships between interests and political action may be further illustrated by examining the sources of Congressional support of high military budgets and anticommunist foreign policies. It is frequently noted that all fifty states and over three-quarters of Congressional districts are the recipients of defense expenditures. But what significance is to be drawn from this fact? Again, there are a number of logically separable (though in practice probably partially interrelated) possibilities:

1. Economic interests within Congressional constituencies are responsible for Congressional hawkishness; that is, the existence of such interests precedes and explains Congressional votes. This is the usual implication—rarely stated explicitly—of the military-industrial complex literature. For example, Henry Jackson of Washington is frequently referred to as "the Senator from Boeing," clearly suggesting that Jackson's hawkishness is a function of the prominence of Boeing in Washington's economy. This

view, however, cannot be entirely correct, as it is easy to point to a number of nonhawkish Congressmen and Senators, past and present, from constituencies with high military expenditures (e.g., Cranston and Tunney from California, Goodell and Robert Kennedy from New York, Clark from Pennsylvania, Young from Ohio, Edward Kennedy from Massachusetts, etc.). Moreover, a number of recent Congressional studies suggest that there is little or no correlation between defense expenditures and Congressional support of military appropriations bills and general cold-war legislation[47]—it need only be recalled that until quite recently there was next to *no* Congressional opposition to such measures.

2. Hawkishness, especially in Congressmen in key committees, is rewarded by defense expenditures; votes precede and explain such expenditures. Whereas in the first view it is implied that the military-industrial complex deliberately spreads its largesse around *broadly* so as to create and maintain the interests which are its main source of power, here it is suggested that the military-industrial complex deliberately spreads the largesse *unevenly*, so as to reward its friends and punish its enemies. The favorite examples in the literature are those of the late L. Mendel Rivers, former Chairman of the House Armed Services Committee, and Richard Russell, former Chairman of the Senate Armed Services Committee, superhawks about whose constituencies it has been said, that "if Charleston (or in the case of Russell, Georgia) had one more military installation, it would sink into the Atlantic." But this view cannot be entirely correct, either, for many key Congressmen with outstandingly good pro-military voting records are rewarded in relatively niggardly fashion (George Mahon of Texas, Chairman of the House Appropriations Committee, John Stennis of Mississippi,[48] Chairman of the Senate Armed Services Committee), whereas many nonsupporters do very well indeed (Kennedy, Cranston, etc.).

3. The last possibility is that there is no relationship between hawkish voting and military expenditures at all. Hawkish voting is a function of attitudes, beliefs, and ideologies, not of the economic interests of one's constituency, and the location of defense expenditures is based on factors having nothing to do with Congressional voting (Charleston has so many naval installations because it has an excellent harbor, Georgia has military bases because of its good climate and favorable terrain, Massachusetts has defense contracts because it has become a center of scientific and engineering expertise, etc.).

We will not take this analysis further or attempt to sort out these possibilities and reach judgments about their relative validity. What we hope is clear is the extent to which theories of the military-industrial complex rest upon unacceptably narrow and simplistic assumptions about individual and group motivation which, uncritically accepted and applied, result in a sadly partial and misleading analysis of American politics.

Who Are the Members of the Complex?

Closely related to the question of motivation is the question of whether it makes sense to conceive the military-industrial complex as a group actor with sufficient internal coherence and group-consciousness to have and act upon "interests." We have already noted how usual it is for the phrase "military-industrial complex" to be used as if it referred to such an entity. Others, too, have observed that the notion of a military-industrial complex suggests "an organized decision-making entity which poses goals, weighs alternative strategies, makes decisions, marshals and arrays its forces, and behaves as a unit."[49] An initial problem here is that most of the literature is vague or inconsistent concerning the kinds of individuals or subgroups that "belong" to the military-industrial complex, and seldom are the criteria for belonging the subject of explicit discussion. Nearly all accounts agree in including as central to the complex the higher officials of the executive branch, particularly those in the Department of Defense; high-ranking military leaders; the top managers and principal owners of industrial corporations judged significantly dependent on military contracts; and Congressional leaders, especially the ranking members of committees consistently supporting high military expenditures. Beyond this inner core, however, there begins to be disagreement with respect to membership in the complex, and it is often unclear whether these other groups are properly regarded as members of the complex, "associate members,"[50] or merely as a sympathetic environment for the complex. Among these other groups are the leadership of labor unions whose members are dependent upon military related and generated employment, and at times even the entire membership of those unions; industrial and military associations of various kinds; veterans groups; many of the nation's scientists and engineers; universities in which military research is being undertaken or which are otherwise dependent upon financial support from the Department of Defense; Congressmen belonging to military reserve units, holding stock in defense corporations, or simply supporting high military budgets and sharing the cold-war consensus; the foreign service, intelligence agencies, and the Atomic Energy Commission; parts of the mass media; local business associations and civic groups in communities which benefit from heavy defense spending; and various religious bodies and spokesmen.

It is apparent that the criteria for membership in the complex are unclear and shifting, and to a considerable extent they undermine other premises of the military-industrial complex theory as an account of who makes high policy and for what ends. At least six criteria for membership can be discerned: participation in high-level policy making (the inner core); participation, at any level, in any government agency involved in foreign or military policy (the foreign service, intelligence agencies, AEC); economic, bureaucratic, or career interests (corporations, unions, scientists, academicians, etc.); ideological support for cold-war policies (conservative Congressmen, church groups, editors, etc.); and emotional attachments to the military (veterans groups, Congressmen in reserve units). Yet once membership in the complex is conceived to include groups beyond those identified as the inner core, the military-industrial complex theory loses most of its force, which rests on the premise that high policy in the United States is the work of a small, largely nonofficial, and unrepresentative elite group or coalition. In some versions, indeed, the complex seems to include most of both national and local government, as well as a substantial proportion of the population at large. While this inclusive concept may reflect an insight into the pervasiveness of militarism in American society, it is certainly inconsistent with the notion of a military-industrial complex as a coherent entity possessing interests and powers. For one thing, insofar as the existence of the complex itself is thought to be explained by the power of vested economic or institutional interests, then the inclusion of groups which have no such interests denies the premise.[51] Moreover, the more inclusively one conceives the military-industrial complex, the less sense it makes to speak of it as an entity, until (in the more extreme versions) it is a mere list of all groups or individuals within American society, with or without "power," that support high military expenditures and the main lines of American foreign policy since 1945, for whatever reasons.

While a less inclusive concept of the complex is thus required if the theory of the military-industrial complex is to make sense, such a concept would not necessarily be correct. That is, there would still be room for debate concerning the internal coherence and agreement of even the least-inclusive collections of men and groups that have been proposed as constituting the military-industrial complex. Any such debate would have to come to grips with the fact that the history of American foreign and defense policy is replete with examples of disagreement among the presumptive members of the complex.[52] The response of defenders of the military-industrial complex theory to this argument is usually that the *range* of disagreement, however significant it might appear to some participants and outside observers, is "really" quite narrow. All policy members are said to share the same cold-war perspective, the same "military definition of reality," as Mills put it, the same devotion to capitalist expansion. Thus, Pilisuk and Hayden argue that the political elite share three crucial "core beliefs:" (1) "efficacy is preferable to principle in foreign affairs . . . [which in practice] means that violence is preferable to non-violence as a means of defense"; (2) "private property is preferable to collective property"; (3) "the particular form of constitutional government, which is practiced within the United States is preferable to any other system of government."[53] Insofar as there is internal disagreement within the complex, then, it is solely over how the shared goals of its members are to be pursued.

A particularly interesting case study on the problem of whether it is more persuasive to emphasize agreement or disagreement within the military-industrial complex would be an examination of Robert McNamara's tenure as Secretary of Defense. From one perspective, certainly that of the majority of writers on the complex, McNamara stood at its very center, indeed was perhaps the prime example of the intertwining of business, bureaucratic, political, and military power at the highest levels of policy-making. Yet, from another perspective—that held by a wide variety of former policy-makers and outside observers—McNamara was the center of raging conflict that rent the complex, if he was not in fact "the 'complex's' greatest foe."[54] How are such differences of interpretation to be resolved? Clearly it is the case that in any group there will always be *some* commonalities and areas of agreement as well as *some* diversity and disagreement. Whether it is what unites or what divides which is more significant is a question to which there can be no general answer; one must ask "significant for what?" If we take as the criterion of significance in the present dispute the ability to explain particular policy outcomes (such as high military expenditures), as writers on the military-industrial complex largely do, then the kinds of agreement among those said to comprise the complex seem to be of such generality as to permit marked disagreement at the level of operational policy. Besides this, some of the generalizations about consensus (such as those of Pilisuk and Hayden concerning "core beliefs") are pretty plainly false, or at least in need of substantial qualification.

Does the Complex Have Power?

The concept of a military-industrial complex as an entity coherent enough to have and pursue interests of a certain kind is incomplete, within the framework of assumptions we are discussing, without the attribution of power to the complex. For it is power which completes the picture of an American society whose purposes and policies are distorted by the complex, and provides the explanatory link between the existence of a complex and these distortions. The concept (or concepts) of power presupposed by the theory of the military-industrial complex must therefore be examined. As the subject is a large one, our discussion is limited to a few points which are critical in evaluating the claims of the theory. In particular, we examine the *criteria* according to which power is attributed to the complex, the *scope* of the power attributed to it, and the *kind* of power it is thought to have.

What criteria are used, explicitly or implicitly, in the military-industrial complex literature for determining the extent to which the postulated complex has power? There appear to be three main approaches to this question. One approach is to infer power by examining who benefits from particular policies: those who gain are presumed to be powerful. This method is implicit in much of the military-industrial complex literature. The crucial point to be made about it is that it assumes rather than demonstrates that there is a causal relationship between (a) the desires and demands of some group and (b) outcomes which satisfy those desires. But this assumption rests on a fallacy. Not only is it the case that in the absence of evidence supporting a causal relationship we cannot assume that outcomes are explained by the desires or demands of particular groups rather than by other factors, but strictly speaking, we cannot even exclude the possibility that the outcomes occurred *despite* those demands.[55]

Another common assumption of the military-industrial complex literature is that power can be inferred from institutional position: the elites of the major economic, military, and political institutions are presumed to be powerful. This view is central to the analysis of Mills, who supported it with the argument that those major institutions constituted the principal means of power in modern society; the elite, by definition, comprised those who because of their positions in these institutions had access to means for satisfying their gratifications and realizing their will which are denied to the ordinary person.[56] While there is certainly something in this view, as it has been applied in discussions of the power of a military-industrial complex it has become misleading. For one thing, those who have adopted this approach have tended to equate a general capacity to achieve ends with the capacity to produce specific results: to have power in general is not necessarily to have the power to achieve some specific end. Another mistake is to equate prospects with success: to assume that because someone *might* have brought about a certain state of affairs, that he *did* bring it about. With respect to particular outcomes, then, institutional elites may or may not have had power, for institutional position provides us mainly with information about general and potential power, which in fact are not always translated into specific and actual power when relevant policy issues are decided.[57]

A third method of ascertaining power would be to examine specific cases of decision making to see who participates, and with what results. We have already observed that case studies are rare in the military-industrial complex literature; when they occur, they quite frequently fail to support the attribution of power to business firms or military agencies. What we know in general about the foreign policy decision-making process in the United States suggests strongly that the main participants are official elites, especially in the executive branch, rather than any behind-the-scenes unofficial elites. In particular, businessmen appear to play only the most minimal role, and the military participate mainly as distinct subordinates to the President and his advisors, and even then usually make their weight felt only on matters directly within their realm of presumed expertise. This is not to say that various business or military groups are without indirect influence on policy (for example, through legislative lobbying or campaign financing),[58] only that there is very little evidence of direct or unusual participation by them in the decision-making process. Finally, the case studies do not support attributions of power to a coherent military-industrial entity for, as we have already argued, there exist conflicts of interest, as well as common interests, among military and industrial groups. Therefore, proven instances of military or industrial influence on decision-making still fail to support attributions of power to a military-industrial *complex*.

Implicit in the decision-making case study approach is the assumption that power consists in being able to "prevail" over opposition. Those whose views or ends most often prevail in policy conflicts have the most power. This criterion for inferring power, though common, is a bad one.[59] But even if we follow the military-industrial complex literature for the moment in adopting it, the results are inconclusive. From one perspective it would appear that if there is a military-industrial complex, it has suffered a whole series of setbacks in recent years.[60] One notes:

1. The mushrooming growth of public and Congressional opposition to the war in Vietnam, general military spending, and to a considerable extent even to the military establishment as such.

2. The decline of military spending in terms either of its percentage share of the federal budget or of overall gross national product.[61] Indeed, if one discounts for inflation, non-Vietnam defense spending has declined in absolute as well as relative terms.[62] Yet another way of viewing the matter, and one which casts particular doubt on the notion of a powerful military-industrial complex, is to note that "the cost of all research and development, construction and all major procurement from industry together has grown just $300 million in the past nine years";[63] it is military pay raises (a total of $21 billion since 1964[64]), voted for by a diverse Congressional majority including doves seeking the establishment of an all-volunteer military, that have accounted for most of the recent increases in the absolute size of the military budget.

3. The elimination or substantial cutback of many weapons systems strongly urged on the executive branch by the defense establishment and its industrial allies, including nuclear-powered airplanes; the Skybolt, Navaho, Snark, and Nike-Zeus missiles; the B-70 bomber; and the ABM.[65] It is quite characteristic of the literature to point with great alarm to the "pressures" of the complex on behalf of these and other weapons systems but somehow to fail to notice how often those pressures *fail*.

4. The present ailing state of the aerospace industries, the heart of the industrial sector of the military-industrial complex.[66]

Certainly, however, from another perspective what is more impressive is what the military and its suppliers continue to get even in the face of these apparent adversities: the defense budget is still over $80 billion, most of the recent Congressional attacks on specific weapons projects have been weathered, the SALT agreements seem to have had little immediate impact on the arms race, and so on. What this juxtaposition of two reasonable perspectives suggests, of course, is the frequent extreme difficulty of ascertaining who "prevails" in conflicts. Take, for example, the ABM conflict prior to the SALT agreements— did the pro- or anti-ABM forces prevail when Congress decided to build two missile sites rather than the twelve initially requested by the Nixon Administration and its corporate and military allies? Or, take the recent Congressional decision in which by a margin of one vote a large loan to the Lockheed Corporation was authorized.[67] Should we be more impressed with the power of Lockheed to get the Nixon Administration and Congress to subsidize its operations, or with the fact that a major corporation presumably standing at the very heart of the complex barely was able to avoid bankruptcy? Congressman William Moorhead likened Lockheed's tactics to that of "an 80 ton dinosaur who comes to your door and says, 'If you don't feed me, I will die.' And what are you going to do with 80 tons of dead, stinking dinosaur in your yard?' "[68] To be sure, the threat to commit an inconvenient suicide carries "power" of a sort, but hardly the kind suggested by the military-industrial complex literature. Attributions of power to a military-industrial complex, at least insofar as power is associated with the notion of prevailing, thus vary according to whether it is the successes of the complex or its reverses, what it gets or what it fails to get, that strike the observer as most significant. But the criterion of prevailing is too crude a notion, and one too closely tied to one's judgments about how much military spending is justified or rational, to bear the theoretical weight it has been asked to carry.

Thus, the criteria according to which power is attributed to a military-industrial complex are indecisive, and involve logical fallacies or conceptual confusion. What about the *scope* of power attributed to the military-industrial complex? Over what range of public policy is the complex said to have power? There seem to be five main possibilities envisaged in the literature, listed here in order of increasing scope: the distribution of the military budget, the overall size of the military budget, foreign and military policy in general, the entire range of public policy, and the structure, ethos, and direction of American society. The scope of power enjoyed by the complex is commonly taken to be very great, including at least the determination of American foreign and defense policies and the general setting of priorities within American public policy.[69] Most of the *specific arguments* made by theorists of the military-industrial complex, however, are relevant only to the complex's alleged power over the distribution of the military budget or, at most, to its overall size.

In essence, the argument concerning the distribution and size of the military budget is that a close, nonadversary, symbiotic "team" relationship has developed between the military and its industrial suppliers, because of (1) the interchange of personnel between the two institutions (over 2000 former high-ranking officers are employed by the 100 largest military contractors; top industrialists move from their corporations to stints in the Defense Department and back again); (2) the practice of letting arms contracts and deciding their terms through industry-Pentagon negotiations rather than through competitive bidding; and (3) the mutually-dependent relationship between the Pentagon and its top suppliers—in contrast with the past, most of the largest defense industries (aircraft, electronics) are not diversified but do the overwhelming majority of their business with the government, and conversely, the Pentagon is dependent on the experience, technological expertise, and massive production capabilities of the largest of its suppliers. This close relationship, in turn, is thought to lead to favoritism, waste, inefficiency, and even corruption. The evidence most commonly presented in behalf of this argument is that over two-thirds of military prime contracts go to the 100 largest companies, enormous cost overruns are typically tolerated by the Pentagon, and that billions of dollars worth of new military weapons systems have had to be cancelled because of their poor operational performance or instant obsolescence.

Two points may be noted about this argument. First, the facts do not necessarily support the conclusions drawn from them. While the military-industrial complex literature is persuasive in demonstrating that there is at least *some* waste, corruption, and inefficiency is attributable to an excessively close industry-Pentagon relationship, other factors are clearly also important.

The uneven distribution of military largesse can be explained by factors other than political influence or favoritism: the largest corporations can afford huge outlays for research and development and have the experience and technological skills necessary to produce advanced weapons systems;[70] climate and geography also play important roles (aircraft and missile work takes place where the climate permits all-year testing and launching, large military bases are thought to be most appropriately located in outpost areas like Alaska or Hawaii or in less densely populated areas like the South and Southwest, Naval installations and shipbuilding facilities obviously have to be in ports, etc.);[71] lack of competition in the awarding of major contracts is often unavoidable for various nonpolitical technical reasons.[72] Similarly, cost overruns, late deliveries, and poor performance are not due simply to inefficiency or corruption but also to the inherent problems and uncertainties involved in advanced technology.[73] Finally, the disposition of the Pentagon to overlook poor performance and to "bail-out" floundering corporations with government loans or subsidies is in great part explained by the prevalent belief that, come what may, the national interest requires the continued existence of the military's major industrial suppliers.[74]

As for the effects of industry-Pentagon relationships on the overall size of the budget, what is "waste" or evidence of corruption, and what are the inevitable byproducts of technological change, healthy interservice and industrial competition, a sound policy of covering all bets even when it is known that some will not work out, and so on, are all matters of perspective, values, and judgments over a wide range of matters, including the nature of the international environment and the appropriate American response to it. Put differently, the implicit argument that the relationship between the military and the defense industry biases the weapons procurement process to such a degree that the United States spends far more on defense than is "necessary," or than it otherwise would, cannot be proven by simply pointing to the amount of money spent on weapons systems that cost more than original estimates or proved to be less adequate or reliable than expected.

Secondly, and for our purposes more importantly, even if the facts cited by theorists of the military-industrial complex contributed to a valid argument concerning military spending, they would be relevant primarily to that part of the argument concerned with the distribution of the military budget, only partially to its overall size,[75] and not at all to the alleged power of a military-industrial complex over matters of broader scope. Thus the centrally-important theme, implicit or explicit, that there is a military-industrial complex which exercises a broad range of power within American society is not supported by relevant evidence or argument, but rests instead upon assertion or indirection.

The final critical problem we wish to examine concerning the analysis of the power of a military-industrial complex has to do with the *kind* of power attributed to it. Implicit in most of the military-industrial-complex literature is the argument that the source of the complex's power lies in the availability to it of both positive and negative sanctions: the complex has power because it is able to use its extensive economic and political resources to reward its friends and punish its enemies. Such a conception of power overlooks a number of possibilities, however, one of which is that a complex might achieve its ends (assuming, again, for purposes of discussion that it existed as an entity, had ends, and succeeded in furthering them) not because it had power in the sense of control over sanctions, but *influence*, defined as the capacity to persuade both public officials and public opinion of the validity of its preferred policies without recourse to sanctions.[76] Thus, to the extent that various supposed members of a military-industrial complex have "prevailed" in decisions concerning military policy, it may be because Presidents and Congressional committees have been convinced by their arguments or deferred to their presumed expertise, rather than that they have brought irresistible economic and political power to bear. Perceptions of whether it is power or influence that is at work vary in quite predictable ways: those who disagree with the rationale of particular policy decisions usually explain them as the result of the exercise of power, whereas those who agree with them rarely see "power" or "pressures" at work, let alone illegitimate power, but only persuasion, or perhaps simply a necessary response to an obvious reality.

Yet another possibility is that an agent's power is not based on his capacity to overcome resistance, whether by sanctions *or* by persuasion, but on the absence of any opposition at all, or the availability of positive support. For most of the postwar period there existed a cold-war consensus in America (shared by groups with no "interests" in the cold war as well as by those who might be said to have such interests) so deep that there were few significant conflicts over military expenditures, and hence little opposition over which a military-industrial complex would be forced to prevail.[77] Indeed, if we were to accept the usual concept of power as the capacity to achieve ends over opposition, we would be forced to conclude that for most of the postwar period in the United States there was little basis at all for attributing power to a military-industrial complex. On the other hand, if power is conceived simply as the capacity to achieve ends, then it would make sense to attribute power of a kind to the executive bureaucracy, the military, and perhaps other institutions alleged to form part of a military-industrial complex, but it would be power which derived primarily from the fact that such institutions gave expression to and were supported by a widely shared public consensus.[78]

A few writers on the military-industrial complex, notably Pilisuk and Hayden, are aware that the existence of a general cold-war consensus in American society throughout most of the postwar period poses serious problems for the more typical view of the complex as an unrepresentative elite imposing its will on society. They meet this problem by claiming that the consensus was not spontaneous or in some sense "genuine," but was created, imposed, or manipulated by the complex itself, through its control over the instruments of mass communication, education, and socialization. In this way the power of the complex manifests itself not, or rather not only, in concrete policy decisions but in its ability to determine what issues become matters of public decision at all and to shape the terms in which such issues are framed. If there is no overt conflict of interests between the majority and the elite, it is because the majority are victims of a "false consciousness" of their true interests, deliberately fostered by a controlling military-industrial complex. Thus, it is not so much that the complex prevails over opposition as that it prevails by ensuring that no opposition arises in the first place.[79]

The argument does not seem very persuasive. The notion that a single coherent elite with a vested interest in the cold war or militarism controls the major instruments of information and education is not demonstrated but simply asserted, and moreover is implausible on its face. The media, the schools, the churches, etc., are neither controlled by such an entity nor are they monolithic in their content. Moreover, most careful studies of the influences of the mass media conclude that their capacity to mold attitudes is highly exaggerated.[80] Finally, the notion of an elite-controlled consensus is embarrassed by the recent explosion of very real popular *dissent* over American foreign and military policies.

The major fallacy in the kinds of analyses we have been discussing is that they rest on a false underlying premise, namely that the existence of a "wrong" or "false" consensus (i.e., one based on erroneous or oversimplified concepts of reality) can only be explained by the actions of an identifiable group with both the power and motivation to create it.[81] Because this premise is wrong, our rejection of the notion that the cold-war consensus in the United States has been deliberately created from above by no means commits us to the view that this consensus was (or is) either substantively correct or rationally arrived at. The irrationalities of American foreign and military policies are better explained by a pattern of fears, misconceptions, myths, and desires, shared by elites and masses alike, and historically rooted in the unwilled structure of American norms, practices, and institutions.[82] The current state of American society is not explained primarily by *anyone's* power, let alone the alleged power of a military-industrial complex; or, alternatively, if the elites and the mass public share the same basic beliefs and values, we could just as well conclude that power "really" resides with the mass public. If this analysis is correct, then some of the central claims of the military-industrial complex theory concerning power collapse.

Conclusion

To reject the framework of assumptions within which discussion of American militarism and the military-industrial complex has been largely carried out is obviously not to deny everything that has been said in the course of that discussion. Clearly one may reject the explanatory theory developed within this framework, while accepting the contentions of the military-industrial complex literature that there are things seriously wrong with American politics and society which constitute or are traceable to militarism, that there exist individuals and groups with a stake in high military expenditures and militarist policies, and that they may have some effect on the process and substance of policy making. Nor is to reject the theory necessarily to deny the value of the military-industrial complex literature as exposé or as a source of information on military procurement practices and the like. What is objectionable in this literature is the inflation of its observations about American politics into an overblown theory which exaggerates the unity and coherence that exists among these groups, their efficacy in controlling policy, and the scope of policy affected by their actions; which neglects other crucially important factors that must be taken into account in understanding the military aspects of American society; and which is tied to a restrictive and misleading model of explanation in terms of the deliberate actions and powers of agents.

The problem with the more recent fashion of adopting the phrase "military-industrial complex" as a catchall under which to carry out studies of military policy-making, civil-military relations, the economics of military spending, and the like, is that the assumptions of the military-industrial complex theory will often by unwittingly borrowed along with the phrase. The tenacious hold of these assumptions over the way in which the concept of a military-industrial complex is actually used is apparent from the few attempts which have been made to revise the concept so that it is no longer associated with an analysis of militarism in terms of entities, actions, and powers. In these attempts the intention has been to conceive the complex as a systemic attribute of American society, the social structure of which is "organized to create and protect power centers with only partial accountability" (Pilisuk and Hayden), or as an institutionalized pattern of beliefs and practices which constitute a distinctive American subculture (Stackhouse). But in these analyses such language co-exists with references to the actions and power of a personified military-industrial complex.[83] It is therefore hard to resist the conclusion that, so far at least, the main consequence of the reliance on the concept of a military-industrial complex has been to oversimplify and misdirect the analysis of power and militarism in American politics.

Notes

1. An earlier version of this paper was presented in 1971 at meetings of the American Political Science Association and the Inter-University Seminar on Armed Forces and Society. We are indebted to many persons for helpful discussions of our subject, especially to John Champlin, David Kettler, Clark Murdock and R. Harrison Wagner, each of whom also provided us with a written critique of the initial version.

2. Respectively, Cook (1964); Melman (1970); Barnet (1969 and 1972); and Tyrrell (1970). Perhaps it is not wrong to speculate that the search for ever more catchy labels is sometimes motivated as much by commercial as by scientific considerations.

3. A typical comment: "The pattern of militarism in American life cannot be measured solely in terms of military control of foreign policy or economic life or any particular institution. It has pervaded the whole American system of values so that there is no longer an effective counter-force to the military in American political life." (Swomley, 1964, p. 244.)

4. For some recent examples see the symposium on the military-industrial complex in the JOURNAL OF INTERNATIONAL AFFAIRS 26, No. 1 (1972), as well as some of the other essays in the present volume.

5. For example see Baumgartner, 1971, and the sections on the defenders of the military-industrial complex in Davis, 1971, and Schiller and Phillips, 1970.

6. In this category we would place Duscha, 1964; Kaufman, 1970; McGaffin and Knoll, 1969; Mollenhoff, 1967; Proxmire, 1970; Tyrrell, 1970; Rice, 1971.

7. Barnet, 1969 and 1972; Cochran, 1965; Coffin, 1964; Cook, 1964; Galbraith, 1969; Lapp, 1969 and 1970; Lens, 1970; Melman, 1970; Perlo, 1963;

Pilisuk and Hayden, 1965; Rodberg and Shearer, 1970; Schiller and Phillips, 1970; Swomley, 1964 and 1968.

8. Note that in a period of similar disenchantment with American foreign policy during the 1930s, similar notions (the "Merchants of Death") had widespread popularity. See Engelbrect and Hanighen, 1934; Ferrell, 1972; Koistinen, 1967 and 1970; Wiltz, 1963.

9. See, for example, Hobson, 1938 (first published 1902). The logical structure of Hobson's analysis of imperialism is strikingly similar to contemporary analyses of the military-industrial complex. Both focus on a phenomenon viewed as irrational for the nation as a whole, but rational from the standpoint of certain groups within the whole. The phenomenon is explained by invoking the power of those groups which benefit from it. Such groups work covertly, hide behind the flag, and not only overcome opposition but forestall it by controlling the media and education.

10. Domhoff, in Domhoff and Ballard, 1968, pp. 275-76.

11. Ibid., p. 257.

12. Ibid., p. 261, 276. For other works in this vein see Domhoff, 1970, and Kolko, 1969. Cf. Miliband, 1969.

13. Mills, 1956, especially Chapter 1. Mills defends his distinction between a power elite and a ruling class on p. 277.

14. Potter, 1962, p. 375.

15. Swomley, 1964; Cook, 1962; Lens, 1970; Barnet, 1969 and 1972.

16. Barnet, 1969, p. 97.

17. Barnet, 1972, p. 341.

18. See especially Melman, 1970. Here the conceptual similarity with Mills' theory is apparent.

19. Cochran, 1965, p. 123. See also Galbraith, 1971: "The bureaucracy, the military and intelligence bureaucracy in particular, operates not in response to national need, but in response to its own need, and carries a too passive Commander-in-Chief along with it. . . . But it would be a mistake to picture bureaucratic need in terms of a too specific bureaucratic self-interest. A more important factor is pure organizational momentum." (1971, p. 37.) Despite this disclaimer, Galbraith continues to speak of "the bureaucracy" as if it were an entity, rather than of bureaucracy as a principle of organization or a kind of phenomenon.

20. Schumpeter, 1955, p. 25, (first published 1919).

21. Claims of this sort, however, are often contradicted in practice by statements referring to the interests, actions and powers of the complex—attributions which presuppose an entity to which they apply.

22. McConnell, 1966, Wolf, 1969, Stackhouse, 1971, and others have argued that there are several such "complexes" in American society; that is, powerful private groups closely collaborating with sectors of the government and exercising largely autonomous power over areas of public policy. Among the areas in

which such complexes have been said to operate are health, education, transportation, labor, agriculture and business.

23. Speech to U.S. Naval Academy, 1961, in PROCEEDINGS OF THE U.S. NAVAL INSTITUTE (June 1971), p. 21.

24. Galbraith, 1969; Yarmolinsky, 1971; Pilisuk and Hayden, 1963.

25. Pilisuk and Hayden, 1965, p. 98.

26. Ibid., p. 103.

27. Cf. Barnet, 1972: "The world in which they [the "National Security Managers"] moved—the Metropolitan Club, the Council on Foreign Relations— ... bore little ... resemblance to the America in which most citizens were struggling to make their lives," p. 57.

28. See Lapp, in Carey, 1969: "the military-industrial complex is a " 'Second Government' existing almost independently within our democracy"; (p. 43); Melman, 1970: "In the name of defense, and without announcement or debate, a basic alteration has been effected in the governing institutions of the United States. ... The state-management has ... become the most powerful decision-making unit in the United States government. ... The joining of the economic-managerial and top political power has been done in an unannounced and, in effect, covert fashion." pp. 1, 2, 5.

29. Popper, 1966, pp. 94-95.

30. Barnet, 1972, p. 126.

31. Galbraith, in Davis, 1971, p. 92; Lens, 1970, p. 47; Yarmolinsky, 1968, p. 43.

32. Popper's idea is further elaborated by Kaplan, 1964, p. 364 and MacIntyre, 1971, pp. 80-81.

33. Even within this framework, such explanations emphasize the actions of the conspirators while overlooking the actions, or failures to act, of other participants in the situation. Exceptions to this would include the emphasis by Mills, Eisenhower, and others on the absence of countervailing power to that of military-industrial elites, and the attention given by reformers like Proxmire to failures and omissions in the military procurement process such as loose auditing, absence of congressional scrutiny of military appropriations, lack of competitive bidding or a uniform accounting system, and absence of information because of all the secrecy surrounding the process (Proxmire, in Davis, pp. 87-88).

34. Peck and Shearer, 1962, p. v.

35. Lens, 1970, p. 14.

36. Melman, 1970, p. 4.

37. Quoted in Proxmire, 1970, p. 111.

38. See Kolkowicz, 1971 and the articles in the JOURNAL OF INTER-NATIONAL AFFAIRS symposium. Also see the discussion of the international "milorgs" in Boulding, 1967 and 1970.

39. Enthoven and Smith, 1971, write that in building new weapons systems,

"the dictum seemed to be, 'I can, therefore I must.' Thus, new technological possibilities became new military requirements." (p. 27). Cf. also Robert Oppenheimer's famous remark on the building of the hydrogen bomb: "When you see something that is technically sweet you go ahead and do it." (Quoted by Peck and Scherer, 1962, p. 294). For similar views on technology as the driving force behind the military-industrial complex see York, 1970; Kolkowicz, 1971; Lapp, 1970; and Yarmolinsky, 1971. Analyses linking the nature of military organization to stages of political development or forms of social structure may be found in Huntington, 1968, and Andreski, 1968.

40. A recent newspaper story discussed the impact of the SALT arms-control agreements on the town of Conrad, Montana, where construction for an ABM site had been abruptly cancelled, badly harming the immediate welfare of the town's inhabitants. The reporter claimed to be able to find no one who objected to the action, and quoted as typical of local reactions the following remark: "Nobody questions the President's move. Nobody in his right mind would question a treaty that's designed to help us all" (THE NEW YORK TIMES, June 4, 1972).

41. We examine this question further in the section titled "Who Are the Members of the Complex?"

42. Barnet, 1969, p. 99. Or, as Aspaturian, 1972, p. 25, puts it:

Perception . . . is frequently a reflection of self-interest rather than objective reality . . . That groups favored by a particular policy or situation have a greater inclination to perceive objective reality in terms of their self-interest is, then, entirely natural.

43. Lens, 1970, pp. 11 and 1.

44. Cook, 1964, p. 112.

45. Melman, 1970, p. 4.

46. Barnet, 1972, p. 67.

47. Cobb, 1969; Gray and Gregory, 1968; Russett, 1970.

48. It has only been in the last few years that Mississippi has received any major defense contracts.

49. Kindleberger, 1969, p. 59. In a similar vein, Aspaturian (1972, p. 1) remarks that the military-industrial complex notion implies an entity that behaves "as a distinctive political actor separate from its individual components."

50. Galbraith, 1969.

51. However, some writers argue that ideological support is itself an artifact of the power of the military-industrial complex to mold opinion. See p. 48.

52. See, for example, the extensive literature written within the pluralist perspective (that is, those who characterize the policy process in terms of conflict and negotiation) as well as memoirs by former insiders. Moreover, even Barnet (1972), who wishes to characterize the "national security managers" as

sharing a "remarkable consensus" ends by providing much more persuasive evidence on their *disagreements*, especially over Vietnam, his main policy case study.

53. Pilisuk and Hayden, 1965, p. 91.

54. Congressional Quarterly Report, p. 1155.

55. For an example of a case study in the weapons procurement process that is sensitive to this problem, see Art, 1968. One of Art's conclusions is that the evidence is insufficient to establish whether political pressures had anything to do with the awarding of the huge TFX contract to General Dynamics, since that award could plausibly be explained by other factors as well. For a general analysis on the problems of deducing power from outcomes, see Wolfinger, 1971.

56. Mills, 1956, Chapter 1.

57. For discussions of the distinction between potential and actual power see Dahl, 1958; 1968; Lasswell and Kaplan, 1950; Oppenheim, 1961. Also, see Bauer, Pool, and Dexter, 1963, on the impact of business groups on trade policy; the authors argue that the feared costs of exercising its potential power severely inhibits big business from pressing its views, even on matters of direct concern to it.

58. We will discuss such "pre-decisional" influence when we take up the question of the *kinds* of power attributed to a military-industrial complex.

59. The notion of "prevailing," widely shared among both "power elite" theorists and their "pluralist" critics, obscures just those distinctions (for example, among coercion, persuasion, exchange, and authority) which are crucial for the resolution of debates about the nature of power, power elites, power structures, and the like.

60. For such a view see Huntington, 1969; Wolf, 1969; Goldwater and Baker in Davis, 1971.

61. The projected figures for FY 1972 showed military expenditures to be 33 percent of total federal outlays and less than 7 percent of GNP, the lowest such figures since the period preceding the Korean War. (Schultze, 1972.)

62. Huntington, 1969.

63. Assistant Secretary of Defense Moot, NEW YORK TIMES, July 30, 1972, 6, p. 38.

64. Ibid.

65. See Baldwin, 1967, pp. 121-22.

66. See the WALL STREET JOURNAL, February 23, 1971, for an analysis of the allegedly deep financial troubles of the defense industry.

67. It is also of interest that Barry Goldwater and several other conservative Senatorial stalwarts of the "military-industrial complex" voted *against* the loan, on the grounds that such Congressional subsidies were inconsistent with the free enterprise system.

68. Quoted in Rice, 1971, p. 183.

69. Some examples:

1. Tyrrell, 1970: "The New Nobility . . . control or influence most of the positions of power in our society . . . " (ix-x).
2. Cook, 1964: the complex "dominates our society." (369)
3. Lapp, 1969: "Gradually the U.S. involvement with defense industry has proceeded to the point where weapons-making begins to dominate our society." (177)
4. Clayton, 1970: "Has the power of the military-industrial-scientific complex reached such proportions that it can now determine its own needs and dictate to the American people the sacrifices that are expected of them in order to sustain this complex in power?" (p. 240).
5. Barnet, 1969: World War II catapulted "the military establishment from a marginal institution without a constituency to a position of command over the resources of a whole society." (p. 69).
6. Melman, 1970: "The new state-management combines peak economic, political and military decision making. . . . Never before in American experience has there been such a combination of economic and political decision-power in the same hands. . . . Rarely does a singly social force have a controlling influence in changing, swiftly, the character of life in a large and complex society. The expansion of the Pentagon and its state-management is such a force." (pp. 1, 5, 227).

70. Novick and Springer, 1959; Baumgartner, 1970; Peck and Scherer, 1962, discuss these factors.

71. See Yamolinsky, 1971; Weidenbaum, 1968; Hitch, in Javits, Hitch and Burns, 1968; Baldwin, 1967.

72. Art, 1972; Baldwin, 1967.

73. Peck and Scherer, 1962; Moore, 1964.

74. Rice, 1971; Baldwin, 1967; Art, 1968. For example, Rice considers that the primary reason for the Nixon Administration's support of a major loan to the Lockheed Corporation, despite its terrible performance on the C-5A contract, was that it was the sole source of Polaris and Poseidon missiles and dozens of other major weapons systems. More generally, in their major study, Peck and Scherer conclude that "Our research disclosed no instances in which firms were selected for which a nonpolitical justification could not be made." (1962, p. 381-82).

75. Few writers claim that without the structural biases embedded in the military industrial complex the United States would spend little or nothing on defense. Most detailed studies of the military budget process minimize the importance of industrial lobbying, especially its importance in determining overall policies and budget levels. For example, Huntington concludes that group pressures focus almost exclusively on contract awards, with "no one group or

even coalition of groups [seeking] to mobilize support for the defense program as a whole.... It is unlikely ... that their activity significantly increased the overall defense effort." (1961, p. 216-7). Of course, it does not necessarily follow that because no groups lobbied for the whole spectrum of military spending that lobbying on behalf of individual projects cannot have a cumulative impact on the size of the total military budget.

76. In making this distinction between power and influence we follow Partridge, 1963, and Parsons, 1963.

77. In fact, there is much evidence that, if anything, mass public opinion was even more militarist than that of the political elites. On the importance of the cold war consensus as opposed to the "power" (in the traditional sense) of a military-industrial complex, see Schultze, PROGRESSIVE, 1969: "The real problem with military budgets and military commitments is that the great majority of the American people will buy anything once it is wrapped in the flag and the Joint Chiefs say it is necessary for security." (p. 54).

78. This conclusion is consistent with the surmise of many writers on elites (notably Pareto, 1966; Mosca, 1939; Mannheim, 1950; and Keller, 1963), that elites have power mainly insofar as and as long as they perform functions widely valued in their societies.

79. Pilisuk and Hayden argue that public opinion "tends to be much more manipulated and apathetic than independent," (1965, p. 82), which results in a "forced or acquiescent consensus." (p. 94). Similarly Lens speaks of "an orchestrated effort by all segments of the military-industrial complex to guide public opinion in a single direction." (1970, p. 50). Others emphasizing the deliberate and successful efforts of the complex to inculcate in mass public opinion a false view of the world are Melman, 1970; Cook, 1964; Barnet, 1969 and 1972; Rodberg and Shearer, 1970. For a similar analysis emphasizing power as the capacity to confine politics to certain "safe" areas, see Bachrach and Baratz, 1962 and 1963.

80. See, for example, Key, 1961.

81. This is the conspiracy theory of society again, invoked in this case to explain a consensus which is disapproved.

82. Cf. Edelman, 1971, especially on the power of the myths of "defense" and "the national interest." A now little read analysis of militarism in American politics during the First World War comes to a similar conclusion:

The root of the trouble ... goes far deeper than the arms industry. It lies in the prevailing temper of peoples toward nationalism, militarism, and war, in the civilization which forms this temper and prevents any radical change.... If the arms industry is a cancer on the body of modern civilization, it is not an extraneous growth; it is the result of the unhealthy condition of the body itself. (Englebrecht and Harrighan, 1939, pp. 8-10).

83. Pilisuk and Hayden, 1965; Stackhouse, 1971. Similarly, as we earlier observed, the one or two promising starts toward an analysis of militarism in

terms of the dynamics of bureaucracy or a state-managed economy soon relapse into accounts of the interests, actions, and powers of *the* bureaucracy or state-management.

References

Andreski, Stanislav. MILITARY ORGANIZATION AND SOCIETY. Berkeley: U. of Cal. Press, 1968.

Art, Robert J. THE TFX DECISION. Boston: Little, Brown, 1968.

Aspaturian, Vernon J. "The Soviet Military-Industrial Complex—Does It Exist?" JOURNAL OF INTERNATIONAL AFFAIRS 26, No. 1 (1972).

Baldwin, William L. THE STRUCTURE OF THE DEFENSE MARKET, 1955-1964. Durham: Duke U. Press, 1967.

Barnet, Richard J. THE ECONOMY OF DEATH. New York: Atheneum, 1969.
_____. THE ROOTS OF WAR. New York: Atheneum, 1972.

Bauer, Raymond A., Ithiel de Sola Pool, & Lewis A. Dexter. AMERICAN BUSINESS AND PUBLIC POLICY. Atherton, 1963.

Baumgartner, John S. THE LONELY WARRIORS. Los Angeles: Nash, 1970.

Boulding, Kenneth. "The Role of the War Industry in International Conflict," JOURNAL OF SOCIAL ISSUES 23, No. 1 (January 1967).
_____. (ed.) PEACE AND THE WAR INDUSTRY. Chicago: Aldine Publishing Co., 1970.

Carey, Omer L. (ed.) THE MILITARY-INDUSTRIAL COMPLEX AND U.S. FOREIGN POLICY. Washington State University Press, 1969.

Clayton, James L. (ed.) THE ECONOMIC IMPACT OF THE COLD WAR. New York: Harcourt, Brace & World, 1970.

Cobb, Stephen A. "Defense Spending and Foreign Policy in the House of Representatives," JOURNAL OF CONFLICT RESOLUTION (September 1969).

Cochran, Bert. THE WAR SYSTEM. New York: MacMillan, 1965.

Coffin, Tristam. THE PASSION OF THE HAWKS. New York: MacMillan, 1964.

Congressional Quarterly Weekly Report. THE MILITARY-INDUSTRIAL COMPLEX (May 24 1968).

Cook, Fred J. THE WARFARE STATE. New York: Collier Books, 1964.

Dahl, Robert A. "A Critique of the Ruling Elite Model." THE AMERICAN POLITICAL SCIENCE REVIEW 52, No. 2 (June 1958).
_____, "Power." INTERNATIONAL ENCYCLOPEDIA OF THE SOCIAL SCIENCES 12 New York: MacMillan 1968.

Davis, Kenneth S. (ed.). ARMS, INDUSTRY AND AMERICA. New York: H.W. Wilson Co., 1971.

Domhoff, G. William. THE HIGHER CIRCLES; THE GOVERNING CLASS IN AMERICA. New York: Random House, 1970.
_____ and Hoyt B. Ballard (eds.). C. WRIGHT MILLS AND THE POWER ELITE. Boston: Beacon Press, 1968.

Duscha, Julius. ARMS, MONEY AND POLITICS. New York: Ives Wasburn, Inc., 1964.

Edelman, Murray, POLITICS AS SYMBOLIC ACTION. Chicago: Markham, 1971.

Eisenhower, Dwight D. Speech to the U.S. Naval Academy, 1971. PROCEEDINGS OF U.S. NAVAL INSTITUTE (June 1971).

Engelbrecht, H.C. and F.C. Hanighen. MERCHANTS OF DEATH. New York: Dodd, Mead, & Co., 1934.

Enthoven, Alain C., and K. Wayne Smith. HOW MUCH IS ENOUGH? New York: Harper & Row, 1971.

Ferrell, Robert F. "The Merchants of Death, Then and Now." JOURNAL OF INTERNATIONAL AFFAIRS 26, No. 1 (1972).

Galbraith, John Kenneth. HOW TO CONTROL THE MILITARY. Signet, 1969.

Gray, Charles H. & Glenn W. Gregory. "Military Spending and Senate Voting." JOURNAL OF PEACE RESEARCH 5, No. 1 (1968).

Hobson, John. A STUDY OF IMPERIALISM. London: George Allen and Unwin, Ltd., 1938.

Huntington, Samuel P. THE COMMON DEFENSE. New York: University Press, 1961.

_____. POLITICAL ORDER IN CHANGING SOCIETIES. New Haven: Yale University Press, 1968.

_____. "The Defense Establishment: Vested Interested and the Public Interest." See Carey (1969).

Javits, Jacob B., Charles J. Hitch, and Arthur E. Burns. THE DEFENSE SECTOR AND THE AMERICAN ECONOMY. New York University Press, 1968.

Kaplan, Abraham. THE CONDUCT OF INQUIRY. California: Wadsworth, 1964.

Kaufman, Richard F. THE WAR PROFITEERS. Indianapolis: Bobbs-Merrill, 1970.

Keller, Suzanne. BEYOND THE RULING CLASS. New York: Random House, 1963.

Key, V.O., Jr. PUBLIC OPINION AND AMERICAN DEMOCRACY. New York: Alfred A. Knopf, 1961.

Kindleberger, Charles B. POWER AND MONEY. New York: Basic Books, 1970.

Koistinen, Paul A.C., "The Industrial-Military Complex in Historical Perspective." BUSINESS HISTORY REVIEW 16, No. 4 (1967).

_____. "The 'Industrial-Military Complex' in Historical Perspective: The Interwar Years." JOURNAL OF AMERICAN HISTORY 56, No. 4 (March 1970).

Kolko, Gabriel. THE ROOTS OF AMERICAN FOREIGN POLICY. Boston: Beacon Press, 1969.

Kolkowicz, Roman. "Strategic Parity and Beyond." WORLD POLITICS (April 1971).

Lapp, Ralph. THE WEAPONS CULTURE. Baltimore: Penguin Books, 1969.

_____ . ARMS BEYOND DOUBT. Chicago: Cowles Book Co., 1970.

Lasswell, Harold D., and Abraham Kaplan. POWER AND SOCIETY. New Haven: Yale University Press, 1950.

Lens, Sidney. THE MILITARY-INDUSTRIAL COMPLEX. Boston: Pilgrim Press, 1970.

MacIntyre, Alasdair. MARCUSE. New York: Viking Press, 1971.

Mannheim, Karl. FREEDOM, POWER, AND DEMOCRATIC PLANNING. New York: Oxford U. Press, 1950.

McConnell, Grant. PRIVATE POWER AND AMERICAN DEMOCRACY. New York: Alfred A. Knopf, 1966.

McGaffin, William and Erwin Knoll. SCANDAL IN THE PENTAGON. New York: Fawcett, 1969.

Melman, Seymour. PENTAGON CAPITALISM. New York: McGraw-Hill, 1970.

Miliband, Ralph. THE STATE IN CAPITALIST SOCIETY. London: Weidenfeld & Nicolson 1969.

Mills, C. Wright. THE POWER ELITE. New York: Oxford U. Press, 1956.

Mollenhoff, Clark R. THE PENTAGON: POLITICS, PROFITS AND PLUNDER. New York: G.P. Putnam's Sons, 1967.

Moore, Frederick T. "Efficiency and Public Policy in Defense Procurement." LAW AND CONTEMPORARY PROBLEMS 29, No. 1 (Winter 1964).

Mosca, Gaetano. THE RULING CLASS. New York: McGraw-Hill, 1939.

Nieburg, H.L. IN THE NAME OF SCIENCE. New York: Quadrangle Books, 1966.

Novick, David & J.Y. Springer. "Economics of Defense Procurement and Small Business." LAW AND CONTEMPORARY PROBLEMS 24, No. 1 (Winter 1959).

Oppenheim, Felix E. DIMENSIONS OF FREEDOM. New York: St. Martin's Press, 1961.

Pareto, Vilfredo. SOCIOLOGICAL WRITINGS. London: Pall Mall Press, 1966.

Parsons, Talcott. "On the Concept of Influence." PUBLIC OPINION QUARTERLY. (Spring 1963).

Partridge, P.H. "Some Notes on the Concept of Power." POLITICAL STUDIES 11, No. 2, 1963.

Peck, Merton J. and Frederic M. Scherer. THE WEAPONS ACQUISITION PROCESS. Division of Research, Graduate School of Business Administration, Harvard University, 1962.

Perlo, Victor. MILITARISM AND INDUSTRY. London: Lawrence and Wishart, 1963.

Pilisuk, Marc and Thomas Hayden. "Is There a Military Industrial Complex Which Prevents Peace?" JOURNAL OF SOCIAL ISSUES 21, No. 3, (July 1965).

Popper, Karl R. THE OPEN SOCIETY AND ITS ENEMIES. 2. New York: Harper & Row, 1967.

Potter, Allen. "The Elite Concept." POLITICAL STUDIES. 14, No. 3, (October 1966).

Progressive, The. POWER OF THE PENTAGON. (June 1969).

Proxmire, William. REPORT FROM WASTELAND. New York: Praeger, 1970.

Rice, Berkeley. THE C-5A SCANDAL. Boston: Houghton-Mifflin, 1971.

Rodberg, Leonard S. and Derek Shearer (eds.). THE PENTAGON WATCHERS. New York: Doubleday, 1970.

Russett, Bruce M. WHAT PRICE VIGILANCE? New Haven, Conn.: Yale University Press, 1970.

Schiller, Herbert I., and Joseph D. Phillips (eds.). SUPERSTATE: READINGS IN MILITARY-INDUSTRIAL COMPLEX. Urbana: University of Illinois Press, 1970.

Schultze, Charles L., et al. SETTING NATIONAL PRIORITIES; THE 1972 BUDGET. Washington, D.C.: The Brookings Institution, 1971.

Schumpeter, Joseph A. IMPERIALISM AND SOCIAL CLASSES. New Jersey: Augustus M. Kelley, 1951.

Stackhouse, Max L. THE ETHICS OF NECROPOLIS. Boston: Beacon Press, 1971.

Swomley, John M., Jr. THE MILITARY ESTABLISHMENT. Boston: Beacon Press, 1964.

_____. "The Military-Industrial Alliance," in Neal D. Houghton, (ed.), STRUGGLE AGAINST HISTORY. New York: Simon & Schuster, 1968.

Tyrrell, C. Merton. PENTAGON PARTNERS, THE NEW NOBILITY. New York: Grossman Publishers, 1970.

Weidenbaum, Murray L. "Arms and the American Economy." AMERICAN ECONOMIC REVIEW (May 1968).

Wiltz, John E. IN SEARCH OF PEACE. Louisiana State University Press, 1963.

Wolf, Charles, Jr. MILITARY-INDUSTRIAL COMPLEXITIES. The Rand Corporation, P-4177, September, 1969.

Wolfinger, Raymond E. "Nondecisions and the Study of Local Politics." AMERICAN POLITICAL SCIENCE REVIEW (December 1971).

Yarmolinsky, Adam. "The Industrial-Military Complex," In E. Mansfield (ed.), DEFENSE, SCIENCE AND PUBLIC POLICY. New York: W.W. Norton, 1968.

_____. THE MILITARY ESTABLISHMENT. New York: Harper & Row, 1971.

York, Herbert. RACE TO OBLIVION. New York: Simon & Schuster, 1970.

3

An Empirical Study of Military-Industrial Linkages

Stanley Lieberson

A major controversy exists in macrosociology over the forces which influence national policy in the United States and other advanced industrial societies.[1] On the one hand, the elitists argue that a relatively small group of people, representing a narrow range of interests, determine national policy across a range of domains including foreign affairs, military spending, and major domestic programs. By contrast, the pluralist school views national decision-making as a process influenced by a broad and diverse array of interest groups, with no single group or set of groups powerful enough to consistently dominate the national political system. Although the two schools are not diametrically opposed, as Kornhauser's comparison (1968) suggests, they are contradictory on a number of counts.[2] However, despite the fact that national political systems are a central concern in sociology, efforts to untangle the conflicting theories often appear more like ideological debates than contributions to scientific knowledge.

There are two special obstacles to overcome before the contradictory implications of elitism and pluralism can be resolved. First, scholarly positions on this subject must be judged by their ability to develop a comprehensive system that takes account of the available information rather than by their implications for contemporary politics. Because of the political overtones, both the elitists and pluralists approach the issues polemically, as if total rejection of the rival theory is the only possible way such a dispute can be resolved. It is true that some scientific controversies are eventually resolved when a body of empirical research persistently supports one theory and is incompatible with another.[3] But rival theories in the social sciences often turn out to be incomplete and distorted parts of a greater truth, such that neither is consistently supported by empirical research. The theoretical controversy over heredity versus environment, for example, is now rejected because it involved a false and unnecessary polarization.

The second major obstacle stems from the difficulties of conducting empirical research relevant to these theories. Not only are sociologists unable to make direct observations on the decision processes, but it is difficult to design research that encompasses the broad range of political events covered by these conflicting theories. No single research effort can be sufficiently comprehensive or critical, for example, to provide a conclusive test of the Marxist argument that capitalism generates a surplus that can only be used up through war and waste (see Baran

1957; Baran and Sweezy 1966). As a consequence, overinterpretation of the results is all too easy. Actually, each empirical study must be viewed only as contributing to an aggregate of investigations that deal with national power.

Military-Industrial Linkages

This study focuses on one facet of the theoretical controversy, the relation between military expenditures and large corporations in the United States, the so-called military-industrial complex. According to one leading elitist (Mills 1959, p. 276), "American capitalism is now in considerable part a military capitalism, and the most important relation of the big corporation to the state rests on the coincidence of interests between military and corporate needs." Mills goes on to assert that there is a "coincidence of interest between those who control the major means of production and those who control the newly enlarged means of violence." Pluralists also recognize the existence of a military-industrial complex (see, e.g., Rose 1967, pp. 94-98), but they view this as but one of many interest groups. Accordingly, they deny the elitist claim that this particular complex has unique breadth, scope, and coordination (see the review by Pilisuk and Hayden 1968).

Several facets of the dispute can be submitted to empirical study. Indeed, unless one claims that power and influence are unrelated to position in the social structure, it is clear that many of the issues raised by the elitists and pluralists call for a quantitative approach, dealing with matters of degree and frequency rather than absolutes. How extensive are the overlapping interests of major institutions? To what degree, and in what domains of national policy, do these connections modify and influence the decision-making processes? Has there been a substantial change in these relations over time?

There is little reason to doubt that a "military-industrial complex" exists if by this phrase is meant a set of commonly shared interests between the military and some major corporations. Certain striking features of these linkages, recognized by both theoretical schools, are: the interchange of personnel between the military and their corporate suppliers, the network that exists within the business sector, and the role of large corporations as suppliers to the military.

Circulation of Personnel

The 100 largest primary military contractors in the 1957-58 fiscal year, recipients of three-quarters of the money awarded, employed 218 former generals or admirals (Janowitz 1960, p. 376). Altogether, these 100 contractors employed some 768 former military officers who had retired with at least the rank of colonel or naval captain. The linkages have increased several-fold during the past decade. The 100 largest primary military contractors in the 1968 fiscal year employed 2,072 former military officers who had been colonels, naval captains, or higher.[4] Excluding five companies for which data are not available, this means an average of twenty-two former officers per major contractors.

The increasing interlock between suppliers and the military during the decade suggests the possibility of a growing community of interest between the two sectors of the society. Personal contacts between high-ranking officers and their former colleagues can affect negotiations, particularly when the military officers themselves may soon seek employment from the corporations after their military retirement (U.S. Congress, Senate 1969, p. S3072-3). Admiral Hyman Rickover has described a number of ways that military contracts may be negotiated to maximize the contractor's gain, for example, contract manipulation, research and development advantages, patents, shoddy procedures for cost accounting, and the like (Joint Economic Committee 1968).

Coordination Among Corporations

Underlying the power-elite thesis is the proposition that large corporations operate in concert, coordinating their activities and interests. "Would it not be strange," Mills (1959, p. 123) asks about large businesses, "if they did *not* consolidate themselves, but merely drifted along, doing the best they could, merely responding to day-to-day attacks upon them?" One indicator of this elite community is the degree of interlocking directorships among large corporations. "As a minimum inference, it must be said that such arrangements permit an interchange of views in a convenient and more or less formal way among those who share the interests of the corporate rich."

Interlocks among boards of directors is a major topic for research in itself. However, an illustration based on leading banks does give the reader a perspective on the kind of linkages that do occur and the economic resources involved. Listed in Table 3-1 is the board composition of the fifth-largest New York City bank in early 1965. The board represents leading corporations from many sectors of the national economy, creating the potential for a rather extensive and diverse communication network. In parentheses, alongside the name of each corporation, is its national rank. The sweep of interlocks is understated, actually, since only the primary affiliations of outside members of the bank board are shown.

Altogether, the boards of the seven largest New York City banks in 1965 include officials from fifty-one of the largest 500 industrial companies. There is a particularly heavy concentration from the fifty largest companies, with nineteen represented on the boards of at least one of the seven banks. The boards also have officers from some of the largest transportation, merchandising,

Table 3-1
Outside Board Members of the Morgan Guaranty Trust Company, New York,
1965, by Primary Company Affiliation

Corporation (and Rank)	Principal Activity
American Machine and Foundry (150)	Bowling, leisure time products, specialty industrial machinery
American Telephone and Telegraph (*U*-1)	"Bell" system, electronics
Bethlehem Steel (18)	Steel
Campbell Soup (93)	Soup, other food products
Coca Cola (68)	Soft drink syrup, juices
Columbia Gas System (*U*-10)	Natural gas distributor
Continental Oil (39)	Crude oil, fertilizer, petrochemicals
E.I. duPont de Nemours (12)	Chemicals, synthetic fibers
Gillette (204)	Razors, wave kits, pens
International Nickel (*F*-70)	Nickel, platinum, copper
New York Life Insurance (*I*-4)	Insurance
Pennsylvania Railroad (*T*-2)	Railroad
Procter and Gamble (24)	Soap, foodstuffs from vegetable oils
Singer (60)	Sewing machines, calculators
Standard Oil of New Jersey (2)	Petroleum
J.P. Stevens (86)	Textiles
State Street Investment	Mutual fund

Note.—Data not available on two additional organizations represented on the bank's board: Bechtel Corporation; The Duke Endowment. Letters *F*, *I*, *T*, and *U* indicate corporation is ranked, respectively, as foreign, life insurance, transportation, or utility. All other rankings refer to 500 largest industrial corporations.

Source.—Rankings from *Fortune* (1965*a*, 1965*b*); principal activities from Standard and Poor's (1965).

and life insurance companies.[5] Total employment in 1964 among the companies represented on these bank boards ranges from 400,000 to 1.65 million, with the median bank board representing the employers of 1.5 million.[6]

Major Contractors

Clearly a segment of American industry is deeply dependent on the military for survival. Attempts by the aircraft industry, for example, to diversify and reduce their dependency on the government have been unsuccessful for the most part (Weidenbaum 1963, pp. 79-83). Even more significant, major industrial corporations obtain a lion's share of the largest primary military contracts. Three-fifths of the fifty largest industrial corporations (as measured by sales in 1967) are among the 100 largest military contractors for the 1968 fiscal year (see Table 3-2). Altogether, sixty-eight of the 100 biggest contractors were among the 500 largest industrial corporations in the United States. Moreover, the remaining thirty-two contractors include two leading utilities (ranking first and forty-third

Table 3-2
Overlap Between 100 Largest Primary Military Contractors and 500 Largest Industrial Corporations, 1968

Rank of Industrial Corporations	Number among 100 Largest Contractors
1-50	29
51-100	11
101-150	5
151-200	7
201-250	3
251-300	4
301-350	5
351-400	1
401-450	1
451-500	2
Other[a]	6
Total	74

[a]Includes nonindustrial companies that are among the fifty largest commercial banks, life insurance companies, merchandising firms, transportation companies, and utilities.

Source.—One hundred largest military contractors in 1967-68 fiscal year from *Congressional Record* (U.S., Congress, Senate 1969). Largest 500 industrial corporations and other leading nonindustrial corporations obtained from *Fortune* (1968).

in assets among U.S. utilities) and four leading transportation companies (ranking among the leading fifty in operating revenues). In short, three-fourths of the largest military contractors are major corporations.

Implications

The results reported above, like those in a number of earlier studies, are suggestive of a close tie-up between the military and at least some industrial companies. But these reports are peripheral to an evaluation of the two theoretical approaches. For pluralists and elitists do not differ on the question of whether there is a close tie-up between some industrial companies and the military, rather they differ on the *magnitude* of the interlock and its *causes*. In order to evaluate these approaches, it is necessary to examine the relative importance of military spending for large businesses. Pluralists view military-industrial relations as but one of many powerful influences on government policy, whereas the elitists see this as a dominant and pervasive influence caused by an inherent necessity for the survival of a capitalistic system.

Dependence of Industry on a War Economy

Military Contracts

As indicated in Table 3-2, the very largest corporations obtain most of the major military contracts. However, the issue now is the importance of these contracts for such corporations. Both Weidenbaum (1965, pp. 113-14) and Lapp (1968, pp. 186-87) have demonstrated that the ratio of military contracts to total sales varies widely among leading contractors. In order to obtain some estimate of the role of military expenditures for large businesses generally, it is more appropriate to focus on leading industrial companies in the nation rather than on simply the leading contractors.

Among the fifty largest industrial companies, all with sales well over $1 billion in 1967, primary military contracts vary greatly in significance (see Table 3-3). Contracts obtained by General Dynamics, the largest military contractor in the 1968 fiscal year, were nearly equal to its total sales in 1967 (the ratio is 0.993). Another corporation has a contract-sales ratio of more than 0.75; one has a ratio of 0.60; and there are seven others with ratios exceeding 0.25. Twelve of the fifty largest industrial companies, on the other hand, have ratios of 0.04 or less—even though they are among the 100 largest military contractors. Military ties are very minor for an additional twenty-one companies that are not listed among the top 100 contractors. Even if we make the extreme assumption that the contracts received by these companies are only $1,000 less in value than the one-hundredth-largest contractor, the ratio of military to total sales would be between 0.03 and 0.04 for eleven companies and 0.02 or less for ten companies. Altogether, then, thirty-three of the fifty largest industrial corporations have contract-sales ratios of 0.04 or less.

Among the fifty next largest industrial corporations, there are thirty-nine that are not on the list of 100 leading military contractors in 1968. Again making the extreme assumption that each of these holds contracts that are only $1,000 less than the one-hundredth-largest military contractor, the ratios would be 0.04, 0.05, and 0.06 for, respectively, fifteen, nineteen, and five of these corporations (Table 3-3).

Table 3-3
Ratio of Military Contracts to Total Sales Among 100 Largest Industrial Corporations, 1968

	Number	
Ratio	50 Largest Corporations	50 Next Largest
0.75 and above	2	0
0.50-0.74	1	2
0.25-0.49	7	4
0.10-0.24	1	5
0.05-0.09	6	24[a]
Under 0.05	33	15

[a]Ratios for all twenty-four of these companies are estimated in terms of maximum possible values. Undoubtedly, most would have lower ratios if actual contract data were available (see text).

Source.—See Table 3-2.

It is clear that the majority of the largest industrial corporations derive only a small portion of their total business from primary military contracts. Moreover, there are numerous merchandising companies that do not enjoy any direct benefits from military contracts. Among these companies, there are twenty-one with sales equal to at least the one-hundredth-largest industrial company (eight have sales greater than the fiftieth-largest industrial company). Undoubtedly, stores are located in communities that receive sizable military contracts, but military expenditures per se, as opposed to government spending in other sectors, are probably not particularly beneficial to major retailers.

Although the data reported above fail to support the notion that American industry is deeply dependent on a military economy, the results are hardly conclusive. First, they fail to take into account the indirect consequences of military spending for the nation's major corporations. Large corporations may supply many of the primary contractors and thus benefit from the demands created by military expenditures. Steel mills, for example, produce the armor plate used in tanks or needed for the hulls of war vessels. Further, there may be general indirect benefits that are based on the prosperity generated by military expenditures. If military spending pumps large amounts of money into the economy, then consumer and industrial demands may be of substantial benefit to all sectors of the economy, not merely the "munitions makers." Finally, military contracts may still be very important if they are unusually profitable or utilize plants and equipment that might otherwise be idle. For General Motors, the largest industrial corporation in the nation and the tenth-largest military contractor, the ratio of military contracts to total sales is only 0.031. However, the contracts do amount to nearly two-thirds of a billion dollars, a sum that can hardly be considered trivial.

In short, the data fail to support the hypothesis that large American businesses are deeply dependent on military spending. The results are inconclusive, however, because there may be substantial indirect benefits for a broad spectrum of American businesses that are not military contractors.

Regression Analysis

Regression analysis provides another method for estimating both the absolute and relative influence of military expenditures on *total* corporate income. The dependent variable, Y, is corporate income after taxes for each year between 1916 and 1965. Two independent variables are used: government expenditures in each year for "major national security" (X_1); government expenditures that are not for national security (X_2). Although the latter includes veterans benefits and other costs reflecting earlier military efforts as well as space explorations, X_1 essentially measures current military expenditures over which the government has some option, and X_2 reflects the nonmilitary expenditures of the government.

Overall, there is a high association between corporate income and the two facets of government expenditures; the coefficient of multiple determination $R^2_{y.z1z2}$, is 0.88. This is not altogether surprising, given inflationary trends through the period as well as the necessary relationships between corporate income and government expenditures. On the zero-order level, corporate income is more closely linked to nonmilitary expenditures than to military spending (see Table 3-4). Even more significant, military expenditures have less impact on corporate income than does an equivalent amount spent by the government on nonmilitary items (compare b_{yx1} with b_{yx2}). Both the correlation and regression of corporate income on military expenditures are virtually nil after nonmilitary spending is taken into account. By contrast, the partial correlation and regression for income on nonmilitary expenditures remain very high, 0.82 and 0.89, respectively.

Table 3-4

Regression Analysis: Corporate Income as a Function of Federal Government Expenditures, 1916-1965

Variable	r	b
YX_1	0.68	0.30
YX_2	0.93	0.77
X_1X_2	0.76	1.42
$YX_1{\cdot}X_2$	−0.08	−0.02
$YX_2{\cdot}X_1$	0.82	0.89

Source: X_1 based on U.S. Bureau of the Census (1960; 1965a; column Y358; 1965b, table 534); X_2 based on U.S. Bureau of the Census (1960; 1965a, column Y357 minus column Y358); Y based on U.S. Bureau of the Census (1960; 1965a, column Y283 minus columns Y288 + Y289); and 1962-1965 data based on U.S. Bureau of the Census (1968, table 694).
Note: X_1 = federal government expenditures for national security (in millions of dollars); X_2 = federal government expenditures not for national security (in millions of dollars); Y = net corporate income after taxes (in thousands of dollars).

Following the procedures described by Blalock (1961, 1964) and Fendrich (1967), the zero-order and partial correlations fit two models. The first one shown below is supportive of Mills, whereas the second model is not. Both models suggest that: $r_{yx1.x2}$ be approximately zero; that r_{yx1} be lower than either r_{yx2} or r_{x1x2}; and that r_{yx1} be approximately equal to the cross product of the other two correlations. All of these conditions are met. Without additional variables, it is impossible to distinguish between them.

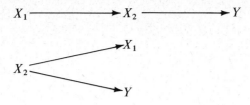

Even under the first causal model, however, efforts to increase corporate income would be directed towards raising nonmilitary spending rather than the military budget. First, it is necessary to recognize that the two facets of government spending operate somewhat independently of each other (r^2 is 0.58). This means that there are other factors influencing nonmilitary spending. Since the regression coefficients indicate that a unit change in nonmilitary spending will increase corporate income far more than will an equivalent military expenditure, the first model would still suggest that nonmilitary spending receive preference by those seeking to raise corporate income. In short, during the past fifty years a dollar spent on the military appears to have generated far less corporate income than a dollar spent by the government in other realms.

Although the results fail to support the contention that corporate income is deeply dependent on military expenditures, again the analysis is not conclusive. For one, the relationship between government spending and corporate income involves some feedback, a complexity not found in the models reported above. In addition, other lag combinations could be used besides the one where corporate income trails government expenditures by a half year. Moreover, it is entirely possible that the political limits on nonmilitary spending are much greater than for military spending. If a shift from the military budget to nonmilitary needs interferes with private enterprise, then the military option might be encouraged. Finally, elitists can argue that military spending provides an umbrella for foreign investments. Such expenditures are therefore necessary, the argument would run, even if a greater immediate return is possible from a budgetary shift to nonmilitary spending.

Input-Output Analysis

An additional method for determining both the indirect and direct consequences of military spending for various sectors of the economy is provided by input-output economics. For each specific industry, this quantitative tool in economics considers the role of every supplier and every market, yielding an interindustry matrix of economic supply and demand. Dealing with the production of automobiles, for example, this method indicates the amount of rubber, steel, glass, copper, aluminum, etc., required and then, in turn, the supplies needed by the producers of these products, say sulfur for rubber, and so on.

Leontief and his associates (1966, pp. 184-222) investigated the role of military expenditures through this perspective. A 20 percent cut in armament expenditures accompanied by a compensating increase in nonmilitary expenditures would mean a reduction in total output and employment in only ten of the nation's fifty-six industrial sectors (Leontief et al. 1966, pp. 194-97). Among the ten industries with declines, five would suffer percentage losses exceeding the percentage gain enjoyed by any single one of the remaining industries. These five industries are: aircraft (−16 percent), ordinance (−15 percent), research and development (−13 percent), electronics equipment (−5 percent), and nonferrous metals (−2.2 percent). The sector with the greatest increase, agricultural services, stands to gain only 2.1 percent.

These results, although basically an exercise in economics, have profound sociological implications for the pluralism-elitism controversy. They mean that the economic consequences of a substantial step toward disarmament are lopsided; most industries would gain, but the percentage of business lost in each of five industries (particularly the first three named above) would be far greater than the percentage gained in any single sector. Although the economy as a whole is not harmed by such military cutbacks, the small number of industries with a substantial vested interest in military spending would suffer far more than other industries would gain. This means that the industries benefiting from military expenditures are more narrowly concentrated than are the economic interests that stand to gain through disarmament. The implications of these conclusions are considered in greater detail later.

An even more elaborate application of input-output analysis by Kokat (1967, pp. 805-19), based on the assumption of a 50 percent cut in the defense budget, also leads to the conclusion that a shift to nondefense expenditures would have an expansionary impact on the majority of industries. If there are compensating increases within either the private or public sectors, only a very limited number of industries would suffer from such a severe cutback in military expenditures.

Although input-output analysis fails to support the hypothesis that military spending is a prerequisite to corporate prosperity, an alternative interpretation is possible that is consistent with elitist theory. Despite the results reported above, an elitist might argue, a shift to peacetime consumption would be resisted if the transitional costs were very high in comparison with the gains that might ensue. Retooling, new marketing procedures, investment in specialized plants and equipment, greater competition, and other costs might well outweigh the small benefits in sales and employment that most sectors of industry would enjoy through a shift from military to nonmilitary expenditures. Moreover, an abrupt cutback in military spending would have serious social and economic consequences in a number of communities. Large cities such as Fort Worth and

Seattle, as well as some industries, would be particularly affected by drastic changes in military policies (Halverson 1969; Ames 1969).

Historical Trends

Rather than restrict the issue to elitism versus pluralism, at this point one could argue that neither theory provides an adequate interpretation of the available data. Although reinterpretation consistent with the elitist perspective is possible, the data above suggest that a high level of military spending is not vital to the prosperity of either the nation or its largest businesses. On the other hand, given the findings of Russett (1969a, 1969b) that a wide variety of consumer and other public civilian activities suffer when there are substantial military expenditures, the pluralist perspective is not entirely satisfactory. For, if more interest groups would benefit from alternative government-spending policies, then how can pluralist theory explain the maintenance of such a substantial military commitment?

Since it is almost inevitable that any valid macrosocietal theory have implications for social change, an historical perspective provides additional clues to the theoretical issues at hand. The historical trends for both government spending, generally, and military spending, in particular, fail to fit neatly into either the pluralistic or the elitist interpretations.

The percentage of federal expenditures devoted to the armed forces has fluctuated considerably during the nation's history, ranging from about 10 percent during the Great Depression to over 90 percent during the Civil War (Figure 3-1). There is no evidence that military spending currently occupies an unusually large proportion of the total federal budget; rates during the 1960s are no higher than those in the 1830s and 1840s. The United States, compared with other nations, spends a relatively large part of its gross national product (GNP) on the military (see Benoit and Boulding 1963, pp. 301-6), but the current percentage is by no means uniquely high when compared with the nation's past record. In this regard, there is no support for the thesis that the role of the military in the government has expanded in recent decades (Mills 1959).

On the other hand, there is some evidence that military spending after the Second World War failed to drop as sharply as it had after previous wars. The War of 1812, the Mexican War, the Civil War, and World War I were followed by periods of very low levels of military spending—even when compared with the period preceding the war. By contrast, military expenditures after World War II never declined to the levels found in the 1930s. This feature is compatible with the elitist perspective which emphasizes the change in military-industrial relations that occurred in recent decades.

Although the proportion of government expenditures devoted to the military shows no clear-cut temporal trend, a historical analysis does reveal that the role

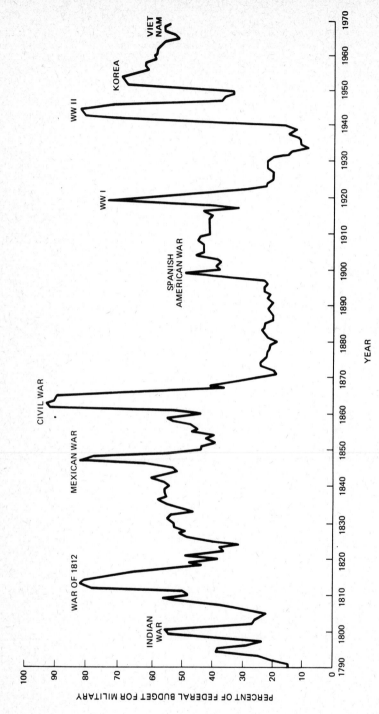

Figure 3-1. Percentage of the Federal Budget for the Military, 1790-1969. Sources: U.S. Bureau of the Census (1960, columns Y350 and Y358; 1965a, columns Y350 and Y358 and Y358a; 1965b, table 534; 1968, tables 538 and 544), based on expenditures for the "armed services" before 1900 and for "major national security" or "national defense" after 1900. There are some minor inconsistencies among sources.

of government in the national economy has consistently increased through the years. From the postbellum period until the First World War, government expenditures ranged between 2 and 3 percent of the GNP (Figure 3-2). After a sharp increase during World War I, the percentage remained above earlier peacetime levels. The federal budget increased to 10 percent of the GNP during the 1930s and reached even higher levels after the emergencies created by World War II had ended. Current government expenditures are about 15 percent of the GNP.

Figures 3-1 and 3-2 suggest that changes in the role of the military in the national economy are to be seen largely as a consequence of changes in the role of government in the economy. Consumption of an increasing portion of the total national output by the federal government means that both its nonmilitary and military expenditures are of growing significance to the total economy. Therefore, although the elitists are correct in arguing that military spending amounts to an expanding part of national productivity, the fact remains that the federal government's impact on many other sectors of the society is also growing. In the case of research, for example, the government plays an exceedingly important role (Barber 1968, p. 225). Likewise, there is some evidence of an "education-industrial complex" that operates with considerable effectiveness in influencing federal expenditures for education (Miller 1970). The government's ability to command an increasing portion of national productivity through taxes and other revenues means that a focus solely on the changing military-industrial relations could lead to a very misleading conclusion.

In short, since this brief review of historical trends fails to consistently support either the elitist or the pluralist approaches, it appears all the more reasonable to consider another perspective. Suggested below is an alternative interpretation of military-industrial relations based on what might be called the mechanism of compensating strategy.

An Alternate Perspective

A high level of military expenditures is not necessarily due to a broad set of intense vested interests in such a policy. To be sure, there are both industries and entire communities that are deeply dependent on military expenditures. Moreover, once a pattern of military consumption is established, a shift to nonmilitary spending would be costly for some industries and regions that were not initially dependent on military spending. Nevertheless, when compared with the consequences of alternate government policies, most sectors of American industry gain very little from a high level of military expenditures.

On the other hand, the absence of widely shared direct benefits from military spending need not be taken as evidence that a small segment of American industry is dominant. Given the different economic and organizational resources

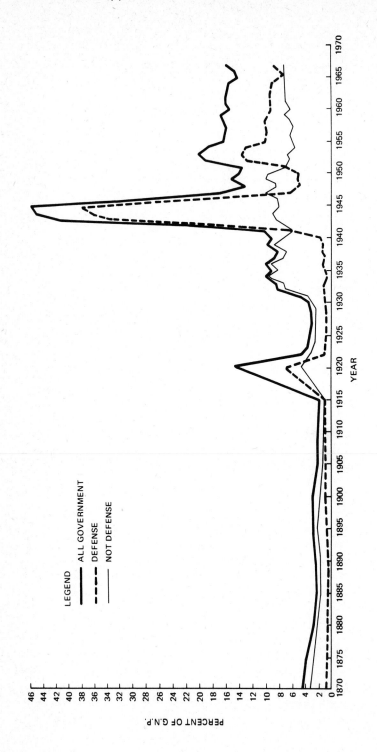

Figure 3-2. Expenditures of the Federal Government as a Percentage of the GNP, 1869-1967. Sources: In addition to those listed under Figure 3-1. U.S. Bureau of the Census (1960; 1965a, column F1; 1968, table 454).

that various segments possess, obviously interest groups in the society do not have equal power. Compare, for example, the resources available to the urban poor with those available to the petroleum industry. Nevertheless, policies detrimental to the numerical majority will occur even if a smaller group does not dominate the entire political system. Rather, a process of decision making may be postulated in which the political system's output can fail to reflect the interests of the majority without this necessarily meaning that a power elite controls the government. Even if interest groups were alike in organization, wealth, and other competitive resources, under certain conditions a "compensating" strategy could be pursued such that political decisions would not invariably reflect the direct interests of the majority.

In order to specify the conditions necessary for a compensating power system to operate, two additional characteristics of interest groups should be noted. First, populations within advanced industrial societies are atomized into a highly diverse set of groups, with interests that are neither fully harmonious with one another nor fully competitive. Not only does an expanding division of labor subdivide a nation into increasingly specialized needs and vested interests, as Durkheim noted, but there is also an increased territorial division of labor such that spatial subunits of a nation also develop distinctive concerns. A second key element involves recognition of the fact that interest groups differ more than in terms of whether they are for or against a specific proposal. Rather they also differ in the *degree* of importance that each issue holds. What this means is that groups vary widely in how far they are prepared to go to achieve a specific end.

Accordingly, an advanced industrial society, regardless of its political ideology, must be viewed as one in which a wide variety of interest groups are each attempting to balance an array of potential gains and losses in order to generate the maximum net gain. Advantages that might accrue from opposing another segment are not necessarily pursued if even larger gains are possible through the expenditure of an equivalent amount of political capital in some other government domain. In other words, if interest groups are not by themselves able to obtain the political outcomes they desire, then it is necessary for them to form alliances and coalitions with other interest groups. Such combinations mean that each interest group sacrifices some issues in order to obtain the greatest net rewards. As a consequence, a political body's decision with respect to a particular issue may reflect the intense concern of a minority of interests coupled with the support obtained from other segments whose major interests are found elsewhere.

Four conditions are necessary for a "compensating" power situation to operate. First, power must be an exhaustible commodity such that each interest group has limited political influence. Second, the interests of the population must be diverse enough so that a given proposal will not have an equal impact on all segments. Third, governmental actions that favor a particular interest group must not eliminate the disadvantaged majority's potential for other gains. In the case at hand, it means that funds are available for more than the military budget or that nonbudgetary legislation can be passed that will yield sufficient gains for other segments of the population. Fourth, legislation beneficial to a specific interest must not at the same time create too great a loss for the majority of other interests. Otherwise, a concerted effort to combat the legislation will provide a net gain to the majority that is even greater than would occur under their use of a compensating strategy.

When these conditions are met, it follows that a given group will not attempt to exert its influence on all issues to the same degree, but rather will concentrate on those that generate the greatest net gain. To obtain passage of particularly beneficial legislation, an interest group may in turn support other proposals that, by themselves, create small losses (see Coleman 1964). The third and fourth conditions are suggested by the controversy over military spending during the Vietnam war. The "guns and butter" policy first meant that other sectors of the population could pursue compensating strategies, such as are required by the third condition. On the other hand, the monetary and domestic crises generated by this series of compensating gains, coupled with the unpopularity of the war, make it increasingly hard to meet the last condition. That is, the potential net gains that would be achieved by the vast majority of the population through a decline in military spending begins to approach or exceed the gains that many segments obtain through a compensating strategy.

According to the notion of compensating strategies, military spending can be explained by a high level of interest on the part of one segment of American business accompanied by a relative lack of concern on the part of other segments of industry. The majority of industries disregard the small losses they incur from defense spending and turn their attention to other aspects of government policy that affect them more directly. Defense spending will influence the profits of dairy farmers, for example, but so too will other government policies such as price supports, marketing restrictions, exports and imports on dairy products, grading practices, trucking costs, and so forth. Accordingly, the area of government action with the most substantial direct impact on the goals of the dairy industry is probably not the military.

Indeed, barring a major war emergency, there are other facets of federal activity that are far more crucial to the interests of many industrial segments. The relevance of the federal government is hardly restricted to the military budget; decisions affecting taxes, antitrust laws, foreign markets, imports, minimum-wage laws, and a wide variety of other government regulations are extremely important to business. These facets of government policy often have far greater short-term consequences for a specific industry than do military expenditures. The tobacco companies, for example, stand to lose far more from restrictions on cigarette advertising than they are likely to gain in the event of disarmament.[7] The petroleum industry would also enjoy a small gain if there was a compensated cutback in military expenditures; however, federal budgetary decisions with regard to their special depletion tax advantages are far more significant. The largest gain would be enjoyed by agricultural services, but obviously agriculture is influenced by many other areas of government legislation and control.

Senate Committees

This propensity for each segment of the society to pursue its areas of greatest direct interest is illustrated by the states represented on various congressional committees. Although residents of all states are in some manner affected by the policies of any committee, it is clear that political efforts emphasize those areas with the greatest potential returns. Hence, each state tends to be represented on committees affecting those facets of the legislative process that are of greatest importance to the state. The House Agriculture Subcommittee on Tobacco, for example, is loaded with legislators from tobacco-producing states; six of the seven members come from Virginia, North Carolina, South Carolina, and Kentucky.

Table 3-5 illustrates the association between special interests and membership among several Senate committees. A crude index of vested interest is developed for each committee. States ranking above the national average on this indicator are classified as states with a special *primary* interest in the committee's work; states below the national average are classified as having a *secondary* interest. The index of vested interest for the Senate Agriculture and Forestry Committee, for example, is the percentage of the 1960 labor force in agricultural and related industries. There are thirty states with a higher percentage than the national figure of 6.7 and twenty states with a lower percentage. These thirty states supply all thirteen members of the Senate's Agriculture Committee.

Although the residents of all states are affected by the prices for food and other agricultural products, the Agriculture Committee is almost entirely in the hands of southern and midwest senators from states with a particularly high vested interest in this domain. Such a pattern is consistent with the proposition that an unequal distribution of potential gains and losses will generate different political thrusts for various interest groups.

Other committees also consist of senators from states with the greatest stake in their activities. The Indian Affairs Subcommittee consists entirely of senators from states with a high proportion of Indians. The Minerals and Fuels Committee is loaded with senators from states with relatively large segments of the labor force engaged in these extractive industries. Merchant Marine draws senators from coastal states. States with large metropolitan populations are overrepresented on the Housing and Urban Affairs Subcommittee, just as the Labor Subcommittee draws senators from states relatively high in union membership.

Table 3-5

Vested Interests of States and the Membership of Senate Committees, 91st Congress, 1969-1970

Committee	All States		States on the Committee	
	Primary Interest[a]	Secondary Interest	Primary Interest[a]	Secondary Interest
Agriculture and Forestry	30	20	13	0
Indian Affairs	17	33	10	0
Minerals, Materials, and Fuels	20	30	8	1
Merchant Marine	30	20	9	1
Housing and Urban Affairs	20	30	7	8
Labor	15	33	7	5
Armed Services	25	23	14	3
International Organization and Disarmament	23	25	5	2

[a]Primary interests of the states in various committees based on the following criteria: AGRICULTURE AND MINERALS—states whose labor force in 1960 exceeds the United States percentage in the agriculture and mining industries, respectively; INDIAN AFFAIRS—states in which the Indian percentage of the population exceeds that for the total United States; MERCHANT MARINE—states contiguous to an ocean, the Gulf, or the Great Lakes; HOUSING AND URBAN AFFAIRS—states exceeding the national percentage of residents who reside in standard metropolitan statistical areas; LABOR—states exceeding the national percentage of population in the AFL-CIO (data available for forty-eight states); ARMED SERVICES—states that would suffer a net loss in output and employment after compensated cut in armament expenditures (Leontief et al. 1966, p. 197) (data available for forty-eight states); INTERNATIONAL ORGANIZATION—same as above, except states gaining in output and employment (data available for forty-eight states).

Note: Committee membership based on CONGRESSIONAL INDEX (no date).

In this context, the composition of the Senate Armed Services Committee is not entirely surprising. The committee is loaded with senators from the states that would suffer a net loss if there was a compensated 20 percent cut in armament expenditures (based on the input-output analysis reported by Leontief et al. 1966, Table 10-2). Only three of the seventeen members of this committee are from the twenty-three states that would enjoy a net gain. On the other hand, the small Subcommittee on International Organization and Disarmament Affairs is disproportionately composed of senators from states that stand to gain through a military cutback.

Obviously other forces influence committee assignments in the Senate. Some committees are attractive simply because they may catapult members into the national limelight, for example, Foreign Affairs. Budgetary and procedural committees are extremely powerful, covering a wide range of activities, although it is difficult to link them with specific vested interests. In addition, some assignments are influenced by tradition and seniority. Moreover, this brief examination does not cover the complex exchange and trade networks that may exist between different congressional blocs.

Nevertheless, the results reported above do serve to illustrate the selective pursuit of vested interests. The fact that all activities of the Congress are of consequence in some direct or indirect way to every resident and every organization does not prevent each segment of the society from emphasizing those areas where maximum net gains may be obtained. In this regard, the composition of the Senate's Armed Services Committee may be viewed as but another manifestation of this organizational principle.

Discussion

No single empirical study can determine the nature of military-industrial relations, to say nothing of resolving the elitist-pluralist controversy in which it is enmeshed. However, the data are suggestive both about the empirical question and the theoretical restatement that may be necessary.

In terms of the empirical facets of the study, several elements of the elitist position are supported. Some major corporations are deeply dependent on armament contracts; and the decline after World War II in the proportion of government spending on the military is less than would be expected from the patterns after earlier wars. Moreover, the federal government is a growing factor in the national economy, and hence its expenditures for the military are of increasing importance to the business world. There is no reason to doubt the existence of a military-industrial complex *if* by that phrase is meant an intense dependency on military contracts among some very large corporations.

On the other hand, there is no evidence to support the contention that the general success of large businesses in the nation depends on substantial expenditures for the military. Indeed, there is evidence to indicate that most would benefit from alternative government spending or from equivalent expenditures in the private sectors of the economy. For the majority of the largest corporations, military contracts at most amount to a very small portion of their total business. Moreover, both the regression and input-output analyses suggest that corporate prosperity would be increased in the absence of military spending.

To be sure, a substantial and sudden drop in military expenditures would create difficulties for a few sectors of the economy and certain cities and regions that are deeply dependent on the military. Nevertheless, the consequences of disarmament should not be interpreted as the cause of its initial buildup. Cities do not first grow and then develop military industries that support them, rather the growth of cities may reflect the expansion of their economic base. Moreover, the bulk of American industry would gain under alternative spending policies.

If these inferences about military-industrial relations are valid, then both of the major current theories provide inadequate perspectives on the nature of societal power. Crucial to the reconceptualization suggested earlier is recognition of the fact that each of the diverse interest groups may, under some circumstances, take stands that are counter to their interests. This will occur when four necessary conditions are met such that a "compensating" strategy is possible. If each group attempts to generate the greatest *net* gain for itself, then a given policy need not be the product of simply the majority of interests, nor need it mean that a small set of interests is dominant. Rather, the policy may mean that the losses to a majority of interests are small, whereas the gains to some sectors are substantial.

From this perspective, military spending is but one among many sets of vested interests. To be sure, this domain could reach the point where it dominates the entire economic and social life of the nation. However, the results suggest that military expenditures are not, currently, a vital and necessary prerequisite to general corporate prosperity. Using the hypothesis of compensating strategies, the high level of military expenditures need not be interpreted as the product of a common vested interest in such spending among major businesses. Rather, extensive military spending may be viewed as reflecting the operations of an important and powerful interest group in a setting where other legislative issues have an even greater direct bearing on the prosperity of the remainder of economic segments. In the same fashion, senators tend to concentrate on areas of greatest direct benefit to their states despite the fact that all legislation is in some way relevant to all states.

Admittedly, this position must be treated as an alternative hypothesis since the results reported earlier may be reinterpreted so as to be consistent with either the pluralist or elitist schools. For example, the latter may claim that large businesses will support military expenditures, even when not directly beneficial, in order to provide a military umbrella for overseas investment. The hypothesis developed here of a "compensating" strategy and its application must be viewed as an initial effort to take into account some of the difficulties that are faced by an unyielding advocacy of either the pluralist or elitist perspectives.

Unless one is prepared to evaluate existing theories in terms of the results obtained from studies of the empirical reality, a basic issue such as the structure of power in the nation will forever remain beyond the purview of sociology. Rather, we shall continue to be sociologists who subject the topic only to polemics, speculation, anecdotal arguments, and the use of models that would be rejected as "stereotypes" if analogous reasoning were applied to other facets of the social world in which we live.

Notes

Reprinted with permission from THE AMERICAN JOURNAL OF SOCIOLOGY, January 1971.

1. I am deeply indebted to Mrs. Lynn K. Hansen for her invaluable research assistance and critical suggestions. The paper also benefited from a critical

reading by Mr. Gordon W. Clemans and helpful suggestions from Professors Herbert L. Costner, Richard M. Emerson, and S. Frank Miyamoto. In addition, I received many comments from colleagues and students in the Center for Studies in Demography and Ecology, University of Washington. The figures were prepared by Mr. Charles B. McVey, former draftsman in the Center for Studies in Demography and Ecology.

2. Both Rose (1967) and Pilisuk and Hayden (1968) provide excellent reviews of the rather extensive literature developed by both the elitists and pluralists. There are some particularly useful evaluations of the power-elite theories of C. Wright Mills. See the criticisms by Bell (1958) and by Gracey and Anderson (1958), as well as the extensive list of reviews and evaluations compiled by Horowitz (1963).

3. I assume that empirical research also supports those implications on which the two theories do not differ.

4. Based on employment on February 1, 1969 (U.S., Congress, Senate 1969).

5. Among the fifty largest in each category, there are two utilities, three transportation, five merchandising, and six life-insurance companies directly linked with one or more of these banks.

6. Based on employment figures reported in FORTUNE (1965a, 1965b, 1966).

7. A gain of 1.76 percent under the conditions described by Leontief et al. (1966).

References

Ames, William E. "Seattle Payrolls Fattened by War." CHRISTIAN SCIENCE MONITOR (May 23, 1969), p. 3.

Baran, Paul A. THE POLITICAL ECONOMY OF GROWTH. New York: Monthly Review Press, 1957.

Baran, Paul A., and Paul M. Sweezy. MONOPOLY CAPITAL: AN ESSAY ON THE AMERICAN ECONOMIC AND SOCIAL ORDER. New York: Monthly Review Press, 1966.

Barber, Richard J. "The New Partnership: Big Government and Big Business," in THE TRIPLE REVOLUTION: SOCIAL PROBLEMS IN DEPTH, edited by Robert Perrucci and Marc Pilisuk. Boston: Little, Brown, 1968.

Bell, Daniel. "The Power Elite—Reconsidered." AMERICAN JOURNAL OF SOCIOLOGY 64 (November 1958), pp. 238-50.

Benoit, Emile, and Kenneth E. Boulding, eds. DISARMAMENT AND THE ECONOMY. New York: Harper & Row, 1963.

Blalock, Hubert M., Jr. "Evaluating the Relative Importance of Variables." AMERICAN SOCIOLOGICAL REVIEW 26 (December 1961), pp. 866-74.

_____. "Controlling for Background Factors: Spuriousness Versus Developmental Sequences," SOCIOLOGICAL INQUIRY 34 (Winter 1964), pp. 28-40.

Coleman, James S. "Collective Decisions." SOCIOLOGICAL INQUIRY 34 (Spring 1964), pp. 166-81.

CONGRESSIONAL INDEX. 91st Cong. New York: Commerce Clearing House, 1969-70.

Fendrich, James M. "Perceived Reference Group Support: Racial Attitudes and Overt Behavior." AMERICAN SOCIOLOGICAL REVIEW 32 (December 1967), pp. 960-70.

FORTUNE. "The Fortune Directory of the 500 Largest U.S. Industrial Corporations." (July 1965a), pp. 149-68.

_____ . "The Fortune Directory: Part 1." (August 1965b), pp. 169-80.

_____ . "The Fortune Directory of the 500 Largest U.S. Industrial Corporations." (July 1966), pp. 230-64.

_____ . "The Fortune Directory of the 500 Largest U.S. Industrial Corporations." (June 1968), pp. 186-220.

Gracey, Harry L., and C. Arnold Anderson. "Review of the Power Elite." KENTUCKY LAW JOURNAL 46 (Winter 1958), pp. 301-17.

Halverson, Guy. "Air Power Propels Fort Worth's Upward Economic Spiral." CHRISTIAN SCIENCE MONITOR (March 28, 1969), p. 14.

Horowitz, Irving Louis, ed. POWER, POLITICS, AND PEOPLE: THE COLLECTED ESSAYS OF C. WRIGHT MILLS. New York: Oxford University Press, 1963.

Janowitz, Morris. THE PROFESSIONAL SOLDIER: A SOCIAL AND POLITICAL PORTRAIT. Glencoe, Ill.: Free Press, 1960.

Joint Economic Committee. ECONOMICS OF MILITARY PROCUREMENT, PART 2. Washington, D.C.: Government Printing Office, 1968.

Kokat, Robert G. "Some Implications of the Economic Impact of Disarmament on the Structure of American Industry." In Joint Economic Committee, ECONOMIC EFFECT OF VIETNAM SPENDING. Washington, D.C.: Government Printing Office, 1967.

Kornhauser, William. "Power Elite or Veto Groups." In READER IN POLITICAL SOCIOLOGY, edited by Frank Lindenfeld. New York: Funk & Wagnalls, 1968.

Lapp, Ralph E. THE WEAPONS CULTURE. New York: Norton, 1968.

Leontief, Wassily, Alison Morgan, Karen Polenske, David Simpson, and Edward Tower. "The Economic Impact—Industrial and Regional—of an Arms Cut." In INPUT-OUTPUT ECONOMICS, edited by Wassily Leontief. New York: Oxford University Press, 1966.

Miller, Norman C. "How Educators Build Support in Congress for Fatter School Aid." WALL STREET JOURNAL (January 20, 1970), p. 1.

Mills, C. Wright. THE POWER ELITE. New York: Oxford University Press, 1959.

National Resources Committee. THE STRUCTURE OF THE AMERICAN ECONOMY. I. BASIC CHARACTERISTICS. Washington, D.C.: Government Printing Office, 1939.

Pilisuk, Marc, and Thomas Hayden. "Is there a Military-Industrial Complex Which Prevents Peace?: Consensus and Countervailing Power in Pluralistic Systems." In THE TRIPLE REVOLUTION: SOCIAL PROBLEMS IN DEPTH, edited by Robert Perrucci and Marc Pilisuk. Boston: Little, Brown, 1968.

Rose, Arnold M. THE POWER STRUCTURE: POLITICAL PROCESS IN AMERICAN SOCIETY. New York: Oxford University Press, 1967.

Russett, Bruce M. "Who Pays for Defense?" AMERICAN POLITICAL SCIENCE REVIEW 63 (June 1969a), 412-26.

_____. "The Price of War." TRANS-ACTION 6 (October 1969b), pp. 28-35.

Standard and Poor's Corporation. SECURITY OWNER'S STOCK GUIDE, OCTOBER 1965. New York: Standard & Poor's Corp, 1965.

U.S. Bureau of the Census. HISTORICAL STATISTICS OF THE UNITED STATES, COLONIAL TIMES TO 1957. Washington, D.C.: Government Printing Office, 1960.

_____. HISTORICAL STATISTCS OF THE UNITED STATES, COLONIAL TIMES TO 1957; CONTINUATION TO 1962 AND REVISIONS. Washington, D.C.: Government Printing Office, 1965a.

_____. STATISTICAL ABSTRACT OF THE UNITED STATES, 1965. Washington, D.C.: Government Printing Office, 1965b.

_____. STATISTICAL ABSTRACT OF THE UNITED STATES, 1968. Washington, D.C.: Government Printing Office, 1968.

U.S. Congress, Senate. CONGRESSIONAL RECORD 115 (March 24, 1969), pp. S3072-81.

Weidenbaum, Murray L. "Problems of Adjustment for Defense Industries." In DISARMAMENT AND THE ECONOMY, edited by Emile Benoit and Kenneth E. Boulding. New York: Harper & Row, 1963.

_____. "Defense–Space Business." In POLITICS, ECONOMICS, AND THE GENERAL WELFARE, edited by Michael D. Reagan. Chicago: Scott, Foresman, 1965.

4

Military Spending and the U.S. Economy

Michael Reich

Since 1950 the U.S. government has spent well over a trillion dollars on the military, or about one-tenth of total economic output; in recent years $30 billion has been spent annually on destruction in Southeast Asia alone. Why does this murderous and seemingly irrational allocation of resources occur? Why give the Pentagon $80 billion per year in spending money when so many basic social needs go unmet both in the United States and in the rest of the world? What sorts of changes in our political-economic system are needed to reorder fundamentally the militaristic priorities of the United States?

I shall argue in this paper that a major shift in social and economic priorities would require a fundamental transformation of the U.S. capitalist economy.[1] The growth and persistence of a high level of military spending is a natural outcome in an advanced capitalist society that both suffers from the problem of inadequate private aggregate demand, and plays a leading role in the preservation and expansion of the international capitalist system.[2] In my view, barring a revolutionary change, militarism and military spending priorities are likely to persist for the foreseeable future.

In what follows, I shall present three principal propositions on the role of military spending in the U.S. economy. (1) In the period that begins in 1950, if not earlier, the United States economy was not sufficiently sustained by private aggregate demand; some form of government expenditure was needed to maintain expansion. Without such stimulus, the growth rate of the U.S. as well as the international capitalist economy would have been substantially lower; (2) The U.S. government turned to military spending as the outlet for needed government expenditures precisely because military spending provides the most convenient such outlet. In a capitalist context, spending on the military is easily expandable and highly attractive to corporations; military spending supplements rather than competes with private demand, more is always "needed" for adequate "defense," it is highly profitable to the firms that receive weapons contracts, and no interest group is explicitly against it. (3) Federal expenditures on socially useful needs on a scale comparable to the military budget are not a feasible substitute. Massive social expenditures would tend to undermine profitability in many sectors of the private economy, remove potential areas of profitmaking, interfere with work incentives in the labor market, and weaken the basic ideological premise of capitalism that social welfare is maximized by giving primary responsibility for the production of goods and services to profit-motivated private enterprises. In short, military spending is much more consistent than is social services spending with the maintenance and reproduction of the basic social relations of capitalism.

These propositions contrast sharply with the conventional wisdom. The dominant view among economists is that military spending is not necessary for the prosperity of the U.S. economy and should not be blamed on capitalism per se. To stimulate the economy any form of government spending is about as good as any other; the *aggregate* amount of demand is what matters and not its composition. Expenditures on social needs could easily replace military spending, provided demand is maintained by a proper mix of monetary and fiscal policies. The implication is that, apart from the difficulties of converting a few large military contractors and the retraining of specialized engineers and scientists, the problem of "conversion" is political rather than economic. Many economists have also argued from analogy with other capitalist nations: advanced capitalist economies in Europe and Japan have experienced fairly high rates of economic growth with considerably lower proportions of their GNP allocated to military expenditures. Finally, many economists point to the changing composition of government spending in the U.S. in recent years: while military spending has declined slightly as a percentage of GNP, the total of Federal, state and local nonmilitary expenditures has been increasing as a percentage of GNP. Thus, the U.S. seems to be moving away from dependence on military spending. None of these points is convincing, and in what follows I will try to answer each of them.

The Inadequacy of Private Demand

Let me turn now to my first proposition. Private investment and consumption demand have by themselves been insufficient to maintain low unemployment and an adequate rate of growth; some form of government expenditure has been necessary since at least the late 1940s to stimulate the U.S. economy and maintain expansion. This proposition has been amply verified by historical evidence and needs little substantiation here. For example, Hickman's elaborate econometric analysis of postwar investment demand showed that sluggish growth in the period 1948-63 was caused by a *downward* trend in business fixed investment as well as a full employment surplus in the government budget.[3] Without the stimulus that was provided by government spending, economic growth in this period would have been substantially lower. In other words, autonomous investment demand has not been constrained by the claims on economic resources induced by government expenditures.

The government stimulation that is necessary must include increased government expenditures as well as tax cuts. While the economy can be stimulated for a time without increased government expenditures by reducing taxes and running larger deficits, such tax cuts cannot be used indefinitely. As the tax rate approaches zero, a further decrease in taxes has very little leverage effect on the economy, and further stimulus will necessarily involve increasing government expenditures; a large budget with a small deficit can have as stimulating an effect on the economy as a small budget with a large deficit.[4] So expenditures can and must play a role in stimulating the economy. Since 1950, military expenditures, averaging about ten percent of GNP, have played this stimulative role. And within the strategic capital-goods-producing industry, the sector of the economy that is most subject to cyclical fluctuations and is most affected by secular declines in business fixed investment, military spending plays a stimulative role that is twice as great as in the economy as a whole.[5]

Note that I am not asserting here that every capitalist economy must at all times be suffering from inadequate aggregate demand. Nor am I offering an explanation of *why* the private sector has been inadequate.[6] I am asserting *only* that the U.S. economy has been sick in this regard for the last several decades.

It may also be the case that the international capitalist system as a whole has been suffering the disease of inadequate demand in recent decades. By seeing each capitalist nation as part of a larger international system, we can explain the apparent ability of some developed capitalist countries within that system to prosper without leaning so heavily on military spending. Although I have not engaged in any quantitative calculations, it seems plausible to hypothesize that military spending by the U.S. in the postwar period has not only been a direct prop for the American economy but also an indirect prop for the economies of Europe and Japan as well. Certainly, the export performance of these economies would have been substantially less conducive to growth had the major U.S. market for imports been much softer. The prosperity of these capitalist economies is thus related to the growth of the U.S. market, partially caused by U.S. military expenditures.

The Attractions of Military Spending

My second proposition is that, given the necessity of some form of government expenditures, military spending provides the most convenient outlet for such expenditures. Military contracts are both easily expandable in the economy without confronting any corporate opposition and highly attractive to the firms that receive them.

Military spending is easily expandable basically because it adds to rather than competes with private demand. The amenability of military spending to expand to fill the need can be easily outlined as follows.

First, a convenient rationalization of the need for massive armaments expenditures exists. The ideology of anticommunism and the Cold War has been drummed into politicians and public alike for over twenty years. This is a powerful force behind military spending as well as a general legitimizer of capitalism. The U.S. government's role as global policeman for capitalism has reinforced this rationale for military expenditures.

Second, armaments are rapidly consumed or become obsolete very quickly. Bombers are shot down in Southeast Asia, ammunition is used up or captured, etc. The technology of advanced weapons systems becomes obsolete as fast as defense experts can think of "improvements" over existing weapons systems (or as soon as Soviet experts do). So the demand for weaponry is a bottomless pit. Moreover, the kind of machinery required for armament production is highly specific to particular armaments. So each time a new weapon is needed or a new process is needed or a new process created, much existing production machinery must be scrapped. Extensive retooling at very great new outlays is required. Since the technologies involved tend to be highly complex and exotic, much gold-plating can occur; only specialists know how superfluous a particular frill is, and whether a $1 billion missile would work as well as a $2 billion missile.

Third, there is no generally-agreed-upon yardstick for measuring how much defense we have. The public can't recognize waste here as it would in education or public housing. How do we know when an adequate level of military security is achieved? National security managers can always claim that by some criteria what we have is not enough. Terms like missile gaps and nuclear parity and superiority are easily juggled. Military men always have access to new "secret intelligence reports" not available to the general public. Since few people are willing to gamble with national defense, the expertise of the managers is readily accepted. Politicians and the general public have little way of adequately questioning their judgment.

Fourth, military contracts are highly advantageous to the firms that receive them. Boondoggling and profiteering are endemic in the nature of the "product" and the nature of the buyer-seller relationship in the military "market." While the structure and performance of the military "industry" has been analyzed in detail elsewhere,[7] a few summary comments here will indicate the inherent structural reasons for waste and profiteering.

Briefly, it has always been presumed that as much as possible, and ideally all, armaments production should be carried on by private profit-seeking corporations. Theoretically, the government, as sole buyer, would purchase from the most efficient, least-cost firms. But given the long lead times and the inherent cost and technological uncertainties in developing and producing complicated weapons systems, the government would find it difficult to identify in advance and reward the most efficient military contractors. In fact, the Pentagon has rarely shown any interest in holding down costs or identifying efficient firms, since until recently, it has not faced a real budget constraint of its own. The reality is that contractors and Pentagon both follow the maxim of socialized risk, but private profits—in C. Wright Mills' term, "socialism for the rich."

The profit incentives in the military contracts reward boondoggling and waste.[8] The Pentagon provides without charge much of the fixed and working capital for major military contracts, underwrites and subsidizes the costs of technological research and development for firms that engage in civilian as well as military production, and negotiates (and when necessary, renegotiates) cost-plus contracts that virtually guarantee the contractors against any losses. It is thus not surprising that careful and objective studies of profit rates on investment in military contracts have found that such profits are significantly and substantially higher in military work than in comparable civilian work.

Nor is it surprising to find that most of the major corporations in the United States have become involved in military contracts. Yet the image of the weapons industry often projected is of a small, albeit powerful, group of contractors, many of whom owe their existence solely to defense work. Producing exotic military hardware, these corporations form an economic *enclave* somehow separated from the remainder of the economy.[9]

According to the enclave view, most corporations in the country are not affected one way or another by the military budget (except, of course, insofar as aggregate incomes and demands are stimulated). There is some superficial evidence for this image. After all, only one hundred corporations receive over two-thirds of all prime contract awards each year and 50 corporations receive 60 percent, and the list of the top one hundred contractors has exhibited very little turnover in the last twenty years.[10] Prime contract awards are concentrated among just four industries: aircraft (43 percent), electronics and telecommunications (19.3 percent), shipbuilding and repairing (10.3 percent), and ammunition (5 percent).[11] Moreover, subcontracts appear to be just as concentrated among the big firms.[12]

But this enclave image is highly misleading. First, a list of the top military contractors is virtually a list of all the largest and most powerful industrial corporations in America (see Table 4-1). Nathanson estimates that of the 500 largest manufacturing corporations in 1964, *at least* 205 were significantly involved in military contracts, either in production or in research and development.[13] Among the top 100 firms, 65 are significantly involved in the military market. As Table 4-1 shows, all but five of the largest twenty-five industrial corporations in 1968 were among the 100 largest contractors for the Defense Department. Of these five, one—Union Carbide—is the largest Atomic Energy Commission contractor, two are oil companies indirectly involved in military sales, and one is a steel company also indirectly involved. It is difficult to think of these top corporations as constituting an "enclave."

Second, there are no self-contained enclaves in the American economy. As the study of input-output economics has revealed, the structure of American industry is highly interdependent. Focusing only on the prime contractors is like looking at only the visible part of an iceberg. This is only the direct impact of the military budget; the indirect impact on subcontractors, on producers of

Table 4-1
Military Contractors in the American Economy

Pentagon[a]	Largest Defense Contractors A.E.C.[b]	NASA[c]	Largest Industrial Corporations[d]	
1 General Dynamics	1 Union Carbide	1 North American Rockwell	1 General Motors	(10)[e]
2 Lockheed	2 Sandia Corp.	2 Grumman	2 Standard Oil (N.J.)	(25)
3 General Electric	3 General Electric	3 Boeing	3 Ford	(19)
4 United Aircraft	4 DuPont	4 McDonnell-Douglas	4 General Electric	(3)
5 McDonnell-Douglas	5 Reynolds Electrical	5 General Electric	5 Chrysler	(43)
6 A.T.&T.	6 Westinghouse	6 I.B.M.	6 Mobil	(51)
7 Boeing	7 Bendix	7 Bendix	7 I.B.M.	(30)
8 Ling Temco Vought	8 Holmes & Narver	8 Aerojet-General	8 Texaco	(46)
9 North American Rockwell	9 Douglas United Aircraft	9 RCA	9 Gulf Oil	(78)
10 General Motors	10 Dow Chemical	10 Chrysler	10 U.S. Steel	(60)
11 Grumman	11 Goodyear Atomic	11 General Dynamics	11 A.T.&T.	(6)
12 Avco	12 Idaho Nuclear	12 TRW	12 Standard Oil (Calif.)	
13 Textron	13 Aerojet-General	13 General Motors	13 DuPont	(49)
14 Litton	14 Atlantic Richfield	14 Ling Temco Vought	14 Shell Oil	(38)

15 Raytheon	15 E.G.&G.	15 Lockheed	15 RCA (26)
16 Sperry-Rand	16 Gulf General Atomic	16 Philco-Ford	16 McDonnell-Douglas (5)
17 Martin Marietta	17 Monsanto	17 Sperry Rand	17 Standard Oil (Ind.) (27)
18 Kaiser Industries	18 Kerr-McGee	18 Martin Marietta	18 Westinghouse (7)
19 Ford	19 National Lead	19 T.W.A.	19 Boeing (7)
20 Honeywell	20 Mason & Hanger	20 Federal Electric	20 Swift
21 Olin Mathieson	21 North American Rockwell	21 Catalytic-Dow (joint venture)	21 ITT (29)
22 Northrop	22 Homestake-Sapin	22 United Aircraft	22 Goodyear Tire & Rubber (48)
23 Ryan Aeronautical	23 United Nuclear	23 Brown Engineering	23 General Telephone and Electronics
24 Hughes	24 Pan American	24 Honeywell	24 Bethlehem Steel (41)
25 Standard Oil (N.J.)	25 Phillips Petroleum	25 Control Data	25 Union Carbide

a100 Companies and Their Subsidiary Corporations Listed According to Net Value of Military Prime Contract Awards (Fiscal Year 1968), Department of Defense.

bAnnual Report for 1968, Atomic Energy Commission.

cAnnual Procurement Report, NASA (Fiscal Year 1968).

d500 Largest U.S. Industrial Corporations, Fortune Directory (1968).

eNumber in parentheses indicates rank among 100 largest Defense Department contractors.

Source: Richard F. Kaufman, "We Must Guard Against Unwarranted Influence by the Military-Industrial Complex," NEW YORK TIMES MAGAZINE, June 22, 1969.

intermediate goods and parts, and on suppliers of raw materials ties military spending into the heart of the economy. For evidence, look at Table 4-2, which indicates the wide range of industries over which direct and indirect effects of military spending were distributed in 1967. With the exception of the aircraft

Table 4-2

Sectoral Distribution of Private Employment Attributable to Military Expenditures in 1967

Sector	Percent of Total Military-Related Employment in Sector
1. Agriculture, forestry, and fisheries	2.5
2. Mining	1.3
3. Construction	2.3
4. Ordnance and accessories	6.2
5. Textile and apparel products	3.4
6. Chemicals and allied products	2.1
7. Petroleum and refining	0.5
8. Rubber and plastic products	1.1
9. Other nondurable goods manufacturing[a]	3.5
10. Primary metals	4.5
11. Fabricated metals	2.9
12. Machinery, not electrical	5.9
13. Electrical equipment and supplies	13.3
14. Aircraft and parts	16.0
15. Other transportation equipment	3.2
16. Instruments	1.9
17. Other durable goods manufacturing[b]	2.6
18. Miscellaneous manufacturing	0.3
19. Transportation and warehousing	6.9
20. Communications and public utilities	2.1
21. Wholesale and retail trade	5.6
22. Finance, insurance and real estate	2.1
23. Business services	4.3
24. Medical, educational services and nonprofit organizations	3.2
25. Other services	1.7
Total, manufacturing	68.0
Total, all private employment	100.0

[a]Food and kindred products, tobacco, paper and related products, printing and publishing, leather and leather products.

[b]Lumber and wood products, furniture and fixtures, stone, clay, and glass products.

Source: R. Oliver, "The Employment Effect of Defense Expenditures," MONTHLY LABOR REVIEW, September, 1967, Table I, pp. 10-11.

and electrical equipment industries, no one industry accounted for more than seven percent of total private military-related employment. Aircraft and parts accounted for fifteen percent, and electrical equipment and supplies accounted for thirteen percent. This industrial profile shows that despite the enclave image, a broad spectrum of the domestic corporate economy is involved in military production.

Third, corporations in the civilian market have been racing to get a piece of the military action. Between 1959 and 1962, years for which a study was done, "manufacturing firms outside the defense sector purchased 137 companies in the defense sector (i.e., aircraft and parts, ships and boats, ordnance, electrical machinery, scientific instruments and computers)." By 1966, 93 of the top 500 manufacturing firms had diversified into the defense sector from a traditional nondefense base.[14]

Military spending is very important for a large number of industries within manufacturing. As Table 4-3 shows, about 11.5 percent of all manufacturing output as early as 1958 is attributable to military-related expenditures; the corresponding figure is 20 percent for the metalworking production sector, comprised of metals and metal products, nonelectrical machinery, electrical equipment and supplies, transportation equipment, ordnance, and instruments.[15] The percentage of profits attributable to military spending is probably even higher, given that profit rates are higher on military contracts.

Within the key metalworking sector, a broad range of industries is dependent on military sales, as Table 4-4 shows. The importance of the metalworking sector in the domestic economy can be seen from the following statistics cited by Nathanson: in 1962, metalworking industries accounted for more than 47 percent of all manufacturing employment, 41 percent of total expenditures for plants and equipment, and 40 percent of the total value added in manufacturing.[16] And Table 4-4 indicates that military-related demand accounted for at least 10 percent of 1958 sales for every detailed industry in the sector. A 1964 *Steel* magazine survey of 5,000 metalworking plants found that 2,000 were producing directly for the Pentagon; of these, 1,400 reported that at least 31 percent of their output was for the military.[17]

The attraction of military spending to the major corporations is also apparent when one examines the impact of military contracts on sectoral growth and on the concentration of economic power. We have already observed that prime contract awards are concentrated among a small number of corporations; fifty firms in an average year get 60 percent of the procurement contract dollar and about 94 percent of the research, development, and testing contract dollar.[18] This makes the war industry much more concentrated than the economy as a whole, where the top one hundred firms usually account for only 35 percent of the manufacturing sales. The business of the war industry goes to the biggest firms and is used by them as a base from which to expand their area of control. It is not surprising that between 1947 and 1963 the top two hundred industrial corporations boosted by defense business, increased their share of total value added in the economy from 30 to 41 percent.[19]

Table 4-3

Direct and Indirect Dependence of Industrial Sectors on Military Expenditures, 1958

Sector	Percent of Total Output Attributable to Military
1. Food and kindred products	1.6
2. Apparel and textile mill products	1.9
3. Leather products	3.1
4. Paper and allied products	7.0
5. Chemicals and allied products	5.3
6. Fuel and power	7.3
7. Rubber and rubber products	5.6
8. Lumber and wood products	3.9
9. Nonmetallic minerals and products	4.7
10. Primary metals	13.4
11. Fabricated metal products	8.0
12. Machinery, except electrical	5.2
13. Electrical equipment and supplies	20.8
14. Transportation equipment and ordnance	38.4
15. Instruments and allied products	20.0
16. Miscellaneous manufacturing industries	2.8
17. Transportation	5.9
18. Construction	2.1
Average, metalworking industries (Sectors 10-15)	19.9
Average, all manufacturing (Sectors 1-16)	11.5
Average, Sectors 1-18	9.6

Source: Computed from Leontief and Hoffenberg, "The Economic Impact of Disarmament," SCIENTIFIC AMERICAN, April, 1961.

Let's look at the increasing concentration produced by military spending on an industry level. Almost all of military spending goes to the most concentrated industries in the economy. The standard measure of concentration in an industry is the percentage of sales accounted for by the top four firms. Industries in which 4 firms monopolized over 50 percent of the sales accounted for about one-quarter of all sales by manufacturing industries in 1958.[20] But 90 percent of all military contracts go to these most concentrated industries.[21] Certainly, an expenditure program that benefits twenty of the top twenty-five corporations, and contributes to the concentration of economic power among the corporate giants, is going to enjoy a political power base that lies deep in the heart of the U.S. economy.

Military spending is easily expandable, is highly profitable and amenable to

Table 4-4
Dependence of Selected Industries on Military Expenditures

Industry	Percent of Total Industry Sales Attributable to Federal[a] Expenditures, 1958	Percent of Total Industry Employment Attributable to Defense Expenditures, 1967
Ordnance and accessories	86.7	64.8
Primary iron and steel manufacturing	12.5	8.8
Primary nonferrous metals	22.3	13.6
Stamping, screw machine products	18.2	10.2
Other fabricated metal products	11.9	6.4
Engines and turbines	19.7	11.5
Materials handling machinery and equipment	17.2	7.7
Metalworking machinery and equipment	20.6	11.2
General industrial machinery and equipment	15.3	7.7
Machine shop products	39.0	23.3
Electric industrial equipment and apparatus	17.0	11.3
Electric lighting and wiring equipment	14.5	8.0
Electronic components and accessories	38.9	26.1
Miscellaneous electrical machinery, equipment and supplies	15.1	8.3
Aircraft and parts	86.7	59.1
Other transportation equipment	10.1	22.5
Scientific and controlling instruments	30.2	14.2

[a]Military sales account for 85 percent of total Federal government demand in these industries.

Sources:
1. U.S. Dept. of Labor, MONTHLY LABOR REVIEW, September 1967.
2. U.S. Dept. of Commerce, SURVEY OF CURRENT BUSINESS, November 1964.

boondoggling, and benefits the major corporations in the economy. These factors combine so that military expenditures can be enormous and expandable almost without limit and not incur major corporate opposition. But the same cannot be said for the nonmilitary sector.

The Opposition to Social Service Expenditures

The last of my three major propositions was that Federal spending on socially useful needs on a scale comparable to the military budget is not a feasible substitute. The contrast between government spending on the military and government spending on social services indicates how post-Keynesian macroeconomic theory has artificially separated economics from politics, i.e., from power relationships. Social services spending is unlikely to be as profitable and expandable as is military spending. Social expenditures have never had the blank check that the military until recently have enjoyed.

Investments in social facilities are usually durable—they do not become obsolete very quickly and are not rapidly consumed. Right now, of course, there are plenty of unmet needs in these areas. But once taxes have been increased and everyone is provided with a decent house, once there are new schools and health clinics stocked with materials, then what? They cannot be immediately torn down and built all over again.

The technology of social welfare facilities is not particularly exotic. Very conventional standards exist to tell us how much a house or a hospital should cost. The possibility for enormous padding to absorb funds, is much less, since there are readily accessible yardsticks to ascertain how well social needs have been met. The public knows when adequate and convenient public transportation is available. No one would want to extend it out to a suburb that did not exist.

In general, social spending beyond a certain point cannot be rapidly and wastefully expanded. The difference here is that investment in social services deals with people, not remote objects like weapons. People are resistant to allowing their lives to be dominated and their tax dollars used up by the priorities of waste—even if it does help to keep the economy running. For example, what would happen if a housing project or a school were built in the same way as a new missile? If a missile doesn't work, the company is excused and the planners go back to their drawing boards armed with another huge contract. Since it already has the expertise, the same company is more than likely to get a new missile contract. Imagine the political repercussions of an inadequate, but expensive, school or housing project? The community complains, a public scandal is declared, and all contracts with the offending company are cancelled. The school or housing bill has rougher going the next time it comes up in the legislature.[22]

Social spending cannot provide the opportunities for waste that are provided by military spending. But more important, massive social spending inevitably interferes with the existence and reproduction of the social relations of production under capitalism.[23]

First, many kinds of social spending put the government in direct competition with particular industries and with the private sector as a whole.[24] This goes against the logic of a capitalist economy. For example, government production of low-cost housing in large amounts would reduce substantially profits of private builders and landlords who own the existing housing stock. The supply of housing would be increased and land would be taken away from private developers who want to use it for commercial gain. Similarly, building *effective* mass public transportation would compete with the automobile interests.

Any one of these interests taken by itself might not be sufficient to put insurmountable obstacles in the way of social spending. Most social service programs affect only one particular set of interests in the private economy. But there are so many forms of potential interference. Each of the vested interests are explicitly, or through their ideology, aware of this problem and work to help one another out. They adopt a general social ideology that too much social spending is dangerous and that governmental noninterference is good.

Furthermore, the capitalist system as a whole is threatened by massive governmental social spending because the very necessity of private ownership and control over production is thereby called into question. The basic assumption in capitalist society that goods and services should be produced by private enterprise according to criteria of market profitability fuels the general ideology limiting social spending. This limits the satisfaction of collective needs such as clean air and water, esthetic city planning, etc., that cannot be expressed in market terms as demand for individually sellable commodities.[25]

Massive social spending also tends to upset the labor market, one of the essential institutions of a capitalist economy. Public expenditures on an adequate welfare program would make it difficult for employers to get workers. If the government provided adequate nonwage income without social stigma to recipients, many workers would drop out of the labor force rather than take low-paying and unpleasant jobs. Those who stayed at jobs would be less likely to put up with demeaning working conditions. The whole basis of the capitalist labor·market is that workers have no legitimate income source other than the sale of their labor power, and capitalist ideology has long made a cardinal rule that government should not interfere with this incentive to work.[26] Powerful political forces operate to insure that direct income subsidization at adequate levels does not come into being.

Social service spending is also opposed because it threatens the class structure. Education, for example, is a crucial stratification mechanism, determining who gets to the top and legitimizing their position there.[27] Good free universal education, extending through college, would undermine the transmission of inequality from one generation to the next. A truly open admission system of higher education would undermine the labor market as well: workers would not settle so willingly for miserable, low-paying jobs.[28] In general, many social service expenditures, because of their public good character, are consumed equally and so the distribution of their benefits is more equal than the overall distribution of income. For this reason, such expenditures are often opposed by the rich.

Finally, good social services, since they have given people some security, comfort, and satisfaction, i.e., fulfill real needs, interfere with the market in consumer goods. Corporations can only sell people goods by playing on their unsatisfied needs and yearnings. New needs are constantly being artificially created: the need for status, security, sex appeal, etc. These needs are based on fears, anxieties and dissatisfaction that people have and that are continually pandered to by the commercial world. But if people's needs were being more adequately fulfilled by the public sector, that is, if they had access to adequate housing, effective transportation, good schools, and good health care, they would be much less prey to the appeals of the commercial hucksters. These forms of collective consumption would interfere with the demand for consumer products in the private market.

Military spending is acceptable to all corporate interests. It does not interfere with existing areas for profit-making, it does not undermine the labor market, it does not challenge the class structure, and it does not produce income redistribution. Social spending does all these things, and thus faces obstacles for its own expansion.

I do not mean to imply by the above analysis that a capitalist economy has not and will not provide any basic social services through government expenditures. Some social overhead investment is obviously important and necessary for the smooth functioning of any economy, and the provision of local and national public goods has always been considered a proper activity for capitalist governments. For example, expenditures on education, highways, and transportation are obviously necessary for the production of workers and for getting them to the point of production; such expenditures are motivated by the needs of production, and only incidentally to fill human needs.[29] In fact, most state and local government expenditures have been directed to these basic infrastructural needs.

In recent decades production has become, as Marx put it, more social in character: the economy has become much more complex, more interdependent, more urbanized, more in need of highly schooled labor. The recent increase in state and local expenditures can be explained by these increases in the social costs of production. Expenditures for such needs would be consistent with and are often necessary for private profitability.[30]

Moreover, state and local expenditures are not motivated by the need to stimulate aggregate demand, for only the federal government is concerned with maintaining aggregate demand.[31] But nonmilitary Federal purchases have barely, if at all, increased as a percentage of GNP since the 1930s. Nonmilitary Federal purchases of goods and services were only 2.3 percent in 1970. By contrast, nonmilitary Federal purchases as a percent of GNP were 4.6 percent in 1938 and 1.9 percent in 1954.[32] Thus, it cannot be said that the Federal government has significantly turned to social services expenditures and away from military expenditures to. meet the problem of inadequate aggregate demand.

This brings me to a final point regarding the meaning of the question, "Is military spending really necessary to capitalism?" I have tried to frame the answer to this question in the following way. A capitalist economy with inadequate aggregate demand is much more *likely* to turn to military than to social spending, because the former is more consistent with private profit and the social relations of production under capitalism. If this military outlet were cut off, say by massive public opposition, it is possible that a capitalist economy might accommodate and transform itself rather than commit suicide. But such reasoning misses the point. Military spending is favored by capitalists and is likely to be defended with considerable vigor, as recent years have shown. Perhaps a parallel with imperialism will clarify this point. It is not essential to a capitalist economy that it be imperialist, for growth can be domestically based. But so long as there are lands to be conquered and markets to be penetrated, it is natural to expect that capitalism will have an imperialist character. Similarly, so long as there is profit to be made in military spending, capitalists will turn to it.

Notes

1. An abbreviated version of this paper was presented at the Annual Meeting of the American Economic Association, December 27, 1971. For many of the ideas in the present paper, I am indebted to the Harvard collective of the Union for Radical Political Economics, and to Paul Baran and Paul Sweezy, MONOPOLY CAPITAL (New York: Monthly Review Press, 1965). Parts of the present paper are based on Michael Reich and David Finkelhor, "Capitalism and the Military Industrial Complex: The Obstacles to Conversion," REVIEW OF RADICAL POLITICAL ECONOMICS 2, no. 4 (Fall 1970), reprinted in T. Christoffel et al., UP AGAINST THE AMERICAN MYTH (New York: Holt, Rinehart and Winston, 1971) and R. Edwards, M. Reich and T. Weisskopf, THE CAPITALIST SYSTEM (Englewood Cliffs, N.J.: Prentice-Hall, 1972). Copyright 1973 by Michael Reich.

2. An important factor in the development of military spending has been the assumption by the U.S. since World War II of the role of global policeman for capitalism. I shall not focus on this issue here because the importance of international operations to U.S. capitalism has been well sketched by others. But it is important at least to mention that the United States emerged after World War II as the dominant power in the international capitalist system, and it took on a correspondingly important role in defending and extending the operation of that system around the world. This role obviously has required high levels of military expenditures. See for example Harry Magdoff, THE AGE OF IM-PERIALISM (New York: Monthly Review Press, 1969); Arthur MacEwan, "Capitalist Expansion, Ideology and Intervention" in Edwards, Reich and Weisskopf, THE CAPITALIST SYSTEM; Harry Magdoff, "Is Imperialism Really Necessary?", MONTHLY REVIEW 22, Nos. 5 and 6 (October and November 1970).

3. Bert Hickman, INVESTMENT DEMAND AND U.S. ECONOMIC GROWTH (Washington, D.C.: Brookings Institution, 1965).

4. See, for example, Richard Musgrave, THE THEORY OF PUBLIC FINANCE, (New York: McGraw-Hill, 1959), pp. 429-43.

5. In 1958, 9.6 percent of total output in the economy was attributable to military spending, while in the metalworking industrial sectors (consisting of primary metals, nonelectrical machinery, electrical equipment and ordinance, and instruments and allied products) an unweighted average of 19.9 percent of output was attributable to military expenditures. See Table 4-3.

6. For recent ambitious, though inadequate, attempts to explain theoretically the insufficiency of investment demand in the U.S. since 1929, see Baran and Sweezy, MONOPOLY CAPITAL, and P. Sylos-Labini, OLIGOPOLY AND TECHNICAL PROGRESS, (Cambridge, Mass.: Harvard University Press, 1969).

7. Walter Adams, "The Military-Industrial Complex and the New Industrial State," PAPERS AND PROCEEDINGS OF THE AMERICAN ECONOMIC ASSOCIATION 57 (May 1968); Richard F. Kaufman, THE WAR PROFITEERS, (Indianapolis: Bobbs-Merrill, 1970); Murray Weidenbaum, "Arms and the American Economy," PAPERS AND PROCEEDINGS OF THE AMERICAN ECONOMIC ASSOCIATION 57 (May 1968); Henry Nieburg, IN THE NAME OF SCIENCE (Chicago: Quadrangle, 1966); Richard Barnet, THE ECONOMY OF DEATH, (New York: Atheneum, 1969); Seymour Melman, PENTAGON CAPITALISM (New York: McGraw-Hill, 1970); Richard B. Duboff, "Converting Military Spending to Social Welfare: The Real Obstacles," QUARTERLY REVIEW OF ECONOMICS AND BUSINESS, forthcoming 1972; U.S. Congress, Joint Economic Committee Print, THE ECONOMICS OF MILITARY PROCUREMENT (Washington, D.C.: U.S. Government Printing Office, 1969).

8. See, for example, Kaufman, WAR PROFITEERS, Chapter 4, and Weidenbaum, "Arms and the American Economy."

9. Emile Benoit, "The Economic Impact of Disarmament in the United States," in S. Melman (ed.), DISARMAMENT: ITS POLITICS AND ECONOMICS (Boston, 1962).

10. W. Baldwin, THE STRUCTURE OF THE DEFENSE MARKET, 1955-64 (Durham: Duke U. Press, 1967), p. 9.

11. Research Analysis Corporation, "Economic Impact Analysis" in U.S. Congress, Joint Economic Committee, ECONOMIC EFFECT OF VIETNAM SPENDING, 1967, 2, p. 827.

12. M. Peck and F. Scherer, THE WEAPONS ACQUISITION PROCESS (Graduate School of Business Administration, Harvard University, 1962), p. 150-52, and M. Weidenbaum, THE MODERN PUBLIC SECTOR, (New York: 1969), p. 40.

13. C. Nathanson, "The Militarization of the American Economy," in D. Horowitz (ed.), CORPORATIONS AND THE COLD WAR (New York, 1969), p. 231.

14. Ibid., pp. 215-16.

15. Note that defense-related employment in 1967 in each industry is lower than defense-related production in 1958. This suggests that defense-related production is more capital-intensive than civilian production, i.e., fewer jobs are generated by each dollar of government military spending than by each dollar of nonmilitary spending. The implications of this result are discussed below. The differences between the columns are *not* accounted for by the use of two points in time, nine years apart.

16. Nathanson, "The Militarization of the American Economy," p. 223.

17. Ibid.

18. A.D. Little Co., "How Sick is the Defense Industry." (1963).

19. U.S. Census of Manufacturers, CONCENTRATION RATIOS IN MANU-FACTURING (1963).

20. J. Bain, INDUSTRIAL ORGANIZATION (New York, 1968), p. 158.

21. Research Analysis Corp., "Economic Impact Analysis." These industries are highly interdependent with the rest of the economy.

22. This is not to deny that there is considerable waste and profiteering in civilian government contracts, for example in housing programs. But the potential magnitudes are much smaller.

23. Recall that capitalist relations of production are characterized by private ownership and control of production, with a hierarchical social division of labor between those who control—the capitalists and managers, and those who are controlled—the wage and salary workers.

24. See Baran and Sweezy, MONOPOLY CAPITAL, Chapter 6.

25. For a discussion of the subordination of collective needs to private profit as well as a general Marxist analysis of civilian government expenditures under capitalism, see Andre Gorz, A STRATEGY FOR LABOR (Boston: Beacon Press, 1967).

26. See Richard Edwards, "Who Fares Well in the Welfare State?", in Edwards, Reich and Weisskopf, THE CAPITALIST SYSTEM.

27. See Samuel Bowles, "Unequal Education and the Reproduction of the Social Division of Labor," REVIEW OF RADICAL POLITICAL ECONOMICS 3, no. 4 (Winter 1971), reprinted in Edwards, Reich and Weisskopf, THE CAPITALIST SYSTEM.

28. See Samuel Bowles, "Contradictions in Higher Education in the U.S.," in Edwards, Reich and Weisskopf, THE CAPITALIST SYSTEM.

29. See Andre Gorz, STRATEGY FOR LABOR, and James O'Connor, "The Fiscal Crisis of the State," SOCIALIST REVOLUTION 1, nos. 1 and 2 (Spring 1970).

30. Nonetheless, a relative impoverishment of living standards has taken place, as the destruction of the city and the environment has far outrun government provision of social goods. See Gorz and O'Connor, "The Fiscal Crisis of the State."

31. Since state and local expenditures tend to be limited by available revenues, a downturn in the business cycle usually results in a cutback in state and local expenditures, as such governments try to maintain balanced budgets. The result is that variations in state and local expenditures usually run counter to the stabilization needs of the aggregate economy.

32. Data from THE STATISTICAL ABSTRACT OF THE UNITED STATES, 1971, (Washington, D.C.: U.S. Government Printing Office, 1971).

5

The Soviet Military-Industrial Complex: Does It Exist?

Vernon V. Aspaturian

Since President Eisenhower's almost casual caveat against the possible emergence of a "military-industrial complex" that might acquire unwarranted and potentially dangerous political power, the phrase has become one of the most durable of polemical cliches. In spite of its casual origins and obvious imperfections—both in conception and as an objective entity—the term "military-industrial complex" has been nevertheless employed usefully as an analytical construct, while retaining ineradicable residues of its abuse as a polemical weapon. Whether a military-industrial complex exists or not is largely determined by definitions and cultural perceptions. Caution must be used in applying the term to the Soviet Union where the possibilities of empirical testing are even more remote than in the United States.

As applied to the Soviet Union, the term "military-industrial complex" suggests, in its broadest sense, a deliberate and symbiotic sharing of interests on the part of the military establishment, industry, and high-ranking political figures, whose collective influence is sufficient to shape decisions to accord with the interests of these groups at the expense of others in Soviet society. In a more restricted sense, the concept implies an interlocking and interdependent structure of interests among military, industrial, and political figures, that enables or impels them to behave as a distinctive political actor separate from its individual components. A complex of this type, interlocked both in terms of organizational structure and interchangeable personnel, would exhibit a high degree of policy unity and act as a single input into the political system. It would be fair to say that such a military-industrial complex is found neither in the Soviet Union nor the United States, nor anywhere for that matter, whereas a military-industrial complex in the broadest sense as defined above probably exists in any country with both a military establishment and an industrial sector.

A Soviet military-industrial complex exists that is much more than the first prototype and something less than the second, and thus falls somewhere along a continuum that separates these two poles, one hypothetical in conception and the other virtually inevitable by definition. The Soviet press, of course, indignantly denies the existence of a military-industrial complex in the Soviet Union, while simultaneously affirming its existence in the United States. Soviet sources, while admitting that a military establishment and an industrial sector exist and that even a "defense industrial" sector functions as a distinct entity in

103

the Soviet system, deny that these add up to a complex. Soviet comment, however, has a curious tendency to affirm the entire Soviet system as an organic and structural military-industrial complex, even as it renounces its existence as a subgrouping. Thus, one commentary in the military newspaper *Krasnaya Zvezda*, the official newspaper of the Soviet Defense Ministry, after charging that the existence of a military-industrial complex in the U.S.S.R. is little more than a figment of the feverish and malign imagination of the bourgeois press, asserts that economic construction, military development, and political power are inseverably linked in a single entity:

The C.P.S.U. [Communist Party of the Soviet Union] coordinates and directs the efforts of Soviet society aimed at strengthening the economic and defensive might of the U.S.S.R. This is the indisputable fact that is being distorted by the bourgeois ideologists, who are now proclaiming the existence in our country of some kind of self-contained "military-industrial complex" and alleging that there are differences between the Soviet military leaders and government leaders. What exists in the Soviet Union is the monolithic social, political and ideological unity of society and the complete identity and inseparability of the interests of the people and the interests of the state.[1]

Soviet Demand Sectors and Issues

Soviet commentators have traditionally denied the existence of not only a military-industrial complex, but of interest groups generally. Soviet institutions supposedly exist only as a reflection of the division of labor, and in this functional capacity do not compete either with one another or with the Soviet system as a whole. This claim, of course, is untenable and corresponds neither with the logic of the Soviet social system nor with the actual course of Soviet politics. From time to time, Soviet observers are forced to concede that perhaps discrete outlooks, attitudes, and even interests—of a nonantagonistic type—do exist.[2]

Since it would be impossible to establish a theory of Soviet politics here, such as I have done elsewhere, no extensive attempt will be made to relate the overall interaction of factions, social classes, institutional, socio-functional, and associational groups to the Soviet political process.[3] It should be pointed out that during the past decade, factional groupings have spilled out of the central organs of the Communist party, subinstitutional groupings have developed within various Soviet institutions, and associational and socio-functional groups have become increasingly characterized by subgroup activity. As a consequence, "interests" have aggregated on the basis of *issues* cutting across institutional and functional lines in which subgroups, as well as the larger groups, make informal alliances with one another in opposition to similar formations on the opposite side.

High on the list of issues that propel forces within the Soviet social system into interest group formations are those concerned with the allocation of resources. Increasingly, it is conceded in the Soviet press that certain decisions affect the fortunes of various groups unevenly and that support for or opposition to various courses of action can often be traced not only to a given policy's abstract merits, but also to the perceptions of different groups and individuals as to how that policy will affect their interests, power, and status. These various interests tend to crystallize into distinctive demand sectors, of which there are principally six in Soviet society: (1) the *ideological demand* sector (the ideologues and conservatives of the Party apparatus); (2) the *security demand* sector (the police, armed forces, and defense industries); which overlaps to some degree with (3) the *producer demand* sector (heavy industry, construction, and transportation); (4) the *consumer demand* sector (light industry, consumer goods industry, trade, and housing); (5) the *agricultural demand* sector; and (6) the *public services and welfare* sector.

These demand sectors by no means correspond with interest group aggregation, nor are all the elements of a given demand sector necessarily in general agreement. In fact, there is often intense intrasector competition; for example, between the police and the armed forces within the security demand sector. These demand sectors have in large measure fractured the Party apparatus, as some Party leaders associate themselves with one sector or another; namely, Kosygin with the consumer sector and Brezhnev with the producer sector.

The important point is that Soviet policy, domestic and foreign, responds primarily to internal constituencies, although residual response to external constituencies (foreign communist parties, communist states, and the international communist movement) continues to persist in some degree. The steady orientation of Soviet policy toward internal constituencies has brought about a polarization of men and institutions into a security-producer-ideological grouping and a consumer-agricultural-public services grouping. Interfaction conflict stems from disagreement over resource allocation and differing perceptions of the state of present and future world tension. This issue of tension versus detente has agitated the Soviet leadership since Stalin's death, with the same time-tested positions adopted by politicians who may once have argued the very opposite when political interest dictated. Periodically, Khrushchev and his successors have vented their frustrations over the tyranny supposedly exercised by the international situation on Soviet budgetary allocations and the fortuitous impact they had on the fortunes, status, rewards, and deprivations of various groups in Soviet society:

It is necessary to state frankly: When the government reviews questions of the distribution of means by branches—where to direct how much of the available resources—difficult puzzles often have to be solved. On the one hand, it would be desirable to build more enterprises that make products for satisfying man's requirements, that produce clothing, footwear and other goods for improving people's lives. It would be desirable to invest more means in agriculture and to expand housing construction. . . . On the other hand, life dictates the necessity for spending enormous funds on maintaining our military power at the required level. This reduces and cannot help but reduce the people's possibilities of obtaining direct benefits. But this must be done in order to . . . keep the imperialists from attacking our homeland, from unleashing a general war. That is why when calculating available resources we must soberly consider the needs of the peaceful economy and the requirements of defense and must so combine the one with the other that there will be no overemphasis on either.[4]

The Continuing Debate

For decades now, the continued postponement of consumer priorities has been officially attributed to Soviet foreign policy obligations and security requirements. At the Twenty-fourth Party Congress, Kosygin revealed that the military establishment had absorbed nearly 25 percent of the funds available for economic development over the preceding five years. Kosygin made his remarks in an attempt to show that development of the consumer sector had been frustrated by the voracious budgetary appetites of the military spokesmen present at the congress. One of the men Kosygin referred to was Marshal Grechko, who believed that Western aggressiveness demanded that an even larger share of resources be allocated to the Soviet military.[5]

The undoubted interests that some groups have in a detente that would force a reordering of priorities is constantly articulated in Soviet speeches and writings. Thus, in 1969, it was pointed out by one source:

Experience has proven that only under conditions of a relaxation of tensions is it possible to concentrate a maximum of resources for accomplishing the plans for building of communism.[6]

On the other hand, a military spokesman writing in *Krasnaya Zvezda* paraphrased Lenin, implying that no ceiling should be placed on military spending:

Everyone will agree that an army that does not train itself to master all arms, all means and methods of warfare that the enemy possesses, or may possess, is behaving in an unwise or even in a criminal manner.[7]

The proponents of greater investment in the consumer sector have articulated a contrary view in what, for Soviet writers, is a particularly audacious manner:

There are objective limits to military spending and if they are exceeded this will have a negative effect not only on expanded production, but also on the strengthening of defense. . . . It is essential to observe definite ratios between the output of armaments and producer and consumer goods. . . . An expansion of military consumption beyond permissible boundaries does not lead to a strengthening of the military power of a state, but to its weakening and an inevitable breakdown of the economy as a whole and military-economic potential in particular.[8]

And even among the champions of the consumer sector, debate may rage over precise allocations and priorities. Myriads of possible conflicts and interest group and subgroup coalitions may develop along essentially functional or "issue" lines, many of them temporary, as well as along more permanent institutional groupings, and subgroupings. All of these cleavages are provoked by high-level decisions that, once implemented, percolate back up to affect the behavior of the Politburo. As conflict below creates opportunities for leaders at the top to mobilize support for themselves, leaders and groupings accommodate to one another to their mutual benefit, just as leaders in need of social support often make common cause with groupings in search of advocates in the system's inner councils. A symbiotic process is thus induced that has increasingly become the norm in the Soviet political system.

In the reports delivered at the Twenty-fourth Party Congress, together with evidence of discussion, controversy, and debate in the Soviet press in the years preceding the congress itself, Premier Kosygin emerges as a subtle and persistent, if not always successful, advocate of shifting greater attention to the consumer sector, with particular emphasis on light industry, consumer durables, and greater efficiency and rational methods of economic management. General Secretary Brezhnev, on the other hand, has demonstrated considerably more partiality to maintaining priority for heavy industry and defense and greater solicitude for enhancing the agricultural branches of the consumer sector of the economy. Like Kosygin, he is essentially a man of the center and tries to meet the demands of heavy industry and defense just sufficiently to keep them from being alienated and allows sufficient increase in the allocation of resources to the consumer sector to prevent it from becoming a source of social opposition. Kosygin, similarly, is willing to trim his demands for light industry and consumer goods in the interests of maintaining a centrist coalition.

Although Brezhnev and Kosygin have attempted to steer a middle course between the two principal demand sector coalitions, on the whole, the military and heavy industry have increased and expanded their influence in shaping Soviet policies, and their preferences continue to be favored as opposed to the policies of the consumptionists. The Brezhnev-Kosygin regime has compromised the issue by supporting detente as well as a high level of defense expenditures and priority for heavy industry in an endeavor to demonstrate that detente policies need not lead to an immediate reorientation of budgetary priorities, and thus to mitigate opposition to detente policies. Expanding Soviet military commitments to Egypt, intensified political commitments to India, the growing Chinese nuclear capability, the deteriorating situation in Czechoslovakia before August 1968, and the ambivalent character of the defense debate in the United States have continued to reinforce the skepticism of the military and its allies as to the desirability of detente-oriented policies. Furthermore, it is possible that the military's opposition to detente policies is also motivated by expectations of new opportunities for expanding Soviet power and influence as Soviet strategic power increases while that of the U.S. wanes in response to domestic social unrest, demoralization and disillusionment over Vietnam, irresolution and paralysis of will, and apparent U.S. willingness to abandon its role as the dominant power in the world. Soviet military leaders apparently perceive these opportunities, but their exploitation involves risks and this, in turn, dictates higher margins of safety and, hence, greater defense expenditures, not less.

The Physical Components of the Soviet Military-Industrial Complex

The Soviet military-industrial complex is a coalition of various institutions and groups largely within the ideological, security, and producer demand sectors. The elements of this complex-share three fundamental positions under which a number of subpositions can be listed. First, they share common perceptions of external dangers and opportunities: (1) continuing danger of nuclear war through inadvertence, accident, confrontation, or political instability in the U.S., China, or both; and (2) new opportunities for expanding Soviet global power by taking advantage of U.S. retrenchment. These perceptions generate the following policy preferences; (1) increasing Soviet forces to a level sufficient to ensure relative victory in the event of nuclear war and to meet commitments and exploit opportunities in Eastern Europe, Asia, and the Mediterranean; (2) preserving a high level of defense expenditures and continuing the priority given to defense and heavy industry; and (3) maintaining strict ideological controls at home to guarantee social unity, particularly in the event of crisis.

Since the priorities advocated by the complex simultaneously serve the functional, socio-political, and economic interests of its four main elements, the question of whether the perceptions supporting these priorities originate in self-interest or in sincere belief naturally arises. This will be examined below.

The physical components of the Soviet military-industrial complex consist of four distinct elements: (1) the armed forces; (2) the defense industries complex and related research and development institutions; (3) heavy industry; and (4) the conservative wing of the Party apparatus. The first two components constitute the "core" of the complex, but it is the association with heavy industry and sectors of the Party apparatus that converts the complex into a political force of some magnitude. Since it would be impossible to describe in detail all four components in this brief account, only the two "core" components will be discussed in connection with the policies advocated by the complex as a whole.

The Soviet Armed Forces

Potentially, the Soviet military constitutes the most powerful institutional interest group in the Soviet system. Since 1956 the Ministry of Defense has been headed by a professional military officer, who is assisted by three first deputy ministers, eight deputy ministers, a general staff of the armed forces with a chief, two first deputy chiefs, and four deputy chiefs. The primary administrative divisions of the Defense Ministry are: Main Inspectorate, Main Political Administration, Rear Services. Its five main service branches include: ground forces, naval forces, air forces, strategic missile forces, and air defense forces. There are four Soviet army group forces stationed abroad, fifteen Soviet military districts, two air defense districts, five naval fleets, and numerous other agencies and academies.

The entire administrative structure of the ministry is staffed with professional military personnel. No civilian ministers or deputy ministers exist, but civilian control is achieved mainly through the integration of the professional military into the political structure of the system. A nonpolitical professional military would be a contradiction in terms; the Soviet officer is ideologically committed and must acknowledge the primacy of the Party.

At the very top, civilian control is exercised through both Party and government organs. The minister and his ministry are constitutionally subordinate to the Council of Ministers. The defense minister, a member of the Party's Central Committee (as are his principal subordinates), is also accountable to the Party in the execution of his duties. Within the Defense Ministry itself is the Main Political Administration, the system of political commissars paralleling the command structure, responsible for the political and ideological indoctrination of the troops and for supervising the execution of Party directives.

The Main Political Administration, headed by General Yepishev, is simultaneously a department within the Party Secretariat's Central Apparatus and an administrative division within the Defense Ministry. The institutional loyalty of the personnel in the Main Political Administration is frequently divided but, as a general rule, the longer individuals serve there, the more they assimilate the armed forces' outlook and adopt its interests as their own. Differences between political and military leaders are frequently reflected in changes in the Main Political Administration; personnel who have identified with the military's point of view are replaced by those whose primary loyalty is to the Party apparatus or the Party faction then in ascendancy.

As an institution thoroughly integrated into both the power and juridical structures of the Soviet political system, the Soviet military has extraordinary channels of access to decision making and policy making organs that are denied to most other military establishments. Over and above this specific institutional input, individual ranking officers can still exercise informal leverage and even become political leaders in their own right, as was the case with Marshal Zhukov. Because the Soviet military as an institution enjoys a bloc of representation in central bodies, there is the temptation for ambitious military leaders to employ it as a vehicle of personal political power, as Zhukov was alleged to have done. It is thus remarkable that the Soviet military has been relatively free of Bonapartist figures within its corps of marshals and generals.

Although the military has been integrated into the Soviet political structure primarily to ensure Party and civilian control over it, the same institutional arrangements simultaneously serve as channels for military input into policy: which of the two functions prevails at a given time depends upon factional quarrels in the political leadership or the state of international tensions. During periods of relative international calm and when the political leadership is relatively free of factional infighting, these channels serve primarily as conduits for the control and direction of the military, as, for example, in January 1960, when Khrushchev announced extensive troop cuts, reduction of defense expenditures, and a new strategic doctrine, all in apparent opposition to the interests and advice of the traditional sectors of the military.[9]

Whenever serious factional quarrels develop within the political leadership—during the period between the U-2 affair and Khrushchev's ouster, for instance—these same channels become instruments of military influence on policy, either because political factions seek military support or because the vacuum at the top created by factional conflict naturally creates opportunities for the military to exploit.

The integration and co-optation of the professional military into the political system is accomplished at four levels:

1. Power-Political: Military Representation in Party Organs. At the power-political level, members of the professional military are admitted to membership in the central organs of the Communist party. There are approximately one million Party members in an armed forces of 3,375,000 men. Of the active officer corps of from 350 to 400 thousand, about 90 percent are members of the Party or the Komsomol. The armed forces are recognized as a distinct institutional constituency for purposes of Party representation, usually accounting for 7 to 8 percent of the delegates elected to Party congresses (see Table 5-1).

The professional military, as an institution, is also amply represented at the Central Committee level, although the precise distribution among various branches of the service can vary from one Central Committee to another. Professional military representation, including retired war-horses and uniformed political commissars, accounts for between 9 and 10 percent of the committee's membership. As the Central Committee has increased in size with each succeeding congress, however, the percentage of the professional military has been reduced, while its absolute representation has gone up. At the Twenty-fourth Party Congress in 1971, twenty professional military officers were elected full members—an increase of six over 1966. Only eleven officers were elected candidate, or nonvoting, members. Thus, the voting membership of the military increased proportionately, but its overall membership was reduced.

Even more important than the size of the military contingent in the Central Committee is the institutional make-up of its membership. Whereas other

Table 5-1
Military Representation in Party and State Institutions, 1956-1971[a]

Party	1956		1961		1966		1971	
	No.	%	No.	%	No.	%	No.	%
Politburo	1	0.05	0	0	0	0	0	0
Central Committee[b]	18	7.0	31	9.3	33	9.7	31	7.8
Congress	116	8.5	305	7.0	352	7.1	287	5.8

State	1958		1962		1966		1970	
	No.	%	No.	%	No.	%	No.	%
Presidium, Supreme Soviet	1	0.03	1	0.02	1	0.02	1	0.02
Presidium, Council of Ministers	0	0.0	0	0.0	0	0.0	0	0.0
Council of Ministers	1	0.01	1	0.01	1	0.01	1	0.01
Supreme Soviet	54	3.9	56	3.9	56	3.7	57	3.8

[a]Does not include Marshals Bulganin and Voroshilov.

[b]Includes candidate members.

Central Committee members are elected essentially as individuals (although institutional association plays a role in their selection), military officers are more clearly institutional representatives because of their lifelong association with the armed forces. The fact that not only the defense minister, but all of his first deputies, most of his deputy ministers, the chiefs of staff, and the chiefs of the major services are members of the Central Committee is a reflection of this situation. No other ministry can boast such a phalanx of representation, because no other ministry is simultaneously a socio-functional institution.

It is at the highest levels of the Party that the professional military appears to be deliberately excluded, that is, in the Politburo and the Secretariat. The only professional military personage to have ever sat in the Politburo/Presidium of the Party in recent decades (if we exclude Marshals Bulganin and Voroshilov, who were politico-military in character) was Marshal Zhukov. No professional military man has ever been admitted to the Party Secretariat and it appears that it is the calculated policy of the regime to keep the doors to the *sanctum sanctorum* of the Party tightly shut to professional military people. A similar situation prevails at the apex of the formal governmental structure, as will be examined below.

2. Constitutional-Juridical: Military Representation in State Organs. As in the case of the Party, the professional military is represented at all levels of the government structure. In the all-Union state institutions, which will concern us here, the armed forces have usually elected just under 4 percent of the total membership of the Supreme Soviet since 1958, with the largest contingent represented in the Council (Soviet) of Union (see Table 5-1). Military representation at higher levels of the all-Union state structure is extraordinarily meager compared to its representation on the central organs of the Party, a situation indicative of the care with which the Soviet regime establishes a clear-cut demarcation between civilian and military authority at the constitutional and juridical level. This virtual exclusion from the top reflects not only the Soviet scrupulousness for confining military officers to essentially administrative matters, but also the ambiguity of constitutional command and control at the apex of the Soviet system. This will be discussed later.

The only professional military figure in the Council of Ministers, which consists of over eighty members, is the minister of defense. But at the higher level of the Presidium of the Council of Ministers, made up of the chairman, his first deputies and deputies, no military representation has ever been permitted. No defense minister, including Marshal Zhukov at the zenith of his power, has ever been appointed a first deputy or deputy chairman of the Council of Ministers. At the apex of the formal state structure (the Presidium of the Supreme Soviet), the only military representative for many years has been Marshal Semyon Budenny, who, like Stalin, Bulganin, and Voroshilov, was a politico-military rather than a strictly professional military figure.[10]

3. Politico-Military: Military Representation in the Command Structure. Another category of decision making bodies that may include military representation is made up of ad hoc politico-military organs established by decrees of the Presidium or statutes of the Supreme Soviet. The most conspicuous of these was the State Defense Committee set up during World War II with Stalin as its chairman, but with no professional military representation. The committee was disbanded after World War II and a peacetime counterpart apparently was never established, although Stalin remained the supreme commander of the armed forces.

The highest politico-military decision making body during World War II with professional military representation was the Supreme Headquarters of the Supreme High Command (*Stavka*), under the chairmanship of Stalin. This agency, which exercised direct wartime control over the armed forces, was also disbanded after 1945 and has not since been revived. Stalin retained the position of supreme commander until his death in 1953, but with his passing a legal vacuum reappeared at the apex of the military command structure—a vacuum that is constitutional and legal because the Soviet Constitution fails to designate a commander-in-chief.

Under the Soviet Constitution, the war and command powers of the state are vested in a collegial chief-of-state, the Presidium of the Supreme Soviet. The chairman of this body, who is often referred to as the ceremonial president of the Soviet Union (Podgorny is the current incumbent) does not exercise the war powers of the Presidium or function as a peacetime supreme commander. Under Article 49 of the Soviet Constitution, the Presidium of the Supreme Soviet is entrusted with a wide array of war and command powers which it may delegate to specific individuals and institutions by decree or other constitutional procedure.[11] Thus the Presidium is empowered, *inter alia*, to institute military titles, appoint and remove the high command of the armed forces, proclaim a state of war, order a mobilization, and proclaim martial law.

There is scattered but persuasive evidence that the absence of a predesignated supreme military commander is a source of continuing anxiety for the professional military. Officers fear that in time of crisis the lack of an unambiguous link between the constitutional authorities and the armed forces may result in indecision, particularly in matters involving the use of nuclear weapons.

Some attempt was made during the Khrushchev period to remedy this deficiency, and a Higher Military Council (*Vyshy Voennyi Sovet*) was established with Khrushchev as chairman, although it remains unclear whether his chairmanship of this body derived from his role as first secretary of the Party or chairman of the Council of Ministers, since he held both positions after 1958. The function of the Higher Military Council was more to advise and recommend than to initiate defense policy or to function as a surrogate for a supreme politico-military body. During the last years of Khrushchev's incumbency, he was occasionally referred to as the supreme commander by various marshals and generals, but the legal significance of this title remains unclear.[12]

The Higher Military Council is rarely mentioned in Soviet literature (and then usually in passing), and its precise functions, composition, structure, and constitutional origins remain shrouded in mystery. Apparently it is or was a body that includes selected members of the Politburo and professional military officers. And, if it still exists, its chairman remains unknown, although some observers conjecture that Brezhnev as general secretary of the Party would be the logical successor to Khrushchev.[13]

The position of supreme commander invests the bearer with the legal capacity to issue binding orders to the entire military establishment and thus, could be a powerful weapon in political struggles. For this reason, a fractured political leadership may be reluctant or unable to delegate such powers to a single man. Although the most powerful political personality in the Soviet leadership is General Secretary Brezhnev, his separation from constitutional decision making positions,[14] which are occupied by Kosygin as chairman of the Council of Ministers and Podgorny as chairman of the Presidium of the Supreme Soviet, suggests that he may be unable to legally lay claim to this position but is sufficiently powerful to deny it to the constitutional decision makers.

The absence of a supreme commander not only means that no individual authority can issue binding commands to the military, but that no single individual is invested with authority to *alert* the strategic nuclear force in an emergency or to give the order to fire. This absence also has become a source of contention between the professional military and civilian authority. Periodic, if enigmatic, items appear in the Soviet press concerning the need to create "the necessary politico-military organs" to insure coordinated, effective, and timely action in the event of a crisis, with some military writers demanding that the professional military be given a more direct role in the determination of defense policy and the development of strategic doctrine.[15] Other observers reaffirm the orthodox view that defense policy should remain completely within the province of the political leadership, but the latter should establish a "supreme military organ" through which the political leadership could exercise this authority. These observers suggest that either the Higher Military Council was disbanded after Khrushchev's ouster, that it does not now have a chairman, or that it does not function as the supreme politico-military decision making organ.

One of the major references made by the Soviet press to the Higher Military Council suggests that even in 1964 the precise nature and constitutional status of this body was in dispute. It was then charged that Marshal Zhukov, the minister of defense and full member of the Politburo, tried to make himself de facto *supreme commander* by subordinating the Higher Military Council to the Ministry of Defense. The defense minister, it was charged:

> tried to subordinate it [the Higher Military Council] to The Ministry of Defense rather than to the decisions of the Central Committee . . . despite the fact that it included members of the Party Presidium as well as military and political leaders of the army and navy.[16]

4. Administrative: Military Control of the Ministry of Defense. As has been explained earlier, the administration of the military rests exclusively with its professional officers, although the Main Political Administration constitutes a Party intrusion into some areas of administration, particularly in the education and political training of troops. Although providing the Party with an input into the military establishment, the Main Political Administration can also serve as an input conduit for the professional military into the Party. Currently, the Main Political Administration constitutes an important institutional link with conservative members of the Party apparatus and Party officials who have traditionally looked with favor upon policies that assign highest priorities to defense and heavy industry.

In the absence of a supreme commander, the complete administrative control exercised by the military over the Defense Ministry—this includes the power to deploy troops and weapons—becomes an important weapon in factional struggles. It was Marshal Zhukov's position as first deputy minister of defense in the post-Stalin government that led to the use of the military as a weapon against Secret Police Chief Beria. Later, Zhukov's position as minister of defense enabled him to employ the armed forces to support Khrushchev in his fight against the anti-Party group, although Khrushchev was outvoted in the Party

Presidium. In each case, Zhukov was rewarded with higher appointments to Party organs, though it dawned upon Khrushchev that Zhukov's administrative control of the Defense Ministry made him, in effect, a kingmaker. This awareness was Zhukov's undoing, and it was shortly thereafter that Khrushchev was referred to as *supreme commander.*

In summary, it should be emphasized that, at all levels of the political integration of the armed forces into the political structure, a systematic attempt has been made to exclude the professional military from the *highest* organs.

The Defense Industries

Although heavy industry as a whole exists in a symbiotic relationship with the military establishment—the two share common outlooks, attitudes, and ideas about policy—it is not absolutely dependent upon military orders. Without the business generated by an extensive and sophisticated military establishment, however, both the share of resources assigned to heavy industry and the prestige it now enjoys would decline. A redirection of heavy industry toward consumer production would cause considerable reorganization, disorientation, and disloca- tion among personnel who are among the best paid in the country. During the past decade the Soviet regime has devoted 50 percent of its durable output to defense, leaving 40 percent for investment and the remaining 10 percent for the consumer sector. About 80 percent of the producer goods output has gone back into the producer sector, with only 20 percent destined for the production of consumer goods. These imbalances in the share of output between the producer and consumer sectors have been the cause of considerable anguish among Soviet leaders, and various reform measures, demands for higher labor productivity, and greater efficiency in utilization of facilities have failed to improve significantly the imbalance. The latest device designed to put off hard and pressing decisions on investment priorities is to stress the need for a greater spillover from defense-oriented activity into the consumer sector. Exponents of this theme conclude that a high priority for heavy industry is important even in raising the Soviet standard of living. Thus, at the Twenty-fourth Party Congress, Brezhnev invested heavy industry with a new multidimensional mission:

The Party's policy of ensuring the priority development of . . . heavy industry has turned our country into a mighty power. . . . High growth rates in heavy industry fully retain their importance in the present conditions . . . be- cause . . . the material and technical bases of communism are all largely de- pendent on the successful development of heavy industry. . . . They also retain their importance because without developing heavy industry we cannot maintain our defense capability at the level necessary to guarantee the country's security. . . . Lastly, the development of heavy industry is of special significance because . . . the basic tasks of improving the standard of living cannot be achieved without it. Heavy industry is to increase considerably the output of the means of production for the accelerated development of agriculture and the light and food industries, for more housing, for the further promotion of trade and community services.[17]

This mild, and perhaps even token, suggestion that heavy industry might devote more of its output to the production of durables for the consumer sector was, however, sufficient to create uneasiness among the traditional executives in heavy industry and the military. Thus, *Krasnaya Zvezda* warned that concern for developing the consumer side of the economy should not compromise the ability of heavy industry to keep abreast of weapons development in an age of almost spontaneous obsolescence.[18]

There exists within heavy industry a cluster of ministries that, together with a network of related research and development agencies, constitute a defense industrial complex. Although some of these institutions produce durable goods for the consumer sector, their relationship to the military is one of near absolute dependency: they would cease to exist in their present form if the military were substantially reduced.

These defense industries consist of eight core ministries that are almost exclusively devoted to production for the military and about five more, a substantial share of whose output is consigned to the defense sector. The defense industries thus produce essentially for one client—the military—although as Soviet military and political commitments to allied and client states expand, these industries are finding new external customers. Because the Soviet Union is one of the world's major arms exporters and a leader in economic assistance programs, countries like India, Egypt, and Cuba, aside from the communist countries of Eastern Europe, are becoming important arms customers. Soviet defense industries may unwittingly be developing a vested interest in an expanding Soviet globalism.

The following eight ministries are responsible for producing the bulk of Soviet military output, including defense-related equipment manufactured by space and atomic industries:[19]

1. *The Ministry of Defense Industry.*, under S.A. Zverev: conventional arms and military equipment.
2. *The Ministry of Aviation Industry*, under P.V. Dementev: aircraft, aircraft parts, and some missile equipment.
3. *The Ministry of Shipbuilding Industry*, under B.E. Butoma: naval ships, ship parts, and ship repair.
4. *The Ministry of Electronics Industry*, under A.I. Shokin: electronic components and parts, which are supplied to the Ministries of Radio Industry, Communications, Instrument Building, Means of Automation and Control Systems, and Electrotechnical Industry, all of which use the components to produce finished electronic equipment.

5. *The Ministry of Radio Industry*, under V.D. Kalmykov: supervises the production of electronic systems and radiotechnical equipment for military uses.
6. *The Ministry of General Machine Building*, under S.A. Afanasev: development and production of strategic ballistic missiles and space vehicles.
7. *The Ministry of Medium Machine Building*, under Ye. P. Slavsky: Soviet atomic energy program, production of fissionable materials, and construction of nuclear weapons.
8. *The Ministry of Machine Building*, under V.V. Bakhirev: established in 1968, probably responsible for the supervision of the civilian space program.

These eight all-Union ministries are not exclusively concerned with the production of defense-related equipment, nor is all military production their exclusive province. Other ministries, oriented toward civilian production, but responsible for a substantial share of military production include:

1. *The Ministry of Instrument Manufacturing, Means of Automation and Control Systems*, under K.M. Rudnev.
2. *The Ministry of Tractor and Agricultural Machine Building*, under I.F. Sinitsyn.
3. *The Ministry of Chemical Industry*, under L.A. Kostandov.
4. *The Ministry of Automobile Industry*, under A.M. Tarasov.
5. *State Committee for Science and Technology*, under the chairmanship of V.A. Kirillin, also a deputy chairman of the Council of Ministers.

All of the above listed ministries and state committees are constitutionally subordinate to the Council of Ministers. Although legally subject to the administrative control of Premier Kosygin, the work of the first eight is in fact highly centralized under Dmitri F. Ustinov. Ustinov, a secretary of the Central Committee and a candidate member of the Politburo, was formerly a first deputy chairman of the Council of Ministers in charge of defense production. At one time he was rumored as the Party leadership's choice to succeed Marshal Malinovsky as minister of defense in a move designed to reassert civilian administrative control over the defense establishment. Although eminently acceptable to the professional military, he was apparently rejected in favor of another professional military man, Marshal Grechko, the current incumbent.

Ustinov's rise to the position of highest direct spokesman for the military-industrial complex in Soviet inner decision making councils dates from March 1963, at a time when Khrushchev was under increasing internal criticism for failures such as the Cuban missile crisis. Khrushchev's economic decentralization program alienated heavy industry; his attempt to downgrade conventional military forces, upgrade the strategic rocket forces, and impose troop cuts alienated the traditional military; and his bifurcation of the Party apparatus into rural and urban organizations alienated the conservative wing of the apparatus. Their interests already injured, these powerful groups probably believed that Khrushchev's "erratic and adventurous" tactics in search of a detente were damaging Soviet prestige and endangering Soviet security.[20]

On 13 March 1963, a joint session of the Party Presidium and the Council of Ministers imposed upon Khrushchev a new Supreme Council of the National Economy to coordinate and supervise the decentralized economic system that was playing havoc with industrial production, particularly in the defense field. Ustinov was apparently foisted upon Khrushchev to serve simultaneously as chairman of the new Supreme Council and as a new first deputy chairman of the Council of Ministers. The emerging military-industrial-apparatus coalition was thus given an important decision making post in the state administration. The significance of Ustinov's appointment was underlined by Khrushchev himself in a speech on 24 April 1963, in which he speculated about his possible retirement from politics (amidst widespread rumors in the West that Khrushchev was about to retire). Even more significantly, he linked the appointment of D.F. Ustinov as economic "tsar" to Western reports about the course and direction of Soviet politics in a way which, curiously, seemed to verify rather than deny the substance of Western speculation which was that Khrushchev was in danger of being dethroned:

Comrade Ustinov, who was responsible for the defense industry, has now been appointed Chairman of the Supreme Council of the National Economy. He knows where, what and how things are in the defense industry too. Therefore we shall hope that he establishes better order in this matter as well. (*Stir in the hall. Applause.*) It is interesting to note how widely astray the capitalist press has gone. When Comrade Ustinov was approved as Chairman of the Supreme Council of the National Economy (they had long ago sniffed out that he was engaged in defense industry matters), this press drew the conclusion that the Soviet Union had taken the course of militarization of the country. They announced: "Ustinov has been made head of the Supreme Council of the National Economy; it follows that the Soviet Union will now make only missiles." What nonsense! We appointed Comrade Ustinov simply because he is well qualified for the post.[21]

After Khrushchev's ouster, Ustinov was shifted out of the Council of Ministers to the Secretariat and Politburo, where he continues to oversee defense production. He is assisted in this work by I.D. Serbin, head of the Department of Defense Industry, and V.S. Frolov, head of the Department of Machine Building, in the Central Apparatus of the Party Secretariat. Both were elected candidate members of the Central Committee at the Twenty-fourth Party Congress.

The division of labor between the Party Secretariat and the Council of Ministers in directing the defense industries complex is such that the ministers are constitutionally and administratively responsible to the Presidium of the

Council of Ministers and its chairman, Kosygin. Ustinov and the Secretariat, however, are responsible for coordinating and supervising the actual execution of their work to ensure that it is in conformity with Party policies. Kosygin's deputies in charge of defense industries appear to be L.V. Smirnov and V.A. Kirillin, deputy chairmen of the Council of Ministers and nonvoting members of its Presidium. Both deputy chairmen have had long experience in the field of defense technology.

The defense industries, however, are subject to still another line of control and supervision, that of the Ministry of Defense. Although Ustinov deals directly with the individual ministries, the Ministry of Defense is continuously consulted to ensure that the work of the industries corresponds to the needs of the military establishment. Information is scanty concerning the exact relationship of these three lines of control over the defense industries, and it is probable that some coordinating body exists, composed of members of the Defense Ministry, the defense industries, the Party Secretariat, and the Council of Ministers.

The signal importance of the defense industries in the politico-economic structure of the Soviet system is reflected in the political stature of the top defense administrators. All eight ministers are in charge of the defense industries and three of the five heading defense-related ministries are full members of the Central Committee, while the other two (Tarasov and Sinitsyn) are candidate members. The core components of the Soviet military-industrial complex alone thus account for 33 full members (20 military, 12 industrial, including Kirillin, Smirnov, and Ustinov) and 15 candidate members (11 military and 4 industrial, including Serbin and Frolov) in a Central Committee of 241 full members and 155 candidate members; that is, more than 13 percent of the full membership.

The highest direct representative of the military-industrial complex remains Ustinov, who, as one of ten secretaries and a candidate member of the Politburo, is the only representative of the complex to sit in the Party's most influential organs. In the state structure, L.V. Smirnov and V.A. Kirillin, both deputy chairmen of the Council of Ministers, are nonvoting members of the Council's Presidium and are, along with Defense Minister Grechko, the military-industrial complex's highest representatives in the government. While this representation in the top Party and governmental structure is not overwhelming, it is substantial. The executives involved in the defense industries complex have spent most of their careers in this area and are among the most experienced, efficient, and dynamic managers in the Soviet economic structure.

The defense industries as a group probably exhibit greater continuity of personnel and organization than any other comparable sector of the Soviet economy. The special character of these industries, as well as their unique relationship to the professional military, was spelled out in 1957 when Khrushchev brutally decentralized the Soviet economic bureaucracy, dissolving the central ministries and scattering their executives to the provinces. Because of the military's crucial support in the confrontation with the anti-Party group, however, the defense industries were exempted from the decentralization scheme, and they remained intact as ministries. Although after Zhukov's downfall these ministries were also disestablished (although not decentralized among the *sovnarkhozy*), they were converted into state committees, presided over by a collegial body rather than an individual minister. They continued, however, to report directly to the Council of Ministers.

With Khrushchev's demise came the abolition of the *sovnarkhozy*, a recentralization of the economic administration, and reconversion of the defense industries to ministerial status. In spite of this repeated reorganization, the defense industries not only preserved their centralized structure, but retained their managerial and executive talent as well.

Just as the Soviet military establishment constitutes an *imperium in imperio*, the defense industries complex constitutes an "economy within an economy." If heavy industry enjoys priority over the consumer sector in terms of investment, managerial talent, and rewards for performance, the defense industries enjoy even greater ascendancy within the heavy industrial sector. These industries receive absolute priority on equipment, materials, and personnel, including first choice in recruiting scientific-technical personnel, managerial talent, and skilled workers, all of whom receive higher pay than their counterparts in the less favored sectors of the economy. Executives in defense industries also enjoy greater administrative freedom and, providing that quotas are met and high production quality maintained, there is minimum bureaucratic interference in their work. The vast qualitative difference between Soviet military and space hardware, on the one hand, and consumer goods, on the other, is eloquent testimony to the effectiveness of this partiality.

The relationship of dependency between defense industries and the military establishment has resulted in an unusual pattern of uniformly held interests. Unlike the so-called military-industrial complex in the U.S., that of the Soviet Union possesses a negligible interlocking of personnel: although executives in the defense industries may hold high military rank in the reserve (they rarely serve on active duty except in time of war), high-ranking Soviet military officers do not retire to accept lucrative positions in the defense industries. Because of the fundamental difference in incentive structures, the relationship between the military establishment and the defense industries in the two countries is reversed. Soviet defense industries always strive to satisfy the military establishment, their sole client, and little incentive exists for the Soviet military to please their suppliers. On the other hand, the American military is often more interested in pleasing its suppliers than the suppliers in pleasing them, because of the rewards and favors business can often extend to officers.

Corruption for private or personal material gain is rarely a part of the client-supplier relationship in the Soviet military-industrial complex, since Soviet defense industries have, in effect, one permanent client capable of absorbing their entire output. The Soviet complex has little incentive to develop new internal markets and thus, even less inducement to adapt or develop technological innovations to the civilian sector. As noted earlier, there has been precious little spillover into the nondefense sector, much to the chagrin of Soviet political leaders who are both dazzled and envious of how advanced defense-related technology finds its way into the consumer sector of the U.S. economy.[22]

The U.S. military, in spite of its size, has few captive suppliers in an economy predominantly geared to consumer production. The overall military output constitutes a small, though often important, fraction of the sales of particular American firms and industries; hence there exist powerful incentives for military contractors to adapt innovations generated by defense production to the consumer area. This versatility also creates vast possibilities for conflict of interest, as private industry seeks to maximize military profits in order to subsidize nondefense production. While there is little corruption or conflict of interest in the Soviet military-industrial relationship (other equally venal vices are associated with the Soviet scene), neither is there significant technological spillover from defense production to the civilian economy.

Although there is little or no overlapping, interlocking, or rotation of personnel between the military bureaucracy and the defense industrial bureaucracy in the Soviet Union, the two bureaucracies are nevertheless uniquely intertwined because of the proliferation of numerous subgroups within them. These establish customer-supplier relationships of a specifically and narrowly conceived mutuality of interests. For example, production units involved in the manufacture of ballistic missiles in the Ministry of General Machine Building may establish subgroup alliances with military representatives of the Strategic Rocket Forces. Similarly, Khrushchev's plan to reduce conventional forces probably impelled the Ministry of Defense Industry, a principal supplier of these forces, to act in concert with the conventional services to protect their interests. Other subgroup interests may exist between the air force and the aviation industry, and between the Soviet Naval Forces and the Ministry of Shipbuilding. These subgroup alliances become critical when general defense allocations are cut and various sectors of both the military establishment and the defense industries scramble for support in protecting their own special interests. Ambitious political leaders can exploit these cleavages for their own purposes, as did Khrushchev in planning to augment the Strategic Rocket Forces, a move that earned him the support of the Rocket Forces as well as that of missile and space executives in the defense ministries.

The Soviet Military-Industrial Complex and International Tensions

What converts the functional role of the military establishment and the defense industries—the core of the Soviet military-industrial complex—into a political role is the support they receive from and, in return, give to heavy industry and the conservative wing of the Party apparatus. The two latter groups have long shared a wide spectrum of views, perceptions, and policy positions with the military and its dependent industries. Between 1957 and 1960, when Khrushchev was at the height of his power, these commonly held opinions were congealed into similar, if uncoordinated policy outlooks. Unfavorably affected by Khrushchev's policies of detente and consumer investment, and endowed with new prestige after the U-2 incident, these groups probably played a crucial role in Khrushchev's ouster. The military establishment, heavy industry, and apparatus conservatives all receive more favorable attention from the Brezhnev-Kosygin regime, although it appears that the priorities dilemma is once again generating the same kinds of tensions that plagued Malenkov and Khrushchev in their attempt to readjust the balance between the producer-defense and the consumer sectors of the economy.

The military establishment, heavy industry, and the conservatives in the Party apparatus are not, of course, united on all issues. Powerful individuals and subgroups within them frequently engage in expedient political alliances with factions in other camps. An ambitious marshal or industrial executive may easily "betray" his group in return for the rewards of high office and position, and skillful Soviet politicians have been particularly adept in exploiting the conflicting ambitions and jealousies of Soviet marshals and generals to good advantage.

Bearing this in mind, the views, perceptions, and policy positions shared in considerable measure by the four major components of the Soviet military-industrial complex can be summarized as follows:

Military Policy:
1. Aggressive circles still prevail in the West and present a continuing threat to Soviet security. Khrushchev's view that "peaceloving" forces have assumed a permanent ascendancy in capitalist "ruling circles" is disavowed.
2. Nuclear war is always a possibility, either through Western aggression, accident, or confrontation with China or in the Third World, as the Soviet Union expands its global commitments in this area. Prospects for stable nuclear deterrence are believed to diminish as the number of nuclear powers increases.
3. Given that the possibility of nuclear war will always exist, the Soviet Union should develop the capabilities to deter or preempt a nuclear attack and to survive and *win* such a war, in a relative sense, if it transpires. Nuclear war will not necessarily end in total destruction; a proper defense posture can limit damage to the Soviet Union while allowing Soviet forces to inflict massive damage elsewhere.
4. Soviet military capabilities should be expanded in all directions, without overall reliance on a single branch and should be "balanced" in order to provide Soviet policy makers with more options ("flexible response") in local confrontations. Soviet conventional capabilities of all types should be sufficient to meet commitments to allies and client states and to deter the United States from intervening in the Third World. Strategic capabilities should be constantly expanded to contend with possible attack from several

directions simultaneously (namely, the U.S. and China) or sequentially. The concepts of "overkill" and "parity" are rejected as either undesirable or unworkable.

Economic Policy:

Continuing high priority must be given to defense production, heavy industry, and research and development. Lip service is paid to the necessity of raising the standard of living, but heavy industry is emphasized as the necessary foundation for the creation of an effective consumer sector. The complex continues to call for a postponement in the shift of priorities until absolute security is achieved.

Ideological Policy:

1. The preservation of tight ideological controls at home, particularly over the sciences, professions, education, culture, and the arts is necessary in order to ensure unity and high social cohesion and morale in time of crisis. Relaxation of ideological controls is viewed as responsible for the generation and dissemination of divisive and dissident views, the introduction of pacifist, antimilitary, and unpatriotic themes in literature and the arts.
2. Citizens and intellectuals who dissent, oppose, or mock the Soviet system and its official ideology and policies must undergo punishment and deprivation.
3. Continued de-Stalinization is harmful, except in very selected areas and only after careful consideration of the implications.
4. There must be a partial rehabilitation of Stalin as a person (in contrast to "Stalinism" as a system) and, in particular, of Stalin's image as an effective, wise, and brilliant wartime commander—in short, a more "balanced" image of Stalin must be forged.

Foreign Policy:

1. Negotiations that might lead to arms control or disarmament are at best futile and at worse crippling to the development of Soviet military capabilities. The Soviet military-industrial complex has opposed the Test Ban Treaty and is unenthusiastic about the strategic arms limitation talks (SALT) (although it may have tacitly favored the Non-Proliferation Treaty). The Soviet military insists upon separate representation in delegations to such negotiations.
2. The Soviet grip on its sphere in Eastern Europe must remain tight even if this policy requires military intervention and the risk of war with China or the U.S.
3. Germany must remain divided and West Germany impotent—militarily and politically—and isolated from the U.S.
4. The Soviet territorial status quo must be preserved, particularly against Chinese encroachment.
5. Political commitments made to allied and client states should be matched with the military assistance necessary to honor them.

It should again be emphasized that the principal components of the complex are not in agreement on all issues, and the above is essentially an inventory of some of the views that they appear to hold in common. The military and the conservative wing of the Party apparatus remain divided on a number of serious issues, among which are the following:

1. The military desires greater institutional autonomy, minimum Party interference within the command structure, and little Party control in general, whereas the conservative wing of the apparatus shares the overall apparatus view that the military should be unambiguously subject to Party (i.e., apparatus) control, and that the apparatus is the best judge of how these controls should be implemented.
2. The Soviet military is relatively tolerant on ideological matters as long as ideological deviations do not seriously affect the effectiveness of the Soviet military or Soviet security and foreign policy interests. Thus, the professional military has been a supporter of rapprochement with Marshal Tito and Yugoslavia and has been less concerned with Yugoslav "revisionism" than the conservative members of the apparatus who view with concern the reacceptance of Yugoslavia as a "socialist" state, since this would tend to legitimize and encourage Yugoslav type "revisionism" elsewhere in Eastern Europe and even in the Soviet Union.
3. The Soviet military, however, appears to be less tolerant concerning the Chinese "deviation" and, although the conservative wing of the apparatus is more prone to make ideological concessions to the Chinese if this would improve relations, the Soviet military increasingly views China as an enemy and threat to Soviet security and would tend to oppose any gestures that might convey an impression of weakness and irresolution where China is concerned. Thus, the Soviet military is inclined to be "hard" on China and "soft" on Yugoslavia, whereas the tendencies are reversed in the case of the apparatus.

What ties the major components of the Soviet military-industrial complex together is their understanding of the interdependency that exists between security, heavy industry, and ideological orthodoxy. This perception of interdependence is a complex political relationship, one that transcends the simplistic formula that security requires the primacy of heavy industry and ideological controls, since heavy industrial interests would continue to favor the primacy of heavy industry and conservative Party people would continue to favor tight ideological controls regardless of security considerations. While this linkage between security, ideological orthodoxy, and heavy industry may have been valid at an earlier stage in Soviet development, it is coming under considerable scrutiny from those interests who have suffered under policies promoted by the military-industrial complex and the perceptions of the international situation upon which they rest. While the linkage now may be essentially psychological, reinforced only by habit and tradition, it may also represent an encrusted structure of vested interests that may have little correspondence with, and indeed may hinder, security or economic development.[23]

The economic appetite of the Soviet military-industrial complex has been voracious, as shown in Table 5-2, and is likely to continue to distort the economic development of the country for many years. It is at once obvious that the linkage between security, heavy industry, and ideological orthodoxy and the economic priorities the complex commands can only be legitimized by perceptions of external threat and the state of international tensions. There is little or no claim that these priorities are dictated by external ideological imperatives, i.e., promoting world communism, although feeble and rather implausible attempts are made to justify the priorities in terms of (internal) "building communism."

The question, then, is this: does the structure of priorities respond to special domestic interests or to authentically perceived external dangers? In general, it can be said that, whereas justification for the continued primacy of defense and heavy industry can only originate externally, the need for preserving the existing structure of priorities can find its stimulus internally as well as externally. If the persisting favoritism for defense and heavy industry reflects more the internal institutional and functional needs and interests of the military, heavy industry, and conservative Party leaders than security and foreign policy requirements, then the military and industrial bureaucracies are less institutions serving defense and foreign policy interests than entities being served by a particular defense and foreign policy posture. And, if this be true, the Soviet military and heavy industry constitute a military-industrial complex not only in the physical sense but, in conjunction with the conservative Party leaders, constitute one in the political sense as well.

Perceptions of the international situation thus become crucial, since they can be employed to further purely parochial group and institutional interests in the Soviet Union just as in any other country. There is ample evidence in Soviet theoretical, ideological, and polemical literature—often indirect but persuasive nonetheless—to demonstrate a Soviet awareness that the international situation can be manipulated for purely factional interests. Thus, Khrushchev bluntly stated in 1957 that "Molotov found more convenient a policy of tightening all screws, which contradicts the wise Leninist policy of peaceful co-existence."[24] And, in the polemics with China in 1963-1964, Soviet observers accused the Chinese leaders of manipulating world discord to further their interests, obliquely implying that factional groups within the Soviet leadership were capable of the same thing. In a 1963 "open letter" to the Chinese leaders, it was charged that "one gets the impression that the leaders of the C.P.C. think it to their advantage to maintain and intensify international tension,"[25] and, a year later, the accusation was even more personalized when *Izvestiya* published the substance of an alleged interview in which Mao purportedly said:

Who benefits from international tension? The United States? Great Britain? The world proletariat? In this lies the problem. Personally, I like international tension. The United States will realize that the tension they themselves have created is not advantageous to them, since it can force the supporters of peace and all working people of the entire world to think, and will bring a greater number of people into the Communist Parties. . . . There is a Chinese proverb: "People dare to touch the tiger's whiskers." This is why I think that we should not fear international tension.[26]

Soviet writers are fond of citing Lenin's injunction that the rewards of a particular policy should not be defined narrowly in terms of "who favors" a particular policy, but rather "who benefits."[27] There appears to be little question that the military, heavy industry, and the apparatus have benefited immensely from policies justified by perceptions of external danger, i.e., high international tension. The crucial question then becomes to what degree perceptions of world conflict are a function of institutional interests rather than objective reality. Soviet writers have already conceded that conditions exist in communist countries that can impel individuals and institutions to develop a vested interest in promoting and maintaining international tensions. Thus, the possibility, opportunity, and precedent exist that a Soviet congeries of interests could be united in a military-industrial complex with a vested interest in perceiving conflict, if not precisely in promoting it (although the cognitive relationship between perceptions and self-fulfilling prophecies is subtle, as is the epistemological relationship between these two phenomena and advocacy).

It would be absurd to maintain, as Lenin does implicitly, that because certain individuals and groups are favored by policies flowing from an exacerbation of international conflict, that these groups necessarily favor or deliberately promote policies designed to sustain or create tension. Equally absurd is the

Table 5-2
Soviet GNP Expenditures, Gross Fixed Investments and Budget Expenditures by Sectors, 1950-1970[a]

Use	1950	1960	1965	1967	1969	1970 (Plan)
			Soviet GNP Expenditures (percent of total)			
Consumption	62.4	58.1		56.5		
Investment	21.2	29.9		30.2		
Defense	12.3	9.6		10.6		
Administration	4.1	2.4		2.7		
Sectors			Gross Fixed Investments (in millions of rubles)			
Total Investment	10,903	35,914		56,701	70,500	76,500
Consumer-oriented	5,598	20,737		32,858	41,200	44,700
Agriculture	1,560	4,891		10,014	13,300	14,700
Consumer goods industry	512	1,945		2,678	3,400	4,000
Housing	2,007	8,209		9,643	11,800	12,500
Services	1,519	5,692		10,523	12,700	13,500
Producer-oriented	5,305	15,177		23,843	29,300	31,800
Construction industry	287	1,021		1,785	2,500	3,000
Heavy industry	3,672	10,728		16,831	20,600	22,200
Transport & communications	1,346	3,428		5,227	6,200	6,600

Table 5-2 (cont.)

Category	1965	1967	1969	1970 (Plan)
	Budget Expenditures (billion current rubles)			
Financing the national economy	44.92	52.8	58.32	63.48
Industry and construction	20.99		22.2	23.9
Agriculture and procurement	6.77		9.2	9.5
Trade (foreign & domestic)	2.27		6.5	6.1
Transportation & communications	2.83		2.6	2.8
Municipal economy and housing	4.23		4.9	
Residual	7.83		12.9	21.2
Social-cultural measures	38.16	43.48	51.12	54.85
Education, science, and culture	17.51	20.09	23.2	24.5
Science	4.26	5.05	6.3	
Health and physical culture	6.67	7.45	8.4	9.2
Social welfare measures	13.99	15.94	19.5	21.1
Defense	12.78	14.5	17.70	17.85
Administration	1.28	1.5	1.6	1.71
Loan Service	0.1	0.2	0.2	0.2
Budgetary expenditures residual	4.38	2.76	4.96	6.56
Total expenditures	101.62	115.24	133.90	144.66

[a]Adapted from data and tables in ECONOMIC PERFORMANCES AND THE MILITARY BURDEN IN THE SOVIET UNION, Joint Committee, Congress of the United States, Washington, D.C., 1970, taken from the following contributions: Scot Butler, "The Soviet Capital Investment Program," p. 51; R.E. Steele, "The State Budget for 1970," p. 58; and S.H. Cohn, "The Economic Burden of Soviet Defense Outlays," p. 169.

hypothesis that individuals and groups favored by a peacetime economy automatically defend their self-interest at the risk of endangering national security. Although it cannot be denied that motivations of this character do exist, the problem is much more complicated than conscious motivation. Aside from such ubiquitous phenomena as "false consciousness," false perception, mistaken perception, false or incomplete information, and misinterpretation, there is the more serious problem of genuine and unconscious distortion of the objective situation through the prism of individual or group self-interest. Perception itself is frequently a reflection of self-interest rather than objective reality and, even more frequently, it is simply a distortion of objective reality to a greater or lesser degree. That groups favored by a particular policy or situation have a greater inclination to perceive objective reality in terms of their self-interest is, then, entirely natural.[28]

Consequently, it is extremely difficult to distill from Soviet factional positions those aspects of thought and behavior expressing conflicting perceptions of self-interest from those based on authentic "objective" considerations. All that we can assume at this point is that the fortunes of certain individuals, factions, and socio-institutional functional groups seem to thrive and those of others wither under conditions of greater or lesser international tension.

Since the ouster of Khrushchev in October 1964, the Soviet military-industrial complex has been alive, well, and flourishing. Almost immediately upon Khrushchev's removal, policies detrimental to the complex were replaced by those that favored it. Thus, the economic primacy of heavy industry was reaffirmed and highest priority again assigned to defense expenditures; the centralized structure of industrial ministries was restored and the system of *sovnarkhozy* dissolved; the bifurcated Party apparatus was reunited into a single organization; Party and ideological controls in the arts, sciences, culture, and education were tightened as dissidents were repressed; de-Stalinization was abruptly arrested and a campaign aimed at a partial rehabilitation of Stalin's image, in which the military has played a conspicuous role, was encouraged; Khrushchev's ideological innovations were downgraded and his strategic doctrines renounced. There has been a corresponding escalation of defense expenditures, a rapid and enormous growth in conventional military capabilities, particularly the naval forces, and an astounding expansion in Soviet strategic and missile capabilities, all of which continues unabated in spite of SALT.[29]

These measures were justified by prominent military and Party leaders in the summer of 1965. In a number of speeches and articles, the leaders pressed their demands for a more rapid improvement of weapons technology and called upon the Soviet public to defer its desires for an improved standard of living in light of the continuing threat of the "imperialist" powers.[30]

One of the most important statements of the views of the Soviet military-industrial complex, particularly the military component, appeared in *Krasnaya Zvezda* on 25 September 1969 in an article entitled "The State's Economy and Its Military Might." It virtually asserted that the primary purpose of the Soviet economy was to serve the military establishment. The basic perception of the international situation upon which the complex's policies, and perhaps interests, depends is crystal clear:

V.I. Lenin regarded heavy industry as the fundamental basis of military might, of a country's defense capability. . . . The necessity of further strengthening the material foundation of the Soviet state's armed might stems from the international situation. . . . The Soviet people, like the absolute majority of mankind, do not need war. . . . But imperialist reaction opposes with all its might the establishment of a lasting peace. In present-day conditions, the International Conference of Communist and Workers' Parties noted, the danger engendered by imperialism and its aggressive policy is growing.[31]

Especially notable in this article propounding the basic views of the military-industrial complex, was the emphasis on (1) justifying the continuous growth of the military, (2) keeping abreast with advanced military technology, (3) maintaining a "balanced" military establishment, and (4) maintaining "superiority" in "the balance of forces" and "military equipment":

This growth, in the first place, is connected with the fact that present-day wars can attain vast scope, especially world wars, and this requires maximum mobilization not only of human but also of material resources; . . . Finally, the outcome of the struggle for superiority in military equipment, a struggle that is of very great importance in present-day conditions, depends on economic possibilities. . . .

V.I. Lenin pointed out that in present-day wars victory goes to those who have the highest degree of technology, organization and discipline and the best machines.

At the same time, Vladimir Ilyich taught that one must pay the closest attention to the enemy's possibilities, study his strong and weak points and carefully weigh the balance of forces. "Everyone will agree," V.I. Lenin wrote, "that the army that does not train itself to master all types of weapons, all means and methods of struggle that the enemy has or may have is behaving unwisely or even criminally" (Vol. XLI, p. 81). . . . Here special attention should be given to the words "may have." This means that it is necessary to evaluate the military, economic and scientific potential of a possible enemy on the basis of a careful study both of the existing situation and of realistic prospects. Only with such a sober and scientific approach can one outline the correct path to the achievement of superiority over the enemy in the balance of forces.[32]

While spokesmen for the Soviet military-industrial-apparatus complex were emphatic in their demands for a reversal of the resource priorities established during the Khrushchev era, it should be emphasized that their position was not without opposition within the leadership. Claims for the domestic sectors of the economy were periodically voiced by Kosygin, Podgorny, and Polyansky, among others, but the varying degrees of emphasis given to the priority of heavy industry and defense industry by all spokesmen suggest that the consensus was against them. The escalation of the war in Vietnam and general Soviet disillusionment with the Johnson administration's militancy in foreign policy apparently undermined the position of those who contended that the "peace forces" were dominant in the U.S. and correspondingly served to strengthen the hand of the military and its political allies, but the controversy over resource allocation was by no means definitely settled.

The Brezhnev-Kosygin regime's general posture has been essentially one of seeking a limited detente while maintaining a structure of economic priorities more appropriately justified by conditions of rising international tension. Since relations between the United States and the Soviet Union have been relatively normal during the past several years, the disproportionate character of Soviet military growth and the articulated perceptions of hostility and aggressiveness attributed to the United States by spokesmen for the military-industrial complex suggest one of two things:

1. The Soviet regime's policy represents a tense and delicate compromise dictated by the internal factional balance of forces. Under the terms of this compromise the components identified here as the Soviet military-industrial complex have demanded, in exchange for their willingness to "support" negotiations for disarmament and arms control, that their perceptions and assumptions concerning the international situation be accepted as the basis of policy until conclusively proven otherwise. Proof must come not by negotiations alone under these terms, but by the concrete results of negotiations after they have been concluded.

2. The Soviet regime is engaged in a calculated act of duplicity. Negotiations designed to convey the willingness to reach agreements on disarmament and arms control are in fact being used to paralyze military development in the United States. Soviet military development will proceed unabated until superiority is achieved, whereupon policies will be developed accordingly.

It is the author's judgment that the first possibility is the more accurate approximation of the regime's current general posture. But since the Soviet military-industrial complex is in a good position to frustrate any agreements on arms control or disarmament, we may never know what the authentic intent of the Soviet leaders may be. As Soviet economic development continues to be distorted by the demands of the Soviet military-industrial complex, its continued growth may prove to be as great a danger internally as it will externally—danger not of military takeover, but of economic stagnation and public restiveness, which once again may force the Soviet political leaders, under the pressure of other social forces and institutions, into a confrontation with the complex. But in any event, the confrontation will probably not occur before the Soviet Union achieves some sort of "superiority" in both conventional and strategic capabilities.[33]

Notes

Reprinted with permission from the JOURNAL OF INTERNATIONAL AFFAIRS, Volume 26, Number 1, 1972.

1. Major General Ye. Sulimov, "Lenin and the Defense of the Gains of Socialism: The Unshakable Foundation of Soviet Military Construction," KRASNAYA ZVEZDA (January 15, 1970).

2. Especially on economic issues. See G. Glezerman, "V.I. Lenin on the Interrelation of Economics and Politics in Building the New Society," KOMMUNIST 7 (1963), p. 32.

3. See V.V. Aspaturian, "Internal Politics and Foreign Policy in the Soviet System," In R. Barry Farrell, editor, APPROACHES TO COMPARATIVE AND INTERNATIONAL POLITICS (Evanston, Ill.: Northwestern University Press, 1966); "Social Structure and Political Power in the Soviet System," in H. Albinski and L. Pettit, editors, EUROPEAN POLITICAL PROCESSES (Boston:

Allyn & Bacon, 1968); and "The Soviet Union," In R. Macridis and R. Ward, editors, MODERN POLITICAL SYSTEMS: EUROPE, SECOND EDITION (Englewood Cliffs, N.J.: Prentice-Hall, 1968).

4. PRAVDA, February 28, 1963.

5. See PRAVDA, April 7, 1971; also THE NEW YORK TIMES, April 8, 1971.

6. K.P. Ivanov, LENINISKOYE OSNOVY VNESHNEI POLITIKI SSSR (Moscow: 1969), p. 50.

7. A. Lagovsky, "The State's Economy and Its Military Might," KRASNAYA ZVEZDA (September 25, 1969).

8. P.V. Sokolov, editor, VOENNO-EKONOMICHESKIYE VOPROSY V KURSE POLITEKONOMII (Moscow: 1968), p. 254.

9. For a general discussion of Khrushchev's difficulties with the military during this period, see V.V. Aspaturian, PROCESS AND POWER IN SOVIET FOREIGN POLICY (Boston: Little, Brown, 1971), pp. 534-43. For a discussion of overall Party-military relations, see Roman Kolkowicz, THE SOVIET MILITARY AND THE COMMUNIST PARTY (Princeton, N.J.: Princeton University Press, 1967).

10. It might be noted that Khrushchev, Brezhnev, and other Soviet political leaders also held high military rank during the war, which they retained on a reserve basis after the war.

11. For details concerning the war and military powers of the Presidium and other state organs, see Aspaturian, PROCESS AND POWER, pp. 592-98, 669 ff.

12. See, for example, Marshal Grechko's speech referring to Khrushchev as "our Supreme Commander," celebrating his seventieth birthday, in IZVESTIYA, (April 17, 1964).

13. See Thomas Wolfe, THE SOVIET MILITARY SCENE: INSTITUTIONAL AND DEFENSE POLICY CONSIDERATIONS, RAND Memo R-4913-PR (Santa Monica, Calif.: RAND, 1966), p. 11.

14. Brezhnev, however, is an ordinary member of the Presidium of the Supreme Soviet, the Soviet collegial chief-of-state, and therefore not technically barred from constitutional decision making positions.

15. See V. Zemskov, "For the Theoretical Seminar: An Important Factor for Victory in War," KRASNAYA ZVEZDA (January 5, 1967) and Wolfe, THE SOVIET MILITARY SCENE.

16. Yu. P. Petrov, PARTINOYE STROITELSTVO V SOVETSKOI ARMII I FLOTE, 1918-1961 (Moscow: 1964), as cited in Wolfe, THE SOVIET MILITARY SCENE, p. 12.

17. PRAVDA, March 31, 1971.

18. KRASNAYA ZVEZDA, November 17, 1971.

19. For a detailed description of the Soviet defense industries complex, see Andrew Sheren, "Structure and Organization of Defense-Related Industries," in ECONOMIC PERFORMANCE AND THE MILITARY BURDEN IN THE

SOVIET UNION, Joint Committee, Congress of the United States, Washington, D.C., 1970. See also William T. Lee, "Soviet Military Industrial Complex," in ARMED FORCES MANAGEMENT (May and April 1970), and Richard Armstrong, "Military Industrial Complex—Russian Style," FORTUNE (August 1, 1969).

20. See V.V. Aspaturian, "Soviet Foreign Policy Perspectives in the Sixties," in A. Dallin and T. Larson, editors, SOVIET POLITICS SINCE KHRUSHCHEV (Englewood Cliffs, N.J.: Prentice-Hall, 1968).

21. PRAVDA, April 26, 1963.

22. This issue has become a major preoccupation of top Soviet political, economic, and military leaders. Some deplore the absence of meaningful "spinoff" and others either demand or promise greater payoff for the civilian economy from defense-related endeavors. See V. Novikov (Deputy Chairman, Council of Ministers), "Foundation of Technical Progress," PRAVDA (September 24, 1967); L.I. Brezhnev, "Road of Glory from Space to the Kremlin," PRAVDA (January 23, 1969); speech by I.V. Kapitanov, PRAVDA (April 23, 1969); Brezhnev speech in PRAVDA (June 7, 1969); A. Lagovsky, "The State's Economy and Its Military Might," KRASNAYA ZVEZDA (September 25, 1969); Baibakov (Deputy Chairman, Council of Ministers), report on 1970 Economic Plan, in PRAVDA (December 17, 1969); M.V. Keldysh, "Science and Technical Progress," PRAVDA (February 4, 1970); "Scientific and Technological Progress and the Economic Effectiveness of Production," PRAVDA (September 1, 1970); Brezhnev's report on agriculture, stressing the benefits agriculture derives from defense industries and technology, PRAVDA (July 2, 1970); M.A. Suslov, "Under the Banner of Great October," PRAVDA (November 7, 1970), in which he emphasizes that defense and space technological development "is indicative of the broad potential opportunities for employing high-precision automatically controlled machinery in the national economy"; A. Yepishev, "On the Army and Navy's Right Flank," PRAVDA (March 25, 1971). See also the reports by Brezhnev and Kosygin at the Twenty-fourth Party Congress, where this theme was particularly stressed. The general problem of technological retardation in the Soviet economy is meticulously developed in Gertrude E. Schroeder, "Soviet Technological Lag," Problems of Communism, September-October 1970.

23. See Stanley H. Cohn, "The Economic Burden of Soviet Defense Outlays," in ECONOMIC PERFORMANCE AND THE MILITARY BURDEN IN THE SOVIET UNION.

24. New York Times, July 7, 1957. For a general discussion of Molotov's "tension-producing policies," see V.V. Aspaturian, PROCESS AND POWER, pp. 343-48.

25. PRAVDA, July 14, 1963.

26. IZVESTIYA, June 19, 1964.

27. See, for example, I. Yermashov, "The Warfare State," INTERNATION-

AL AFFAIRS (Moscow) 7 (July 1962), p. 19. For an interesting study relating Soviet defense expenditures to "international tensions," see Raymond Hutchings, "Soviet Defence Spending and Soviet External Relations," INTERNATIONAL AFFAIRS (London), July 1971.

28. Self-interest also makes groups understandably reluctant to permit any diminution of their roles, and such defensiveness may actually result in the expansion of Soviet foreign commitments. The broadening of Soviet power in the Mediterranean, for example, was made possible by a rapid increase in naval capabilities. The Soviet navy may now have a vested stake in an expansive Soviet global policy, although it may have played little or no part in formulating the policy itself.

29. See THE MILITARY BALANCE 1971-1972 (London: Institute for Strategic Studies, 1971).

30. This has, of course, become the standard litany of the Soviet military-industrial complex in its justification of the continued high priority given heavy industry and defense. For an elaboration of this theme see Mikhail Suslov's remarks to Bulgarian party officials, June 2, 1965 (PRAVDA, June 5, 1965); also the statements of many speakers at the Twenty-fourth Party Congress in March and April 1971. For other expressions of the same theme that summer see the Navy Day speeches of Premier Kosygin and Presidium member A.P. Kirilenko; also Shelepin's predictions that the shift back to military priorities would be reflected in the next Five-Year Plan, all in PRAVDA, July 25, 1965.

31. A Lagovsky, "The State's Economy."

32. Ibid.

33. The two possible Soviet positions briefly outlined above represent "stripped-down" basic positions which, of course, can be expressed and manifested in discrete, subtle, and refined variations, both in conception and execution. See also Thomas W. Wolfe, SOVIET INTERESTS IN SALT: POLITICAL, ECONOMIC, BUREAUCRATIC AND STRATEGIC CONTRIBUTIONS AND IMPEDIMENTS TO ARMS CONTROL, RAND Paper P-4702 (Santa Monica, Calif.: RAND, 1971).

6

Aerospace Production Lines and American Defense Spending

James R. Kurth

Competing Explanations of Weapons Procurement

How can the major cases of American weapons procurement be explained? Why, for example, does the United States buy multiple independently-targeted reentry vehicles (MIRVs), despite expert testimony about the grave dangers that they will bring? With their high accuracy in targeting, their high number of warheads, and their high immunity to aerial surveillance, MIRVs can provoke a Soviet fear of an American first strike against Soviet land-based missiles and thereby can provoke the Soviets into acquiring their own MIRVs, perhaps leading again to "the reciprocal fear of surprise attack" and "the delicate balance of terror" of the 1950s. Why does the United States buy a costly ABM system, despite expert testimony that it will not work, given the ease with which the Soviets could overload the system with a dense attack? And why does the United States buy such a costly aircraft as the F-111, with its frequent crashes and repeated groundings, the C-5A, with its mechanical and structural failures, and the B-1, said to be obsolete even before the first prototype is built?

The problem with such questions about weapons procurement is not that there are no answers but that there are too many answers. Around MIRV, or around ABM, or around many cases of aircraft procurement, there has grown up a cluster of competing explanations, a thicket of theories. Does MIRV, for example, result from rational calculations about Soviet threats, or from reckless pursuit by weapons scientists and military bureaucrats of technological progress for its own sake, or from resourceful efforts by weapons manufacturers and their allies in Congress to maintain production and profits, or from some combination of these factors? More generally, we can distinguish in the academic and journalistic literature on military policy four broad, major, competing explanations of weapons procurement: the strategic, the bureaucratic, and democratic, and the economic.

Strategic explanations are familiar enough; they argue that weapons procurement results from rational calculations about foreign threats or from the reciprocal dynamics of arms races. Not surprisingly, policy makers and officials offer strategic explanations. They are less favored, however, outside of official circles. Bureaucratic explanations see weapons procurement as the outcome of bureaucratic politics, competition between bureaucracies, especially the Army,

135

Navy, and Air Force; or as the output of bureaucratic processes, standard operating procedures within bureaucracies. Many liberals favor bureaucratic explanations; for them, the problem is, as the title of a book by John Kenneth Galbraith puts it, "how to control the military."[1] Democratic explanations see weapons procurement as the outcome of electoral politics, e.g., a President's efforts to avoid being vulnerable to campaign charges that he has neglected the nation's security and permitted a "missile gap." Some liberals are drawn to this kind of explanation. Economic explanations see weapons procurement as the result of aggregate economics, the needs of the capitalist system; or, in a less sweeping formulation, as the result of corporate economics, the needs of particular corporations in the aerospace industry. Radicals favor such explanations; for them, the problem is not how to control the military but how to control the economy. The bureaucratic and economic explanations in combination yield, of course, the theory of the military-industrial complex, which in its pure form argues that the military and industry are roughly equal in their influence on policy outcomes.

This essay is an effort to cut away at the thicket of theories. In it we will examine the major cases of aircraft, missile, and antimissile procurement by the U.S. government during the 1960s and 1970s, that is, during the period of the Kennedy, Johnson, and Nixon administrations. These are (1) the F-111 fighter-bomber, (2) the C-5A jumbo transport, (3) the B-1 large bomber, (4) the massive buildup of Minuteman and Polaris missiles from 1961 to 1964; (5) MIRV; and (6) ABM. Each of the six can be defined as a major case because of the large sums ($5 billion or more) that have been or will be spent on procurement of the system. All but the missile buildup also can be defined as a major case because of the intense political debate over the program. And each of the last three also can be defined as a major case because of its impact on the strategic balance between the superpowers. We will also examine the major cases of nonprocurement, that is, the B-70 large bomber and the Skybolt air-to-surface missile.[2]

Aircraft Procurement and Economic Explanations

The two most debated cases of manned aircraft procurement in the 1960s were the F-111 fighter-bomber and the C-5A jumbo transport. Both aircraft became famous, even notorious, because of "cost overruns," mechanical failures, prolonged groundings, and Congressional investigations.[3] Further, in June 1970 the Air Force awarded a contract to produce prototypes of a new, large, manned bomber, the B-1, which begins anew the numbering of the bomber series and which would go into operational deployment in the late 1970s. By that time, given the efficiency of strategic missiles and antiaircraft missiles, the new B-1 would seem to be about as useful and about as obsolete as the first B-1 of the 1920s.

Why does the United States buy such aircraft? There are, of course, the official, strategic explanations: The F-111 is needed for a variety of tasks, such as tactical bombing, strategic bombing, and air defense; the C-5A is needed for massive airlifts of troops and supplies; and the B-1 is needed for strategic bombing and post-attack reconnaissance. But these explanations neglect the fact that the respective tasks can be performed by a variety of ways and weapons, and that these particular manned aircraft are not clearly the most cost-effective (to use the proclaimed criterion of Robert McNamara) way to do so.

Bureaucratic explanations are also possible: The F-111 is needed by the Tactical Air Command to preserve its power and prestige within the over-all balance of the military bureaucracies; the C-5A is needed similarly by the Military Airlift Command; and the B-1 is desired by the aging commanders of the Air Force and of the Strategic Air Command within it, who look back with nostalgia to their youth and to the manned bomber in which they rode first to heroic purpose and then to bureaucratic power. But these explanations are not fully satisfactory: Neither the Tactical Air Command nor the Military Airlift Command is the strongest organization within the Air Force (the strongest is the Strategic Air Command), and probably neither of them could achieve such expensive programs as the F-111 and C-5A without allies. And even the powerful commanders of the Air Force and the Strategic Air Command could not achieve the B-1 on the basis of nostalgia alone, especially in a period of unusually sharp criticism of military spending and after the predecessor of the B-1, the B-70, had been canceled as obsolescent by McNamara several years before. Nor would a democratic explanation which focused on public fears of an "aircraft gap" be persuasive, simply because the public has had no such fears.

An alternative explanation, more economic in emphasis and more general in scope, can be constructed, for these aircraft and perhaps for some other weapons systems also, by drawing some relations between two variables for the period since 1960: (1) aerospace systems which are military or military-related (i.e., military aircraft, missiles, and space systems) and (2) aerospace corporations which produce such systems.

Aerospace Systems

The major military aerospace systems produced since 1960 have been the following: the B-52, B-58, and B-70 large bombers;[4] the F-111 and F-4 fighter-bombers; the C-130, C-141, and C-5A transports; the Minuteman and Polaris missiles and their MIRV successors or "follow-ons," Minuteman III, and Poseidon; and the ABM system including the Spartan and Sprint missiles. In addition, there has been the military-related Apollo moon program. Major military aerospace systems presently planned for production in the mid or late 1970s are the B-1 which can be seen as a long-delayed follow-on to the canceled

B-70; the F-14 and F-15, which will follow the F-4; a lightweight fighter; an STOL transport; the Undersea Long-Range Missile System (ULMS), which will be a follow-on to Poseidon, and perhaps a super-MIRV which will follow Minuteman III; and the military-related space shuttle program. These add up to twenty-two major military or military-related aerospace systems for the 1960s and 1970s.[5]

These various aerospace systems can be grouped into six functional categories or production sectors: (1) large bombers, (2) fighters and fighter-bombers, (3) military transports, (4) missile systems, and (5) antimissile systems, (6) space systems.

Aerospace Corporations

At the beginning of our period, in 1960, there were a large number of aerospace corporations which produced military aircraft, missiles, or space systems. Four stood out, however, in the sense that each received in fiscal year 1961 military and space "prime contract awards" of some $1 billion or more: General Dynamics, North American, Lockheed, and Boeing.[6]

During the decade after 1960, each of these four corporations continued to normally receive each year $1 billion or more in military and space contracts, although Boeing's awards occasionally dropped below that amount. McDonnell, a minor contractor at the beginning of the decade with contracts of $295 million in FY 1961, greatly expanded its military sales, primarily with the F-4 Phantom. In 1967, McDonnell merged with Douglas, another minor contractor. In FY 1961, Douglas was awarded contracts of $341 million, much of which went to research and development programs for Skybolt, an air-to-surface missile canceled in 1962, and for Nike Zeus, the first antimissile missile; in FY 1966, the last year before the merger, Douglas was awarded contracts of $539 million. Since 1967, the merged corporation of McDonnell Douglas has normally received each year contracts of $1 billion or more. Grumman, another minor contractor in FY 1961 with contracts of $249 million, also greatly expanded its military and space sales, primarily with two large subcontracts awarded in the early 1960s, one for the aft fuselage of the F-111 and one for elements of the Apollo moon program. There are now six aerospace corporations which produce military aircraft, missiles, or space systems and which each normally receive some $1 billion or more in military and space contracts each year; in FY 1971, Lockheed, General Dynamics, Grumman, McDonnell Douglas, and North American Rockwell[7] were each awarded contracts amounting to almost $1 billion or more; Boeing was awarded some $800 million.[8]

We can analytically split Lockheed, which is normally the largest military contractor, into its two main military divisions, Lockheed-Missiles and Space, located in California, and Lockheed-Georgia. Similarly, we can split McDonnell

Douglas into its McDonnell division in Missouri and its Douglas division in California. There are thus eight major production lines.

Given these aerospace systems and aerospace corporations, two related but different economic explanations can be constructed, which we shall call the follow-on and the bail-out imperatives.

The Follow-on Imperative

We can chart the major military aerospace systems according to the production line to which the U.S. government awarded the contract and according to the years when major development or production phased in or out or is scheduled to do so.[9] Some interesting patterns result. (See Table 6-1)

About the time a production line phases out production of one major government contract, it phases in production of a new one, usually within a year. In the case of new aircraft, which usually require a development phase of about three years, the production line normally is awarded the contract for the new system about three years before production of the old one is scheduled to phase out. In the case of new missiles, the development phase usually is about two years. Further, in most cases, the new contract is for a system which is structurally similar while technically superior to the system being phased out, i.e., the new contract is a follow-on contract. (An exception is Apollo, but even here North American was NASA's largest contractor before the Apollo contract was awarded; in the case of the B-1, the follow-on is one step removed from the B-70.)

A large and established aerospace production line is a national resource—or so it seems to many high officers in the armed services. The corporation's managers, shareholders, bankers, engineers, and workers, of course, will enthusiastically agree, as will the area's Congressmen and Senators. The Defense Department would find it risky and even reckless to allow one of only eight or less large production lines to wither and die for lack of a large production contract. This is especially so because for each of the aircraft production sectors (large bombers, fighters, and military transports), there are actually only four or five potential production lines out of the eight major lines we have listed. Large bombers are likely to be competed for and produced by only General Dynamics, North American Rockwell, Boeing, and perhaps Lockheed-Georgia; fighters and fighter-bombers by only General Dynamics, North American Rockwell, Boeing, McDonnell division, and Grumman; and military transports by only Boeing, Lockheed-Georgia, Douglas division, and, for small transports, Grumman. Thus, there is at least latent pressure upon the Defense Department from many sources to award a new, major contract to a production line when an old major contract is phasing out. Further, the disruption of the production line will be least and the efficiency of the product would seem highest if the new contract is

Table 6-1
The Follow-on Imperative: Major Production Lines and Military Aerospace Systems

	General Dynamics	North American Rockwell	Boeing	Lockheed-M & S	Lockheed-Georgia	McDonnell	Douglas	Grumman
1960	B-58	B-70	B-52	Polaris	C-130	F-4	Nike Zeus d.	Misc.
1961		Apollo d.in	Minuteman Minuteman buildup	Polaris buildup	C-141 d.in			
1962	B-58 out		B-52 out					F-111 sub. d.in
1963	F-111 d.in							Apollo sub. d.in
1964		B-70 out			C-141 p.in			
1965					C-5A d.in		Nike Zeus out Spartan d.in	
1966	F-111 p.in	Apollo p.in	Minuteman III d.in	Poseidon d.in				F-111 sub. p.in Apollo sub. p.in
1967								
1968			Minuteman out Minuteman III p.in	Polaris out Poseidon p.in	C-141 out C-5A p.in			
1969						F-15 d.in		F-14 d.in
1970		B-1 d.in						
1971				ULMS d.in				
1972		Apollo out Shuttle d.in			C-5A out	F-4 out	Spartan p.in	
1973	F-111 out Lightweight fighter in ?	B-1 p.in	Minuteman III out Super-MIRV or SST in ?	Poseidon out ULMS p.in	STOL transport in ?	F-15 p.in		F-111 sub. out Apollo sub. out F-14 p.in

d. = development; p. = production

structurally similar to the old, in the same functional category or production sector, i.e., is a follow-on contract. Such a contract renovates both the large and established aerospace corporation that produces the weapons system and the large and established military organization that deploys it.

This latent constraint or rather compulsion imposed on weapons procurement by industrial structure might be called the follow-on imperative and contrasted with the official imperative. The official imperative for weapons procurement might be phrased as follows: If a military service needs a new weapons system, it will solicit bids from several competing companies; ordinarily, the service will award the contract to the company with the most cost-effective design. The follow-on imperative is rather different: If one of the eight production lines is opening up, it will receive a new major contract from a military service (or from NASA); ordinarily, the new contract will be structurally similar to the old, i.e., a follow-on contract. Relatedly, the design competition between production lines is only a peripheral factor in the award.

The follow-on imperative would have predicted and can perhaps explain the production line and the product structure of eleven out of the twelve major contracts awarded from 1960 through 1972 (1) Minuteman III follow-on to Minuteman, (2) Poseidon follow-on to Polaris, (3) ULMS follow-on to Poseidon, (4) C-141 follow-on to C-130, (5) C-5A follow-on to C-141, (6) F-14 follow-on to F-111 major subcontract, (7) F-15 follow-on to F-4, (8) Spartan follow-on to Nike Zeus, (9) space shuttle follow-on to Apollo, (10) F-111 after B-58 (superficially a less certain case, but the two planes are structurally similar, with the F-111 being a relatively large fighter-bomber and the B-58 being a relatively small bomber), (11) B-1 delayed follow-on to B-70. In regard to the twelfth contract, Apollo, North American might have been predicted to receive the award, because it was already NASA's largest contractor.

The imperatives of the industrial structure are reinforced, not surprisingly, by the imperatives of the political system, as would be suggested by a democratic explanation. Five of the production lines are located in states which loom large in the Electoral College: California (Lockheed-Missiles and Space, North American Rockwell, and Douglas division of McDonnell Douglas), Texas (General Dynamics), and New York (Grumman). The three others are located in states which in the 1960s had a Senator who ranked high in the Senate Armed Services Committee or Appropriations Committee: Washington (Boeing, Henry Jackson), George (Lockheed-Georgia, Richard Russell), and Missouri (McDonnell division of McDonnell Douglas, Stuart Symington).

It might be said, however, that one should expect most contracts to be follow-on contracts. Production of the original system should give an aerospace corporation a competitive edge in technical experience and expertise which will win for it the next system awarded in the same production sector. But in at least three major cases, the Source Selection Board on technical grounds chose a different corporation than the one already producing a similar system; the contract became a follow-on contract only when the Board was overruled by higher officials. With the F-111, the original, technical choice was Boeing, rather than General Dynamics; with the C-5A, it was Boeing rather than Lockheed; and with Apollo, it was Martin rather than North American. More importantly, it is not always obvious that there should be any new system at all in an old production sector. This is especially the case because of the recent evolution of the six functional categories or production sectors. The aerospace systems within them or follow-on contracts are of course becoming progressively more complex and expensive, but they are also becoming progressively more dangerous strategically (MIRV), or operationally (F-111, F-14, and C-5A), or at best dubious (B-1, F-15, ABM, and the space shuttle).

The Bail-out Imperative

A related but inferior economic explanation can be constructed by looking at the annual sales, income, and employment figures for all six (originally seven) aerospace corporations for the period 1960 to 1971. Again, we can chart the major military aerospace systems according to the corporation to which the U.S. government awarded the contract and according to the years in which it did so. But this time we will also include in the table those years in which the corporation suffered either (1) a drop in sales of almost 10 percent or more from the previous year, (2) a deficit in income, or (3) a drop in employment of almost 10 percent or more from the previous year.[10] (See Table 6-2)

There have been many occasions when an aerospace corporation has experienced one or more of these three difficulties. In twelve cases, the U.S. government within the next year has awarded the corporation a new, major, military contract: (1) General Dynamics and the F-111 in 1962, (2) North American Rockwell and the B-1 in 1970, (3) North American Rockwell and the space shuttle in 1972, (4) Boeing and the Minuteman buildup in 1961, (5) Lockheed and the Polaris buildup and the C-141 in 1961, (6) Lockheed and the C-5A in 1965, (7) Lockheed and the development of ULMS in 1971 (as well as a government guarantee of $250 million in bank loans), (8) McDonnell and the Air Force version of the F-4 in 1962, (9) Douglas and Skybolt in 1960, (10) McDonnell Douglas and the Johnson administration's approval of the Sentinel ABM system, including Spartan, in 1967, (11) McDonnell Douglas and the Nixon administration's approval of the Safeguard ABM system, including Spartan, in 1969, and (12) McDonnell Douglas and the F-15 in 1969. These observations suggest that the government comes to the aid of corporations in deep financial trouble, that there is what might be called a bail-out imperative.

In two cases the government has not awarded any new, major contract to the afflicted corporation. General Dynamics did not immediately receive contract aid after its bad year of 1970, but it is in a good position to receive a contract

Table 6-2
The Bail-out Imperative: Corporate Financial Troubles and Military Aerospace Systems

	General Dynamics	North American Rockwell	Boeing	Lockheed	McDonnell	Douglas	Grumman
1960	$27 mil. deficit		9% emp. drop	$43 mil. deficit		$19 mil. deficit 25% emp. drop Skybolt in	
1961	$143 mil. deficit	Apollo in	Minuteman buildup	Polaris buildup C-141 in	21% sales drop 13% emp. drop		
1962	20% emp. drop F-111 in				Air Force F-4 in	32% sales drop 22% emp. drop	F-111 sub. in
1963	25% sales drop						Apollo sub. in
1964				17% sales drop			
1965				C-5A in		Spartan in	
1966			Minuteman III in	Poseidon in		$28 mil. deficit	
1967					McDonnell Douglas merger Johnson ABM decision		
1968					11% emp. drop		
1969		9% emp. drop	13% sales drop 15% emp. drop	$33 mil. deficit	Nixon ABM decision 16% sales drop 13% emp. drop F-15 in		F-14 in
1970	12% sales drop $7 mil. deficit 22% emp. drop	10% sales drop 22% emp. drop B-1 in	34% emp. drop	$86 mil. deficit $13 emp. drop	31% sales drop 14% emp. drop		16% sales drop 21% emp. drop
1971	16% sales drop 17% emp. drop	10% emp. drop 1972: space shuttle in	17% sales drop 16% emp. drop	12% emp. drop $250 mil. govt loan guarantee ULMS in			20% sales drop $18 mil. deficit

for the Air Force lightweight fighter and a large subcontract for the space shuttle in 1972 or 1973. (Similarly, General Dynamics did not immediately receive aid after 1960 but was awarded the F-111 in 1962.) Boeing did not immediately receive aid after 1969, but perhaps this was because the government planned for the SST to fill the gap in 1971; instead the SST was canceled by Congress. In three other cases, the government had just awarded the corporation a development contract for a major weapons system, which could be expected to shortly revive the corporation as the system moved toward production (General Dynamics 1963, McDonnell Douglas 1970, and Grumman 1970). Overall, however, the bail-out imperative is a less general explanation than its follow-on counterpart: three major weapons systems have been awarded without an immediately preceding corporate crisis (Minuteman III, Poseidon, and the F-14).

The follow-on and bail-out imperatives at first glance might seem to explain not only cases of aircraft procurement but also missile procurement (the Minuteman and Polaris buildup of 1961-1964 and, with the follow-on imperative, their MIRV successors, Minuteman III and Poseidon) and antimissile procurement (the Spartan missile of the ABM). But such an extension of the two imperatives is not without problems.

First, a general point, the mere fact that a condition is present in many cases does not in itself demonstrate that it is important or salient in each of them. Alternative explanations may be less general but more real.

Second, in regard to the missile buildup of 1961-1964, the two imperatives are flawed by *overcomplication*. A complex array of economic considerations may not be necessary to explain the outcome; a simpler model may serve just as well.

Third, in regard to MIRV, the two imperatives are flawed by *underprecision*. Neither explains why highly accurate warheads as opposed to merely multiple ones (MIRV as opposed to MRV) were procured; economic needs would have been met equally well with a missile carrying either kind of warhead; and therefore economic needs alone do not explain the most important part, the "I," of MIRV.

Fourth, in regard to ABM, the two imperatives are flawed by *overprediction*. Each would predict large-scale procurement of Spartan; neither explains why the Nixon administration moved in the Strategic Arms Limitation Talks (SALT) with the Soviet Union to limit deployment of Spartan to only 200 missiles.

Given these problems with the extension of economic explanations into the major cases of missile procurement and antimissile procurement, we should examine these cases on their own and in search of alternative explanations.

Missile Procurement and Bureaucratic Explanations

The first case of missile procurement during the period since 1960 was the massive buildup of Minuteman and Polaris missiles from 1961 to 1964. This is also the simplest case of weapons procurement to examine and explain: A decision was made during a relatively limited time and for a merely quantitative change.[11]

Because Minuteman and Polaris were invulnerable and thus second-strike weapons, they had a generally stabilizing impact on the strategic balance between the Soviet Union and the United States. As such, a strategic explanation of the U.S. buildup, focusing on international stability, might seem quite sufficient. However, even Secretary of Defense McNamara in 1967 retrospectively criticized as excessive the *degree* of the U.S. expansion and its effect on the Soviets:

Our current numerical superiority over the Soviet Union in reliable, accurate and effective warheads is both greater than we had originally planned and more than we require. . . . Clearly, the Soviet build-up is in part a reaction to our own build-up since the beginning of the 1960s.[12]

Why did the United States deploy as many missiles as it did? McNamara's own explanation, like almost all official explanations, is a strategic one, but it stresses his lack of information.

In 1961 when I became Secretary of Defense, the Soviet Union possessed a very small operational arsenal of intercontinental missiles. However, they did possess the technological and industrial capacity to enlarge that arsenal very substantially over the succeeding several years. We had no evidence that the Soviets did plan, in fact, fully to use that capability. But, as I have pointed out, a strategic planner must be conservative in his calculations; that is, he must prepare for the worst plausible case and not be content to hope and prepare merely for the most probable.

Since we could not be certain of Soviet intentions, since we could not be sure that they would not undertake a massive build-up, we had to insure against such an eventuality by undertaking ourselves a major build-up of the Minuteman and Polaris forces. Thus, in the course of hedging against what was then only a theoretically possible Soviet build-up, we took decisions which have resulted in our current superiority in numbers of warheads and deliverable megatons. But the blunt fact remains that if we had had more accurate information about planned Soviet strategic forces, we simply would not have needed to build as large a nuclear arsenal as we have today.

Let me be absolutely clear. I am not saying that our decision in 1961 was unjustified; I am saying that it was necessitated by a lack of accurate information.[13]

But McNamara's account does not explain why the U.S. ordered a massive buildup all at once instead of ordering part of the buildup at first and delaying the rest of it until more information became available.

An alternative explanation emphasizing bureaucratic politics is given by Schlesinger in his account of the drawing-up of the Kennedy administration's first full defense budget in the fall of 1961:

The budget . . . contemplated a sizeable increase in missiles; and the White House staff, while favoring a larger Minuteman force than the original Eisenhower proposal, wondered whether the new budget was not providing for more missiles than national security required. But the President, though intimating a certain sympathy for this view, was not prepared to overrule McNamara's recommendation. As for the Secretary, he did not believe that doubling or even tripling our striking power would enable us to destroy the hardened missile sites or missile-launching submarines of our adversary. But he was already engaged in a bitter fight with the Air Force over his effort to disengage from the B-70, a costly, high-altitude manner bomber rendered obsolescent by the improvement in Soviet ground-to-air missiles. After cutting down the original Air Force demands considerably, he perhaps felt that he could not do more without risking public conflict with the Joint Chiefs and the vociferous B-70 lobby in Congress. As a result, the President went along with the policy of multiplying Polaris and Minuteman missiles.[14]

A similar account is given by David Halberstam, one which, however, emphasizes more the power of Congress:

In 1961 some White House aides were trying to slow the arms race. At that point the U.S. had 450 missiles, and McNamara was asking for 950, and the Chiefs were asking for 3,000. The White House people had quietly checked around and found that in effectiveness the 450 were the same as McNamara's 950.
"What about it, Bob?" Kennedy asked.
"Well, they're right," he answered.
"Well, then, why the 950, Bob?" Kennedy asked.
"Because that's the smallest number we can take up on the Hill without getting murdered," he answered.[15]

In summary, the massive buildup of Minuteman and Polaris missiles resulted from a decision for a merely quantitative change and during a relatively limited time. It is best explained by bureaucratic politics: bargaining among different actors within the executive branch over the share and degree of incremental change, with allies within Congress playing a supporting role. Although the missile buildup can also be fitted into the broader economic frameworks formed by the follow-on and bail-out imperatives, it is neither easy nor necessary to do so. Bureaucratic factors were the salient consideration for policy makers at the time, and they are a sufficient explanation for policy analysts looking back.

More generally, the particular quantity bought of any weapons systems ordinarily will be the outcome of bureaucratic politics, of a complex bargaining process of negotiating, logrolling, and trading. Each military service wants more of what it already has or is scheduled to get. The services compete with each other and with other bureaucracies over their share of the budget. Quantitative disputes, being about merely numerical changes and generally familiar weapons, are especially amenable to bargaining and to precise compromises and tradeoffs. The bargaining ordinarily takes place among actors within the executive branch;

it is, as Samuel Huntington long ago pointed out, "executive legislation."[16] Although each service has its own allies in Congress and among the corporations beyond, these normally play only a supporting role.

The Minuteman and Polaris buildup was the first important case of American missile procurement during the period since 1960. But the most important case, because of its potentially destabilizing impact on the strategic balance between the Soviet Union and the United States, was MIRV.[17]

Why did the United States develop and deploy MIRV? The official explanation is again a strategic one, and the usual argument has been that MIRV is needed to penetrate Soviet ABM systems. But this, like the economic explanations, does not explain why highly accurate, as opposed to merely multiple, warheads (MIRV instead of MRV) are needed. Nor does it explain why the U.S. continued to develop MIRV in the mid-1960s after the Soviets limited their development of ABM. A more accurate strategic explanation, suggested by the following censored congressional testimony, would argue that MIRV was developed in order to increase the U.S. capability to destroy Soviet missiles, and, in effect, to give the U.S. a first-strike capability.

Question (by Senator Mike Mansfield, D.–Mont.):

Is it not true that the U.S. response to the discovery that the Soviets had made an initial deployment of an ABM system around Moscow and probably elsewhere was to develop the MIRV system for Minuteman and Polaris?

Answer (by Dr. John S. Foster, Director of Defense Research and Engineering):

Not entirely. The MIRV concept was originally generated to increase our targeting capability rather than to penetrate ABM defenses. In 1961-62 planning for targeting the Minuteman force it was found that the total number of aim points exceeded the number of Minuteman missiles. By splitting up the payload of a single missile (deleted) each (deleted) could be programmed (deleted) allowing us to cover these targets with (deleted) fewer missiles. (Deleted.) MIRV was originally born to implement the payload split up (deleted). It was found that the previously generated MIRV concept could equally well be used against ABM (deleted).[18]

Although Secretary of Defense McNamara had rejected a first-strike targeting doctrine, the Air Force commanders, formally his subordinates, had not. They preferred a first-strike doctrine, with its double implication that the United States could win a war with the Soviet Union and that the Air Force would have the prime role in doing so, to a second-strike doctrine, which implied that the U.S. could only deter a war and that the Air Force would be only an equal of the Navy in the task. Against McNamara, the Air Force commanders could not achieve an official first-strike targeting doctrine for the United States; with MIRV, however, they could achieve a real first-strike targeting capability for the Air Force.[19] The initiation of MIRV in 1961-1962, then, can be explained by bureaucratic politics.

Further, the research and development of MIRV in the mid-1960s was of course highly classified, so that knowledge of it would be kept from the Soviets. But the effect was also to keep knowledge of MIRV from Congress and the public.[20] Nor, in the early phases of the program, did Defense officials have any need to build support in Congress and the public for large expenditures of funds. As a result, the MIRV program faced no political opposition, and it quietly progressed in accordance with technical and bureaucratic procedures of research and development internal to different organizations within the Defense Department.

The MIRV program may have been reinforced by another round of bureaucratic politics in late 1966. McNamara was attempting to prevent the procurement of ABM but was meeting with the united opposition of the Joint Chiefs of Staff, supported by leading members of Congress. One of the main arguments of the proponents of ABM was that the Soviets were going ahead with their own ABM system. One way for McNamara to neutralize this argument was to go ahead with an American offensive system with high penetration capabilities, i.e., MIRV.[21] Thus, in late 1966, MIRV procurement may have been the price for ABM postponement, just as in late 1961, missile procurement was the price for manned bomber postponement. In each case, of course, the price bought only a delay: in the case of the manned bomber, almost a decade; in the case of ABM, less than a year.

The MIRV program continued to quietly progress in accordance with technical and bureaucratic procedures of research and development through 1967 and 1968. By the time the strategic implications of MIRV became public knowledge, it had already been tested, the production of Minuteman III and Poseidon missiles had already commenced, and the conversion of Polaris-launching submarines into Poseidon ones had already begun.[22] Given this momentum generated by bureaucratic processes, the MIRV program could have been brought to a halt in 1969 or after only if the President or leading members of Congress had been willing to expend an extraordinary amount of political capital. And thus MIRV finally reached the point where bureaucratic pressures were reinforced by economic ones, where John Foster, the Director of Defense Research and Engineering, could make before a congressional committee in 1970 an economic argument against stopping the MIRV program much like our earlier argument about production lines:

Another consequence of our stopping at this time would be financial. These programs I am discussing now have a number of years of research and development behind them and have also developed a significant production capability. . . . I do not see how we can justify the added expense that would be incurred as a result of keeping production capability on standby.[23]

Further, once the U.S. had successfully tested MIRV, the Soviets could not be sure that the U.S. had not also deployed it. The Soviets probably then felt themselves compelled to develop, test, and deploy their own MIRV; the Soviet program, in turn, reinforces the pressures behind the American one.

In summary, the procurement of MIRV, of highly accurate as well as multiple warheads, resulted from a developmental process over a relatively lengthy time. It is best explained by a combination of bureaucratic politics and bureaucratic processes: bargaining among different actors within the executive branch and standard procedures for research and development. Although the Minuteman III and Poseidon missile programs can be fitted into the broader economic framework formed by the follow-on imperative (but not by its bail-out counterpart), economic explanations do not capture the most important part of MIRV.

Bureaucratic politics may have structured another aspect of American missile procurement, that is, the close parallelism of the Air Force and the Navy programs. As Table 6-1 indicates, each service took the same steps at the same time: Minuteman and Polaris buildup in 1961, Minuteman III and Poseidon development in 1966, and production in 1968. Indeed, the first flight test for Minuteman III and the first flight test for Poseidon occurred on the same day, August 16, 1968. It is as if the two services had reached an agreement on rough equality, a "minimax" solution, in regard to their respective progress in the prestigious mission of strategic offense. If so, the recent funding for development of the Navy's ULMS has imposed a considerable strain on the Air Force to achieve comparable funding for development of a super-MIRV or a mobile missile system.

The ULMS program is important in another sense. Given the necessity to maintain an invulnerable nuclear deterrent, a long-range, submarine-launched missile system is clearly the most rational way to do so; for the next decade at least, its vulnerability to Soviet attack will be much less than that of land-based missiles, even with such Air Force gimmicks as ever more hardened silos or putting missiles on railroad cars. The present development and eventual procurement of ULMS, therefore, can readily be explained in strategic terms; ULMS is one of the few American weapons systems initiated since 1960 for which the best explanation is the strategic explanation. Bureaucratic and economic interests are present, of course, and may insure that the rational, strategic choice will in fact result. But, overall, ULMS is a salutary reminder that not all cases of American weapons procurement can be reduced to bureaucratic and economic factors.

Anti-Missile Procurement and Democratic Explanations

The ABM is, in many ways, the superlative case of weapons procurement in the period since 1960. In regard to the probable cost of a completed system, it would be the most expensive. In the length of time that the system has been an issue (programs date back to 1955), it is the most extensive. In the scope of actors participating in the decision-making process, it has been the most inclusive; and in the heat of the public debate over procurement, it has been the most intensive.[24]

Why did the United States buy the ABM? More specifically, why did the Johnson administration in September 1967 propose the Sentinel ABM, and why did the Nixon administration in March 1969 and later propose the Safeguard ABM? The official, strategic explanations have been many and varied. McNamara in 1967 argued that the ABM was needed to protect cities from China. Nixon and Laird in 1969 argued that it was needed to protect Minutemen from the Soviet Union. Later, they extended the proposed protection to some cities again. All of the justifications have been questioned by many strategists, scientists, and Congressmen; the most decisive refutation is simply the argument that the ABM will not work, especially given the ease with which the Soviets could overload the system with a dense attack.

Bureaucratic explanations are more helpful. The Army saw the ABM as its way to get again into strategic missile programs, from which it had been excluded while the Air Force had Minuteman and the Navy had Polaris and Poseidon, and thus as its way to restore the bureaucratic balance of power. But as long as the Army was alone in its support of ABM, not much happened. Further, within the Army the air defense and missile defense organizations were not the dominant organizations (these were the ground combat forces); the large-scale deployment of ABM would redistribute bureaucratic power within the Army.

By 1966, however, the Air Force and the Navy each came to see the Army's ABM as the opening wedge and necessary condition for its own entry into the ABM field, and the Joint Chiefs of Staff adopted a unified position in support of ABM procurement. The Joint Chiefs, in turn, were supported by leading members of Congress. This confronted Secretary of Defense McNamara, who was opposed to ABM, with a difficult problem in November 1966, when he was due to make decisions about the next defense budget.[25] But, as we have suggested above, one of McNamara's responses was to trade the procurement of MIRV for the postponement of ABM. Another response was to place a great deal of emphasis on the prospects for successful arms control negotiations with the Soviet Union, as grounds on which to justify postponement. What, then, brought about the decision in September 1967, less than a year later, to procure and deploy ABM?

At this point, a democratic explanation becomes more persuasive. President Johnson feared being vulnerable in the approaching election to charges from the Republicans that he had neglected the nation's security. John Kennedy in 1960 charged a "missile gap"; Lyndon Johnson in 1967 feared an "ABM gap."[26] One possible antidote to the image of gap-maker in a Soviet-American arms race was the image of peace-maker in a Soviet-American arms control agreement. But just as Khrushchev eliminated that possibility for Eisenhower and the Republicans in 1960, when he broke up the Paris summit meeting, so did Kosygin eliminate that possibility for Johnson and the Democrats in 1967, when he was totallly unreceptive to American proposals concerning ABM limitation at the Glassboro summit meeting in June 1967. In September, McNamara announced the decision to procure and deploy ABM.

For the Nixon administration's affirmative decision in March 1969 and later, a democratic explanation is also plausible, but less so. Congress had to be pressured by the administration to approve ABM, the reverse of the situation two years before (in the Senate in 1969, an amendment to prevent deployment was defeated by only two votes), and the public was much more critical of ABM. But Nixon may have reasoned that by 1972 his political situation would more resemble Johnson's in 1967 than his own in 1969, and he may have feared being vulnerable not only to charges of having neglected the nation's security but of having wasted the military assets which he inherited from the Democrats.

By 1972, however, there was even more political advantage to be found in the image of peace-maker. The Nixon trip to China was the most dramatic result, but an arms control agreement with the Soviet Union also offered political advantage in the forthcoming Presidential election. Why ABM, rather than some other weapons system, was the object of a cutback in planned procurement can be explained in several different ways; perhaps the major factor was bureaucratic: it is easier to cut back the major system of a subordinate organization within a service (e.g., the missile defense forces within the Army) than to cut back the major system of the dominant organizations within a service (e.g., the bomber and missile forces within the Air Force and the carrier and missile-submarine forces within the Navy).

In summary, the procurement of ABM and the limitation imposed on that procurement resulted from a political process involving an unusually wide scope of actors and over an unusually great length of time. The major milestones in that process (1967, 1969, and 1972) are best explained by electoral politics, by the efforts of Presidents to satisfy the electorate and to win the next election. Although the Spartan missile portion of the ABM program can be fitted into the broader economic framework formed by the follow-on and bail-out imperatives, economic explanations would have predicted procurement of somewhat more Spartans than will probably happen in fact.

Canceled Procurement and Eclectic Explanations

Any satisfactory analysis of policy outcomes within an issue area must account not only for those outcomes which did occur but also those which, despite similar conditions, did not. In regard to aerospace weapons systems, an analysis must account for the two major cases of nonprocurement or canceled procurement in the period since 1960. These were the B-70 large bomber and the Skybolt air-to-surface missile, designed to be launched from large bombers.[27] Superficially at least, economic explanations such as the follow-on and bail-out imperatives and bureaucratic explanations stressing the dominant role of the "bomber generals" within the Air Force would have predicted large-scale production of the B-70 and Skybolt.

Why did the United States cancel the B-70 and Skybolt? A strategic explanation, focusing on the vulnerability of the manned bomber and on its low cost-effectiveness versus Minuteman and Polaris, might seem quite sufficient. (Although similar strategic considerations have not been sufficient to bring about the cancellation of the B-1.) Such strategic factors may have been reinforced by bureaucratic politics, that is, McNamara's determination to establish his authority over the military services and over the traditional autonomy of their procurement practices. A similar argument has been made to explain McNamara's insistence on commonality between the Air Force and the Navy versions of the F-111, another case which occurred at the same time, 1961-1962.[28] Together, strategic and bureaucratic factors seem to account for the cancellations.

In the case of the B-70, however, cancellation came at the cost of compensation. First, as the account by Schlesinger suggests, the Air Force and its allies in Congress had to be compensated for the cancellation of the B-70 with a massive missile buildup, with its attendant costs of a Soviet buildup and an arms race. Second, as the follow-on imperative suggests, North American had to be compensated for the cancellation of the B-70 with another major contract, in this case the Apollo moon program.

The cancellation of Skybolt a year later does not seem to have exacted such a price. The Air Force and its allies in Congress did not receive any obvious compensation. (Although one could imagine the continuation of the Minuteman buildup and of the MIRV program as part of an over-all compromise.) Douglas, which was a minor contractor at the time, did not immediately receive another major contract comparable to Skybolt. This suggests that the compensation pattern for minor contractors (less than $500 million in military and space contracts per year) may be different than the pattern for major ones (more than $1 billion in military and space contracts per year) and that there may be a sort of class system for weapons contractors.

In summary, then, canceled procurement is best explained by eclectic accounts. Strategic analysis and bureaucratic politics can enact a cancellation, but when a dominant military organization and a major aerospace corporation are involved, bureaucratic politics and economic imperatives will also exact a compensation. Such considerations would predict, for example, that any successful effort in the mid-1970s to cancel the B-1 would be immediately confronted with a super-MIRV for the Strategic Air Command and more space shuttles for North American Rockwell.

The Future of American Weapons Procurement

The analysis of weapons procurement presented in this essay may have other implications for the future. Table 6-1 indicates that recently the pressure on the U.S. government has become especially intense. In 1972, the Nixon administration was confronted with the impending phaseout of the F-111 program of General Dynamics and the C-5A program of Lockheed-Georgia and thus with the impending opening-up of two major production lines. The first was in an important state in the Electoral College, Texas; the second was the largest industrial enterprise in the Southeastern United States.[29] The administration temporarily resolved its dilemmas with a contract to General Dynamics for twelve additional F-111s and a contract to Lockheed-Georgia for twenty additional C-130s. But unless the administration decides to buy yet additional numbers of these older aircraft, it will again be confronted with the same dilemmas in 1973. At the same time, a third production line, Boeing, will open up. How will the administration fill the contract gap?

One answer might seem to lie in conversion of production to commercial aircraft. But here past experience suggests that the cure would be worse than the disease. Thus, General Dynamics in the early 1960s entered the commercial aircraft market with the Convair 880, only to lose so much money that the F-111 contract was needed to save the corporation from bankruptcy. Similarly, Lockheed in the early 1970s entered the market with the L-1011, only to drive Rolls Royce into bankruptcy and consequently Lockheed itself into a position in which only government guarantees of bank loans saved it from bankruptcy. Even the extraordinary government effort to save the L-1011 will not solve the problem of Lockheed-Georgia, to say nothing of any distant problem of Lockheed-Missiles and Space, which is located in Northern California. For the L-1011 is produced at a third, mainly commercial, Lockheed division, Lockheed-California, which is located in Southern California. Conversion might seem more plausible for Boeing, already an established producer of superior commercial aircraft. But its major candidate for a new commercial aircraft, the SST, was canceled by Congress in 1971. Nor is conversion of production away from aerospace to other sections, such as mass urban transportation or waste disposal systems, promising or likely.

The follow-on imperative, however, would suggest other answers. For General Dynamics in the next year or two, it would predict a major contract for the Air Force lightweight fighter, now being planned. For Lockheed-Georgia, it would predict a major contract for the STOL transport, also now being planned. And for Boeing, it would predict a super-MIRV if there is no revival of the SST. Then, at last, with each of the eight major production lines safely supported for the remainder of the 1970s with a major government contract, the follow-on imperative will have done its work and can be laid to rest.

Notes

1. John Kenneth Galbraith, HOW TO CONTROL THE MILITARY (New York: New American Library, 1969).

2. For a study of earlier cases of weapons procurement, see Merton J. Peck and Frederic M. Scherer, THE WEAPONS ACQUISITION PROCESS: AN ECONOMIC ANALYSIS (Boston: Harvard Business School, 1962).

3. For a detailed analysis of the F-111 case, see Robert J. Art, THE TFX DECISION: MCNAMARA AND THE MILITARY (Boston: Little, Brown, 1968). For a critical account of the C-5A case, see Berkeley Rice, THE C-5A SCANDAL (Boston: Houghton Mifflin, 1971); a more sympathetic account is Harold B. Meyers, "For Lockheed, Everything's Coming Up Unk-Unks," FORTUNE 80 (August 1, 1969), pp. 71-81, 131-34.

4. The B-70 was produced only in the sense that two prototypes were built.

5. For descriptions of the aerospace systems and contract awards since 1960, see various annual editions of THE AEROSPACE YEAR BOOK (official publication of the Aerospace Industries of America, Inc.; Washington, D.C.: Books, Inc.) and JANE'S ALL THE WORLD'S AIRCRAFT (New York: McGraw-Hill). For information on recent systems and awards, see recent issues of AVIATION WEEK AND SPACE TECHNOLOGY.

6. See AVIATION WEEK AND SPACE TECHNOLOGY 75 (November 13, 1961, p. 30, and December 25, 1961, p. 66). Annual figures for Department of Defense and NASA prime contract awards are normally published by AVIATION WEEK AND SPACE TECHNOLOGY each November or December.

7. North American merged with a nonaerospace company, Rockwell-Standard, in 1967.

8. These six aerospace corporations are also major corporations in terms of another, related, indicator; total annual sales (commercial as well as government). With the exception of Grumman, each in 1971 had sales of more than $1 billion; Grumman had sales of $800 million. See the FORTUNE Directory of the 500 largest U.S. industrial corporations, FORTUNE 85 (May 1972).

9. See various editions of THE AEROSPACE YEAR BOOK and JANE'S ALL THE WORLD'S AIRCRAFT and recent issues of AVIATION WEEK AND SPACE TECHNOLOGY.

10. Calculated from figures in the annual editions of the FORTUNE Directory of the 500 largest U.S. industrial corporations, normally published in FORTUNE each May or June. Sales and earnings figures can also be found in annual editions of MOODY'S INDUSTRIAL MANUAL (New York: Moody's Investors Service, Inc.) and quarterly editions of MOODY'S HANDBOOK OF COMMON STOCKS (New York: Moody's Investor Service, Inc.).

11. The following discussion of the missile buildup is taken from my "A Widening Gyre: The Logic of American Weapons Procurement," PUBLIC POLICY, 19 (Summer 1971), pp. 380-83.

12. Robert S. McNamara, THE ESSENCE OF SECURITY (New York: Harper and Row, 1968), pp. 57-60.

13. Ibid., pp. 57-58.

14. Arthur M. Schlesinger, Jr., A THOUSAND DAYS (Boston: Houghton Mifflin, 1965), pp. 499, 500.

15. David Halberstam, "The Programming of Robert McNamara," HARPERS 232 (February 1971), p. 54. A similar account is given by Jerome B. Wiesner, President Kennedy's Special Assistant for Science and Technology, in his "Arms Control: Current Prospects and Problems," SCIENCE AND PUBLIC AFFAIRS: BULLETIN OF THE ATOMIC SCIENTISTS 26 (May 1970), p. 6.

16. Samuel P. Huntington, THE COMMON DEFENSE (New York: Columbia University Press, 1961), pp. 146-66.

17. For detailed discussion of the MIRV case, see Herbert York, RACE TO OBLIVION: A PARTICIPANT'S VIEW OF THE ARMS RACE (New York: Simon and Schuster 1970), pp. 173-87; and Ralph E. Lapp, ARMS BEYOND DOUBT: THE TYRANNY OF WEAPONS TECHNOLOGY (New York: Cowles Book Co., 1970), pp. 17-34.

18. Quoted in ibid., p. 21.

19. On the nuclear strategies of McNamara and the Air Force, see Alain C. Enthoven and K. Wayne Smith, HOW MUCH IS ENOUGH? SHAPING THE DEFENSE PROGRAM, 1961-1969 (New York: Harper and Row, 1971), pp. 163-96; and William W. Kaufman, THE MCNAMARA STRATEGY (New York: Harper and Row, 1964), Chapter 2.

20. F.A. Long, SCIENCE AND THE MILITARY, Cornell University Peace Studies Program, Occasional Papers, No. 1 (Ithaca, N.Y.: Cornell University), pp. 11-12.

21. See Morton H. Halperin, "The Decision to Deploy the ABM: Bureaucratic and Domestic Politics in the Johnson Administration," WORLD POLITICS 25 (October 1972), p. 84.

22. See the discussion of MIRV before the Congressional Conference on the Military Budget and National Priorities (March 28 and 29, 1969), especially the statements by Jeremy J. Stone, George W. Rathjens, Leonard Rodberg, and Congressman Robert L. Leggett (Dem.-Calif.), in Erwin Knoll and Judith Nies McFadden (eds.), AMERICAN MILITARISM 1970 (New York: Viking Press, 1969), pp. 70-82.

23. "ABM, MIRV, SALT, and the Nuclear Arms Race," Hearings before the Subcommittee on Arms Control, Committee on Foreign Relations, U.S. Senate, 91st Congress (June 4, 1970) (Washington, D.C.: U.S. Government Printing Office, 1970), p. 428.

24. For detailed analyses of the ABM case, see Halperin, "The Decision to Deploy the ABM"; Aaron Wildavsky, "The Politics of ABM," COMMENTARY 48 (November 1969), pp. 53-63; and Abram Chayes and Jerome B. Wiesner (eds.), ABM: AN EVALUATION OF THE DECISION TO DEPLOY AN

ANTI-BALLISTIC MISSILE SYSTEM (New York: New American Library, 1969).

25. See Halperin, "The Decision to Deploy the ABM."

26. See ibid. and Ralph E. Lapp, THE WEAPONS CULTURE (Baltimore: Penguin, 1969), pp. 150, 151.

27. On these two cases, see Enthoven and Smith, HOW MUCH IS ENOUGH?, pp. 243-62. On Skybolt, also see Richard E. Neustadt, ALLIANCE POLITICS (New York: Columbia University Press, 1970).

28. Art, THE TFX DECISION.

29. Berkeley Rice, "What Price Lockheed? NEW YORK TIMES MAGAZINE, (May 9, 1971), p. 24.

7

The Weapons Procurement Process: Choosing Among Competing Theories

Arnold Kanter
Stuart J. Thorson

Introduction

One aspect of military policy which has received some attention is the topic of weapons production (broadly defined to include development and operation). It is frequently assumed that military procurement is a key indicator of military policy. This assumption is reflected in the view that a nation's defense policy is substantially determined by the forces it chooses to buy and operate. For example, the Eisenhower administration's decisions to emphasize firepower rather than manpower was reflected in the force structure of the 1950s which was optimized for the delivery of nuclear ordinance. These characteristics of a country's force posture have consequences for the range of alternative policies available to decision-makers: when the U.S. Seventh Fleet was ordered to support the Nationalist defense of the Offshore Islands in 1958, it was discovered that the Fleet was substantially limited to threatening the use of nuclear capabilities.[1]

If we accept the stipulation that the production of weapons is a central component of military policy, we are confronted with an important puzzle: given the broad range and large number of weapons systems which could be produced, why do some weapons get produced while others do not? An understanding of the weapons procurement aspect of defense policy would require an answer to at least this question. However, as James Kurth has noted elsewhere in this volume, our search for explanations of weapons procurement decisions seems hampered less by a dearth of theory than by a multitude of explanations. These "theories" represent something of an embarrassment of riches in the sense that each provides a different explanation for a given observation: "The problem . . . is not that there are no answers but that there are too many answers."[2] Moreover, these differences are important. A decision-maker seeking guides for action soon discovers that "each of the major theories or explanations has a different prescriptive implication."[3] Consequently, he runs the risk of becoming ensnarled in what Kurth has described as a "thicket of theories."[4]

What does seem to be in short supply are well understood and agreed upon criteria in terms of which the analyst and the policy-maker can check for defects in particular theories and choose among apparently competing theories which seek to account for the same phenomena. The purpose of this paper is to discuss potential criteria which might provide some guidance out of the thicket. After a brief discussion of some more familiar considerations in theory construction, we will develop the argument that a clear specification of the purpose to which the theory is to be put is an essential prerequisite for evaluating theories and for choosing among them. In particular, we will argue that the sort of theories with which social scientists usually deal are usefully divided into categories by reference to the user's objective. Thus, we will seek to distinguish *point prediction* theories from policy *prediction* theories, demonstrate that rather different criteria of performance and validity should be applied to each, and warn of the pitfalls of indiscriminately applying familiar standards which are appropriate to point prediction theories to the evaluation of policy theories.

Given our interest in choosing among competing theories which we share with James Kurth, as well as his previous work in the area reported in this volume and elsewhere,[5] we will draw heavily on his analysis of the weapons procurement process for illustrations of several of the points we wish to develop. We will examine the consequences of particular classification of phenomena and the problems involved in the operationalization of variables with reference to Kurth's "follow-on imperative." We will discuss criteria for the evaluation and choice among theories by additionally drawing upon his description of the "bail-out imperative" and his earlier analysis of the process of weapons procurement.[6] The reader should bear in mind that our primary intention throughout is to raise several points regarding theory evaluation rather than to undertake a systematic critique of the closely-related research of Kurth.

Classifying Phenomena: The User's Concerns as a Standard

Even if we accept that there is a crucial relationship between military policies and weapons procurement decisions, we still are left with the problem of selecting those weapons decisions upon which to concentrate. We might initially respond that our theory must account for *all* weapons procurement decisions. However, it is commonly recognized that such generality may come only at the expense of either obscuring important differences or being inaccurate with regard to at least some of the theory's claims. At the other extreme, the diversity of phenomena may be so restricted as to produce an accurate (if trivial) "theory" of a unique event. More generally, conclusions regarding the utility and validity of one or another theory depend in large measure on the criteria for delineating the class of phenomena to which the theory is applied. We will explore this issue by examining one theory which seeks to account for weapons procurement—the "follow-on imperative" formulated by Kurth—and the data in terms of which it is evaluated.

The follow-on imperative is classified by Kurth as an "economic theory" of weapons procurement. Such theories argue that the economic need of major defense contractors is highly associated with weapons procurement decisions. Neither the strategic needs of the nation nor the specific weapons requirements of the military services account for procurement as well as do corporate requirements of large defense contractors. The follow-on imperative derives from the observation that:

About the time a production line phases out production of one major government contract, it phases in production of a new one, usually within a year. . . . Further, in most cases, the new contract is for a system which is structurally similar while technologically superior to the system being phased out, i.e., the new contract is a follow-on contract.[7]

It is not the "official imperative" usually found in the public record which accounts for the decisions to develop and produce new weapons systems but rather the follow-on imperative:

The official imperative for weapons procurement might be phrased as follows: If a military service needs a new weapons system, it will solicit bids from several competing companies; ordinarily, the service will award the contract to the company with the most cost-effective design. The follow-on imperative is rather different: If one of the . . . production lines is opening up, it will receive a new major contract from a military service (or from NASA); ordinarily, the new contract will be structurally similar to the old, i.e., a follow-on contract. Relatedly, the design competition between production lines is only a peripheral factor in the award.[8]

Kurth tests the follow-on imperative with data on major weapons procurement contracts awarded during the 1960s. All of the cases he selects are *aerospace* contracts.[9] Later in this paper we will consider the significance of the choice of this particular time period. Now we will address the consequence of his concentration on aerospace contracts for evaluating the follow-on imperative.

Kurth suggests three criteria for identifying "major" cases of weapons procurement: (1) impact on strategic balance between the superpowers; (2) dollar size of the procurement contract; and (3) intensity of the political debate about the weapons program.[10] We will not consider the third standard since it does not appear to identify any weapons system which would not be included by either of the other criteria. (Indeed, it might be hypothesized that intense political debate is a consequence either of the perceived impact of the system on the strategic balance or of the visibility of any large spending program.) Although Kurth is not clear on the point, it appears that, taken alone, meeting either criterion is a sufficient but not a necessary condition for the inclusion of a contract as a "major" case of weapons procurement.[11]

Those public policy analysts who concentrate in the issue-area of defense policy primarily are interested in the relation between changes in the arsenal of weapons and changes in the relative security of the nation. For the past several years this concern has directed attention to the consequences of new weapons for the *stability* of the nuclear balance between the superpowers.[12] Thus, the deployment of Polaris submarines generally was applauded as a contribution to stability while the development of MIRV missile warheads has been condemned by some as a potentially destabilizing factor. As a preliminary (and admittedly crude) indicator of such weapons, we might stipulate that all systems which are (or would be) funded under the Strategic Forces Program of the Defense Department budget will have an impact on the stability of the balance between the superpowers.[13]

Of course, public policy theorists other than those who concentrate solely on the national security issue-area are vitally concerned with weapons procurement. However, such analysts are professionally concerned less because of the nuclear stability consequences than because of the dollar *cost* of weapons programs. The development, production, and operation of weapons systems has accounted for no less than one-third of the very large expenditures for defense in each of the last fifteen years. About $30 billion is accounted for by such weapons in the FY 1972 defense budget.[14] To the extent that an analyst must be concerned with the allocation of limited governmental resources among sectors, he cannot ignore expenditures of this magnitude. Even analysts who concentrate on a discrete issue-area other than national security must be concerned with any powerful competitor for government dollars in an environment of scarce resources. Accordingly, Kurth includes weapons programs in excess of $5 billion.[15]

(The dollar magnitude of defense contracts also would likely attract the interest of analysts who study the domestic economic consequences of government spending programs. Such concerns might direct their attention to defense contractors, the relationship between defense spending in Congressional districts and roll-call votes, and to related topics included under the banner of the military-industrial complex.)

The crucial point is that while a broad range of policy analysts may study weapons procurement decisions, they do so with very distinct objectives in mind. One group might be primarily interested in the *strategic* consequences of weapons while another group might be concerned with the *dollar cost* of the program. Given these separate concerns, there is no reason why these two groups should define the universe of relevant phenomena similarly nor why they should agree on sampling criteria. Theorists from both groups could be expected to focus on the same weapon decisions only if all weapons programs affecting the strategic balance were expensive and all expensive weapons would affect the strategic balance.

However, it has been argued that there is no necessary relationship between a defense program's costs and its impact on the probability of arms races or war. As Morton Halperin has observed: "Some weapons programs may be relatively inexpensive and yet threaten stability."[16] In fact, this argument implies that an analyst who is primarily concerned with the relationship between weapons and stability should concentrate attention on weapons programs funded under the Strategic Forces Program in the defense budget while an analyst primarily interested in affecting the level of defense spending should focus efforts on the programs and activities funded under the General Purpose Forces Program.[17]

If this argument is correct, then theories which relate weapons programs and nuclear stability would not be required to scrutinize the same class of phenomena as theories which relate to the level of defense spending. By confusing one concern with the other, the analyst confounds the evaluation of separate but not necessarily competing theories. For example, a theory which emphasizes the economic incentives of defense contractors may readily accommodate the F-111 (TFX) aircraft program—a very expensive system but one which has only modest consequences for strategic stability—but be insensitive to the distinction between MRV and MIRV missile warheads—a distinction which produces relatively small differences in dollar cost but may have major consequences for the ability of a nation to launch a disarming first strike.[18] Similarly, a theory which seeks to account for weapons systems made possible by unanticipated technological breakthroughs may perform inadequately with regard to "merely" expensive weapons programs.

If the analyst insists that a case be both expensive *and* have an important impact on the strategic balance, he risks excluding from his purview those developments which relate to only one concern—and thereby affect the evaluation of a body of less general theory—because they do not relate to the other as well. Kurth's stipulation that a weapons program be either destabilizing *or* expensive ameliorates the dangers of this pitfall. However, this qualification is purchased at the price of substantially increasing the demands made on any theory of weapons procurement by increasing the diversity of phenomena for which it must account.

Moreover, stipulating the class of phenomena for which the theory must account, without prior careful attention to the concerns and standards which distinguish among phenomena, may neutralize any such safeguards. Thus, generalizing from Kurth's evaluation of the follow-on imperative, it may be concluded that, by confining his attention to cases of *expensive aerospace* procurement, he appears to have neglected both inexpensive programs which affect the strategic balance (e.g., highly accurate missile guidance systems)[19] and expensive programs which seem to have a negligible effect on the stability of the nuclear balance (e.g., the Army's ill-fated Main Battle Tank, and the Navy's proposed aircraft carrier [CVN-70] and destroyer [DD-963] shipbuilding programs, etc.).

Since one way in which we evaluate theories is to compare them with phenomena, our judgments regarding a particular theory's performance will be significantly affected by our prior decisions which identify the relevant class of phenomena. These decisions, in turn, depend upon our requirements regarding the theory's generality and our rules for distinguishing members of the class from other "irrelevant" phenomena. Thus, should we reject a theory because it cannot deal with phenomena as diverse as MIRV warheads and C-5 transport aircraft? Can we accept a theory which purports to account for the B-1 manned bomber and F-111 fighter aircraft but does not address weapons systems such as submarines and helicopters? Although there are no final answers to these questions, the analyst should be sensitive to the fact that the answers crucially depend on how reality is structured and he should recognize the need to link that structuring to his interests and concerns.

Defining Terms in the Theory: Problems of Operationalization

We have argued that one task preliminary to evaluating any theory is to isolate the phenomena the theory is supposed to "be about." Evaluation also entails that the theory be confronted with these phenomena. This requires that the observation terms in the theory be operationalized.[20] We will address this issue by examining Kurth's operationalization of the "defense contractor" term in the follow-on imperative.

In testing of the follow-on imperative, Kurth confines his attention to "major military airframe production lines" operationally defined as contractors who have received an annual average of $1 billion or more in military or space (including NASA) prime contracts since 1960.[21] He identifies five such companies: Lockheed, General Dynamics, McDonnell-Douglas, and North American Rockwell. Grumman is added to this list on the basis of large subcontracts.[22] Thus, firms to be included in the analysis are identified in terms of two characteristics: (1) product specialization—they are *airframe* manufacturers, and (2) volume of defense and space related business—measured in dollar value of average annual prime contract received.

Notice that this operational definition appears to be somewhat narrower than that allowed by the follow-on imperative: nothing in the follow-on imperative seems to restrict its application solely to aerospace firms. Presumably, the follow-on imperative is the result of the joint interest of the government and the contractor in the continuing economic survival of the latter. The Pentagon is said to consider major defense suppliers to be "national resources" which it loathe to allow to die.[23] From the perspective of the Pentagon, the concept of major defense supplier might be operationalized in terms of the proportion of total defense contract dollars represented by any particular contractor: the higher the proportion, the more dependent is the Pentagon on that contractor, and consequently, the greater is the government's interest in continued sustenance.[24] A contractor whose proportion exceeds some threshold may be designated a "major defense contractor." Kurth's $1 billion threshold may be intended to reflect this dimension.

The contractor's interest in defense contracts relates to the contractor's concern for profits. Although we might assume that most contractors would prefer to win defense contracts (assuming projected profits competitive with alternative nondefense contracts), a company's interest presumably increases as the proportion of his sales represented by defense contracts increases (assuming this interest reflects a relative reluctance or inability to shift to production in the civilian sector). Kurth's product specialization criterion may be a surrogate measure of a firm's dependence on government contracts, presumably based on the assumption that *airframe* manufacturers are universally and peculiarly in such a dependent condition.

Thus, the follow-on imperative would seem to apply most forcefully to the overlap of these two classes: to those contractors who are very dependent on defense contracts for economic survival *and* on whom the Pentagon depends for a significant proportion of its contracts. It remains to be seen whether airframe production lines are the exclusive occupants of this territory.

Table 7-1 lists the top ten defense contractors (measured by dollar value of defense prime contracts) for each year from FY 1961 to FY 1970. Seventeen different firms have been among the top ten defense contractors during the past decade, only about half of which ordinarily are identified as airframe manufacturers. Note that in this list, airframe producers do not rank above all other defense contractors. Beginning in FY 1966, only three of the top five defense contractors were airframe manufacturers. Several of the firms which rank in the top ten are best known for products other than aircraft: General Motors, United Aircraft, General Electric, and AT&T. The latter three have ranked in the top ten in every year of the past decade.[25] Even if we restrict our attention (for whatever reason) to aircraft procurement, firms which manufacture aircraft *engines* (e.g., GM, United Aircraft, and GE) frequently receive a larger share of defense prime contracts than do some airframe production lines. On the average, three firms have received a larger dollar amount of defense contracts than at least one of Kurth's major airframe producers.[26] Thus, on the basis of Pentagon dependence on contractors, airframe production lines would not seem to be uniquely subject to the follow-on imperative.

It is somewhat more difficult to measure how dependent a contractor is on defense contracts. This is due in part to the problems of associating annual sales figures (usually recorded on a calendar year basis and sometimes including sales from subcontracts) with multi-year prime contracts (usually recorded on a fiscal year basis). Additional problems derive from a certain ambiguity surrounding Kurth's concept of a "production line" and, in particular, how production lines relate to individual firms.[27] Table 7-2 lists sales to NASA and the Department of Defense as a percent of total annual sales for several large defense contractors. Bearing in mind the reservations noted above, it is possible to glean an impression of the relative dependence of firms on defense and space contracts.

The available evidence does suggest that at least some airframe producers are

Table 7-1
Major Aerospace Contractors, Rank Ordered According to Proportion of DOD Prime Contracts

Rank	FY 61	FY 62	FY 63	FY 64	FY 65	FY 66	FY 67	FY 68	FY 69	FY 70
1	General Dynamics	Lockheed	Lockheed	Lockheed	Lockheed	Lockheed	McDonnell Douglas	General Dynamics	Lockheed	Lockheed
2	North American	General Dynamics	Boeing	Boeing	General Dynamics	General Electric	General Dynamics	Lockheed	General Electric	General Dynamics
3	Lockheed	Boeing	North American	McDonnell Douglas[a,b]	McDonnell Douglas[a,b]	United Aircraft	Lockheed	General Electric	General Dynamics	General Electric
4	Boeing	North American	General Dynamics	North American	General Electric	General Dynamics	General Electric	United Aircraft	McDonnell Douglas	AT&T
5	General Electric	General Electric	General Electric	General Dynamics	North American	McDonnell Douglas[a]	United Aircraft	McDonnell Douglas	United Aircraft	McDonnell Douglas
6	Martin Marietta	Martin Marietta	McDonnell Douglas[a]	General Electric	United Aircraft	Boeing	Boeing	AT&T	AT&T	United Aircraft
7	United Aircraft	McDonnell Douglas[a]	Martin Marietta	AT&T	AT&T	AT&T	North American	Boeing	Ling-Temco Vought	North American Rockwell
8	AT&T	United Aircraft	AT&T	United Aircraft	Boeing	Textron	AT&T	Ling-Temco Vought	North American Rockwell	Grumman
9	McDonnell Douglas	AT&T	United Aircraft	Martin Marietta	Grumman	North American	General Motors	North American Rockwell	Boeing	Litton
10	Sperry Rand	Sperry Rand	McDonnell	Grumman	Sperry Rand	General Motors	Ling-Temco Vought	General Motors	General Motors	Hughes Aircraft
11	RCA	General Motors	Sperry Rand							

[a]Sum of McDonnell and Douglas contracts for indicated year.

[b]McDonnell's contract total ranks third independent of Douglas' contracts.

Source: AEROSPACE FACTS AND FIGURES, various years.

Table 7-2
Annual Sales to DOD and NASA as Percent of Total Annual Sales

Calendar Year	United Aircraft[a]	McDonnell-Douglas[b]	General Electric	General Dynamics	Ling-Temco-Vought[a]	Boeing	General Motors[a]	North American Rockwell	Grumman
1960	72	53	22	–	–	68	03	100[d]	90[a]
1961	77	63	25	–	–	78	03	100[d]	90[a]
1962	80	77[a]	23	–	86	76	03	100[d]	90[a]
1963	79	78[a]	21	75[a]	87	85	03	100[d]	90[a]
1964	71	76	17	–	93	64	02.5	100[d]	–
1965	66	67	17	–	85	50	02	100[d]	90[d]
1966	64	53	18	78[a]	73	48	03	100[d]	90[d]
1967	61	63.2	29	83[a]	28	41	04	74[a]	96
1968	56	50.1	20	–	24	31	03	71[a]	89
1969	57	50.3	29	86[c]	22.5	36	03	61[a]	89
1970	–	–	19	82[c]	–	20	03	58[a]	89
1971	–	–	18	–	–	–	02	54[a]	–

[a]Total sales to entire Federal government.
[b]Pre-1967, Douglas Aircraft only.
[c]Includes some commercial marine sales.
[d]Ambiguous, apparently virtually all sales to U.S. Government.
Source: Annual reports to stockholders.

highly dependent on government contracts. Thus, the major proportion of Grumman's business during the last decade has been with the Federal government. (The same probably is true for Lockheed but the firm's annual report to stockholders does not distinguish between commercial sales and government sales.) In the early 1960s, airframe producers such as LTV, North American, and to a lesser extent, Boeing and Douglas, were similarly dependent.

However, several other features of the data also are significant. Notice (from Table 7-1) that although General Motors ranked in the top ten defense contractors during five of the last ten years, sales to the government represent only a very small proportion of GM's business. That is, heavy government dependence on a particular contractor is not necessarily reciprocated by heavy contractor dependence on the government.

Note also that some contractors who are not best known as airframe producers are about as dependent on government business as are airframe production lines. Thus, by the late 1960s, General Electric was doing about the same amount of business with the government as was Boeing. Based on these data, it does not appear that airframe producers are uniquely dependent on government business for economic survival.

Finally, Table 7-2 indicates that while some firms have done a relatively stable proportion of their business with the government throughout the decade (e.g., General Electric, General Motors, Grumman), the dependence of other contractors on defense and space contracts has undergone considerable change. Thus, early in the decade, virtually all of North American's sales were to the government. By the end of the decade, only about half of North American Rockwell's business was the result of government contracts.

These changes stem from a variety of sources. For example, the North American case substantially can be accounted for by its *merger* with Rockwell in the middle of the decade. The dramatic drop in the proportion of LTV's sales accounted for by government business can be attributed to the operation of an aggressive *conglomerate* acquiring several nondefense companies. Boeing's declining percentage may be attributed to the growth of its commercial aircraft business and to *diversification* of its product line. More generally, measured in terms of proportion of sales represented by government contracts, there is substantial variation over time in the class of defense-dependent contractors, even in the relatively brief period of a decade. Any detailed study of the interaction between contractors and the Pentagon will have to accommodate these variations.

These data strongly suggest that airframe producers are not distinguished by their dependence on defense and space contracts for economic survival. It would further seem that a detailed analysis of the follow-on imperative would require a somewhat more careful definition of major defense contractors.

For example, it may be hypothesized that the more dependent the government is on a particular contractor, the greater the potential influence of that contractor (following a line of reasoning similar to that suggested by the follow-on imperative). It can also be argued that, the more dependent a particular contractor is on the government for annual sales, then the greater his interest in any large contract and the harder he will work to secure a decision to produce the system. If the category of "major defense contractor" is defined as the overlap of these two classes of corporations, it follows that major defense contractors are more influential than either corporations which, although large, do only a small proportion of their business with the Pentagon, or corporations which although highly dependent on defense contracts do not represent a critical Pentagon supplier.

We might operationally define the *mutual* dependence between contractors and the government in terms of the arithmetic product of (1) the proportion of a firm's sales to DOD and NASA, and (2) the proportion of total DOD and NASA prime contracts awarded to the contractor. The larger the product, the greater the mutual dependence. The measure ranges from 0.0 to 1.0. The theoretical maximum mutual dependence equals 1.0 (i.e., if the government were completely dependent upon a single contractor and that contractor did business exclusively with the government). The minimum mutual dependence is equal to zero either when the government awards no contracts to the firm or the firm makes no sales to the government. Contractors might be rank-ordered on the basis of such computations with "major" contractors defined as lying above some arbitrary cutting point.

Some illustrative data on firms which ranked among the top recipients of Pentagon contracts are presented in Table 7-3. The mean mutual dependence between these contractors and the government is shown in column (4). (Since there are relatively few data points, the highest and lowest annual mutual dependence products are given in columns (5) and (6).) Notice that, on the basis of this measure, firms ordinarily considered to be airframe producers tend to outrank other contractors. That is, if this operationalization of major defense contractors is accepted, then Kurth's concentration on "airframe production lines" is a reasonable selection among firms.

Our procedures have produced a sample of defense contractors which is substantially identical to that employed by Kurth to evaluate the follow-on imperative. However, since his analysis did not explicitly identify the operations which led to his choice of airframe contractors, it would be difficult to test the follow-on imperative in other national and temporal settings. As we have seen, a variety of different operational definitions seem consistent with the follow-on imperative, yet each set of operations generates a different set of defense contractors and, presumably, different evaluations of the imperative as a theory of weapons procurement.

Classifying Theories: The User's Concerns as a Standard

While we have noted the relevance of phenomena classification to the evaluation of theories and highlighted some of the pitfalls in operationalizing terms, we

Table 7-3
Mutual Dependence Between Contractors and Government

Contractor (1)	Sales to DOD & NASA/ Total Sales (2)	Prime Contracts from DOD & NASA/Total DOD & NASA Contracts (3)	Mean Mutual Dependency (2) x (3) (4)	High Mutual Dependency (5)	Low Mutual Dependency (6)	No. of Years (7)	Period (8)
North American Rockwell[a]	0.844	0.048	0.040	0.068	0.021	11	1960-1970
General Dynamics	0.812	0.032	0.026	0.038	0.0255	5	1963, 66, 67, 69, 70
Grumman	0.939	0.019	0.018	0.025	0.010	10	1960-69
Boeing	0.489	0.035	0.172	0.044	0.004	11	1960-70
United Aircraft	0.649	0.025	0.016	0.021	0.016	10	1960-69
McDonnell-Douglas[b]	0.582	0.026	0.015	0.035	0.008	10	1960-69
General Electric	0.201	0.038	0.008	0.010	0.006	9	1960-68
LTV	0.345	0.014	0.005	0.009	0.004	8	1962-69
General Motors	0.032	0.015	0.0004	0.0006	0.0003	11	1960-70

[a]North American only pre-1967.
[b]Douglas Aircraft only pre-1967.

Source: Sales data abstracted from annual reports to stockholders contract data from AEROSPACE FACTS AND FIGURES.

have yet to mention the *purposes* to which the theory is to be put, i.e., the objectives of the analyst may have an important impact on the manner in which he constructs theories and the criteria in terms of which he chooses among apparent competitors.

One purpose to which a theory may be put, and in terms of which it would be evaluated, is to make quantitative predictions of the values of specified variables (usually the "dependent variable") at specified points in time (and which generally are optimized for particular time periods, e.g., short-range, middle-range, and long-range predictions). For convenience, we will term theories which have this objective "point prediction theories."

A somewhat different purpose for a theory is to seek to associate changes in the values of variables, parameters, and the relationships among them (i.e., the system's structure) with changes in the behavior of the system. Since this is roughly what is implied in recommendations for changes in policy decisions and actions, we will call such theories "policy prediction theories."

That is, "prediction" is a multidimensional concept. As will be demonstrated below, the theory which predicts well in terms of one dimension may not predict as well as a different theory in terms of another dimension. When confronted with such a tradeoff situation, the theorist's objectives should determine his choice.

It may be argued that these different objectives have no consequence for the construction of theories and the evaluation of competing theories. In principle this is true. The "ideal" theory both would make very accurate point-in-time predictions and unfailing associate changes in the system's structure with changes in the system's future behavior. However, not only is every theory "incomplete" in the sense that it is an abstraction from reality, but at this stage in theory development, "good" policy prediction theories may come at the expense of "good" point predictions. Specifically, it will be argued that when evaluating competing theories, if the objective is to choose the better *policy* prediction theory, the relative accuracy of their point predictions is an inappropriate standard. If the theory which generates superior point in time predictions is always chosen, then we run the risk of selecting the inferior policy prediction theory. This argument will be developed in the context of a comparison of alternative theories which seek to account for the development and procurement of particular weapons systems. The follow-on imperative already has been described. The next task is to sketch another theory of weapons procurement.

Kurth has identified several kinds of theories which are invoked to account for weapons procurement decisions. These are: (1) "strategic theories" which relate weapons decisions to national security requirements and perceived changes in the international environment which affect those requirements; (2) "technocratic theories" which argue that systems are developed because they are intellectually exciting and technically challenging to researchers; (3) "bureaucratic theories" which relate weapons system decisions to interaction of groups within the executive branch bureaucracy, notably the military services; (4) "democratic theories" which relate weapons systems to the domestic political process including electoral politics and Congressional-constituency relationships; and (5) "economic theories" which emphasize the influence of large corporations on those political decisions in which they are interested: for defense contractors these decisions obviously include the allocation of large Pentagon procurement contracts.[28] Both the follow-on imperative and the "bail-out imperative" described by Kurth in "Aerospace Production Lines and American Defense Spending" are examples of economic theories of weapons programs.

Although these "theories" usually are viewed as competing with one another and requiring a choice among them, an alternative is to posit a "meta-theory" which specifies the relationship among them. Based on his earlier discussion of "modes of change and modes of causation"[29] we have pursued this alternative in the following adaptation of Kurth's theory of weapons procurement.

New weapons systems have to be researched and developed before they can go into production. The earlier stages of research and development are characterized by activities of *low visibility* to senior decision-makers within the organization as well as to outsiders (e.g., Congress). This low visibility is a consequence of several features of the early stages of weapons development. First, early research efforts ordinarily entail relatively low dollar expenditures and, in the preliminary stages, the objects of expenditure may not be explicitly identified in the budget. Thus, there is little in the budgeting process which would attract the notice of senior officials or outsiders. Second, the high level of secrecy which characterizes military research combines with the low expenditures to reduce the probability that new developments will be recognized. Third, weapons developments are usually associated with technical and unfamiliar concepts which require more than casual efforts for the laymen to comprehend. Thus, even if senior officials or outsiders should learn of new weapons developments, they would have to be highly motivated before they would expend the efforts required to probe the technical mysteries.

These factors combine to yield a high probability that weapons programs in the early stages of development will proceed unhampered by competition or opposition (assuming there is no important resistance within the R&D community). So long as programs retain low visibility, they are predominantly under the control of the scientists and engineers (if only by default) and, accordingly, the "technocratic theories" perspective would seem most relevant (perhaps embellished by the "standard operating procedure" emphasis of "bureaucratic theories").[30]

However, such theories are inadequate for treating decisions relating to production and deployment.[31] Advanced development and production are associated with heightened visibility and increased opportunities for and probability of opposition to the weapons program. First, actors who would have opposed the program had they known of its existence become alerted and mobilized. Second, as the program becomes more expensive and a more voracious competitor for scarce resources, defenders of other programs (in this and other issue-areas) will enter the ranks of the opposition.

Accordingly, once a program achieves high visibility, its future depends on the strength of its supporters compared to the power of its opponents. Given sufficient visibility, the probability of a system being produced the deployed might be thought of as a function of (1) the strategic environment. (2) the distribution of influence within the military services; and (3) the support available from and opposition generated by coalitions of defense contractors and Congressmen. These sets of variables are related to (1) "strategic theories"; (2) "bureaucratic theories", (3) "economic theories"; and (4) "democratic theories," respectively.

Recall that the decision to produce a weapons system entails visible expenditures. This attribute not only arouses opposition but also stimulates additional sources of support. Since a significant proportion of those expenditures will be in the form of defense contracts, both contractors (according to the "economic theories") and their representatives in Congress (according to the "democratic theories") can be expected to support efforts to bring a system into production.

Moreover, Kurth implies that funded programs are an indication (or perhaps source) of influence within the military services. Thus, powerful branches of a military service (e.g., the Strategic Air Command) can, by virtue of their dominance, prevail over the opposition of their weaker colleagues and (with some assistance) propel a favored program into production and deployment. However, if a relatively subordinate military organization (e.g., the Army Air Defense Command) somehow can succeed in getting one of its weapons programs funded, its success will be followed by an increase in its relative influence within the military services.[32] Similarly, the contract might be awarded to an already major contractor, or it might go to a company usually associated with another industrial sector.[33] Changes in the distribution within the military are not necessarily accompanied by similar outcomes in the economy (and vice versa). For example, a contract which maintains the distribution of influence within the military may redistribute economic rewards among defense contractors.

The subsequent discussion will be clarified if several of the propositions entailed by this weapons procurement theory are identified:

1. The more advanced the research and development (R & D) phase of the program, the higher the visibility of the program.
2. The higher the visibility of the program, the more probable the involvement of participants not members of the research community, both in support and in opposition to the program.

3. The more advanced the (R & D) program, the higher the probability of an affirmative production decision (assuming this represents technical progress and high nonrecoverable costs).[34]

4. The greater the influence of the military organization which will operate the system, the higher the probability of an affirmative production decision.

5. The greater the perceived strategic threat, the higher the probability of an affirmative production decision.

6. The higher the probability that the contract, if awarded, will go to the producer of a structurally similar weapons system, the higher the probability of an affirmative production decision.

7. The higher the level of Congressional support for the program, the higher the probability of an affirmative production decision.

Notice that the weapons procurement theory, as well as the follow-on imperative and the bail-out imperatives discussed by Kurth, seek to account for the decision to produce a particular weapons system. (While the latter two theories focus on the identity of the particular defense contractor which will receive the contract, a decision that the weapons system will be produced obviously is a necessary prerequisite to designating its producer.) However, the set of variables (implicitly) included within each theory is *not* equivalent to the set in the other theories, i.e., each views reality from a somewhat different perspective.

Imagine that, for a given set of weapons system decisions, all three theories yielded the same predictions of the probability of an affirmative production decision (P). On the basis of these results, there would be no way to choose among the theories, even though each theory represents a somewhat different abstraction from reality. More generally, the "validity" of the system's structure cannot be inferred from the results: since different structures may produce identical predictions, the analyst cannot infer from the results of his theory back to the underlying structure. Even if his model has produced predictions which closely approximate his test data, the analyst should not conclude that he has satisfactorily specified the underlying process which in reality produced those observations. Conventional data analytic techniques cannot provide the *theoretical* rationale for selecting and ordering variables. Rather, the analyst must stipulate the system's structure prior to performing the statistical manipulations.[35] In the absence of independent evidence for the stipulated structure, he is confined to claiming that the real world phenomena behave *as if* they were structured like his system. (For a more formal discussion of these points, see the appendix to this essay: "Notes on System Behavior and Structure.") This point might be highlighted by drawing attention to a particular problem involved in identifying structures which is of special significance to policy prediction theories.

If, for a particular set of data, the values of some variable (or its parameter) are equal to zero, those data do not allow one to distinguish between a structure which includes the variable (whose value is zero) and a structure which omits the variable. For example, the variable which measures the intensity of the perceived strategic threat (S) in the weapons procurement theory might be weighted by the perceived responsiveness of the proposed weapons system to the strategic threat. If, in some survey of weapons production decisions, no proposed weapon were perceived to meet any threat, then the weighted S term always would equal zero. In that case, the weapons procurement theory described above would be indistinguishable from a theory which omitted a strategic threat variable. However, the structures in fact would be distinct and policy advice which assumes one structure may lead to inefficient (or perhaps disastrous) consequences if the other structure actually applied. Thus, a decision-maker formulating policies on the basis of a theory which does not include a strategic threat variable would fail to recognize the relationship between policies to reduce international tensions and the probability of future weapons systems being produced.

Since we cannot make high confidence inferences regarding structure from comparing a theory's predictions with data, we cannot choose among theories purporting to account for the same set of phenomena solely on the grounds that one theory is a more "accurate" representation of reality than the other.

However, the competition among theories which seems to require a choice may be more apparent than real: it may be an easy task to choose among two theories, if each is better suited for a different purpose, once that objective is known. A theory which makes very good predictions of the values of a specified variable at selected future points in time *may* be of little use to someone interested in assessing the consequences of changes in policy decisions and actions: superior point prediction theories may not be equally superior policy prediction theories. In such cases, the analyst's concerns should direct his choice. The *kind of variables* included help to distinguish these two purposes of theory.

The follow-on imperative is a good illustration of a point prediction theory: it seeks to predict when production of new weapons systems will be approved (as well as who will produce them). It does not seem well suited to serve as a policy prediction theory because it gives so little attention to the system's structure and, in particular, it omits *variables which seem potentially susceptible to manipulation* by the policy process.[36] Rather, this imperative argues that major defense contractors with open production lines probably (and virtually inevitably) *will* receive new contracts.

With only the follow-on imperative as a basis for policy advice and action, an actor may be able to inhibit growth in the industrial sector but apparently is helpless in the face of an open production line (short of reducing the number of open production lines, perhaps by corporate merger). It would be as if an egregiously overweight person were told by his doctor that a carefully done empirical study of body weight showed that height and age are the best predictors of body weight. Based on this "theory," it is unlikely that anything can be done about the patient's weight problems (short of perhaps cutting him off at the knee). However, if the objective of the follow-on imperative is accurate point-in-time predictions and if this objective is achieved, then its lack of attention to the underlying structure is irrelevant and its deficiencies for generating policy advice reflect an inappropriate standard of validity.

In comparison to the follow-on imperative, the weapons procurement theory serves the objectives of policy prediction somewhat better. The follow-on imperative includes manipulable variables only if the number of production lines somehow can be reduced by means other than by firms going out of business (which would directly contradict the theory's predictions). The weapons procurement theory, by contrast, includes a number of variables which are manipulable. Some examples may illustrate this point: (1) Propositions entailed by the latter theory relate the probability of an affirmative production decision to the costs and technical accomplishments of the development program at the time of decision, and relate the growth of a coalition of participants opposed to the program to the visibility of the project. These relationships suggest that mechanisms which affect the visibility of a project (such as the monitoring capabilities of the budgeting system) would have an effect on the probability of weapons procurement.[37] (2) The ultimate decision regarding production depends upon the "balance of forces" between the program's advocates and opponents. Although the weapons procurement theory is silent on the sources of the size and strength of these coalitions, preliminary research by one of the authors suggests that budget allocations may affect the distribution of influence among military organizations.[38] (3) The theory suggests that changes in perceptions of strategic threats affect the likelihood of affirmative production decisions. Accordingly, actions which alter perceptions of the strategic environment (perhaps the SALT agreements) will be associated with changes in the probability of a particular weapons system going into production.

These arguments imply that the first step in choosing among theories is a *clear* specification of what it is you want to do, a statement of objectives. It would seem that simply a desire to "predict" accurately is *not* an unambiguous enough specification to be helpful in discriminating among theories one is likely to run across in the behavioral sciences.[39] Indeed, a major reason for the "thicket of theories" of the weapons acquisition process is a thicket of nonequivalent objectives by which theories of weapons acquisition are judged. One objective which might occupy a theorist is the prediction of weapons procurement decisions. Another, and potentially competing, objective might be the prediction of how changes in the weapons procurement decision process will affect the probability of procuring particular weapons systems. If the latter describes the theorist's purposes, he should prefer the weapons procurement theory to the follow-on imperative *even if the weapons procurement theory cannot predict as well as the follow-on imperative whether and when defense contracts will be let.*

Evaluating Theories: Examining Propositions Entailed by the Theory

Our discussion of the need to relate a theory's evaluation to its objectives has merely postponed consideration of some of the ways in which theories might be judged and of the appropriateness of a variety of criteria. We will introduce this discussion by a brief examination of some considerations which apply to a variety of theories. We then will consider the relation between a theory's purpose and the criteria appropriate for its evaluation.

Neither point prediction nor policy prediction theories can be considered satisfactory until they have been confronted with data and their empirical assertions compared with the reality to which they refer. Naturally, the theory should include propositions which are liable to empirical falsification and it is those propositions which should be confronted with the data. That is, it is important to distinguish within a theory those statements which are true by the meanings of the words involved (analytic statements) from those which make empirical claims about the phenomena which may be true or false depending on the evidence. Confusing empirical with analytic statements may lead to unwarranted satisfaction with the theory's performance. This point can be illustrated by considering again the specification of "major defense contractors" in the follow-on imperative.

The follow-on imperative does not readily account for contractor *growth*: how do contractors become "major" and thus eligible for sustenance via the follow-on imperative? As Kurth notes, two of his six airframe producers—Grumman and McDonnell-Douglas—were relatively minor contractors at the beginning of the time period he analyzes. Although the act of merger obviously accounts for part of McDonnell-Douglas' growth, both contractors entered the ranks of the major producers by virtue of new contracts let during the 1960s, notably the F-4 contract to McDonnell-Douglas and F-111 fighter aircraft subcontract to Grumman. If these contracts were awarded to McDonnell-Douglas and Grumman even though one or more of the already major contractors had an open production line, then the follow-on imperative would fail to predict the award.[40] If all major production lines were already filled, then the follow-on imperative cannot account for some subset of aircraft procurement decisions and we must resort to some other theory in order to make such predictions.

The fact that companies can enter the ranks of major defense contractors by winning new contracts directs our attention to the relationship between contracts for aircraft procurement and production lines. Recall that the follow-on imperative argues that new contracts are let in order to sustain contractors with open production lines. However, it appears that contractors eligible for such contracts are defined in terms of having been awarded the contract e.g., Grumman and McDonnell-Douglas.

It may be argued that this relationship indicates a process by which the Pentagon creates an increasing number of major contractors which it must sustain via the follow-on imperative. However, in the absence of independent and well-specified criteria for identifying companies eligible for support, the operationalization of major aerospace contracts seems to be interdependent with the operationalization of major contractors. The award of a contract for a major (i.e., expensive) weapons system elevates its recipient into the ranks of major contractors, whereupon it is observed that contracts for major weapons systems typically are awarded to large defense contractors; aircraft procurement contracts typically go to airframe manufacturers. The result is that the follow-on imperative runs the danger of being a self-confirming hypothesis in which support for the argument is embedded in the definitions of the words being used rather than in the phenomena being studied.[41]

Even if we are careful to distinguish analytic from empirical statements, we have not assured that the theory has been submitted to a reasonable challenge to its claims about reality. For example, the data in terms of which the theory is tested may be inadequate for an evaluation of a proposition whose claims are counter to a proposition entailed by the theory. Of special concern is the choice of temporal cutting points which may have an important effect on the findings of empirical analysis.

The follow-on imperative argues that the government will act so as to *sustain* major contractors (however defined). Presumably, a finding of *turnover* among the top ranks of defense contractors would falsify the follow-on imperative since it would imply that while some fluid *group* of defense contractors might be perceived to be a national resource, particular individual contractors were not. That is, the government's incentive to maintain dependable sources of production would not require it to behave in accordance with the follow-on (or bail-out) imperative unless particular production skills were specialized, highly concentrated, and not readily acquired by other firms.

This raises the question of whether the time frame selected by Kurth—the 1960s—is sufficient to allow for turnover to occur. For example, Peck and Scherer argue that the postwar period prior to 1960 was characterized by substantial turnover among major defense contractors.[42] Since development of a complex weapons system typically is measured in years rather than months, and production times ordinarily exceed development times, the time from the letting of the first development contract to the expiration of the final production contract easily could consume the better part of a decade.[43] Accordingly, we cannot exclude the possibility that the absence of turnover of the ranks of the top airframe production lines discovered by Kurth is an artifact of the time frame selected: insufficient time was allowed for turnover to have occurred and for the follow-on imperative to have been challenged.

This familiar relation between the choice of test data and empirical findings suggests a strategy for choosing among theories. Different theories may be said to be in competition when they have the same purpose, e.g., point prediction or policy prediction. If we assume that an analyst's objective is to maximize the accuracy of predicting the probability of affirmative weapon production decision (which requires a point prediction theory), we might exclude from consideration our (policy prediction) theory of weapons procurement. However, on the basis of Kurth's discussion we still are left with two genuinely competing theories: the follow-on imperative and the bail-out imperative. A deliberate and theoretically directed search for particular data may allow us to make a choice between these genuine competitors.

Recall that both the follow-on imperative and the bail-out imperative account for weapons decisions by reference to the condition of the prospective contractor. The former argues that when a production line opens up which had been producing a weapons system which is structurally similar to the system proposed, it is very likely that production of the new system will be approved and that the contractor will be awarded the contract. The latter argues that when the financial condition of the contractor deteriorates, production of the new weapon likely will be approved and the contract awarded in order to financially rescue or "bail-out" the ailing corporation.

Notice that the two imperatives offer somewhat different explanations for contractor selection and therefore allow the possibility of making different predictions in particular cases. This suggests a strategy for deliberately selecting data which relate to these differences, i.e., assembling data which would allow a kind of natural "critical experiment."[44]

To the extent that the onset of a company's financial woes is attributable to the completion of a *defense* contract, we would expect the two imperatives to yield indistinguishable predictions and thus afford no grounds for preferring one theory to the other. So long as the selection of data is confined to cases of defense contract termination, we would expect to have to continue to accept both theories. However, the bail-out imperative would predict that the government would respond with a defense contract to Lockheed's deteriorating financial condition, which is largely attributable to the company's problems with its *commercial* production (notably the L-1011), while the follow-on imperative would not predict any contract award since Lockheed's problems were not the result of a defense production line opening up. If the bail-out imperative better accounted for affirmative production decisions in such cases, and performed as well as the follow-on imperative in other cases, we would prefer the bail-out imperative to the follow-on imperative.[45] That is, we may be able to make a choice among genuinely competing theories if we can design "critical experiments" which allow us to differentiate their performance: although a system's structure cannot be validated by results, some stipulated structures may be rejected in favor of others.

Evaluating Theories: The User's as a Standard

It has been argued that theories well suited for one purpose, such as prediction of the values of specified variables at closely spaced points in time, may not be well-suited for another purpose, e.g., predicting the consequences of changes in policy decisions and actions. Similarly, tests of validity or performance appropriate to one kind of theory may be inappropriate to another.[46] The familiar standards of "goodness-of-fit" and "parsimony" seem appropriate to the evaluation and selection of point prediction theories. They do not appear to be equally relevant to the evaluation and selection of policy prediction theories. Accordingly, if these tests are applied indiscriminately, without regard to the analyst's objectives, the superior theory may be rejected in favor of a less adequate one.

Recall that the follow-on imperative has been characterized as a point prediction theory. Its purpose is to predict whether and when a new weapons system will be procured.[47] A reasonable test of its validity (and, indeed the kind of test which Kurth applies) is how well its predictions correspond to real-world outcomes: the better the fit between its predictions and actual results—perhaps as measured by residual sum of squares—the greater the confidence we should have in the follow-on imperative's predictions regarding future weapons decisions. However, since the imperative is virtually silent on the *structure* which yields the outcomes it predicts, the analyst is confined to saying that defense contracts are awarded *as if* production lines abhor a vacuum. There is nothing in the follow-on imperative itself, *nor in its test of validity,* which requires that this proposition be true nor which allows us to assess whether it be true in fact.

Someone interested in assessing the consequences of changes in policy decisions and actions is particularly interested in the adequacy with which the system's structure is specified. Therefore, we have argued, he probably would prefer the weapons procurement theory to the follow-on imperative. If, in choosing among theories, we apply the decision rule to *always* prefer the theory with the smallest residual sum of squares, then the follow-on imperative will be chosen instead of the weapons procurement theory in all cases in which the latter is inferior as a point prediction theory, *even if it is superior as a policy prediction theory:* if "goodness-of-fit" between the theory's predictions and real-world outcomes is the first standard for a comparative evaluation of theories—without regard to their purposes—then theories which are designed to describe the policy process may be systematically rejected in favor of theories which yield better point-in-time predictions.

Policy prediction theories should not be evaluated and compared solely in terms of the accuracy of their point-in-time predictions: accurate point-in-time predictions appear to be neither a necessary nor sufficient condition for preferring one *policy prediction* theory to another. For the purposes of making policy recommendations, we might prefer a theory whose point-in-time predictions are less accurate than those made by another theory. This point can be illustrated by the following example.

Assume the "true" behavior of a variable "*y*" in relation to time is known and its values are plotted as the dotted line in Figure 7-1. Imagine that two "competing" theories have been formulated which purport to account for the behavior of variable "*y* over time. The predictions of theory$_1$ are illustrated by the solid line parallel to the horizontal axis "*t*". The predictions of theory$_2$ yield the solid line sinewave.

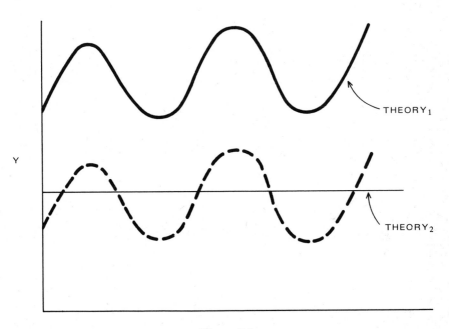

Figure 7-1.

If we calculated the sum of the squared deviations between the observed values of the variable and the values predicted by each of our two theories, we would find that theory$_1$ made more accurate point in time predictions that did theory$_2$. If we are seeking the better point prediction theory, we should prefer theory$_1$. Moreover, if we indiscriminately apply a familiar "goodness-of-fit" test (such as least squares) we will choose theory$_1$ over theory$_2$ *even if we actually were seeking the superior policy prediction theory.*

However, theory$_2$ appears to better characterize the dynamic (over-time) behavior of variable "y". This ability to reflect the dynamic character of behavior would seem to be an important quality of a policy prediction theory. Imagine a third axis added to Figure 7-1 which reflected the behavior of another variable "z" through which the values of "y" could be affected. Although the ability to theory$_1$ to give better point-in-time predictions of the observed values is unimpaired, it would make predictions of the relation between *changes* in "z" and changes in "y" which would be inferior to those of theory$_2$. Theory$_2$, in contrast to theory$_1$, would perform very well in assessing the relative impacts on "y" of various policy changes which affected the value of "z". Accordingly, if we are seeking the better policy prediction theory, we should reject theory$_1$ in favor of theory$_2$.[48]

Reflecting the dynamic character of the behavior is not, of course, a sufficient (although it may be a necessary) condition of a policy prediction theory. It does, however, return our attention to the need for confidence that the system's structure has been appropriately specified. One standard which might be applied to evaluating policy theories is that they be *plausible*.[49]

How do we know whether a policy theory is plausible? One way is to ask the participants in the particular policy process under investigation. All decision-makers have some mental image(s) of the phenomena on which they operate and routinely make informal (and perhaps subconscious) predictions regarding the consequences of alternative policy actions.[50]

The need for explicit policy prediction theories derives in part from the deficiencies of the human mind in intuitively coping with large numbers of variables which may interact in unfamiliar (e.g., nonlinear) ways. However, active participants in the process may have a relatively clear, if only intuitive, sense of the functional form of the bivariate relationships (at least over short time intervals). Consequently they represent a valuable resource for an analyst interested in constructing and validating a policy prediction theory. It recently has been argued, for example, that a major difference between behavioral science applied research and applied research in the physical and engineering sciences is that in contrast to his colleagues in the latter area, the behavioral scientist does most of his research in the university and does not interact in a continuous way with the potential consumers of his research.

The quest for solutions to social problems should involve applied research in a sense that has not usually been understood by the social scientist—a continued and close interaction between those who do the research and those who must make the decisions and policies that result in the application of research. The quest should also include rapid and continuous exchange of information and knowledge between those doing the research and those who are doing the things that research has indicated to be necessary for the solution of the problems. To achieve these interactions, it may be necessary to change . . . the methodology of research. . . .[51]

The point is not that *only* the Secretary of Defense can understand how the Pentagon behaves, but it is to suggest that people involved in the process being theorized about often can be very helpful both in providing "quick and dirty" (and generally very cheap) reality tests and in suggesting the structures *they* impose upon the process in which they operate.[52]

One way an analyst might try to define the structure relating the variables would be to ask policy-makers to specify a number of bivariate relationships. The analyst next would estimate the couplings among these relationships to specify the structure. He then would return to the participants and ask them if the consequences of the structure appeared to be plausible. Repeating this procedure several times with a range of policy-makers hopefully will yield relatively stable estimates of the structural relations. An adaptation of the "Delphi" forecasting technique appears to be a promising mechanism for organizing the involvement of the policy participants and generating consensual estimates of the structural relations.[53]

A related issue concerns the criteria which might be employed to select some finite number of variables for inclusion in the system from the infinite number of variables found in reality. Once again, the analyst's *objectives* should exercise controlling influence over the choice of criteria.

"Parsimony" has been a traditional standard against which theories have been measured. Ceteris paribus, the "simpler" the better. This interest in parsimony has led to widespread acceptance of "proportion of variance explained" measures as criteria for identifying "important" variables and segregating them from "unimportant" variables. Conventionally, a variable which explains more of the variance in real-world outcomes is preferred to a variable which explains less. Similarly, a system of equations composed of a small number of variables which accounts for a given amount of variance usually is preferred to a system composed of a larger number of variables which accounts for the same proportion of total variance. However, just as "goodness-of-fit" may be an inappropriate measure of the adequacy of policy prediction theories, "variance explained" measures may be misleading indicators of which variables are "important" and should be included in such a theory.

If the objective of a particular theory is to parsimoniously describe the "behavior" of the phenomena, then a criterion for including or excluding a given variable such as "proportion of variance explained" makes good sense as a way of isolating "significant" variables. However, if a goal of the theory is to enable its user to somehow change behavior, the import of a standard such as "percent of variance explained" may be greatly reduced.

Recall our "theory" of body weight which found that height and age were the best predictors of body weight, i.e., these two variables explained most of the variance observed in body weight. The doctor, armed with such an elegantly parsimonious theory, could make no realistic recommendations to his overweight patient. If "variance explained" were the primary standard applied to theories without regard to objective, the follow-on imperative always would be preferred to the weapons procurement theory even if both theories yielded equally good point-in-time predictions, since the former theory is more parsimonious. However, the person interested in weight reduction as well as the analyst of policy prediction theories is concerned less with "variance explained" than with identifying variables which he can *manipulate*. Given their respective objectives, *those* are the "important" variables.

Generally, which variables are "significant" depends to a large degree upon the objective(s) of the theory. If one's objectives include the capability to use the theory in evaluating or designing feasible policies, it is critical that the variables be partitioned into the set of those variables which are manipulable by the policy-makers or implementors and those which cannot be so manipulated. However, the criteria often applied by behavioral scientists ordinarily fail to make the distinction between controllable and uncontrollable variables.[54]

Moreover, not all variables are equally susceptible to manipulation by every individual. One's relation to the policy process will have an important effect on partitioning variables according to manipulability. The proverbial New York taxi driver may well understand which actions will influence the probability of weapons procurement, but, for people in his position, few if any variables are manipulable. Presumably, from the perspective of the President, a somewhat larger number of variables are controllable. Since which variables are "important" in a policy prediction theory depends in part on which variables are manipulable, the design of the system and policy prediction theory should be sensitive to the position of the output's consumer. The theory for providing advice to the President will be significantly different from the theory which yields responses appropriate to taxi drivers.

The relation of variable manipulability to the location of various participants in the policy process highlights the contribution which policy-makers can make to the construction and evaluation of policy theories, and underlines the need for close interaction between the analyst and the practitioner.

This discussion has sought to develop the argument that the appropriate criteria for evaluating and comparing theories cannot be identified without reference to the purposes to which the theory is to be put. Thus, conventional goodness-of-fit measures may lead to the discarding of promising policy prediction theories and a concern for parsimony may cause the omission of significant policy variables. Heightened sensitivity to a theory's objectives will help the analyst to discern suitable criteria.

Having tried to draw a distinct boundary between policy prediction theories and point prediction theories, it may now be appropriate to mute that boundary by briefly addressing an apparent paradox. Suppose both the weapons procurement theory and the follow-on imperative predicted a particular weapons system would be produced. However, opponents of the weapons system note that the weapons procurement theory would predict that system would *not* be produced *if* certain variable values somehow were changed. Suppose these variables were changed and the weapons system was not produced. This outcome would corroborate the weapons procurement theory but would falsify the follow-on imperative.

This brief example illustrates two important points. The first has been made elsewhere by Robert Merton: "Public predictions of future social developments are frequently not sustained precisely because the prediction has become a new element in the concrete situation, thus tending to change the initial course of developments."[55] That is, a policy theory becomes a part of the phenomena which it is about. Any tests of it must take this into account. Second, as theories develop, the tradeoffs between "policy" and "prediction" will probably decrease. This is because, as noted above, these two objectives are, in principle, not in conflict. The "ideal" theory will do both (as well as much more) with equal facility. It is only in the early stages of theory building that there will appear to be these tradeoffs.

Improving Theories: The Confrontation of "Competing Theories

Although this essay primarily has been concerned with making choices among already existing theories which refer to the same phenomena, a logical extension of the discussion leads to a consideration of choosing between an existing theory and one which has not yet been explicitly formulated or, more simply, some guides to the modification and improvement of theories.

When different theories lead to incompatible assertions about the same (or closely related) reality, it suggests either that there is more than one referent, or that the system has not been properly identified (or perhaps that the two systems are complementary).[56] A possible heuristic device for identifying defects in a theory is to confront it with incompatible claims made by another theory. As a *heuristic* device, this strategy seems promising even if the latter theory had been intended to serve an objective different than that of the former. This point will be illustrated by confronting the weapons procurement theory (a policy prediction theory) with the follow-on imperative (a point prediction theory).

A close comparison of the follow-on imperative and the weapons procurement theory reveals apparently incompatible assertions. The former argues that an open production line probably will be filled, most likely with a structurally similar system. Thus, the follow-on imperative makes no allowance for, and indeed is insensitive to, the preference ordering of (or distribution of influence within) the consumer (military organization). The weapons procurement theory, by contrast, includes consideration of the distribution of influence within the military services: the greater the predominance of the sponsoring military organization, the higher the probability that the weapons system will be produced. Thus, the latter theory seems to assume that there always will exist a contractor who is eager to produce the weapon and a military group which advocates the proposed system.

These differences between the two theories do highlight an interesting question: viz., are contractor preferences ever in conflict with military-consumer preferences and if so, how is the conflict resolved? For example, what happens when a production line which has been producing a system sponsored by a *subordinate* military organization opens up? The follow-on imperative would predict that a new and structurally similar contract will be forthcoming. However, the weapons procurement theory would argue that a structurally similar weapons system, i.e., one which would be sponsored by and would benefit a subordinate military organization, has a low probability of being produced, regardless of its resemblance to a previous weapons system produced by a now open production line—and perhaps independent of whether there is an open production line of a major contractor.

There are several possible explanations which yield a reconciliation. For example, perhaps contractors with open production lines always are prepared to produce systems advocated by dominant military groups, i.e., all observed follow-on contracts are structurally similar high-priority programs. However, Lockheed-Georgia's string of air transport programs—sponsored by the relatively subordinate Military Airlift Command[57]—would seem to contradict this explanation. Alternatively, perhaps low-priority programs were not funded at the direct cost of high priority programs, so that such programs had only a negligible impact on the distribution of resources within the military services. Such a situation should reduce the intensity of inter- and intraservice rivalries and perhaps reduce the incentives of any military group to oppose any weapons system. This in fact may have been one of the consequences of Secretary of Defense McNamara's budgeting system which prevailed during most of the time period surveyed by Kurth. Or perhaps the explanation lies in an incomplete specification of the structure, i.e., the civilian administration and the extent of the role it plays in such decisions have been omitted. Thus, the weapons procurement theory, as presently articulated, does not seem to readily accommodate differences (if any) between active ("strong") and passive ("weak") Secretaries of Defense and Presidential administrations.

These tentative explanations suggest that the weapons procurement theory may be incomplete in at least two ways. The weapons procurement theory appears both to have omitted important (i.e., manipulable) variables such as differences among Secretaries of Defense, and to have inadequately specified the relationships among these variables. Thus, without further information, the relationship between particular weapons systems and the incentive structure (as reflected by the distribution of influence) of the military organizations cannot be specified nor, accordingly, can the strength of intramilitary opposition to a particular program.

Similarly, assuming that the defense contractor's primary objective is to maximize his profits, it remains unclear which actions best serve that goal. Thus contracts which are structurally *dis*similar might promote a (government subsidized) diversification which will increase expected long-run profits. Alternatively, structurally similar follow-on contracts might represent minimum new investment (in learning time and resources) and thus allow larger short-run profits.[58] Without a better understanding of the contractors' incentive structure and how it responds to changes in the contractors' environment, we cannot choose among competing predictions regarding a firm's behavior nor evaluate the structure underlying the follow-on imperative.[59]

Consider another example. The weapons procurement theory argues that the probability of a particular weapons system being produced is a function of the intensity of the perceived strategic threat, the strength of the military organization promoting the system, and the strength of the coalition of outside allies (composed of Senators and contractors). Kurth hypothesizes the following constraint on the relationship: there is no military organization which is sufficiently dominant to successfully promote a program without additional assistance: even the most dominant services and branches must be reinfored *either* by a high strategic threat *or* outside allies.[60]

Notice that the weapons procurement theory implies that the high economic cost of procurement contracts routinely activates the interest and support both of corporations seeking to increase business and profits and Congressmen who act to service their constituents (and thus to enhance their prospects for re-elections).[61] That is, according to the theory, any procurement contract—because it implies large expenditures—*always* will find an eager outside coalition of Congressmen and contractors. Notice also that for dominant military organizations, outside allies are a substitutable source of support for a highly perceived strategic threat.

Since the theory implies that a supportive coalition always stands ready, and that a dominant military organization requires either a strategic threat or outside support, then the theory must predict that dominant military organizations *always* will be successful in securing favorable decisions regarding weapons which they advocate. In its present form, the theory can account for variations in the probabilities of weapons procurement only by combinations of subordinate military organizations advocating weapons in a situation of an inadequately threatening strategic environment.

These implausible propositions entailed by the weapons procurement theory indicate additional omissions and shortcomings. For example, it is difficult to explicitly identify the motives or the sources of strength of any *opposing* coalition of outsiders in the theory as presently formulated, although casual observation immediately reveals such opposition can (and with increasing frequency does) exist. Similarly, it is difficult to infer any sources of variation in the supportive coalition. Yet, even without reference to the strength of an opposing coalition, it seems reasonable to suppose that support for a proposed weapons system will vary.

Our operational definition of "major defense contractor" developed above in an examination of the follow-on imperative is suggestive of sources of variation among contractors. Perhaps the greater the mutual dependence between the Pentagon and the contractor, the greater the contractor's motivation and influence, i.e., the government's interest in sustaining the major contractors confers more influence on firms which confront the imminent prospect of economic decline (in the absence of contracts for new weapons systems) than on firms which face no such prospect in the near-term. A parallel concept, perhaps related to a Congressman's electoral prospects, might account for variation in aggregate Congressional support.

The purpose of this discussion has not been to reformulate the weapons procurement theory. Rather, it was designed to illustrate how a theory might be improved both by examining the plausibility of the propositions it entails and by comparing its predictions with those of other theories relating to the same phenomena, even when the latter theories were intended for other purposes.

Summary and Conclusion

Using James Kurth's description of the follow-on imperative and weapons procurement theory as examples, we have made a variety of arguments concerning the construction of policy prediction theories and appropriate criteria for evaluating such theories. We have argued that "prediction" is a multidimensional concept. In the short run, there may well be tradeoffs between theories which are useful in predicting (i.e., evaluating) the impacts of various policy actions, and theories which make accurate point-in-time predictions. Accordingly, a theory cannot be evaluated except with reference to its objectives and until those objectives have been clearly specified. These objectives should, in part, determine the phenomena to be studied and the particular variables which are abstracted.

Given certain parameter and variable values, different structures may result in indistinguishable behavior. However, to change these behaviors in a preferred direction requires a knowledge of the underlying structure. Accordingly, a policy prediction theory must give special attention to stipulating the structure from which the system behavior is generated. Conventional data analysis techniques are unable to distinguish among structures of behaviorally identical systems and are of little assistance in identifying structure independent of a theory which suggests the functional forms relating the variables.

Further, it is important for a policy theory to identify those variables which can be *manipulated* by a particular policy-maker or implementor. Conventional "variance explained" measures are not designed to distinguish between controllable and uncontrollable variables (nor are they sensitive to the relativity of the distinction) and therefore should not be used as the sole indicator of which are the "important" variables.

If, as we suspect, there is at this early stage of theory development a tradeoff between such objectives as point-in-time prediction and policy evaluation, an uncritical application of conventional evaluation criteria will, at best, retard the development of useful policy theories and, at worst, will result in disastrous policy advice.

Appendix: Notes on System Structure and Behavior

The points made about distinguishing between the structure being theorized about and the sequences of behaviors produced by that structure can be developed more precisely through the explicit use of a systems vocabulary. A (general) system, S, is defined as a collection of objects—$0_1, 0_2 \ldots 0_n$ together with the relations defined upon these objects $R_1, R_2 \ldots R_n$ and may be designated:

$$S : \langle 0_1, 0_2 \ldots p_n ; R_1, R_2 \ldots R_n \rangle \; .$$

The relations defined upon the objects "structure" the objects and the totality of the relations is referred to as the "structure" of the system. A set of (linguistic) statements which claims to be true of the system is often termed a theory of that system. For a dynamic system (i.e., one directly parameterized by time) we are often interested in the values each of the objects in the system take on at various points in time. A listing of the values of each of the objects at a point in time is the state of the system at that point in time. A sequence of states (ordered by time) is termed the (internal) behavior of the system.

A fundamental point made in this paper has been that the theorist distinguish between structure and behavior since equivalent behaviors by two systems do not imply equivalent structures nor do equivalent (isomorphic) structures imply equivalent strings of behavior. This will be illustrated by the following hypothetical example.

Imagine a political scientist who is very interested in what makes people in a nation "satisfied." After doing some preliminary research, he decides the following three objects (variables) are the important ones:

S_t = overall satisfaction level of the people in a given nation at time t

P_t = performance of the private sector on the nation at time t

G_t = performance of the government of the nation at time t

Recall, however, that this is not enough to identify a system; the variables must be related to each other in some way: the structure of the system must be given. Our political scientist stipulates the system's structure with the following three difference equations:

$$P_t = \alpha S_{t-1} \tag{1}$$

$$G_t = \beta(P_t - P_{t-1}) \tag{2}$$

$$S_t = P_t + G_t \quad \text{where } \alpha \text{ and } \beta \geqslant 0 \tag{3}$$

Equation (1) states that private sector performance will be proportional to the preceding period's level of overall satisfaction. Equation (2) tells us that government performance will be proportional to the change in private sector performance from this period to the preceding period. Finally, (3) is an accounting equation which defines overall satisfaction as the sum of government performance and private sector performance. (Throughout this analysis it will be assumed that S, P, and G are measured in comparable units.)

The state variables of the system are G, P, and S and the state of the system at a particular point in time is therefore given by listing the values of each variable at that time: G_t, P_t, S_t. Variables which are *not* included in the system are called parameters. An "effective" parameter is one which has a discernible impact upon the system's behavior (e.g., and α, β, and t in the set of equations above). The above set of equations describes a *dynamic* system since the system is effectively parameterized by time.

The values of α and β for a particular nation might be estimated by observing over time values of S, P, and G. As Brunner[62] points out, the data analysis problems associated with this estimation are by no means simple. However, let us assume our political scientist is aware of the problems, does his job properly, and from data for the period 1966-1971 estimates $\alpha = 0.5$ and $\beta = 0.0$. He now can use Equations 1-3 together with his estimates of α and β to make the following predictions about future system behavior. (See Table 7A-1.)

Imagine a second political scientist who argues that his colleague has misspecified the system. Contrary to the latter's assumptions, he argues that the people's satisfaction is independent of actions undertaken by the government. Accordingly, Equation (3) should be amended as follows:

$$S_t = P_t \tag{3'}$$

Notice that when β is equal to zero the second political scientist's equations will yield predictions which are identical to those of the first theorist even though the stipulated structures are different. If two structures produce identical behavior strings, most data analysis strategies, e.g., regression analysis, will be of little help in providing criteria for choosing between the posited structures.

Since the consequences of having $S(t) = 0$ are usually thought to be undesirable, the results reflected in Table 7A-1 may be viewed with alarm. Accordingly, both political scientists might be asked for policy advice based upon their respective theories. However, the first set of equations suggest a course of policy which the second set of equations predicts will be irrelevant.

Table 7A-1
Results of Equations 1-3 when $\alpha = 0.5$ and $\beta = 0.0$

		$\alpha = 0.500$		$\beta = 0.000$	
	T	S(T)	P(T)	G(T)
	1966	1.000	0.000	0.000
Already	1967	0.500	0.500	0.000
Observed	1968	0.250	0.250	0.000
	1969	0.125	0.125	0.000
	1970	0.062	0.062	0.000
	1971	0.031	0.021	0.000
	1972	0.016	0.016	0.000
	1973	0.008	0.008	0.000
Predicted	1974	0.004	0.004	0.000
	1975	0.002	0.002	0.000
	1976	0.001	0.001	0.000
	1977	0.000	0.000	0.000
	1978	0.000	0.000	0.000

If the value of α could be increased to 0.8, the value of β raised to 3.0, and the level of $S(t)$ set at 1.0 for one time period (perhaps through the expenditure of vast resources), our first political scientist's equations predict that the people's satisfaction will rise in the quasigeometrical fashion traced in Table 7A-2. However, our second political scientist's equations predict that, after a few time intervals, such policy actions would have *no* impact on the level of the people's satisfaction (see Table 7A-3).

Table 7A-2
Effect of Raising α to 0.8 and β to 3.0 in Equations 1-3

	$\alpha = 0.800$	$\beta = 3.000$	
T	S(T)	P(T)	G(T)
1	1.000	0.000	0.000
2	3.200	0.800	2.400
3	7.840	2.560	5.280
4	17.408	6.272	11.136
5	36.890	13.926	22.963
6	76.267	29.512	46.756
7	155.521	61.014	94.507
8	314.625	124.417	190.208
9	633.549	251.700	381.849

Table 7A-3
Effect of Raising α to 0.8 and β to 3.0 in Equations 1-3′

	$\alpha = 0.800$		$\beta = 3.000$
T	S(T)	P(T)	G(T)
1	1.000	0.000	0.000
2	0.800	0.800	2.400
3	0.640	0.640	−0.480
4	0.512	0.512	−0.384
5	0.410	0.410	−0.307
6	0.328	0.328	−0.246
7	0.262	0.262	−0.197
8	0.210	0.210	−0.157
9	0.168	0.168	−0.126
10	0.134	0.134	−0.101
.	.	.	.
.	.	.	.
.	.	.	.
34	0.001	0.001	0.000
35	0.001	0.001	0.000
36	0.000	0.000	0.000
37	0.000	0.000	0.000

That is, while conventional data analysis techniques cannot distinguish among different structures which yield identical predictions for particular parameter and variable values, different structures will yield different predictions for some parameter and variable values and, as we have seen, differences among structures are important. Specifically while equations

$$S_t = P_t + G_t \tag{3}$$

$$S_t = P_t \tag{3′}$$

will be behaviorally indistinguishable when G (or β) is equal to zero, very different policies will be recommended if the level of satisfaction is a function of the government's performance (although observed government performance is equal to zero) than if satisfaction is unrelated to government performance.

While many uses of mathematics make no *quantitative* distinction between a variable having a value equal to zero and that variable being absent from the system, the theorist who is concerned with system identification in order to influence policy results must be sensitive to the *structural* differences between a variable being absent and a variable being present with value zero.

However, as we have seen, most data analysis strategies do not promote such a sensitivity since they cannot distinguish among structures which yield identical predictions. Rather, the theorist must stipulate the structure *prior* to performing the statistical manipulations. In the case of regression analysis, for example, there are rules for *parameter estimation* provided the *previously stipulated* structure is linear or linearized. As Cain and Watts point out: "Without a theoretical framework to provide order and a rationale for the large number of variables, we have no way of interpreting the statistical results."[63] Conventional analytic techniques cannot provide such a framework and, accordingly, are not sufficient for choosing among competing policy recommendations.

Notes

Published simultaneously in PUBLIC POLICY, Volume XXI, Number 1, by special arrangement.

An earlier version of this chapter was presented at the 1972 Midwest Regional Meetings of the International Studies Association and the Peace Research Society (International), Toronto, Ontario, May 11-13, 1972. We gratefully acknowledge the assistance of Donald L. Cook, Mason Frichette, and Vincent Winterland in the preparation of this manuscript as well as the advice and comments of John R. Champlin and William Harrison.

1. James A. Donovan, MILITARISM, U.S.A. (New York: Charles Scribner's Sons, 1970), p. 20.

2. James R. Kurth, "Aerospace Production Lines and American Defense Spending," hereafter cited as Kurth, "Aerospace Production Lines . . . "

3. James R. Kurth, "A Widening Gyre: The Logic of American Weapons Procurement," PUBLIC POLICY 19, no. 3, (Summer, 1971), p. 377; hereafter referred to as Kurth, PUBLIC POLICY. This article reports an earlier and somewhat more wide-ranging analysis on which his essay in this volume is based.

4. Ibid., p. 373.

5. Kurth, PUBLIC POLICY, pp. 373-404.

6. Ibid., pp. 395-401.

7. Kurth, "Aerospace Production Lines . . . "

8. Ibid.

9. Ibid.

10. Ibid.

11. Ibid.

12. See, e.g., Thomas C. Schelling, ARMS AND INFLUENCE. (New Haven: Yale University Press, 1966), Chapter 6.

13. It should be noted that Kurth rejects this operationalization: the proposed B-1 strategic manned bomber does not meet his strategic balance criterion.

14. Robert J. Art, "Why We Overspend and Underaccomplish," FOREIGN POLICY, No. 6 (Spring, 1972), p. 95.

15. Kurth, PUBLIC POLICY, p. 380. A problem of both theoretical consequence and substantial operational import is that of how to define a weapons *system* and that system's cost. First, it is unclear whether the $5 billion figure is restricted to the direct production costs of the weapon or whether it includes some proportion of R & D and/or indirect costs assignable to the system. Second, *estimated* costs are notoriously unreliable indicators of *actual* costs. Based on the experience of the 1960s, a system estimated to cost $1 billion and to be operational in 60 months can be expected actually to cost between $109 million and $688 million additional. (See: R.L. Perry, et al., SYSTEM ACQUISITION EXPERIENCE [RM-6072-PR], RAND Corporation, November, 1969, pp. 40-41.) Accordingly, it is important to specify more precisely to which set of costs the threshold dollar figure refers. Third and more importantly, the scope of the concept of weapons *system* requires elaboration. Thus, are the costs of the Poseidon and Minuteman launch vehicles included in the cost of the MIRV system? Are the costs of aircraft carriers and submarines included in the price of the F-14 and Polaris/Poseidon systems respectively? If the dollar threshold of a "major" procurement contract is, in the last analysis, arbitrary (but not unimportant) then these questions may be trivial. However, they do seem consequential for one's definition of the universe of major defense contractors and the relation between defense contractors and "production lines" which is at the heart of Kurth's "economic theory." For example, does the electric Boat Division of General Dynamics, which manufactures submarines, constitute a different and relevant production line from that part of General Dynamics which produces the F-111?

16. Morton H. Halperin, "The Good, the Bad, and the Wasteful," FOREIGN POLICY, No. 6, (Spring, 1972), p. 74.

17. Ibid., p. 80. However, Halperin also argues that the size of the annual defense budget is substantially independent of decisions regarding specific weapons programs, regardless of the specific part of the budget in which they are funded.

18. Cf. Kurth, "Corporate and Bureaucratic Imperatives."

19. See, e.g., the statement by Air Force Chief of Staff Ryan regarding an obscure research project to develop a "hard-target killer" capability, in U.S. Congress, House Committee on Appropriations, Subcommittee on Defense Appropriations. HEARINGS ON DEPARTMENT OF DEFENSE APPROPRIATIONS FOR 1970. 91st Congress, 1st Session, Part 7, p. 47.

20. Cf. Carl G. Hempel, ASPECTS OF SCIENTIFIC EXPLANATION, (New York: The Free Press, 1965), p. 123.

21. Kurth, "Aerospace Production Lines . . . "

22. Ibid. It should be noted that it would be difficult to routinely include contractors which hold DOD subcontracts since the Pentagon does not collect exhaustive data on subcontracting. See: William S. Rukeyser, "Where the Military Contracts Go," FORTUNE (August 1, 1969).

23. Kurth, "Aerospace Production Lines . . . "

24. This measure admittedly is insensitive to sole suppliers of relatively inexpensive items.

25. On the basis of *prime* contracts, Grumman ranks in the top ten in only three years. This is the same frequency as another firm which might be considered to be an airframe producer—LTV—which produces the A-7 attack aircraft, a weapons system omitted from Kurth's analysis.

26. Grumman was not counted as lowest-ranking except in those years in which it was among the top ten prime contractors.

27. See, Kurth, "Corporate and Bureaucratic Imperatives," and our note 15.

28. Kurth, "Aerospace Production Lines . . . " Note that "technocratic theories" which were separately identified in his earlier analysis no longer are explicitly distinguished.

29. See our note 6.

30. See, Kurth, PUBLIC POLICY, pp. 375-76.

31. Kurth appears to use the boundary between development and production as a surrogate for increased visibility. However, most programs become expensive—and therefore visible—during the later stages of development and testing, prior to being funded under the procurement section of the defense budget.

32. See: Kurth, PUBLIC POLICY, pp. 398-99.

33. Ibid., p. 399.

34. Cf. Kurth, "Corporate and Bureaucratic Imperatives."

35. Cf. G. Cain and H. Watts, "Problems in Making Policy Inferences from the Coleman Report," AMERICAN SOCIOLOGICAL REVIEW 35 (April, 1970), p. 229.

36. Kurth would be unlikely to accept this restriction; he seems to believe that the follow-on imperative reflects the reality of the decision-making process.

37. The former proposition assumes that the further along the development of a program, the more economically expensive and politically risky is cancellation. Accordingly, the further advanced the development of a program, the lower the probability that it will be cancelled. (Cf. Kurth, PUBLIC POLICY, p. 385). The difficulty of restricting production to one of two obviously duplicative weapons systems is typified by the decision to deploy both Thor and Jupiter IRBMs. See: Michael H. Armacost, THE POLITICS OF WEAPONS INNOVATION, (New York: Columbia University Press, 1969).

38. Arnold Kanter, "Presidential Power and Bureaucratic Compliance: Changing Organizational Objectives," paper prepared for delivery at the 1971 annual meeting of the American Political Science Association.

39. Cf. Kurth, "Aerospace Production Lines . . . "

40. If conscientious bidding for a contract is evidence of an open production line, Boeing was in such a position at the time the F-111 contract was let. See: Richard Austin Smith, "The $7-Billion Contract That Changes the Rules," FORTUNE (March-April, 1963).

41. A related problem emerges in Kurth's conceptualization of "redistributive change," a category which describes contracts which have the effect of redistributing defense contract awards among industrial sectors (Kurth, PUBLIC POLICY, p. 399). The ABM is said to be an example of redistributive change because the prime contractor—the Western Electric Division of AT&T—is not a major aerospace producer. This conclusion, however, seems to be the result of arbitrarily restrictive definitions. AT&T was the sixth largest *defense* contractor in FY 1969 and ninth largest for the period 1950-1964. (AEROSPACE FACTS AND FIGURES 1970, 1965) Moreover, the Safeguard ABM prime contract does not appear to represent a dramatic discontinuity with previous experience but, on the contrary, seems to be yet another follow-on contract awarded to Western Electric in a program of aircraft and missile defense which dates from the Nike-Ajax antiaircraft missiles of the early 1950s (JANE'S ALL THE WORLD'S AIRCRAFT, 1964/64). Cf. Kurth, "Aerospace Production Lines . . . "

42. Merton J. Peck and Frederic M. Scherer, THE WEAPONS ACQUISITION PROCESS: AN ECONOMIC ANALYSIS. (Boston: Harvard University School of Business Administration, 1962), p. v.

43. See: Alvin J. Harman, A METHODOLOGY FOR COST FACTOR COMPARISON AND PREDICTION (RM-6269-ARPA), RAND Corporation, August, 1970; and Kurth, ISA, Table 1.

44. See, Thomas S. Kuhn, THE STRUCTURE OF SCIENTIFIC REVOLUTIONS (Chicago: The University of Chicago Press, 1962).

45. Note that while Kurth employs the same criterion for choosing between the follow-on and the bail-out imperatives, his data suggest that the former theory is superior to the latter.

46. Cf. Charles F. Hermann, "Validation Problems in Games and Simulations with Special Reference to Models of International Politics," BEHAVIORAL SCIENCE 12, (1967), pp. 217f.

47. If stated as a hypothesis relating probabilities, the follow-on imperative would state something like: the larger the number of open production lines, and the greater the structural similarity between the contemplated system and a system previously produced on a presently open production line, the higher the probability that the system will be produced (and, as a corollary, the higher the probability that a contractor with an open production line will receive the contract).

48. The reader may object that our illustration is highly contrived: the inadequacies of theory$_2$'s point-in-time predictions are the result of that theory's predictions deviating from the observed values of "y" by a constant scale factor. Thus, proper parameter estimation would yield a theory which made highly accurate point-in-time predictions as well as superior policy predictions. However, consider the following illustration from Forrester in which the conflict between the two theoretical objectives cannot be resolved by improved parameter estimation. The "true" values of "y" are illustrated by the solid line. The

two theories are illustrated by the broken lines: theory$_1$ is a horizontal straight line and theory$_2$ is a slightly growing sinusoid which has a period of fluctuation about 25 percent shorter than that of the observed values of variable "y". Theory$_1$ yields better point-in-time predictions as measured by least squares.

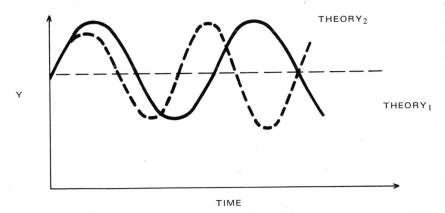

From Jay W. Forrester, INDUSTRIAL DYNAMICS (Cambridge: M.I.T. Press, 1961), p. 126. For problems of parameter estimation, see: Ronald Brunner, "Data Analysis, Process Analysis, and System Change," paper prepared for delivery at the 1970 Annual Meeting of the American Political Science Association.

49. Cf. Hermann's discussion of "face validity," p. 221.

50. Jay W. Forrester, "Counterintuitive Behavior of Social Systems," TECHNOLOGY REVIEW (January, 1971).

51. Harold Gershinowitz, "Applied Research for the Public Good—Suggestion," SCIENCE 176, No. 4033 (April 28, 1972), p. 381.

52. There are obvious problems in pushing the plausibility argument too hard. As Newell and Simon observe:

The plausibility of a fundamental hypothesis about the world is almost always time-dependent. Hypotheses are seldom thought plausible when they are new and have not yet been widely accepted. If empirical evidence supports an hypothesis increasingly, and if the hypothesis succeeds in providing explanations for a significant range of phenomena, it becomes more and more plausible.

Allen Newell and Herbert A. Simon, HUMAN PROBLEM SOLVING (Englewood Cliffs: Prentice-Hall, 1972), p. 19.

53. For a description of Delphi procedures, see, Olaf Helmer, SOCIAL TECHNOLOGY (New York: Basic Books, 1966).

54. For an extended treatment of these problems, see, G. Cain and H. Watts, "Problems in Making Policy Inferences from the Coleman Report," AMERICAN SOCIOLOGICAL REVIEW 35 (April, 1970), pp. 228-42.

..

55. Robert K. Merton, "The Unanticipated Consequences of Purposive Social Action," AMERICAN SOCIOLOGICAL REVIEW 1, No. 6 (1936), pp. 903-04.

56. Werner Heisenberg, "Quantum Theory and Its Interpretation," in S. Rozental, editor, NEILS BOHR: HIS LIFE AND WORK AS SEEN BY HIS FRIENDS AND COLLEAGUES (New York: John Wiley, 1967).

57. See: Kanter, "Presidential Power and Bureaucratic Compliance . . . "

58. This leads to a consideration of Kurth's distinction between the "official imperative" and the "follow-on" imperative (See: Kurth, "Aerospace Production Lines . . . "). The former argues that the most cost-effective bid will be awarded the contract. The latter argues that open production lines receive contracts, relatively independent of performance in design competition, and that such a contract will be structurally similar to the previous weapons system produced. However, a contractor's prior manufacturing experience with a structurally similar system would likely yield a unique expertise which would allow it to reduce anticipated production costs and, accordingly, to submit a low bid (in much the same way that a development contract usually gives a company an insurmountable competitive advantage when bidding for the production contract). Thus the *official* imperative would predict that on the basis of *economic* criteria most contracts which are awarded will be follow-on. The follow-on imperative as presently formulated requires that the recipient of the contract not submit the most cost-effective bid (however measured). Kurth's finding that in three of twenty-two cases contracts were awarded to companies other than those with the highest technical scores (without regard to dollar cost) fails to relate promised performance to the amount of the contract bid and therefore does not address the distinction.

59. Some indication of how little is understood about a firm's incentive structure and its responses to stimuli is given in the analysis of the Pentagon's experience with incentive contracts. See: Irving N. Fisher, A REAPPRAISAL OF INCENTIVE CONTRACTING EXPERIENCE (RM-5700-PR), RAND Corporation (July, 1968).

60. Kurth, PUBLIC POLICY, pp. 398-99.

61. Ibid., p. 398.

62. See our footnote 48.

63. Cain and Watts, p. 229.

8

The United States Senate and the Impact of Defense Spending Concentrations

Stephen Cobb[1]

For the past several years, one of the major controversies in sociology has concerned the question of how national policy is determined and by whom. Many authors have suggested that the foreign and domestic policy of the United States may be unduly influenced by what some have termed a "military-industrial complex," (Mills, 1956; Cook, 1962; and Lens, 1970). A quotation from Mills reveals many of the standard themes of these writers (1960:66-67):

Since the end of World War II many in elite circles have felt that economic prosperity in the U.S. is immediately underpinned by the war economy and that desparate economic—and so political—problems might well arise should there be disarmament and genuine peace. . . Leading corporations profit from the preparation of war. In so far as the corporate elite are aware of their profit interests—and that is their responsible business—they press for a continuation of their sources of profit, which often means a continuation of the preparation for war.

Mills in his work *The Power Elite* describes a society controlled in its important aspects by three major power centers acting in concert. They are the top military leaders, the big businessmen, and the highest governmental officials of the Executive Branch in Washington. Mills believed that these three groups controlled society for their mutual benefit. The basis of their coordination is not conspiracy but the overlapping of the interests of the major societal institutions they control.

According to this theory, the career interests of the high military officers lead them to support a large military establishment. Under conditions of peace and a small military machine such as we have had throughout much of the history of this country, the opportunities for advancement and satisfying careers are severely limited for the professional officer. The officer corps has repeatedly been the "victim" of massive cutbacks in defense spending at the termination of the various conflicts in which the United States has participated. In short, this thesis would maintain that top military officers need a high level of defense spending and the belligerent foreign policies which would justify that spending if their career possibilities are to be maximized and the presitge and importance of the military maintained.

The theory also suggests that the economic dependence of some private firms on government contracts for war materials leads them to work with military officers to keep up the level of defense spending.[2] Cook (1962) details at great length the governmental ties with big business which originated in connection with the "war effort" in the early 1940s and continued after the war. Lieberson (1971:564) notes the high number of former military officers employed by major defense contracting firms. Domhoff (1967) cites the interconnections among businessmen in different firms. In general, the economic power controlled by the defense industry is thought to be so large that cutbacks in its sector are feared to threaten the economic prosperity of the whole nation (Bolton, 1966). It is felt that the financial resources, public relations abilities, and political connections of business afford it an ability to influence or control government officials and office-holders responsible for making decisions regarding a broad range of national policies.

High governmental officials are hypothesized to be in favor of actions which increase their power and importance. Any type of situation that resembles war has always strengthened the hand of the Executive Branch in this country. Furthermore, many of the top leaders in government are actually businessmen spending a few years in "public service." They would share the interest of their business colleagues in economic prosperity.

Sympathetic authors such as Cook (1962) and Lens (1970) add new elements to the military-industrial complex model. Both Lens and Cook give considerable attention to the fact that major labor leaders have come to share at least as much benefit as top business leaders from the high levels of defense spending that have prevailed in recent years. Without government defense contracts, many union members would be at least temporarily laid off, and areas like California would become severely depressed unless massive rehabilitation programs were undertaken. Therefore, it is in the best interests of organized labor to promote the military-industrial complex.

Lens (1970) also adds a discussion of what he terms "academia in harness." He notes the extreme dependence of many scientists on government funds in general and on the more lavishly available Pentagon funds in particular. Scientists who need large sums of money for their research (such as experimental nuclear scientists or survey method sociologists) may be tempted to find it in their own best interests to keep the defense dollars coming. In addition, it is likely that even nonresearch-oriented college administrators in need of government funds for their institutions and needy graduate students being offered *National Defense* Education Act fellowships and loans, will come to see a certain propriety in present governmental spending policies.

In general the "military-industrial complex" is felt by all these theorists to be pressuring Congressmen, Senators, and members of the Executive Branch both directly and by generating support for aggressive foreign policies and larger defense spending among the general public. The government is induced to act more belligerently than it might and purchase more defense equipment than might be needed.

One specific hypothesis which may be derived from the notion of a military-industrial complex is that members of Congress are being pressured specifically to vote for high levels of defense spending and aggressive foreign policies by the forces discussed in the preceding paragraphs. As Turner (1951) has noted, Congressmen and Senators are usually quite responsive to the major, organized members of their constituencies. As noted, Bolton (1966) has shown the size and importance of the defense industry.

As we have noted elsewhere, (Cobb, 1969: 358-59):

The implications of this theory are very serious. It predicts an electorate becoming increasingly militant and chauvinistic in response to the appeals of businessmen and military leaders. More importantly, this belligerence of public utterance combined with heavy armaments purchases is likely to stimulate similar actions on the part of other countries, which in turn can be used to justify still further armaments increases on our part, and so tension spirals upward.

Defense Spending and Congressional Voting

There have been a number of empirical studies of the relationship between defense spending and congressional voting in several areas. Cobb (1969 and 1972) has studied this relationship in the House of Representatives. He found almost no evidence that concentrations of defense spending had an influence on how members of the House voted on a series of foreign policy issues he labeled "the jingoism scales." The only exception to this general lack of relationship occurred among the representatives with a great deal of seniority and, to a lesser degree, among those who were members of important House committees such as Ways and Means or Armed Services.

Investigations into this relationship have also been performed for the United States Senate. Gray and Gregory (1968) found there were small but statistically significant (Tau) correlations between their measure of defense spending based on total military spending as a percentage of total income in a state and two of their five voting scales. Correlations of -0.14 (in the expected direction) were found between defense spending and their scale of "liberalism" and between defense spending and their scale entitled "foreign aid-test ban." Three other scales including one labeled "cold war-ethnocentrism" were not significantly related to defense spending. They used votes from the 88th Congress (1963-64).

Russett (1970) investigated the relationship between several different measures of defense spending and several scales of Senate voting.[3] He was concerned with the 87th Congress (1961-62) and the 90th Congress (1967-68). For the 87th Congress he constructed three separate Guttman scales covering somewhat different content areas which he called "general defense," "military assistance," and "aerospace." For the 90th Congress he constructed four scales entitled "general defense," "NASA," "gun control," and "arms sales."

For the 87th Congress, Russett found that his general defense scale was significantly correlated with only one of the five measures of defense spending he used. Using a rank-order correlation (Kendall's Tau), he obtained a figure of 0.14 (in the expected direction) between this scale and Department of Defense military payrolls index.[4] When he controlled for region, his only significant correlation disappeared leaving no significant correlations between defense spending and the general defense scale of Senate voting. When controlled for party, the correlation between Defense Department military payrolls increased to 0.21 and a formerly nonsignificant correlation between Defense Department civilian payrolls and general defense became significant (0.13).

There were other significant correlations between various measures of defense spending and his other two scales, military assistance and aerospace. However, the direction of the correlations presented an unstable pattern in that it would be in the expected direction (positive) in one instance and in a direction conflicting with Russett's hypothesis in another. Perhaps the most consistent finding was that prime contract awards showed no correlation with any scale under any controlled or uncontrolled conditions.

For the 90th Congress, Russett found somewhat more impressive evidence of a relationship between defense spending and voting. He found that both military and civilian Defense Department payroll indices showed significant or near-significant (if relatively small) relationships with the general defense scale. This pattern held up under uncontrolled conditions and when party or region was controlled. The correlations range from 0.11 to 0.28. Again, he found no relationship between prime contract allocation and voting on the general defense scale. He also found no relationship between three other measures of defense spending and voting on this scale. Several of his defense spending measures were correlated with NASA voting. The figures ranged from below 0.10 to 0.17 (in the expected direction). There were considerably fewer correlations between spending and the arms sales scale (ranging from below 0.11 to 0.14). The relationships were somewhat higher between various measures of spending and voting on the gun control scale (ranging up to −0.27) but were not consistent in direction. He concludes;

Clearly, Department of Defense expenditures for military installations go to support and reinforce if not to promote a set of hawkish and strongly anti-communist postures in American political life, (Russett, 1970:75).

Later he adds:

The correlations are not, it must be noted, astonishingly high—nor did our original expectations, which recognized the data handicap of using heterogeneous states as units of analysis and identified the probable sources of many deviations from the simplest expectations, anticipate very high correlations, (Russett, 1970:77).

In short, though his pattern of correlations appears rather weak and somewhat inconsistent, he concludes that there is support for the hypothesis that defense spending concentrations do affect the voting of U.S. Senators. His results and the results of Gray and Gregory contradict those of Cobb to the degree that the limited pattern of significant correlations in the former studies is taken as support for the basic hypothesis of these studies. In this paper, we shall investigate the relationship between senate voting and defense spending and try to resolve the discrepancies between the previous studies.

The Jingoism Scales

We have constructed two separate scales of roll-call votes in the United States Senate. Based on roll-call votes from the first session of the 89th Congress (1965) and the first session of the 90th Congress (1967), we have been able to develop two five-item Guttman scales which we interpret to reflect dimensions of jingoism analogous to those reported in Cobb (1969 and 1972).

The years 1965 and 1967 were chosen because defense spending data were readily available for the years and because there were votes on relevant issues in the Senate with sufficient variance to allow us to attempt to construct a Guttman scale. Further, it was of some interest to correlate the analysis of the Senate with the earlier analyses of the House (Cobb, 1969 and 1972) in order to eliminate differences in years as a possible source of different findings.

Investigation of the relationship between defense spending and voting is perhaps more difficult in that states are very large and heterogeneous. It is unlikely that a state will be as dependent on any one industry as can be the case in some congressional districts. However, there are a number of reasons for studying the Senate including that body's historic concern with foreign and defense policy. Even today the Foreign Relations Committee is accorded the highest prestige. The senate shares with the House the power of the purse. The cost of foreign and defense policy today is very great. This increases the potential importance of the legislature in the conduct of foreign affairs and increases the need to understand voting patterns on these issues.

The Democrats and the Republicans could be scaled together in both 1965 and 1967. We interpret this to mean that members of both parties view these issues as representing points along the same dimension and that they felt that the particular issues were ordered along that dimension in one particular array.

Measuring Defense Spending

We have computed six measures of defense spending: one was based on Pentagon-supplied figures on defense-created jobs and one on FY 1964 data, and

Table 8-1
The 1965 Senate Jingoism Scale

Number	Issue	Difficulty[a] (Percent)
CQA 155[b]	Young Amendment to reduce $124,370,000 Defense Department civil defense funds to $97,190,000 as passed by the House[c]	15
CQA 28	Foreign Relations Committee amendment to reduce Arms Control and Disarmament Agency funds from $40 million to $20 million	41
CQA 12	Appropriations Committee move to strike House prohibition of Food for Peace sales to Egypt and substitute a somewhat less restrictive clause	49
CQA 90	Miller Amendment to prohibit aid to any country more than 1 year behind in its payment of U.N. assessments unless President determines and reports otherwise	67
CQA 29	Passage of bill authorizing $20 million for the Arms Control and Disarmament Agency	84

The coefficient of reproducibility is 0.944.

[a]Difficulty is measured by the percentage of all Senators who voted in a nonjingoistic manner. All signs of intent were used including voting, pairing, the announcement of preference, and responses to the CQA poll.

[b]CQA refers to the Congressional Quarterly Almanac.

[c]"Yes" votes on items 1, 3, and 5 were considered nonjingoistic while "no" votes on items 2, and 4 were considered nonjingoistic.

both will be correlated with the 1965 jingoism scale; four were based on FY 1967 data and will be correlated with the 1967 jingoism scale. It would be preferable to have to compute only one, accurate measure of defense spending reflecting jobs generated in an area as a percentage of total employment or similar figure for each year of the study. This has not been possible because the Pentagon will not release detailed and accurate data on things like subcontracting, which would make the computation of such figures possible. These data are not available because of security considerations and because the government desires to protect the proprietary information of the companies which furnished it to the government in confidence.

The first measure is called "defense involvement" or DI and is defined as the total value of all Defense Department prime contracts allocated to a state as a percentage of the total value added by manufacture in that state.[5] The value of

Table 8-2
The 1967 Senate Jingoism Scale

Number	Issue[b]	Difficulty[a] (Percent)
CQA 91	Selective Service Act of 1967. Morse Amendment to permit a registrant to be represented by a lawyer when appearing before his draft board	21
CQA 106	Selective Service Act of 1967. Adoption of the conference report extending draft and forbidding the institution of a lottery	24
CQA 156	Tower Amendment restoring authorization of Department of Defense revolving funds for arms sales aid	49
CQA 46	Mundt move to prevent pending consular treaty with the Soviet Union from taking effect until the President determined that U.S. troops were no longer needed in South Vietnam or that U.S. troop removal was not being hampered or delayed by Soviet military aid to North Vietnam	72
CQA 79	Amendment declaring that Congress would provide all necessary support to U.S. servicemen fighting in Vietnam and that Congress supported (1) persons trying to bring about an honorable settlement in Vietnam and (2) persons trying to convene an international meeting to plan an end to the War	79

The coefficient of reproducibility is 0.94.

[a]Difficulty is measured as the percentage of all Senators who voted (or paired, announced, etc.) against the jingoistic vote.

[b]A "yes" vote on issues 1 and 5 was considered nonjingoistic. "No" votes on all other issues were considered nonjingoistic.

the prime contracts is divided by this measure of industrial activity because the impact of a contract of a given size would vary depending upon how large a percentage of the state's economy it constituted.

An important defect involved in using prime contract data as an indicator of defense spending concentrations is that approximately 50 percent of all prime contracts are in turn subcontracted out to another firm. These subcontracting firms may be, but often are not, in the same state as the firm to which the contract was originally let. Therefore, knowing where a prime contract is allocated is not the same as knowing where the money involved is actually spent and has its impact. It is possible that public announcements of contracts by important political figures may help to overcome this difficulty to some extent by making the Senator and his constituents feel dependent on these contracts even when a part is to be subcontracted out of the state. Bolton (1966:17) discusses these problems in greater detail.

$$DI \quad = \quad \frac{\text{prime contract value–fiscal 1964}}{\text{value added by manufacture}}$$

Cobb (1969) discusses other types of errors which may be expected when using prime contract and value added by manufacture statistics. The measures used in his article are analogous to the first two measures of defense spending we utilize in this paper.

The second measure of defense spending is defined as total number of defense generated jobs in a state divided by the total state work force. It is entitled "defense dependency" or *DD*.

$$DD \quad = \quad \frac{\text{total state defense generated jobs}}{\text{total state work force}}$$

Buehler (1967) reports a defense dependency score by states which we have utilized. His figures for *DD* include work done on all prime contracts over $10,000, all military and civilian employment at defense installations, and an estimated 12 percent of the total indirect employment generated in everything from raw materials to finished product manufacture (DOD Bulletin, 1966). It includes subcontracted work only at the top 400 companies (in terms of defense contract allocation) surveyed. This measure is based on data gathered by the Pentagon's Economic Information System's Plantwide Economic Report and Individual Project Report Program which were begun in 1966.

The next measure of defense spending is based on the allocation of military prime contracts for FY 1967. It is entitled "defense involvement (military)" or *DIM* and is defined as the total value of military prime contracts allocated to a state as a percentage of the total value added by manufacture.

$$DIM \quad = \quad \frac{\text{military prime contracts–fiscal 1967}}{\text{value added by manufacture}}$$

The effects in this measure are similar to those discussed with regard to *DI*. Prime contracts are often subcontracted out in whole or part and our data do not contain information on this subcontracting. Therefore, this measure does not indicate as well as might be hoped where defense spending actually becomes wages and profits. The problems associated with the use of "value added by manufacture" are present. It should be noted that unlike *DI* which is based on both military and civil functions prime contracts together, *DIM* is based only on the military prime contract.

There is another source of error in this indicator. The numerator is taken from the fiscal year in question (fiscal 1967) while the denominator comes from the 1963 Census of Manufactures. If, for example, all areas did not grow at an equal rate between 1964 and 1967, some error will be introduced.[6] Due to the short period of time involved, the error is likely to be minimal.

The second measure of defense spending is called "defense involvement (civilian)" or *DIC*. *DIC* is the total value of civil functions prime contracts as a percentage of the total industrial activity, again measured by "value added by manufacture" in the state.

$$DIC \quad = \quad \frac{\text{civil functions prime contracts--fiscal 1967}}{\text{value added by manufacture}}$$

The problems associated with this measure are approximately the same as were discussed with reference to *DIM*. The reason for creating a separate index based on civil functions contracts was to determine if the absence of correlations between prime contracts and voting found in certain studies (Cobb, 1969 and 1972), was attributable to the fact that civil functions prime contracts might be less visible or dramatic in their impact on a district, and hence serve to reduce the correlation between spending and voting.

The third measure of defense spending is called "defense dependency (military)" or *DDM*. It is defined as the total military payroll in a state as a percentage of the total income of that state.

$$DDM \quad = \quad \frac{\text{total military payroll--fiscal 1967}}{\text{total income}}$$

The figure for the total income of the state is based on the 1960 census figures. The military payrolls are taken from Pentagon data furnished for FY 1967. If income has grown unevenly among the states, some error will be introduced.

The final measure of defense spending is called "defense dependence (civilian)" or *DDC*. This is defined as the total Department of Defense payrolls in a state paid to civilian employees as a percentage of the total income of the state.

$$DDC \quad = \quad \frac{\text{total civilian payroll--fiscal 1967}}{\text{total income}}$$

The difficulties with this measure are the same as those experienced with *DDM*. The advantage of separating the two kinds of payrolls again hinges on the possibility that military payrolls have a more obvious impact on a district. The shopkeeper who lives by the trade of uniformed military personnel is perhaps somewhat more likely to be aware of the source of his prosperity than is the merchant whose customers are civilian employees of the Department of Defense.

Findings

Table 8-3 lists a series of correlations between defense spending (*DI* and *DD*) and the 1965 Senate jingoism scale under various controlled conditions. None of the

Table 8-3
Correlations Between 1965 Senate Voting and Measures of Defense Spending

Correlation Type[a]	N=99 DD	DI	Criterion[b]
Uncontrolled	−0.029	0.074	−0.197
Controlled for Region[c]	−0.040	0.038	−0.195
Controlled for Party[c]	−0.072	0.058	−0.195
Controlled for Region and Party	−0.120	0.007	−0.193

[a]All correlations, except when otherwise noted, are product-moment.

[b]The criterion level is the level a correlation must attain to be statistically significant at the 0.05 level.

[c]Coded and entered by means of dummy variables.

correlation coefficients shown in Table 8-3 are significant at the 0.05 level. Party and region (coded as a series of dummy variables) were expected to show a strong relationship with voting on our scales (Turner, 1951). Therefore, it was conceivable that the effects of these variables might have been obscuring a small but statistically significant relationship between *DI* and 1965 jingoism or *DD* and 1965 jingoism. However, Table 8-3 shows that even when controls are imposed, in no case does the relationship between spending and voting reach the level of statistical signficance.[7]

Half of the small correlations found in Table 8-3 do not have the expected sign. From the method of construction of our scales of Senate voting it is clear that the correlation between spending and voting should be strongly negative if our hypothesis of a relationship is true. In the case of the relationship between jingoism 1965 and *DD*, the correlations are in the expected direction though not statistically significant. In the case of the relationship between 1965 jingoism and *DI*, the correlation coefficients are both statistically nonsignificant and in the wrong direction. Even if they were significant, they could hardly be viewed as confirmation of our hypothesis. Were we to find significant, positive correlations we would be forced to conclude that the more dependent a Senator is on defense spending, the less likely he is to vote for belligerent, jingoistic foreign policies. While extremely interesting, if a pattern of such correlations were found it would not constitute support of our original hypothesis.

Therefore, we find in Table 8-3 no support for the hypothesis that the votes of United States Senators on the foreign and defense policy issues listed in our 1965 jingoism scale are influenced by the amount of defense spending in their districts. This result does not really contradict the findings of Russett for 1961-62. He finds few significant correlations in the expected direction between his various measures of defense spending and his scales, especially the important general defense scale (Russett, 1970:72).

Table 8-4

Correlations Between 1967 Senate Voting on Jingoism Scale and Several Measures of Defense Spending with Controls

Correlation Type	DIM	DIC	DDM	DDC	Criterion
		N = 99			
Uncontrolled	0.138	0.165	−0.036	−0.007	−0.197
Controlled for Region	0.145	0.247*	0.002	−0.021	−0.195
Controlled for Party	0.083	0.107	−0.107	−0.081	−0.195
Controlled for Party and Region	0.065	0.210*	−0.021	−0.059	−0.193

*Statistically significant.

Table 8-4 reports a series of correlations between defense spending measures based on 1967 data and voting on the 1967 Senate jingoism scale. For the Senate as a whole, only two of the correlations are significant at the 0.05 level. These two significant relationships are between dependency on civil functions prime contracts and voting controlled for region and controlled for region and party. These two significant correlations are not in the expected direction. The interpretation would have to be that a Senator from a dependent state would be less likely to vote for jingoistic foreign policy measures. This would not support our hypothesis. Russett found no instances of significant correlations between prime contract allocation and voting either in 1961-62 or 1967-68.

All of the correlations between prime contract data and voting are in a direction which does not confirm our hypothesis. Seven of eight correlations between defense spending measures based on 1967 payrolls (*DDM* and *DDC*) are in the expected direction. None, however, are statistically significant. Therefore, we find no support in Table 8-4 for the hypothesis that the votes of United States Senators on foreign policy issues studied are influenced by the amount of defense spending in their states. The findings of Table 8-4 are in partial disagreement with the findings of Russett. He too found no relationship between voting and prime contract allocation. He did however find a series of small but significant rank-order correlations between voting and spending measures based on payrolls of the Department of Defense.

Table 8-5
Variance Explained in 1965 Senate Voting on the Jingoism Scale by Independent Variables in a Given Order

Variable	N=99 Percent of Variance	Sign
Party Affiliation	6.2	−
Region Represented	20.9	
DI	0.0	

When entered in this order, region makes the largest contribution to the explanation of variance in the 1965 jingoism scale. Party explains a substantial portion of the total explained variance, though it is not as powerful as region. When *DI* is added, no additional variance in the jingoism scale is explained. Though not a surprising finding in view of the pattern of correlations found in previous tables, it reinforces those findings.

Table 8-6
Variance Explained in 1965 Senate Voting on the Jingoism Scale by Independent Variables in a Given Order

Variable	N=99 Percent of Variance	Sign
Party	6.2	−
Region	20.9	
DD	1.0	−

Table 8-6 reports the use of a substantially similar test, this time using *DD* as the measure of defense spending. *DD* explains 1 percent of the variance in the 1965 jingoism scale after that attributable to party and region has been removed. It is consistent with Russett's findings to have a larger effect for a jobs-based measure of defense spending than for prime contracts. The effect in this table, though present, is not large.

Table 8-7 reports the results of a similar regression computation explaining the 1967 jingoism scale and using 1967 defense spending measures. Party and region are first entered and the variance explained by them listed. *DIT*, the measure of defense spending used here, is a composite of *DIM* and *DIC* representing the total military and civil functions prime contracts in a state as a percentage of the value added by manufacture in that state. Party explains almost 11 percent of the variance in 1967 jingoism while region explains about 15 percent. *DIT* explains only an additional ½ of 1 percent.

Table 8-7

Variance Explained in Senate Voting on 1967 Jingoism by Independent Variables in a Given Order

| | $N=99$ | |
Variable	Percent of Variance	Sign
Party Affiliation	10.7	−
Region Represented	14.7	
DIT	0.5	+

Table 8-8

Variance Explained in 1967 Senate Voting on Jingoism by Independent Variables in a Given Order

| | $N=99$ | |
Variable	Percent of Variance	Sign
Party Affiliation	10.7	−
Region Represented	14.7	
DDT	0.0	

Table 8-8 is identical to Table 8-7 except that the defense spending measure used is *DDT*. *DDT* is the total dependency on both military and civilian payrolls measured as a percentage of total state income. *DDT* adds no additional variance to that explained by region and party. This finding is not consistent with Russett's findings in that he found that payroll based spending indices (such as our *DDM, DDC,* and *DDT*) were better able to explain voting than prime contract allocation based indices (such as our *DIM, DIC,* and *DIT*). While the spending figures in our study for 1965 and 1967 are not perfectly comparable, the findings in Table 8-7 and 8-8 appear to be inconsistent with our findings reported in Tables 8-5 and 8-6. In short, while *DIT* did show a small effect on 1967 jingoism, these two tables give little support to the contention that there is a relationship between defense spending and the way a Senator votes on foreign and defense policy issues.

We hypothesized that membership on a powerful committee or high seniority would be related to spending and voting and would serve to obscure the relationship between voting and spending (Cobb, 1972). We therefore correlated *DI* and *DD* with the 1965 jingoism scale under controlled conditions. The partial correlations and the zero-order relationship for comparison are reported in Table 8-9. None of the correlations obtained were significant at the 0.05 level. Table 8-10 reports similar tests for the 1967 data.

In this table, the correlations between *DIC* and voting on the 1967 jingoism scale and *DIM* and jingoism are larger than those reported between *DI* and the

Table 8-9

Correlations Between Senate Voting on 1965 Jingoism and Measures of Defense Spending

Correlation Type	$N = 99$		
	DI	DD	Criterion
Uncontrolled	0.074	−0.029	−0.197
Controlled for Membership on Important Committees[a]	0.069	−0.032	−0.195
Controlled for Seniority	0.071	−0.050	−0.195

[a]For the purposes of this study, the important committees are Appropriations, Foreign Relations, and Armed Services.

Table 8-10

Correlations Between Senate Voting on 1967 Jingoism Scale and Various Measures of Defense Spending

Correlation Type	DIM	DIC	DDM	DDC	Criterion
Uncontrolled	0.138	0.165	−0.036	−0.007	−0.197
Controlled for Membership on Important Committees	0.139	0.169	−0.003	−0.040	−0.195
Controlled for Seniority	0.135	0.205[a]	−0.005	−0.051	−0.195

[a]Statistically significant but not in the expected direction.

1965 jingoism scale. However, they like those between *DI* and 1965 jingoism are not in the expected direction and, hence, do not confirm the hypothesis. The only significant correlation in Table 8-10 (between *DIC* and 1967 jingoism controlled for seniority) is not in the expected direction. Tables 8-9 and 8-10 do not lend much support to the hypothesis.

It could be hypothesized that those Senators whose power and seniority were especially needed to pass defense and foreign policy would be especially likely to be rewarded with the allocation of defense spending to their states if they voted jingoistically. Cobb (1972) has demonstrated such a pattern in the House of Representatives. We have divided our sample into two groups; those with high seniority and those with less. In this manner we hoped to uncover any relationship between spending and voting that might be occurring in only one of the groups. The results are reported in the first part of Table 8-11 and do not lend support to the original hypothesis for the 1965 jingoism scale and the measures of spending shown. The correlations between *DI* and jingoism (1965) remain small and in the direction opposite that expected. While the correlation between spending and voting was higher and in the expected direction among the nonsenior members of the senate, the coefficients are not statistically

Table 8-11

Correlations Between Senate Voting on 1965 Jingoism Scale and Measures of Defense Spending

Power Group	N	DI	DD	Criterion
Whole Senate[a]	99	0.074	−0.029	−0.197
Senior Members	54	0.069	−0.033	−0.268
Nonsenior Members	45	0.036	−0.116	−0.294
Powerful Committee Members	54	0.138	0.071	−0.268
Nonpowerful Committee Members	45	0.000	−0.127	−0.294

[a]Mean number of terms in the Senate for this group is 3.97 (almost 24 years). The mean for the nonsenior group is 1.61 terms (almost 10 years).

[b]Member of the Appropriations, Foreign Relations, or Armed Services Committees.

Table 8-12

Correlations Between Senate Voting on 1967 Jingoism Scale and Measures of Defense Spending

Power Groups	N	DIM	DIC	DDM	DDC	Criterion
			N=99			
Whole Senate	99	0.138	0.165	−0.036	−0.007	−0.197
Senior Members	54	0.145	0.193	−0.018	−0.126	−0.268
Nonsenior Members	45	0.063	0.222	−0.130	−0.499[a]	−0.294
Powerful Committee Members	54	0.217	0.196	−0.031	0.005	−0.268
Nonpowerful Committee Members	45	0.057	0.134	−0.050	−0.012	−0.294

[a]Statistically significant.

significant. It should be noted that the correlation which was higher was not the figure which was expected to increase.

The Senate was also divided by committee membership. Those Senators who were members of powerful committees might be expected to be especially likely to be rewarded for jingoistic voting. The correlations reported in the second part of Table 8-11 do not support this belief and therefore provided no support for the original hypothesis.

Table 8-12 reports the results of similar tests with the 1967 defense spending and voting data. The correlations based on prime contract measures of defense spending are not significant and are positive. Most of the correlations based on payroll measures of spending are in the expected negative direction. However, only one of them is statistically significant. It is somewhat surprising to find that the correlation between the 1967 jingoism scale and a spending measure based on civilian payrolls is larger than that between 1967 jingoism and military payrolls. This correlation appears to be essentially random and generates little confidence in the original hypothesis in the face of the lack of significant correlations in most of the other attempts.

Table 8-13
Mean Change in *DI-DIT* by Changes in Jingoism[a]

	N=99	
Group	N	Mean Change
Those Who Became Less Jingoistic	29	0.111
Those Who Stayed the Same in Jingoism	31	0.083
Those Who Became More Jingoistic	39	−0.003
Total Sample	99	0.057

[a]Change = 1967 *DIT* − 1964 *DI*.

Before attempting to draw final conclusions, we shall examine two tables which make use of the limited over-time changes possible with our data. For Table 8-13, we have divided our sample into three approximately equal groups, on the basis of a comparison between their 1965 jingoism and their 1967 jingoism scores. The first group is comprised of those whose jingoism scores went up between 1965 and 1967.[8] This indicates that the Senator became less jingoistic in his voting between the years. The second group is comprised of those whose scores remained the same, while the final group had scores which decreased, indicating that they were voting in a more jingoistic manner. If our original hypothesis is true, we should expect to find that those Senators who became more jingoistic should have a greater increase in dependence on defense spending than the other groups. That is, we would expect that as a man became more jingoistic, he would be rewarded by the allocation of more military funds to his state.

Inspection of Table 8-13 indicates that this expectation is not supported by the data. What effect there is operates in a manner contrary to our expectations. Those whose voting became less jingoistic were on the average more dependent on defense spending. Those who became more jingoistic in their voting were on the average slightly less dependent on defense spending in their areas. Those whose voting had remained the same had become more dependent upon defense spending, though to a lesser degree, than those who became less jingoistic. This pattern lends little support to the contention that military spending concentrations influence Senators to vote more jingoistically.

Table 8-14
Mean Change in *DI* by Power Groups[a]

Power Group	N	Mean Change in *DI*
Whole Senate	99	0.045
Senior Members	54	0.037
Nonsenior Members	45	0.046
Powerful Committee Members	54	0.053
Nonpowerful Committee Members	45	0.031

[a]Change—1967 *DIM*—1964 *DI*. This measure will probably underestimate changes slightly.

Table 8-14 is an attempt to determine whether Senators with high seniority, or those who are members of powerful committees, are more likely over-time to see jingoistic voting rewarded by increases in defense spending in their states, sufficient to increase the dependence of those states on that spending. The findings again lend little support to the original hypothesis. Those who are members of powerful committees are more likely to increase their dependence on defense spending more than those who are not members of such committees. However, those with high seniority are actually increasing their dependence on defense spending less than those with less seniority. The first result supports the original hypothesis while the latter does not.

Conclusions

The findings reported in this paper do not support the contention that defense spending concentrations have a significant influence on the manner in which Senators vote on issues in the area of foreign policy. In the first place, of all the correlations reported, only *one* was significant in the hypothesized direction. There were in addition three significant correlations whose signs precluded their consideration as support for the original hypothesis.

In the second place, the pattern of correlations—significance tests aside—was rather inconsistent. In one instance a correlation will be found to be small but in the hypothesized direction, while in another instance, in which controls are introduced in some manner, the correlation reverses and becomes positive. These reversals do not appear to have a meaningful interpretation.

Our findings support the conclusions reached by earlier studies of the House of Representatives (Cobb, 1969, and 1972), but conflict with at least the interpretations of the findings of the earlier studies of the Senate (Gray and Gregory, 1968, and Russett, 1970).

In a communication to the *Journal of Conflict Resolution*, Russett (1970b) discusses the possible reasons for the differences found between his study of the Senate and my earlier study of the House (1969). While not designed to be a replication of Russett's work, in this paper we have been able to reduce in some measure the number of possible explanations for the differences found in these two studies. Russett lists six possible differences:[9]

1. Different subjects of analysis—Russett studied the Senate while Cobb studied the House.
2. Different dependent variables—Russett used a long Guttman scale for each of several dimensions while Cobb utilized a short, six-item, one-dimensional Guttman Scale.
3. Different sources for the data—Published sources of data differ though data appears to be the same. The denominator differs in that Russett uses total income while Cobb uses value added by manufacture.
4. Different years under examination—Russett studied the 87th (1961-62) and the 90th (1967-68) Congresses while Cobb studied the 89th first session (1965).
5. Different correlation coefficients and underlying statistical assumptions—Russett used rank-order correlations (Kendall's tau) while Cobb used product moment and other interval measures.
6. Different treatment of independent variables—Russett disaggregated defense spending by creating several separate measures while Cobb used only two, one of which was based on prime contracts.

The present study eliminates *point one,* since the subject of our analysis is also the United States Senate.

With regard to *point two*, in this study we rely on a short, five item scale which is not identical to Russett's longer ones. Also there is only one scale for each year studied while Russett included several. However, inspection reveals that our 1967 jingoism scale contains three of the same items Russett includes in his basic 1967-68 general defense scale and that one of our items is included in his arms sales abroad scale. In short, four out of five items on our scale appear in Russett's scales. As he states in this rejoinder (Russett, 1970b) to the earlier article on the House (Cobb, 1969), this is probably *not* an important point of difference between our earlier work on the House and his work, since we appear to be measuring essentially the same phenomenon. ("While I cannot establish the fact with certainty, it is very likely that Cobb and I measured essentially the same phenomenon and that his scale and mine would correlate highly with each other. . . ." Russett, 1970b). By 1972, however, Russett had apparently changed his mind. In a criticism of an earlier draft of this paper he stated, "I doubt that we are in fact measuring the same thing." This criticism, which he terms his most important one, does not appear to be warranted on the basis of any change in the content of the scales from 1969 to the present work.

Point three discusses the source and to some degree the nature of the measure of defense spending employed in the analysis. While some of Russett's measures are different from those utilized in the present study, and his use of total income rather than value added by manufacture as a denominator when dealing with prime contract based measures remains a difference, the two most important measures in his study appear to be identical with our *DDM* and *DDC* (Russett, 1970:59-61). Thus, while some difference exists between his data and ours, sufficient overlap exists to enable judgments to be made as to the importance of this factor in creating differing results.[10]

While certain differences remain with regard to the years under study (*point four*), the 1967 jingoism scale is essentially drawn from the same year as the later Russett scales. Russett includes items from both the first and second sessions of the 90th Congress, while we use items only from the first session. Our 1965 jingoism scale is somewhat later than the first Russett scale. Our spending data appear to be drawn from approximately the same time period with regard to the analysis for the later scale (1967 versus 1967 and 1968 for Russett).[11]

The basic difference with regard to the statistic employed to ascertain the relationship between spending and voting remains in this paper as it did in the earlier study of the House. We have used the product-moment correlation, with its assumptions of linear relationship and interval level of measurement, while Russett uses the Kendall's tau with its rank-order assumptions. In the following discussion, we do not wish to suggest that Russett was in error when he used the tau correlation, but that he *was* in error when he objected to the use of the product-moment correlation in the earlier study of the House and presumably to its use in this paper. We have continued the use of the product-moment statistic because it is as important to us to replicate our earlier study of the House (1969) as it is to replicate Russett's later study of the Senate (1970).

Russett (1970b) objects to what he terms the unwarranted use of interval level procedures. He states, "The distribution of military spending by state is notably skewed, with a few states such as Alaska emerging as extreme outliers. Under these conditions, with interval correlations, the outliers exert extreme influence on the presence or absence of an apparent relationship."

Statistically, his contention is true, but an examination of Figures 8-1 and 8-2 would indicate that elimination of the highly dependent states would not materially affect the correlation, except to raise the strength of the relationship necessary to attain statistical significance. Contrary to Russett's contention, examination of these figures does not constitute "lopping off outliers" when the preferred procedure would have been to "normalize the distribution by some transformation, such as $\log_{10}$." What it does constitute is a refutation of the statistically plausible but factually inaccurate contention that the "extreme outliers" in this case greatly affect the correlation coefficient.

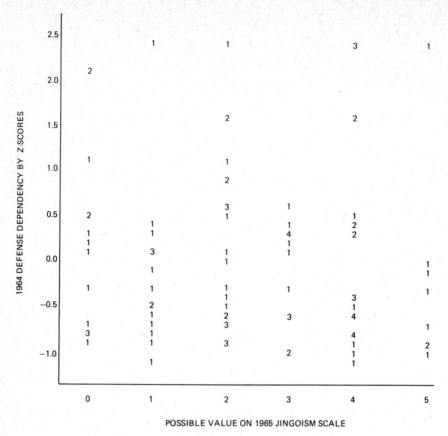

Figure 8-1. Possible Values on 1965 Jingoism Scale.

Russett also objected to the use of the product-moment statistic, on the basis of a refusal to assume a linear relationship between spending and voting. This is a valid concern, in that certain curvilinear relationships of high strength may result in a product-moment correlation of near zero, because of the assumption of a nonexisting linear relationship.

However, examination of Figures 8-1 and 8-2, *reveals no pattern of curvilinear relationship between spending and voting*, such as would have been obscured by the use of the product-moment correlation. He also indicates a concern that a relationship between spending and voting may exist up to a certain degree of dependence, after which increments of dependence do not result in increased concern by the Senator for his constituents. A Senator might fear or respect a large defense contracting firm just as much as a very large defense contracting firm. Figures 8-1 and 8-2 lend no support to this contention either.

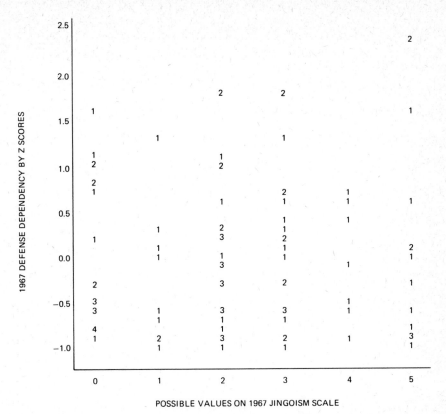

Figure 8-2. Possible Values on 1967 Jingoism Scale.

Russett reports that when he computed product-moment correlations using his data, what had been strong rank-order correlations disappeared and were replaced by product-moment correlations near zero. Such a reduction does not appear to be attributable to any of the factors he mentions, assuming that scatter-grams of his data approximate our Figures 8-1 and 8-2. Russett does not show any scatter-grams in his work.

Table 8-15 reports both the product-moment correlations we have discussed in this paper and rank-order, Kendall's tau correlations computed from the *same* data. None of the product-moment correlations taken from earlier tables in this paper are significant. When tau correlations are computed from the same data, one of the correlations does become significant. Our index of defense spending based on military payrolls is significantly correlated with Senate voting when the statistic used is tau, but not when the product-moment correlation is used. In addition, the correlations between *DD* and voting and *DDC* and voting increased when computed with rank-order methods.

Table 8-15

A Comparison of Product-Moment and Rank-Order Correlations Between Various Measures of Defense Spending and Senate Voting on Jingoism Scales Computed for the Same Data

Type of Correlation	1965			1967		
	DI	*DD*	*DIM*	*DIC*	*DDM*	*DDC*
Product-Moment	0.074	−0.029	0.138	0.165	−0.036	−0.007
Rank-Order TAU	−0.031	−0.061	0.026	−0.008	−0.202[a]	−0.109

[a]Statistically significant at the 0.005 level.

However, across all measures of defense spending, the pattern is quite inconsistent and certainly does not reveal any uniform depressing effect of the use of product-moment correlations. As Russett points out, each of the employment based measures does increase when recomputed with rank-order methods. He indicates that there are good reasons to believe that employment-based measures would be more highly correlated with voting. He does not, on the other hand, indicate why rank-order recomputation should result in increasing correlations more with employment based indices, rather than increasing both types of spending measures equally, with employment based measures being higher when computed both ways. He certainly does not indicate why the other measures of defense spending should have lower correlations with voting after recomputation with rank-order procedures.

We conclude, on the basis of examination of the scatter-grams in Figures 8-1 and 8-2 and the recomputations reported in Table 8-15, that there is no basis for the contention that our negative findings (and probably those of the earlier House study) are based on the erroneous use of interval level procedures.

There are, in addition, a number of reasons for exercising caution in the choice of nonparametric statistics such as Kendall's tau. Cohen (1965:119) states, "I would conclude, therefore, that since the premises which underlie the current widespread use of nonparametric methods are generally false, they be relegated to those restricted and infrequent circumstances where they are uniquely appropriate." Cohen indicates that nonparametric statistics are useful for Chi-square with nominal data since there is no parametric alternative, when the data originally come in the form of ranks, and when one wants to quickly screen out clearly nonsignificant relationships as a preliminary step before the use of other, parametric statistics. It appears that Russett's use of the nonparametric statistic would not be viewed as the correct choice by Cohen.[12]

In his discussion of *point six*, Russett suggests that the combining of contract data, payrolls, and other military spending into one indicator (in the manner of Gray and Gregory) is likely to result in the reduction of the correlation between spending and voting, because some types of spending are not related closely to voting while others do show such a relationship. He also criticizes the earlier House study because of its reliance upon indices based on the allocation of prime contracts. He too found no relationship between prime contracts data and voting. In the present study, we have been able to utilize defense spending measures based on payrolls as well as indicators based on prime contracts. Although the relationships between voting and payroll-based spending measures do increase in strength when recomputed as rank-order correlations, the data presented do not confirm Russett's contention of a connection between voting on foreign and defense policy issues and the concentrations of defense spending in the districts of Senators.

In summary, our figures reveal neither a significant nor a consistent pattern of correlations between defense spending and foreign and defense policy voting. It would perhaps not be too inaccurate to say that the results of this study and that of Russett differ less than our respective interpretations of them.

In any event, we suggest that a pattern of results this inconsistent and weak, especially if it is dependent for its existence on the somewhat controversial choice of a nonparametric statistical method, is insufficient evidence to support the original hypothesis.

Discussion

A substantial proportion of the variance in jingoism can be explained by the Senator's party and the region he represents. We perceive these variables to represent relatively long-term ideological predispositions of the Senators, growing out of their own experiences and those of their states. It does not appear that votes are being crudely traded for defense spending, at least in the area of foreign policy. The Senator appears to be free to vote his convictions, those of his party, and those of his general constituency in broad, ideological terms.

Under the basic military-industrial complex model of artificially elevated defense spending levels, it would be more likely that an issue like actual defense appropriations voting would be strongly related to defense spending concentrations. Appropriations voting is much more of a bread and butter issue than the rather esoteric foreign policy issues which make up the majority of the dependent variable scales in this paper and all the other papers cited in this area. In the years between 1960 and 1967 at least, there is very little variance on appropriations voting in the area of defense. All Senators usually vote in favor of defense spending measures. This makes it impossible to correlate spending concentrations with voting for more spending.[13]

Even if we accept high levels of military spending as the explanation for this pro-defense voting by certain Senators, we still need to explain why Senators from relatively nondependent states also vote for almost all defense appropriations measures during the period under study. Our data do not provide direct answers to this question, but certain hypotheses are possible.

There have been no strong forces opposing defense spending since the Second World War.[14] Under these circumstances, there has been no strong reason to vote against defense expenditures, since there was no political opposition to punish pro-defense votes. On the other hand, there were a series of factors which promoted pro-defense voting. All Congressmen and Senators, including those from nondependent areas of the nation, have been made aware of the real and suspected dangers posed by other nations. Further, the "norm of reciprocity" Matthews (1960) has demonstrated, indicates that there would be pressure on nondependent Senators to vote for bills benefitting the states of dependent Senators, in the expectation that the dependent Senator would return the favor by voting for measures designed to help his nondependent colleague (e.g., an increased level of farm supports).

The effect of this "log-rolling" habit would be to pressure nondependent Senators into voting for defense spending measures which would not benefit their districts. Fears of foreign threats would serve to justify such votes in the eyes of the Senator and his constituents. Until opposition develops to military spending per se, any relationship between spending and voting that potentially exists will remain obscured by these other factors.

Lieberson (1971) has called this situation the "hypothesis of compensating strategies." For him "military spending can be explained by a high level of interest on the part of one segment of American business accompanied by a relative lack of concern on the part of other segments of industry," (Lieberson, 1971:578).[15] We conjecture that this lack of concern is shared for similar reasons by powerful nonindustrial constituents in a Senator's district.

We would expect that as pressure grows against military spending bills, either from other industries needing funding or from the public on the basis of ideological opposition, research opportunities in this area should increase. Under such circumstances, any relationship between Senate voting on defense appropriations and the concentration of defense spending in a Senator's state should be most apparent. To the extent that foreign policy issues are publicly tied into debates over the course of governmental policy on military preparedness, any connections between defense spending and foreign policy voting should also become apparent.

Notes

1. I would like to thank Nancy Hendrix Cobb for her support and critical readings of earlier drafts of this paper. In addition I would like to thank Richard A. Peterson, John McCarthy, and Leo Rigsby for their time and suggestings. I

also wish to thank Barbara Jones for her very helpful work in the computation of several of the tables and figures. A greatly revised paper based on this data is scheduled to appear under the title, "The Impact of Defense Spending on Senatorial Voting Behavior: A Study of Foreign Policy Feedback," in THE SAGE INTERNATIONAL YEARBOOK OF FOREIGN POLICY STUDIES, edited by Patrick McGowan, forthcoming 1973.

2. As we shall note below, discussions of domestic economic considerations in the decision-making process are not meant to exclude other factors such as real or perceived foreign threats.

3. The necessity of using several scales of defense spending points up the fact that the accuracy of information we have is not optimal. Due to problems like subcontracting of prime contracts to unknown locations, many of our indices do not reflect as precisely as we might wish the actual area in which funds are spent. Better data exists on subcontracting for example but has been classified by the Pentagon on grounds of security and because it is proprietary information of the companies involved.

4. A tau of 0.12 is significant with 100 cases while a Pearson product-moment correlation must attain the level of 0.197 to be significant at the 0.05 level with the same 100 cases.

5. A prime contract is the original award of a contract to a private firm. That firm may, and usually does, subcontract out a part of the job to other firms or subsidiaries. Prime contracts covered include only those $10,000 or larger.

6. There is also some possibility of error in that the spending data are based on FY 1964 while the voting data are from 1965. This should not represent a major source of difficulties.

7. The use of tests of significance does not imply an intent to generalize to any population greater than the sample. In this case, our sample is almost identical to the population. The use of tests of significance here is justified as a method of comparing these results with results that might have been obtained by chance had these Senators been rated on the two variables by random methods, (Russett, 1970:240).

8. Strictly speaking the unit of analysis is the state. However, there was little turnover between 1965 and 1967 so the unit may meaningfully be thought of as the Senator.

9. These six items are listed in Russett (1970b). The explanations of the items are not Russett's but are an attempt to summarize the content of each item briefly.

10. In his criticism of this paper, Russett disparaged the use of "value added by manufacture" in some of the indicators of defense spending though he did not note why his was more appropriate. Another critic of this paper indicated that both this work *and Russett's* were weak on substantive reasons for using various defense spending and impact measures. The use of value added by manufacture seemed most appropriate when dealing with contract data and was retained in order to insure maximum comparability with the 1969 House study.

11. In the case of the years chosen for analysis as well as in the case of several other procedures, we have elected to use different methods than those of Russett. We have been very concerned to maintain comparability with our earlier study of the House which appeared before the Russett Senate study. When the difficult choice had to be made, we felt that comparability with that study was as important as comparability with the work of Russett. Since our results support the conclusions of the earlier House study, relatively little attention was paid to comparisons between the earlier paper and this one. We have, however, devoted considerable attention to differences between this study and that of Russett because of the differing findings. We have made every effort to delineate just where our procedures differed and to estimate just how important those differences are in order to obtain as much of the value of a true replication as possible under the circumstances.

12. Cohen (1965:119) suggests that parametric tests should be used in preference to nonparametric tests like Kendall's tau because (1) the parametric tests are quite robust with regard to failure of assumptions like linearity and normality in a wide range of practical conditions; (2) are not crucially dependent on scaling assumptions while nonparametric tests have several major failings including (1) the fact that they are *not* distribution-free in the desired sense; (2) lack relative power and adequate methods of power analysis; and (3) lack the development necessary for any but the simplest of experimental designs and data-analytic forms. In addition, as Russett himself notes, nonparametric tests—including those such as the Kendall's tau which he uses—generally do not have an interpretation of variance-explained thereby making it difficult to decide what a given value means.

13. We were able to include one item on the 1965 scale that might be construed as an appropriations vote. Russett included a number of defense spending measures in his 1967-1968 scale. He notes however (Russett, 1970:34) that he excluded votes on which the division was more extreme than 95 to 5 percent. This was a somewhat less stringent criteria than we adopted. The inclusion of roll-call votes was limited to those on which the division was 80-20 percent in order to prevent increasing the coefficient of reproducibility by large numbers of votes on which the chance of error was small.

14. Opposition to the war in Vietnam has shown some possibilities to become an exception to this rule.

15. It should be noted that he is concerned also with why some industries are willing to take the small economic losses incurred when funds go to defense production rather than other segments of industry. This industry willingness to "look after its own business" in the hope that all will be provided for parallels and influences the "log-rolling" process in the Senate.

References

Bolton, Roger E. (ed.). DEFENSE AND DISARMAMENT. Englewood Cliffs: Prentice-Hall Spectrum Book, 1966.

Buehler, Col. Vernon. "Economic Impact of Defense Programs." STATISTICAL REPORTER 68, No. 1 (July 1967), pp. 1-9.

Cobb, Stephen A. "Defense Spending and Foreign Policy in the House of Representatives." JOURNAL OF CONFLICT RESOLUTION 13, No. 3 (September 1969), pp. 358-69.

_____. "Defense Spending, Foreign Policy Voting, and the Structure of the U.S. House of Representatives." Read at the 1972 Meetings of the Southern Sociological Society at New Orleans, Louisiana.

Cohen, Jacob. "Some Statistical Issues in Psychological Research," in Benjamin B. Wolman (ed.), HANDBOOK OF CLINICAL PSYCHOLOGY (1965), pp. 95-121.

Cook, Fred J. THE WARFARE STATE. New York: Collier Books, 1962.

Department of Defense Bulletin. "Defense Generated Employment, December 1966." Washington, D.C. (1966).

Gray, Charles and Glen Gregory. "Military Spending and Senate Voting." JOURNAL OF PEACE RESEARCH (1968), pp. 44-54.

Lens, Sidney. THE MILITARY-INDUSTRIAL COMPLEX. Philadelphia: Pilgrim Press and the National Catholic Reporter, 1970.

Lieberson, Stanley. "An Empirical Study of Military-Industrial Linkages." THE AMERICAN JOURNAL OF SOCIOLOGY (1971), pp. 562-85.

Lowi, Theodore J. "American Business, Public Policy, Case Studies, and Political Theory." WORLD POLITICS (July 1964), pp. 677-715.

Mills, C. Wright. THE POWER ELITE. New York: Oxford University Press, 1956.

Russett, Bruce. WHAT PRICE VIGILANCE? New Haven: Yale University Press, 1970.

_____. "Communication to the Editors." THE JOURNAL OF CONFLICT RESOLUTION 14, No. 2 (June 1970b).

Turner, Julius. PARTY AND CONSTITUENCY: PRESSURES ON CONGRESS. Baltimore: Johns Hopkins University Press, 1951.

9

Testing Some Economic Interpretations of American Intervention: Korea, Indochina, and the Stock Market

Betty C. Hanson and
Bruce M. Russett

Some Theories about Investors' Attitudes

By 1970 casual observers, as well as seasoned analysts, had begun to anticipate a rise in the stock market each time a major peace move was made in Southeast Asia. Such a market response would appear to challenge Marxist-Leninist theses that capitalist economies profit by—indeed require—periodic wars. The available "evidence" on these matters, however, is merely anecdotal, sometimes contradicted by the response to other events. Is there in fact a positive statistical relationship between de-escalatory moves in Indochina and stock market rises; or does the memory of a few dramatic examples merely give this impression? If such a positive pattern of response could be systematically established, would this be a phenomenon of the later stages of the war? If so, when did the shift occur and what kind of pattern, if any, emerges from the early period? Is the recent pattern similar to, or quite different from, earlier overseas United States wars?

Any effort to understand the causes of contemporary American military activity abroad must address itself to the perceptions and preferences of American investors; analysts of every ideological persuasion must face the evidence on these questions openly. This study is concerned *not* with the effect of war on the *economy*, but with the *attitudes* prevalent in the financial community about the economic consequences of military intervention. Two recent military involvements are examined, in Korea and in Indochina—by far the longest and most costly of American military conflicts since 1945. The attempt is made to ascertain the relationship between stock market fluctuations and important escalatory and de-escalatory events in the Indochina war, in order to test several hypotheses about these attitudes. For additional insight into these attitudes, the relationship between these same events and the stocks of a selected group of corporations with substantial investment in less developed countries (LDC stocks) is investigated. Finally, in order to provide some basis of comparison and historical perspective, the relationship between important escalatory and de-escalatory events and stock market fluctuations during the Korean War is analyzed.[1]

The direction and magnitude of the net changes on the days the events are reported is used as an indicator of the financial community's attitudes. The primary concern is the immediate response of the financial community to dramatic and salient events indicating a widening or termination of military hostilities. Thus, the focus is not the economy but the investor. This is not an analysis of market trends nor an exercise in forecasting. Certainly it is not an investor's guide to future international crises, although a more comprehensive analysis of international crises for three decades might yield some insights regarding tendencies of the market to respond in particular ways at certain points in each crisis.[2]

The abrupt involvement of the U.S. in an international crisis is generally expected to be accompanied by a decline in stock prices, or at least a "dull" market, while buyers "wait and see" what course of action will be taken. After the uncertainties of the new situation have been removed and the nation is committed to military involvement, the chief reason for buying or selling, rather than simply holding, is the belief that the new situation is likely to mean greater or lesser profits for the corporation or corporations involved in the transaction. Expectations about a corporation's prospects are influenced by the view held concerning the effect of military involvement on the economy in general as well as that corporation in particular.

This paper will consider four alternative perspectives for explaining and "predicting" the probable response of the market to the escalating Indochina War, based upon different expectations about the way the financial community views the economic consequences of military intervention.

A *simple Marxist* perspective might impute to businessmen a belief that war is good and necessary for the capitalist American economy. Wartime mobilization provides "assured demand at assured profits for the specific interests in armaments research and production and a powerful stimulant to demand and production throughout the economy."[3] According to this perspective, war is bullish. Investors would be expected to respond positively to escalation and negatively to conciliatory moves throughout the war.

An opposite perspective, which will be called *simple inverse Marxist*, might assume that there are other effective ways of stimulating the economy without the negative side effects commonly resulting from war, such as inflation, increased deficit, adverse effect on balance of payments, and the possibility of wage and price controls. This view recurred throughout the war in the "Abreast of the Market" column of the *Wall Street Journal* in the informal samplings of opinion taken on the current market scene. In a typical example the author estimates that "most brokers asked for an opinion on the market's strength in the light of U.S. peace feelers expressed the view that a cessation of hostilities would be bullish." One particular broker is then quoted as saying, "Peace is never bearish. It could be disruptive in some stocks for a short period, but in the long run the investor always makes more money out of butter than he can out of guns."[4] According to this view, enough investors will recognize that in the long run peace is more beneficial to the economy than war, and that the market would respond negatively to escalation and positively to conciliation from the very beginning of the war.

The third perspective, *modified Marxist/inverse Marxist*, is a combination of the first two. This view might assume that by increasing the aggregate demand, a *little* war is good for the econmy—as long as there is a prospect of victory, there is little risk of escalation into a major confrontation with another major power, or that the negative side effects on the economy will become serious enough to outweigh the benefits. This belief in the positive effect of a limited military effort is demonstrated in two more quotations from the *Wall Street Journal* analysis columns. When the market rose slightly in the middle of the Tonkin Gulf crisis, one commentator was quoted as saying: "We are on a war footing in localized areas. If we can keep it that way, this good market performance probably will get better. If the war spreads, though, we could go a lot lower."[5] When the crisis appeared to be simmering down the analyst estimated that "the consensus of the Street is that the primary threat of more than a brush war developing in Asia is past and stocks could be in for a sizable rally."[6] According to this perspective, the market would respond positively to escalation and negatively to conciliation, in the early period, and in the reverse manner in the later period, when the military stalemate as well as the negative effects of the war upon the economy became apparent.

According to the fourth perspective, the *Neo-imperialist*, businessmen might regard war as necessary to protect vital economic interests abroad, actual or potential. As much of the world as possible must be kept open for United States trade and investment and utilization of resources. Communist revolutionary movements and other nationalist movements, which would restrict or hamper American capitalist enterprise abroad, must be resisted for the following reasons. First, the immediate interests of the investors in the threatened country must be protected. These interests in Vietnam are generally regarded as more potential than actual. Banning Garrett argues in *Ramparts*[7] that the Indochina War has been one to create economic opportunity rather than merely seize existing resources. The necessity of a military protection force for this "compulsive capital development" and the feedback between the two is discussed. But the point is made even more clearly in a *Fortune*[8] editorial on war aims, which reminded the reader:

Even now as the fighting rages, the U.S. is building in Vietnam and neighboring Thailand the "infrastructures" of future economic development. Once the drain of the war is ended, these harbors, bridges, roads, power stations, and other facilities will pay enormous dividends. Unless we glimpse the opportunity behind the agony in Vietnam, recognizing the strategy and economic imperatives of our commitment in Asia, we won't really understand what the war is about.

Because the costs of protection are so disproportionate to any gains which can be envisaged in Indochina itself, the potential availability argument is often expanded. Competing multinational corporations with conflicting interests are seen as united in wanting "the world of nations in which they operate to be as large as possible."[9] Moreover, the U.S. "requires the option to expand to regions it has not yet penetrated."[10] For these opportunities to remain profitable as well as available, it is necessary that the "political and economic principles of capitalism should prevail and that the door be fully open for foreign capital at all times."[11] Thus, it is necessary to forestall that particular kind of domino effect which might result from another communist or nationalist takeover. But the economic domino theory also has an ideological component. Even those corporations without specific interests in Vietnam or Southeast Asia will share a general concern for perpetuating the "rules of the game" that "guarantee the sanctity of private property and other essentials of capitalism."[12] Because of Vietnam's modest economic value, military intervention there is all the more significant "as an example of America's determination to hold the line as a matter of principle against revolutionary movements."[13]

According to this perspective, corporations with substantial overseas investment, especially in less developed countries, will support military intervention more strongly and for a longer period of time than will other corporations. However, the potential availability rationale, as well as the fear of falling dominos, gives rise to a certain predilection towards intervention on the part of the entire business community. Hence, the overall market should respond positively to U.S. escalatory and unconciliatory moves for most of the war, with a similar but stronger response by stocks of firms with large holdings in LDCs. In contrast to the simple Marxist perspective, however, no strong opposition to Communist conciliation would be expected nor would there be any approval of Communist escalation—the stakes abroad, rather than the domestic level of economic activity, are of central importance here.

Method of Analysis

All Vietnam events between August 1964 and December 1970 which appeared on page 1 of the *Wall Street Journal*, in the first paragraph of the "World-Wide" news summary column, were coded when they indicated a "positive event" with a relatively clear message for escalation or de-escalation of the war, and they fit into certain categories specified below. A positive event is defined as the actual occurrence of an event, indicating a military action, a statement, decision, opinion or judgment. "Reportedly" and "implies" statements were included for the Communist side in order to amplify the number of entries, but were not for the United States and South Vietnam.

From this list, one day per month was selected as the one on which the most important event or events of the month occurred. Occassionally more than one type of event occurred on the same day and both were reported in the top paragraph. We chose to use only the most prominent event or events of the month, rather than to look at the effect of *all* Vietnam-related events, on the assumption that the effect of less-prominent events would likely be masked by the "noise" of other events. This allows us to compare the relative effect of the various types of events we are concerned with; it is not our intention to compare the effect of these events with that of all other national and international events.

The *New York Times Index* was also coded according to similar procedures and a monthly event selection made from this list. The concurrence of events on the two lists was a factor in the final selection. When a choice between two or three days was difficult, all were included. In some months no events were coded. The resulting list consisted of 93 event-days. In the analysis, each of these event-days was related to the net change in the stock market on the day the event was *reported* in the *Wall Street Journal*, except when the market analysis column or news report indicated that the news had reached the investing public before closing time the previous day, in which case that day's net change was used.

For the purposes of coding, the events have been divided into six categories, two military and four political. *Military escalation,* which is divided into United States (including South Vietnam) and Communist subcategories, is defined as an increase in weapons, troops, advisors, ships, or the use of new tactics or techniques. "Record number" and "first time" are two key phrases indicating escalation. De-escalation is confined to the two political categories designated as United States (and South Vietnam), and Communist *conciliatory* actions. In addition, there are two political escalatory categories termed United States (and South Vietnamese) and Communist *unconciliatory* actions.

Conciliatory actions are defined as those which indicate a peace initiative; i.e., a proposal to reduce military operations or initiate talks leading to a settlement of the war; any other kind of effort to de-escalate the war or reduce military operations; a softening of previous terms for de-escalation or political settlement. Unconciliatory actions indicate a negative response to a peace initiative; a nonmilitary escalatory event; a hardening of peace terms; threats to expand or prolong the war or accusations that the opponent does so. Statements indicating determination to win or to continue until the opponent stops aggression are included on the grounds that this necessitates continuation of hostilities. Statements about vital interests or ideological principles being involved in the war are also included in this category. Increases in economic aid and all aid offers are regarded as nonmilitary escalatory actions; only military aid actually granted or agreed upon is considered military escalatory. Thus, the six categories are: (1) U.S. military escalation (2) Communist military escalation (3) U.S. conciliation (4) U.S. unconciliation (5) Communist conciliation (6) Communist unconciliation.

The sources of the actions, statements, decisions, and opinions coded for the United States are the President or White House; Vice-President; Secretary of Defense, Department of Defense or Pentagon; Secretary of State or State Department; or Military Command, Saigon. The sources for South Vietnam are the President, Vice-President, diplomatic representatives in Paris, and other government spokesmen. For the Communist side the official statements of North Vietnam, the NLF, the People's Republic of China, and the Soviet Union as well as reports from their official publications have been coded. The categories were separately coded by two independent coders with an inter-coder reliability of 0.95. All these independent variables are essentially uncorrelated with one another.

This investigation into the relationship between stock market fluctuations and Indochina war events consists of three separate analyses. First, the response of the overall market is examined. A multiple regression analysis with each class of events, i.e., the occurrence or nonoccurrence of each event on that day, was run against the net change in the closing Dow Jones Industrial average on the 93 selected days. The 1964-70 years were cut up in several different ways and separate regressions run against the events in different periods, so as to estimate the approximate timing of any shift that occurred.

Second, the response of ten selected LDC stocks to the war is analyzed. The corporations were selected using the following criteria (see Table 9-1): foreign content, i.e., percentage of sales, earnings, and assets abroad; LDC content, i.e., percentage of less developed countries out of the total number of countries in which a firm has operations; size; representation according to type with emphasis on raw materials. All corporations selected made at least 20 percent of their sales abroad and held over 30 percent of their assets abroad. Of the total number of states in which they had operations, at least 45 percent for each firm were LDCs. All of the firms were ranked in the top quartile of the *Fortune* listing of the largest 500 U.S. corporations. We did not use any single criterion (e.g., size, or percentage of sales abroad) mechanically because we wanted to cover a fairly broad range of different products and industries. A multiple regression analysis using each class of events as an independent variable was run against the net changes in prices for each stock, as well as the standardized composite value for the group of stocks, for the overall period and for the pre-Tet and post-Tet periods separately.

Finally, a regression attempt was made to "predict" net changes in the Dow Jones Industrial averages on the days the weekly casualty lists were reported from July, 1965 through 1970, using the Defense Department's official report of the number of deaths.

The Stock Market as an Indicator:
Some Explanations and Some Caveats

A number of difficulties, of varying degrees of seriousness, accompany our effort. We are trying to impute the "average" investors' attitudes from the

Table 9-1
Foreign Content of Selected U.S. International Corporations

	Fortune Rank[a]	% Foreign Sales[b]	% Foreign Earnings	% Foreign Assets	#States with Operation LDC/Total[d]
Boise Cascade (Paper products)	100	20	25	33	4/5
Corning Products	66	43	47	43	13/29
Goodyear Tire & Rubber	20		36	38	16/34
IBM	9	29	29	34	55/81
ITT	30	60	54	56	12/25
Pfizer (chemicals, pharmaceuticals, cosmetics)	125	46	60	56	24/44
Reynolds Metals (aluminum products)	91	26	4	32	7/12
Singer	65	54		64[c]	35/61
Socony Mobil	6	48	59	46	37/52
Standard Oil (N.J.)	3	33	60[c]	52[c]	25/54

[a]FORTUNE, 57, 8 (Sept. 15, 1968), p. 105.

[b]Figures for foreign sales, assets, and earnings for 1964 operations from Nicholas K. Bruck and Francis A. Lees, "Foreign Content of U.S. Corporate Activities," FINANCIAL ANALYST'S JOURNAL, 22, 5 (Sept.-Oct. 1966), pp. 127-131.

[c]Nicholas K. Bruck and Francis A. Lees, FOREIGN INVESTMENT, CAPITAL CONTROLS, AND THE BALANCE OF PAYMENTS (New York: New York University Press, 1968), pp. 83-85.

[d]Juvenal L. Angel, DIRECTORY OF AMERICAN FIRMS OPERATING IN FOREIGN COUNTRIES (New York: World Trade Academy Press, 1966, 6th ed.).

behavior of those investors who choose to buy or sell stocks on a particular day, or specifically from the prices at which stocks were bought and sold. In principle, of course, it would be better to have conducted depth interviews with a large and properly selected sample of investors, probing directly for their attitudes toward war, peace, intervention, and the health of the American economy in general and of certain segments in particular. We are in fact now engaged in such a study. But the interviewing approach has its own limitations; for example, the difficulties of obtaining accurate data on such sensitive subjects from highly sophisticated interviewers. Another limitation is even more compelling. The "modified Marxist/inverse Marxist" hypothesis predicts a shift, perhaps a reversal, in investors' attitudes over the course of some wars. We might even find a reversal in attitudes toward military intervention in general. That is, an investor may, in the 1950s or early 1960s, have felt that a little war, far away, was a good thing for the economy. But after observing the Indochina debacle he may have changed his mind, on the ground that such wars carry very great risks of a "quagmire effect," with economic and political upheaval at home. Thus, he may reason, even little wars should in the future be avoided. Asking people directly about such changes in perceptions is tricky; memories are untrustworthy. Hence, the information one obtains from interviewing is not fully reliable either. The method we use here, despite the limitations we are about to specify, at least does tap the *actual behavior of investors at the time* of the political and military events that concern us.[14]

One caveat nevertheless concerns the limited impact the war itself will have had on investors' behavior, especially in the early stages where it was not so salient, or in periods when other events—domestic and international, political and economic, general or concerning particular firms or industries—were occurring. Surely these will have greatly affected the selling prices of stocks, and we do not introduce them directly into the analysis. What we do, however, is to assume that to the extent they matter they will reduce any correlations we find with our war-related events, appearing as random error. The evidence, then, that a particular kind of war event is an important influence will be in the correlations we do find. Since our concern is with war-related behavior rather than with explaining the course of the market generally, we can leave to others the addition of other sorts of variables to our equations.

The selection of the war events themselves has its problems. Those critical turning points of the war which are seen in retrospect were not always viewed as such at the time; conversely, certain crises, fraught with dire consequences, passed without altering the course of the war. The main criterion must be salience at the time, and thus the events selected cannot comprise a list of *the* important events of the war from a historical point of view. But all the events included on the list were probably regarded as important at the time, by virtue of the location in which they were reported in the newspapers.

Another problem is possible ambiguity in the implications of the various events for the termination of the war. A highly escalatory event could be favored as the best means for bringing about an early ending to the war, and conversely, a de-escalatory event opposed on the grounds that such an approach merely prolonged the war. That such interpretations are not merely theoretical possibilities can be seen in the view expressed by a major securities firm about the implications of Nixon's May 8, 1972 decision to resume the bombing of North Vietnam, to mine that nation's major ports, and to interdict rail transportation. Asserting that these moves could very well serve as "the final major battle of the war," the author expresses the belief that "if we are correct in assuming that this latest military venture is the key to an eventual termination of the conflict, it is possible to assume that in the next few months a settlement will be reached."[15] The political and economic significance of any item of news is not clearly and immediately self-evident; consequently, "Hardly any event can happen of sufficient importance to attract general attention which some process of reasoning cannot construe as bullish and some other process as bearish."[16] In spite of the variety of interpretations which could be given to the meaning of the various events, escalatory and de-escalatory events are coded literally to minimize the use of arbitrary judgments.

The problem of signal ambiguity is further compounded by the manner in which major escalatory and de-escalatory events in the Indochina war were announced. The former often were de-emphasized with the insistence that this event did not represent a departure from past policies. On the other hand, peace moves were generally accompanied by assurances that the war would continue until a just peace was achieved and aggression ended. But again, it is the literal meaning of the event that is used in the coding.

In addition to problems relating to the significance of events, there is the question of the point in time at which to measure the response of the market to any given event. The full effects of an event may not be felt until days, weeks, or even months later. An analysis with a lag is not made in this study because the main concern was the *immediate* response of the financial community.[17] Furthermore, the "noise" of extraneous events obviously increases with each day that passes after an event. A more serious problem is the impact which events often appear to have upon the market even *before* they occur, i.e., traders buy or sell in response to advance information that a certain event is imminent. By the time the event does occur, it may already have been discounted in the market and produce little or no further reaction—or even a reversal of the initial response. Peace moves, such as the extension of peace feelers and announcements of impending troop withdrawals, are particularly prone to generate rumors and premature market responses with resultant diluted, altered, or reversed effects by the actual occurrence of the events. For example, although President Johnson's announcement of a partial bomb halt in April 1968 had sent the Dow Jones Industrial averages up 20 points, and throughout the month of October rumors that a total bomb halt was imminent gave rise to a so-called "peace rally," the market in fact dipped two points when the long-awaited complete bomb halt was announced on November 1. Obviously premature market responses to rumors of an event obscure the meaning of the response to the actual occurrence. This is particularly true in the case of the wilder and more drastic rumors that circulate. In July of 1965 the market declined on several occasions, according to analysts, because of rumors that the economy was about to be put on a war-type footing with wage and price controls and an excess profits tax instituted. However, when President Johnson finally made his statement on forthcoming war measures, he called for *only* doubling of the draft, and consequently the market was said to rise out of relief that nothing worse was contemplated.[18] Similarly a six-month high in stock prices, which occurred during the Korean War when President Truman declared a state of emergency and announced forthcoming wage and price ceilings, was attributed to the fact that the mobilization message was "milder than expected" and "contained no surprises."[19]

Advance information varies greatly in its accuracy from speculative rumor to the texts of statements released before their delivery. Because the market immediately takes into account any new information which appears to have economic consequences, it is quite possible that its responses to rumors are stronger than its responses to actual occurrences. Indeed the "Abreast of the Market" column in the *Wall Street Journal* frequently refers to the apparent effect of some rumor which in fact was reported in a relatively insignificant position as a news item or not at all. At one point in 1969 the columnist estimated that the spring rally from mid-April to mid-May was "based almost entirely on peace hopes," the hopes being inspired by a series of rumors.[20] But aside from the difficulties that would be involved in systematically locating and coding rumors, there is their tendency to convey unclear messages and to evoke denials and conflicting rumors to further cloud the message. Therefore, in spite of the obvious responsiveness of the market to rumors, these are not included among the events. Official statements about intentions are included as a means of obtaining some of the early responses.

One final clarification should be made regarding the possibility of an upward bias or trend in the market as a methodological problem. An examination of the daily closing averages for the Dow Jones Industrials indicates there was no major upward trend in the market during the period covered. The average for July 31, 1964 was 841 and for December 31, 1970 it was 838. There were of course fluctuations but these ranged between a low of 631 on May 26, 1970 and a high of 995 on February 9, 1966. All fluctuations were within a range of 25 percent of the mean, not enough to cause any methodological difficulties. (See Figure 9-1 for the range of averages for war event-days.)

The above caveats warn us not to expect very high correlations between the market behavior of stocks and various wartime events as reported in the newspapers. Other factors will introduce a good deal of additional variation that will seem, on the basis of our very imperfect knowledge, to be virtually random noise. But despite these other influences, we shall nevertheless show some important and statistically significant relationships.

Findings Concerning the Indochina War

Table 9-2 outlines the various predictions we have attributed to the four perspectives, and summarizes the results of our analysis for the Indochina War from 1964 to 1970. Table 9-3 presents the results in more detail.

The only statistically significant results from the analysis concern *conciliatory* acts. Such acts in the latter period of the war, whether by the United States-Saigon side or the Communist forces, regularly are associated with *rising* stock prices on that day. This applies to the set of LDC stocks as well as to the overall Dow Jones Industrial average, and holds as well for the period starting in the beginning of 1967 as it does for a time-period commencing with the start of 1968 and the Tet offensive. Thus, the financial community did not wait for Tet or President Johnson's bombing halt to favor conciliation; rather, the market shift coincides closely with a discernible shift in the mass public's approval of the war, also in early 1967.[21]

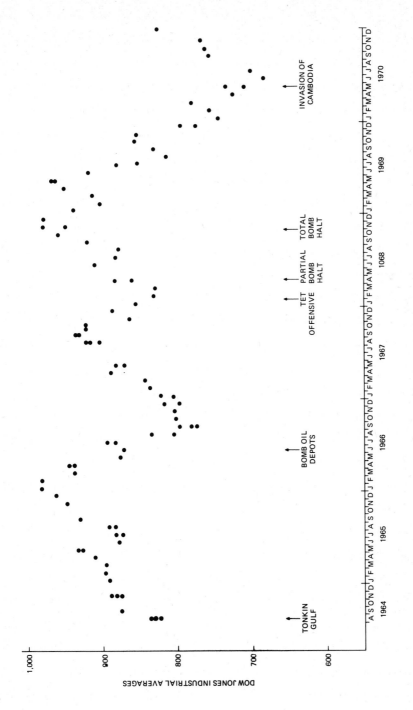

Figure 9-1. Dow Jones Industrial Average on Days of Important Vietnam Events, 1964-70

Table 9-2
Predictions Attributed to Various Perspectives, and Summary of Empirical Results for Indochina War

	Simple Marxist	Inverse Marxist	Modified Marxist/ Inverse Marxist		Neo-imperialist	Results (DJI)			Results (LDC)		
			Early	Late		Early	Late	Total	Early	Late	Total
U.S. Escalation	+	−	+	−	+	−	+	−	−	+	−
Communist Escalation	+	−	+	−	−	+	−	−	+	−	−
U.S. Conciliation	−	+	−	+	−	+	+a	+a	+	+a	+a
U.S. Unconciliation	+	−	+	−	+	−	+	+	+	+	+
Communist Conciliation	−	+	−	+	+	...	+a	+a	...	+a	+a
Communist Unconciliation	+	−	+	−	−	−	+	−	−	+	+

aIndicates statistically significant finding (see Table 9-3).

Table 9-3
Stock Changes Against Indochina Events: Regression Coefficients

	1964-70 Total	1964-66 Early	1964-67 Pre-Tet	1967-70 Post Disillusionment	1968-70 Post-Tet	1964-70 LDC (cv)[a]	1964-67 LDC (cv)	1968-70 LDC (cv)
Multiple Correlation Coefficient (r)	0.58	0.38	0.41	0.68	0.71	0.56	0.45	0.69
F ratio	7.35	1.11	2.04	6.90	5.62	6.58	2.54	5.02
Regression Coefficient[c]								
(1) U.S. Escalation	-1.19 (0.60)	-1.18 (0.25)	-4.17 (0.15)	1.22 (0.65)	1.72 (0.65)	-0.01 (0.95)	-0.25 (0.40)	0.22 (0.45)
(2) Communist Escalation	-2.47 (0.40)	0.12 (0.90)	0.30 (0.90)	-2.90 (0.40)	-4.12 (0.30)	-0.09 (0.70)	0.02 (0.95)	-0.14 (0.65)
(3) U.S. Conciliation	*5.14 (0.025)	0.62 (0.50)	1.39 (0.65)	*7.07 (0.01)	*7.23 (0.025)	*0.54 (0.001)	0.41 (0.20)	*0.63 (0.01)
(4) U.S. Unconciliation	0.84 (0.70)	0.19 (0.85)	-0.38 (0.85)	1.95 (0.45)	0.18 (0.90)	0.20 (0.25)	0.05 (0.80)	0.26 (0.25)
(5) Communist Conciliation	*11.64 (0.001)	-[b]	-	*13.4 (0.001)	*12.85 (0.001)	*0.93 (0.001)	-	*1.07 (0.001)
(6) Communist Unconciliation	-0.54 (0.90)	0.49 (0.65)	-3.62 (0.35)	0.73 (0.80)	4.15 (0.50)	0.12 (0.60)	-0.13 (0.70)	0.51 (0.35)
	N=93	N=38	N=54	N=55	N=38	N=93	N=54	N=38
Bivariate Correlations Between Independent and Dependent Variables								
(1) U.S. Escalation	-0.27	-0.32	-0.33	-0.21	-0.12	-0.28	-0.34	-0.13
(2) Communist Escalation	-0.18	0.09	0.08	-0.31	-0.37	-0.16	0.02	-0.35
(3) U.S. Conciliation	0.35	0.26	0.28	0.35	0.35	0.36	0.39	0.31
(4) U.S. Unconciliation	-0.07	0.04	0.10	-0.12	-0.24	-0.03	0.06	-0.13
(5) Communist Conciliation	0.42	-	-	0.50	0.52	0.37	-	0.51
(6) Communist Unconciliation	-0.11	-0.03	-0.11	-0.17	0.09	-0.07	-0.07	-0.03

[a]LDC (cv) = less developed country stocks, composite value.

[b]_ = No entries coded for this variable during this period.

[c]Significance levels in parentheses. Levels at 0.10 and smaller asterisked.

No clear pattern of response to *escalation* appears, whether early or late, for American or Communist escalation, for the overall market or for the LDC stocks. The only relationship which even approaches a level of statistical significance applies to United States-Saigon escalation in the pre-Tet period.

No statistically significant relationships whatever appear in the *early* years of the war, regardless of precisely what time-division is taken.

Supplementing the material in the tables, *no* relationship for either the earlier or later periods was found between net changes in the averages and the number of *casualties* reported by the Department of Defense. The correlation coefficient (r) for the Dow Jones Industrial average and casualties was 0.02 for the pre-Tet period and 0.15 for post-Tet.

Table 9-4 reports the results from examining changes in the price of each of the 10 LDC stocks individually for the overall period. Essentially the same pattern prevailed as with the market as a whole. Five of the 10 stocks responded *positively* to United States *conciliatory* acts, and four of the 10 responded positively to Communist conciliation. There are only two significant correlations with *escalatory* acts, one each with United States and Communist escalation. Both correlations are *negative*. There are two significant *negative* relationships with *unconciliatory* acts (one to United States unconciliation and one to Communist acts of that type), substantially countered by two *positive* responses to United States *nonconciliation*. Lest much be made of the latter, however, stocks of these same two firms (Singer and Standard Oil) also went up when the United States side took conciliatory actions.

In comparing these findings with the predicted results outlined in Table 9-2, it is clear that none of the four perspectives exactly predicts the findings.

The *"simple Marxist"* proved to be wrong even in the signs of its predictions in appreciably more cases than it was right; even where the sign was right the results were not statistically significant.

The *"inverse Marxist"* position works fairly well for the later period, but not for the earlier one.

Thus, the *"modified Marxist/inverse Marxist"* position accurately predicts the shift, in 1967, to a positive response to conciliation, a response that was statistically significant. Furthermore, with the nonsignificant coefficients, the sign predicted by the "modified Marxist/inverse Marxist" is correct in all but one case during the later period (a very insignificant positive coefficient appears for United States unconciliation). Nevertheless, the approval of escalation in the early period that was anticipated by this perspective clearly was not borne out by the results. If anything, the results show a moderate disapproval of American escalation in the early period of the war.

The *"neo-imperialist"* perspective seems to have mixed results, being right slightly often (especially in the later period) than it was wrong. This is deceptive, however, since in most of the cases where it was right, its detailed predictions were no different from the predictions of the "inverse Marxist" position. In the

Table 9-4
LDC Stock Changes Against Indochina Events, 1964-70: Regression Coefficients

	Boise Cascade	Corning Products	Goodyear	IBM	ITT	Pfizer	Reynolds Metals	Singer	Socony Mobil	Standard
Multiple Correlation Coefficient (r)	0.36	0.32	0.33	0.39	0.45	0.32	0.27	0.38	0.28	0.41
F Ratio	2.28	1.72	1.86	2.74	3.83	1.74	1.10	2.45	1.27	2.99
Regression Coefficient[a]										
(1) U.S. Escalation	-0.45 (0.25)	*-0.64 (0.01)	-0.40 (0.15)	0.07 (0.95)	0.35 (0.35)	0.14 (0.70)	-0.07 (0.80)	0.05 (0.90)	0.39 (0.20)	0.17 (0.50)
(2) Communist Escalation	0.04 (0.30)	-0.19 (0.45)	*-0.66 (0.05)	-2.39 (0.35)	-0.52 (0.20)	0.12 (0.80)	0.01 (0.95)	-0.47 (0.90)	-0.12 (0.70)	-0.01 (0.95)
(3) U.S. Conciliation	-0.03 (0.95)	-0.34 (0.15)	-0.04 (0.85)	*4.95 (0.05)	*1.01 (0.01)	*0.84 (0.05)	0.23 (0.50)	*0.57 (0.10)	0.12 (0.70)	*0.72 (0.02)
(4) U.S. Unconciliation	-0.55 (0.15)	*-0.33 (0.10)	-0.39 (0.12)	2.22 (0.25)	0.41 (0.20)	0.21 (0.60)	0.09 (0.70)	*0.50 (0.10)	-0.03 (0.90)	*0.50 (0.10)
(5) Communist Conciliation	*0.95 (0.10)	0.30 (0.45)	-0.01 (0.70)	4.79 (0.12)	*1.38 (0.01)	0.63 (0.30)	0.71 (0.15)	*0.81 (0.10)	0.31 (0.45)	*0.92 (0.02)
(6) Communist Unconciliation	0.41 (0.45)	*-0.51 (0.05)	-0.25 (0.40)	0.19 (0.45)	0.42 (0.30)	-0.26 (0.60)	-0.35 (0.40)	0.24 (0.50)	0.02 (0.95)	0.01 (0.95)

[a]Significance levels in parentheses. Levels at 0.10 or under asterisked.

crucial case of predicting market response to United States conciliatory actions, the sign of the coefficient was highly significant in the direction opposite to the "neo-imperialist" prediction.

Perhaps we have caricatured the four labeled perspectives, though we have tried our best to extract fairly a set of empirically testable predictions from each. Whether or not we succeeded, it nonetheless emerges sharply from our results that *by the beginning of 1967 the American financial community in general clearly wanted to see the Indochina War de-escalated.* (We cannot say anything about the amount of de-escalation desired, or the price they were willing to pay for it.) Moreover, the corporations with substantial investment in less developed countries were no exception to this pattern. In fact, the upward movement of LDC stocks in response to United States conciliatory acts was slightly stronger than was the movement of the overall Dow Jones average, suggesting that investors in those firms were, if anything, still more anxious to end the war.[22] However, the fact that the stock movements of two firms were upward with United States unconciliation, as well as with United States conciliatory acts, suggests that concern for the specific interests of these firms made their investors more particular about the terms of any settlement.

Although some slight disapproval of escalation in the early period is indicated, the absence of any strong relationship with that variable was unanticipated by any of the perspectives we examined. In offering some post-hoc explanation of the lack of relationship, we can only tentatively suggest the following: (1) There may be some flaw in our data-making procedures, especially in the coding or selection of events, that is not apparent to us. Future research will have to check this possibility. (2) The response to escalation may have indicated mixed or unclear expectations about its military consequences. That is, a positive response to escalation at that point, might have stemmed as much from a hope that the extra effort would end the war quickly, as from a disapproval of the war; similarly, negative responses to escalation may have been rooted in quite differing expecations. (3) Alternatively, the unpatterned response to escalation may have stemmed from a substantial degree of ambivalence within the financial community toward the military intervention in its earlier stages. The lure of a higher level of economic activity at home with a small limited war, plus the hope of containing communism and other nationalist movements in Asia, could have been motivating factors. But at the same time, those attractions could have been offset for many other investors by the expectation of inflation and other negative effects of an escalating war—not to mention the risk that the small conflict might become a super-power confrontation.

Korean War Results, and Overall Conclusions

As the Korean War probably antedates the widespread acceptance within the business community of Keynesian tenets that prosperity could be maintained by public spending for *civilian* needs, the Korean experience is presumably a good test of the proposition that businessmen used to (even if they don't now) think that a little war is a good thing. We investigated the relationship of stock market fluctuations to Korean war events according to procedures similar to those of the Indochina War, but with two variations. In this case, the selection of important events was based upon the location in the top paragraph of the *Wall Street Journal* news summary column, in conjunction with the length and location of headlines in the *New York Times* itself, rather than the *Index*. We also added two categories, United States victory and Communist victory. (These initially had been used in the Indochina coding, but the final selection of events yielded such a small sample of these two types that they were excluded.) A victory was defined in terms of a defeat for the opponent, defeat being indicated by words clearly expressing military setback, such as destroyed, wiped out, crushed, and overrun. The period covered was from June 1950 through July 1953; a total of 76 event days resulted from the selection. Only the net changes for the overall market were examined.

The results of this analysis (see Table 9-5) showed a strong negative correlation between the Dow Jones Industrial averages and both Communist escalation and Communist victory. Hence there certainly was Wall Street

Table 9-5
Stock Changes Against 76 Korean Events: Regression Coefficients

	June 1950-July 1953 Overall	October 1950-July 1953 Post-China Entry
Multiple Correlation Coefficient (*r*)	0.45	0.45
F ratio	2.2	1.65
Regression coefficient[a]		
(1) U.S. Escalation	0.35 (0.70)	−0.23 (0.80)
(2) U.S. Victory	−0.21 (0.80)	−0.51 (0.60)
(3) Communist Escalation	−3.02 *(0.005)	−2.29 *(0.025)
(4) Communist Victory	−1.80 *(0.05)	−1.86 *(0.05)
(5) U.S. Conciliation	−0.90 (0.25)	−1.12 (0.15)
(6) U.S. Unconciliation	−0.12 (0.90)	−0.47 (0.45)
(7) Communist Conciliation	−0.79 (0.35)	−1.13 (0.15)
(8) Communist Unconciliation	0.10 (0.90)	−0.09 (0.90)

[a]Significance levels in parentheses. Levels at 0.10 or under asterisked.

displeasure at prospects that the Communists might gain the upper hand. But there were *no* systematic patterns of response to United States escalation, victory, conciliation, or nonconciliation, nor to Communist conciliation or nonconciliation. Thus, whereas the financial community had turned against the Indochina War by 1967, there was *no particular Wall Street enthusiasm either for the Korean War or for its end*. No division of Korean War events significantly affects this statement.[23]

The strong positive correlation between de-escalatory events and stock price increases during the Indochina War, and the absence of any such relationship for the Korean War, might be explained by two alternative propositions: (1) the economic effects of the Indochina War were perceived by investors as more serious than were those of the earlier war, or (2) a shift in investors' attitudes concerning the economic effects of military intervention occurred in the interim. Or both propositions may have partial explanatory value.

Domestic economic conditions of June 1950 were somewhat different from those of August 1964. The buildup of the Korean War was more rapid, on a larger scale, and utilized a larger fraction of the nation's resources than the later war. However, inflationary pressures in the Korean War were most serious during the first year, after which they were checked in part by the correction of overstocked civilian inventories, and in part by three major pieces of tax legislation and by the introduction of wage, price, and credit controls. Hence, the consumer price index rose by only two percent from 1951-1952 and less than 1 percent in 1952-1953.[24] By contrast, the military spurt of the Indochina War came at a time when the United States was rapidly approaching the full utilization of its resources. The operating rate of industry was higher than at the onset of the Korean War (90 percent versus 80 percent) and the unemployment rate lower (4.5 percent versus 5.4 percent).[25] The stimulus of defense outlays creates problems of economic stabilization and allocation, in any circumstances. If there is a high level of employment and little slack in the economy, the aggregate demand becomes excessive, and inflation serious, unless the government takes neutralizing actions. For a variety of political, economic, and other reasons, the right mix of appropriate monetary and fiscal policies and reduction in nondefense government outlays needed to curb the inflationary pressures of the late 1960s was not achieved,[26] and by 1969 the consumer price index had increased 6.1 percent for that year.

It could be argued that the investor might welcome inflationary tendencies created by war, that the value of common stocks is increased by inflation and therefore preferable to fixed-yield investments. There are indications of this view in the financial press at the time of the Korean War. On the other hand, a casual survey of the financial analyses in the *Wall Street Journal* during the Indochina War seems to indicate a much more negative attitude toward inflation as a market factor. Perhaps by the 1960s investors had begun to decide that inflation may boost stock prices, but at the same time it may decrease corporate profits and dividend values. Tax increases and the introduction of controls to curb inflation tend to have—at least in the short run—a further negative impact on profits. According to the *Wall Street Journal* report from the semiannual meeting of the Business Council in May 1967: "The consensus of 100 leading industrialists was that business will be further strained by the Vietnam War, shrinking profits, higher taxes, a ballooning federal budget deficit, more militant labor, and more skittish shoppers."[27]

Such a changed attitude toward inflation could be part of an increasing appreciation among investors of the destabilizing effects of war upon the economy and the difficulty of selecting, timing, and legislating the appropriate combination of measures that would make a war economy substantially more profitable than a peacetime one. Evidence of a shift in attitudes toward war among business leaders may be found in a 1969 series of Fortune-Yankelovich surveys of more than 300 chief executives of companies listed in the annual *Fortune* 500 directory. When asked which national problems seemed "most pressing and critical," 49 percent cited the Indochina War and 43 percent inflation.[28] In answer to another question 56 percent cited the Indochina War as "one of the most serious threats to the economy at the present time." Another survey in this series indicated a great reluctance to see the United States involved in future wars.[29] Not one of the seven potential *casus belli* listed was cited by a majority of the business leaders as worth fighting for. "Protecting our national interest" ranked highest with 40 percent; only 19 percent indicated "containing the Communists." A later survey of American elite by the Bureau of Applied Social Research at Columbia also found "dovish" attitudes among its selection of business leaders.[30]

Lest we conclude that the business community will keep us out of war, the following points should be made. First, both the Dow Jones Industrial averages and the survey results reflect disillusionment in the later stages of a prolonged war with particularly detrimental effects upon the economy, a war initiated in a period of prosperity. Second, the absence of any negative pattern of response to escalation in either war at least leaves open the possibility that a future war initiated under different economic circumstances, e.g., a recession, might generate a different set of attitudes and responses, despite the "lessons" which appear to have been learned in Indochina. Third, neither the results of this paper nor those of the surveys cited indicate anything about the business community's attitudes towards defense spending or its influence in maintaining these expenditures at a certain level. Insofar as negative attitudes are indicated, they are to war, not weapons. War might well be perceived as creating too many imponderables, carrying too many risks, and further complicating the adjustments necessary to maintain the balance between aggregate demand and productive capacity. At the same time, a sustained high level of defense spending might be regarded as a more practical stimulus than war itself for assuring demand, as planning and adjustments could be made with a greater degree of predictability and, perhaps, with less drastic measures. This is not to imply that such views do or did prevail in the business community, but simply to emphasize the point that the economic propositions tested in this paper were by no means exhaustive.

The fact that investors showed no particular enthusiasm for the continuation or escalation of the Korean or Indochina wars, as indicted by the stock market response to certain events, does not eliminate the economic factor as *a* root of war. But the results do suggest that economic influences may operate in more subtle ways than is generally recognized, and that they may be inseparably linked with other variables. We suspect that an important variable, as yet not very systematically investigated, is the ideological predisposition both of elites and of the public.[31]

Notes

Research on this paper was supported by contract N-0014-67-A-0097-0007 from ARPA, Behavioral Sciences, monitored by the Office of Naval Research.

1. Yet another analysis might look specifically at the reaction of stocks of firms heavily dependent on Vietnam or other military sales. In the extreme case this would merely prove the obvious, that investors in firms profiting greatly from the war would approve its escalation and regret its de-escalation. We have not investigated this here, although some aspects will receive attention in a later report.

2. The substantial evidence available that stock prices follow a random walk demonstrates that there are no systematic patterns of response to cyclical, periodic, or otherwise predictable events. This does not preclude the possibility of finding systematic responses to unpredictable events. See the collection of papers in Paul H. Cootner ed., THE RANDOM CHARACTER OF STOCK MARKET PRICES (Cambridge: M.I.T. Press, 1964).

3. Ronald Aronson, "Socialism, the Sustaining Menace." In K.T. Fann and Donald C. Hodges (eds.), READINGS IN U.S. IMPERIALISM, (Boston: Porter Sargent, 1971), p. 334. See also Ernest Mandel, MARXIST ECONOMIC THEORY, tr. Brian Pearce (New York: Monthly Review Press, 1970), Vol. 2, p. 524. Mandel does point out, however, that the arms economy implies a permanent tendency to inflation.

4. WALL STREET JOURNAL, December 31, 1965, p. 13.

5. Ibid., August 6, 1964, p. 27.

6. Ibid., August 10, 1964, p. 23.

7. "The Strange Economics of the Vietnam War," RAMPARTS 10, No. 5 (November 1971), p. 34.

8. "Needed: Better War—and Peace Aims," FORTUNE 73, No. 1 (January, 1966), pp. 116-17.

9. Paul A. Baran and Paul M. Sweezy, "Notes on the Theory of Imperialism." In K.T. Fann and Donald C. Hodges, p. 81.

10. Gabriel Kolko, THE ROOTS OF AMERICAN FOREIGN POLICY (Boston: Beacon Press, 1969).

11. Harry Magdoff, THE AGE OF IMPERIALISM (New York: Monthly Review Press, 1969), p. 85.

12. Ad Hoc Committee on the Economy and the War, "Economic Interests and American Foreign Policy," REVIEW OF RADICAL POLITICAL ECONOMICS (August, 1970), p. 26.

13. Gabriel Kolko, THE ROOTS OF AMERICAN FOREIGN POLICY, p. 85.

14. One analyst, for example, recently described stock and bond prices as "the most accurate gauge of Wall Street's real views." John H. Allan, "McGovern Speech Affects Stock Prices Only Slightly," NEW YORK TIMES, August 30, 1972, p. 23.

15. Harris, Upham & Co., MARKET INTERPRETATIONS 10, No. 30 (August 7, 1972).

16. G.C. Selden, PSYCHOLOGY OF THE STOCK MARKET (New York: Ticker Publishing, 1912), p. 66. Quoted in Arnold M. Rose, "A Social Psychological Approach to the Study of the Stock Market," KYKLOS 19, No. 2 (1966), p. 273.

17. There is independent evidence that our procedure taps the strongest reaction. An earlier study of the market's reaction to a variety of world events found a plunge on the first day following bad news, with rises on subsequent days. See Victor Niederhoffer, "The Analysis of World Events and Stock Prices," JOURNAL OF BUSINESS OF THE UNIVERSITY OF CHICAGO 44, No. 2 (April 1971), p. 211.

18. WALL STREET JOURNAL, July 29, p. 23 and July 30, p. 25.

19. Ibid., December 18, 1950.

20. Ibid., June 9, 1969, p. 33.

21. A Gallup survey was conducted at brief but irregular intervals from August, 1965, posing the question, "In view of the developments since we entered the fighting in Vietnam, do you think the U.S. made a mistake sending troops to fight in Vietnam?" In early February 1967 52 percent of the national sample gave a negative response; this figure dropped to 50 percent in May, 48 percent in July, and 42 percent in October. It did not subsequently fall below 40 percent until August 1968. See GALLUP OPINION INDEX, Report No. 39, September 1968, p. 3.

22. For this comparison, one must compare the significance level for the Dow Jones average with that for the LDC stocks. Due to the way the averages were constructed, the regression coefficients are not comparable between the two analyses (though they are of course comparable between classes of events within either analysis).

23. The only logical time division would be the entry of China which presaged a sharp decline in popular support for the war. The shift in support was the only significant one of the war. (See John E. Mueller, "Trends in Popular Support for the Wars in Korea and Vietnam," AMERICAN POLITICAL

SCIENCE REVIEW 65, No. 2 (June 1971), pp. 358-75. The analysis of events from November 1950 through July 1953 yielded results similar to those for the entire period.

24. Alvin Hansen, "Inflation: Korea vs. Vietnam," WASHINGTON POST (November 30, 1969), vi, p. 1.

25. Figures supplied by Murray L. Weidenbaum in Center for Strategic Studies, ECONOMIC IMPACT OF THE VIETNAM WAR (Washington: Georgetown University, 1967), p. 19.

26. An extended explanation is contained in Arthur Okun, THE POLITICAL ECONOMY OF PROSPERITY (Washington, D.C.: Brookings, 1970), pp. 62-99.

27. WALL STREET JOURNAL, May 16, 1967, p. 23.

28. "What Business Thinks," FORTUNE 80, No. 4 (September 1969) pp. 93, 94, 208.

29. "What Business Thinks," FORTUNE 80, No. 5 (October 1969), pp. 139-40.

30. NEW YORK TIMES, Aug. 17, 1972, p. 9.

31. For some important suggestions see Wayne Moyer, "House Voting on Defense: An Ideological Explanation," and Douglas H. Rosenberg, "Arms and the American Way: The Ideological Dimensions of Military Growth," both in Bruce M. Russett and Alfred Stepan (eds.), MILITARY FORCE AND AMERICAN SOCIETY (New York: Harper & Row, 1973).

10

Why We Overspend and Underaccomplish: Weapons Procurement and the Military-Industrial Complex

Robert J. Art

Whether measured by dollars spent or people involved, the procurement of major weapons systems consumes huge resources.* For the last 15 years, at least one-third of the defense budget each year has been devoted to the development, production, and maintenance of aircraft, missiles, tanks, surface ships, submarines, and associated electronic gear. The amount spent for fiscal year 1972 on these systems will be close to $30 billion. In any given year, at least 30 major systems are in various stages of development and production. Several hundred thousand soldiers and civilians in the Defense Department are concerned with defense procurement. If we add to this the number of people employed by firms doing defense work, the figure runs into the millions. Weapons system management is big business—on a gigantic scale.

Where such sums and numbers of people are involved, continuing close scrutiny and periodic public criticism by the Congress, press, and attentive academics can be expected. In past years, defense procurement has been scrutinized and criticized and has had its share of exposés of mismanagement, the C-5A being the most recent example. What is significant about the present, however, is, first, that the criticism points unanimously to a widespread inefficiency *inherent* in the weapons acquisition process and, second, that much of this criticism comes from *within* the defense establishment. In August of 1970, for example, in delivering an address to the Armed Forces Management Association—a who's who of the military industrial complex—then Deputy Secretary of Defense David Packard spoke bluntly: "Frankly, gentlemen, in defense procurement, we have a real mess on our hands. Let's face it—the fact is there has been bad management of many defense programs in the past." In its report on the FY 1972 defense budget, the Senate Armed Services Committee said: "if the geometric cost increase for weapons systems is not sharply reversed, then even significant increases in the defense budget may not insure the force levels required for national security." The House Appropriations Committee has stated that what we need now is, "not more dollars for defense, but more defense for the dollars." One pundit summarized the matter this way: "while weapons performance is poor and deliveries are late, costs are overrunning right on schedule."[1]

Why the current spate of criticism? The antimilitary climate created by the Vietnam War is part of the answer; the need to reorder priorities for domestic problems is another. But when the establishment begins to criticize itself publicly, something deeper is at work. What has happened, in effect, is that civilian officials responsible for procurement have recognized that past procedures have not worked well because they have failed to correct the causes of waste rooted in the system. A brief review of past practices will shed some light on what future improvements are urgently needed in order to control the astronomical cost growth of major weapons.

The 1950s and 1960s

Two terms characterize the way development programs were managed in the 1950s: crash programs and massive cost overruns. The sense of urgency surrounding our missile programs in the mid-1950s led to the practice of spending whatever sums were necessary to realize them as quickly as possible. The major device used by the government to get defense firms to undertake these programs on a crash basis was the cost-plus-fixed-fee (CPFF) contract. This type of contract transferred the risks of development inherent in most new weapon systems from the defense firm to the government. With the CPFF contract, the firm was guaranteed a fixed fee, or profit, no matter how high the total cost of the system; the government bore all the costs incurred by the contractor in developing and producing the weapon. The result was massive cost overruns. Studies done by the RAND Corporation and Harvard Business School found that in the 1950s the average weapon's cost was three times as much as expected.[2]

Reading these results, the McNamara team in the Pentagon devised new procedures to procure major weapons systems. The hallmark of the 1960s became incentive-type contracts and "contract definition." Reasoning that a defense firm had no contractual incentives to control costs under CPFF contracts, defense officials sought to create such incentives. Instead of guaranteeing a contractor a fixed profit no matter how large his costs, they related profits inversely to costs: the higher a contractor's costs, the lower his profits; and the lower his costs, the higher his profits. In short, through the device of incentive contracting, the government sought to share the risks of development with the defense firm.[3]

In order to make these risks manageable, the Defense Department resorted to the device of "contract definition." For most programs designed to advance "the state of the art"—to provide the Pentagon with a new, more effective capability—numerous uncertainties exist—whether the new capability can be provided at all; if so, what is the best way to do it; and, of course, how much will it cost to do it. Most programs in the 1950s experienced such large overruns because they were initially poorly defined; the uncertainties, that is, were not located and delineated early enough in these programs. As a consequence, expensive solutions were required for unanticipated problems. In the 1960s, therefore, the McNamara team tried to define a project more clearly at the outset, before substantial sums were committed to it. The device of contract definition was intended to reduce the unknowns as much as possible and then to put a price tag on them. Contract definition was a competition carried on, usually between two companies, for a period of several months in order to determine which firm would receive the development contract. Each company prepared extensive technical designs and cost estimates—all on paper—of its proposed solutions to the government's requested new capability. Often these "paper competitions" generated studies standing eight feet high and weighing over one ton.

Contract definition and incentive contracts thus went hand in hand. The former was intended to reduce the risks in developing a new weapon by eliminating many uncertainties; the latter, to divide the reduced risks between the government and the firm competitively chosen to develop the weapon. Both devices, if they worked, should have reduced cost overruns. If the developer had a clearer idea of what he was doing, then presumably he could price it more accurately. If his profits were related inversely to his costs, then presumably he would keep his costs as low as possible.

Did the devices of the 1960s work any better than those of the 1950s? The evidence is still tentative, but the answer appears to be "no." Cost overruns in the 1960s were less on the average than they were in the 1950s: close to twice instead of three times the estimated cost.[4] The reduction in cost overruns, however, can be misleading; and in this case, it does not signify a substantial improvement in the efficiency of the weapons acquisition process. A cost overrun is a difference between an initial estimate and a final figure. The difference can be narrowed either by raising the initial estimate or by lowering the final figure.[5] The earlier in the life of a program an estimate of its total cost is made, the more optimistic (low) the estimate is likely to be. Hence, high overruns can be produced merely by using very early estimates. In the 1950s such early estimates were used as the base figures and accounted in part for the high average overruns.[6] In the 1960s a conscious effort was made not to use such early estimates as base figures. The reduction in average overruns for the 1960s can thus be partially accounted for by a systematic shift in the base figures used. Moreover, the weapons systems of the 1960s were carried on with less urgency and incorporated smaller technological advances than did those of the 1950s. To the extent that urgency is reduced and the state of the art not pushed so far, cost overruns are likely to be smaller.[7] Again, we can partially account for the reduction in overruns, not by any significant improvement in the efficiency of the acquisition process, but rather by a change in the nature of the programs.

The significance of reduced cost overruns in the 1960s becomes even more dubious when we look at how incentive-type contracts affected prices. Under CPFF contracts, firms understated their estimated costs because they would suffer no penalty by doing so. "Optimism," or unrealistically low bids, characterized the 1950s. In the 1960s, in many cases, the reverse seems to have occurred: "pessimism" took over and unrealistically high bids replaced unrealistically low ones. Under incentive-type contracts, if a firm could negotiate a price (a target cost) with the government well above what it thought the program was likely to cost, it would then make a much larger profit than would otherwise be the case if its actual costs turned out to be well below the price set with the government. If a defense firm has reduced its cost overrun by inflating the total contract price, the government and the taxpayer have not saved money! Recent studies by the RAND Corporation suggest that precisely this situation occurred on many programs in the 1960s.[8]

The effects of these three factors—a change in base figures, a change in the nature of programs, and the inflation of target costs—should make us skeptical about the meaning of the average overrun reduction of the 1960s. We should not feel confident, that is, that we could in the 1960s more accurately predict the likely cost of *any given program* than we could in the 1950s. But greater accuracy in predicting final costs is integral to attaining an efficient, effective defense posture. Two types of questions must be asked and answered in defense procurement: first, how many and what kinds of major new weapons should we buy; second, once these decisions have been made, how can we spend the monies allocated as efficiently as possible? Neither of these questions is easy to answer.[9] The answers to the first, moreover, depend partly upon the answers given to the second. In an intelligent approach to defense, one considers the likely cost of a new program when evaluating its potential usefulness. For example, the military effectiveness of a new bomber will depend in part upon how many are available for use. If the bomber turns out to cost twice as much as estimated, two choices can be made: first, fewer bombers can be bought than originally planned; second, the original quantity can be purchased, but then decisions will have to be made on what other programs to cut in order to provide the additional funds required.[10] In the first case, the effectiveness of the bomber may be degraded if fewer are available; in the second case, other programs will suffer and an unbalanced overall military posture may result. Because an effective defense posture depends upon how we allocate our scarce resources, we need to know the likely cost of a new program *before* we begin to spend significant sums on it. Better choices will result only if the real costs of future alternatives are known at the time the choices are made.

The System Corrupts

Why have we not been able to control the costs of acquiring new weapons? Why has nothing worked well in the past? Even a cursory look into the weapons acquisition process reveals, first, that the causes of waste are endemic to the way the process is structured and, second, that past reforms have not touched these causes. Not the quality or the motives of the people involved, but rather the incentives of the system are responsible for the inefficiencies. Money is wasted because the system rewards waste and penalizes efficiency. It is the system itself that corrupts, and it does so because of five factors.

Gold-plating. First is the inherent bias of the military services toward what is called "gold-plating"—the design of weapons that are more sophisticated technologically than they need be for the task specified. Combat is a risky, often fatal, and always highly uncertain business. The military services naturally want to cope with the uncertainties of combat by doing everything possible to make the outcome certain—to guarantee victory. This means obtaining as many forces as they can get and also the best weapons they can buy. General Carl "Tooey" Spatz put the military perspective well: "a second-best airplane is like a second-best poker hand. No damn good!"[11]

We should not buy "second best." But how much do we need to spend in order to make certain that what we have is good enough? The question has no definite answer. Each weapon must be analyzed in terms of both the mission it is to perform and the desirability of the mission itself. Buying what is sufficient, but not that which is gold-plated, requires continuous monitoring by civilians in the Pentagon. Such oversight has not been consistently exercised in the past, as former Deputy Secretary Packard made clear in testifying before a Congressional subcommittee: "Many of our new weapons programs have been in trouble from the very beginning because of a tendency toward overambition for what is wanted, and overambition on what is thought can be done." He put the point more prosaically at a news conference when he referred to the MBT-70 (main battle tank)—a program plagued by overruns and delays: "the boys wanted everything but the kitchen sink on the tank."[12]

The military services are the consumers of the weapons the Pentagon buys. They have been able to retain considerable control over weapons procurement no matter who the top team of civilians has been. The military consequently, are the ones the defense firms seek to satisfy. Not too little, but too much competition and over the wrong things have therefore characterized the contests to get defense contracts. Big firms heavily engaged in defense business need contracts to survive. The technical expertise they develop on one contract enables them to compete more effectively on future contracts. The military services demand the most technology can offer. The firms compete to give it to them. What the Armed Services Procurement Regulations call "source selection competitions," the defense firms term "the bidding and lying competitions."

Bidding and Lying. The second factor driving up the costs of new weapons is that defense firms have not been penalized for their "bidding and lying." Only about 10 percent of all defense procurement dollars is awarded on the basis of price alone in "formally advertised" competitions. The remaining 90 percent is awarded in a "negotiated" environment, where design and technical performance are as important, if not more so, than price. Negotiated procurement consists of two types: "competitive," where two or more firms bid for a contract; and "sole-source," where the government negotiates the terms of the contract only with one firm. Sole-source procurement accounts for 50 to 60 percent of all procurement dollars awarded each year. This was so in 1962; it is so today.[13]

Most negotiated and single-source procurement is unavoidable. The government *must* work closely with defense firms in defining what it wants from them. Often the government is not certain exactly what it does want, or whether what it wants is technologically feasible. Equally as often, defense firms are not completely clear about what the government is asking of them. A certain amount of give-and-take, or negotiation, is inherent in the process. Also, design and technical performance *are* important. The government wants to do business with the firm that promises to produce the "best looking" system. The government *does* become "locked-into" the developer of a weapons system. The costs in delay and dollars are too high for the government to switch and award the production contract to a different firm.[14] The advantages for the contractor are evident: if he has bid low in order to obtain the development contract, he can make up his losses and "get well" on the production contract. He can do so because only 20 percent of the total costs of a weapon is spent on development; the other 80 percent is incurred in the production phase.

In their considerations of costs, the armed services are at a disadvantage. Their cost estimates have usually been dependent upon data supplied to them by the contractors. In order to avoid this dependence, the armed services have resorted to producing estimates derived from historical experience by a technique called "parametric costing"—a technique that incorporates all the inefficiency of past programs and therefore projects past waste into future programs.[15]

The contractor, moreover, has many devices available to evade the price commitments he has made. The one most frequently and effectively used is the "contract change order"—a mechanism for changing the stipulations of the initial contract while the program is in progress. Most major programs have experienced literally thousands of change orders. Some are necessary because of unforeseen technical difficulties; some, beneficial because they simplify things and reduce costs; and some, desirable because they incorporate new technology that has become available after the initial contract was signed. Too many, however, are unnecessary because they needlessly gold-plate the product *during* development.

Because change orders have been so numerous and so costly, they have rendered incentive-type contracts ineffective in controlling costs. When a change order is proposed, the government has usually had no clear idea of its exact cost; and when the government does settle accounts, it does so long after the work has already been completed. Through this process the government in effect re-imburses the contractor for the costs he has incurred. Change orders thus convert any contract into a cost-reimbursable type. Since the contracting firm is, moreover, entitled to a profit on changes in specifications, the more expensive and numerous the changes, the greater the total cost of the program for the taxpayer and the larger the total profit for the contractor. The defense firm therefore has a positive incentive to gold-plate during development: it makes more money by doing so.

Military service-industry relations have thus been akin to labor-management collective bargaining. Each side has some leverage over the other, but neither can live without the other. Some interests are opposed, but many are shared. Too often the shared interests have predominated. The military have stressed promised performance; the contractors have given it to them. The contractors have taken advantage of contractual loopholes; the military have encouraged them to do so. The weapons acquisition environment has been conducive, not to realistic price competition, but to extravagant performance promises and overoptimistic (low) bids.[16]

Profits for Inefficiency. The third factor responsible for driving the costs of procurement up is the manner in which profits are figured. Many critics claim that defense firms earn a much higher rate of profit on defense contracts than do comparable firms engaged in commercial work. This may be so, although recent studies do not conclusively confirm the claim.[17] In terms of the total cost of a program, however, the size of the profit is not significant. This is so because profits on defense contracts amount to only about 5 percent of sales. Cost overruns on a program can run anywhere from 100 to 600 percent of estimated costs. An example will clarify the point. Assume that the initial cost of a program is estimated to be $2 billion. Assume an overrun of 100 percent, or $2 billion. With a total cost of $4 billion, and with profits 5 percent of total cost, a profit of $200 million results. The overrun is $2 billion. The profit accounts only for 10 percent of the overrun. What accounts for the other 90 percent?

Not the absolute size of profits, but the *way* they are determined accounts for much of the overruns. On defense contracts profits are negotiated as a percentage of sales. This means simply, as we saw in the case of contract change orders, that higher profits result if larger costs are incurred. The method of determining profits as a percentage of costs, moreover, rewards and thereby perpetuates inefficiency because of the way costs are defined. Simply put, costs are determined by totaling what the firm spends on labor, materials, and overhead in order to fulfill the terms of the contract. Notice, however, that in doing so the amount of capital investment a firm makes is *not* included in the costs on which profits are figured.[18]

Two things result from this anomaly: first, the defense contractor has no incentive to make those capital investments that will improve his efficiency on a current contract; second, if such investments increase his overall efficiency, he will be penalized on future contracts. An increase in efficiency will mean a reduction in total labor, material, and overhead costs. And if total allowable costs are reduced, so too are profits. The result is that a firm can make larger profits by remaining inefficient. Once again, the system rewards waste and penalizes economy.

Managers Without Power. A fourth cause of high costs is what we may call "bureaucratic foul-ups." All major weapons programs, in fact almost all programs, are headed by a "program manager" who is usually a middle-ranking military officer, supposed to have the authority to run the program, to make the countless daily decisions that any complex project entails. In the past, however, he has not had this authority.[19] Officers who rank above him in the chain of command interject themselves into these daily decisions in one of two ways. Either they demand to be kept constantly informed of the progress of the program, or they require that they be consulted on the daily decisions. The result of the first is to convert the program manager into an information errand boy—the ever-ready "oral briefer." The result of the second is to convert him into a "base-toucher"—the man who must check out every proposed decision with innumerable people before he finally makes it.

Neither result has permitted the program manager to exercise effective control. But another, subtler factor is also at work. Because the program manager is a middle-ranked officer, he is dependent for career advancement upon the evaluations of his performance by those very superiors who are constantly harassing him. The desire for promotion pressures the program manager to please his superiors, to give them what they want, which is, of course, the best system produced in the shortest time possible, regardless of the cost. The situation the program manager finds himself in was described pointedly by a civilian procurement official for the Navy before a Congressional subcommittee: "if the heads of all the contract divisions in the Navy are captains and four stripers and they are under a lot of admirals, they do not stand up when they have not yet been selected [promoted] . . . when they are told to do something by the admiral, his finger is right on their number."[20]

The services, moreover, operate under the "every-man-is-a-potential-chief-of-staff" theory. Besides good performance, wide experience is essential in order to advance to the pinnacles of power. Wide experience means frequent rotation (every two or three years) from one assignment to another. The effect on major weapons programs is a disaster: just when a man has developed real expertise and the program reaches its crucial stage, the program manager is rotated and replaced with someone who has no idea about what is going on. The crowning touch is that program management is not thought a particularly valuable or important assignment. The military rely totally on major weapons, but they do not consider the job of developing them either glamorous or desirable!

Concurrency. The fifth and final factor that has kept procurement costs higher than need be is something called "concurrency," a practice prevalent in the 1960s and designed to reduce the lead time of a weapon system (the time between the beginning of development and the putting of the weapon into use). Concurrency means that substantial production of a weapon begins before development is finished. The result is costly. If difficulties are encountered during development (which always happens), corrections have to be made on all the items being produced or already finished. Concurrency means that every mistake is repeated a large number of times and implies a multiplication of corrections. And, of course, the costs of these corrections. . . .

Packard's Reforms

We can readily understand why Deputy Secretary Packard said that defense procurement is "a real mess" and due to "bad management." Ever since the mid-1950s, when the government brought the defense sector of the American economy into being, it has laid down the rules according to which weapons systems are procured. If a mess exists, the government bears the primary responsibility for creating it. What the government has created it can modify. The causes of the high costs of procuring weapons point unmistakably to this conclusion: the system itself needs to be reformed if the costs are to be reduced.

This was precisely the conclusion that Packard himself reached after a few months in office. He moved vigorously to improve the efficiency of the weapons acquisition process, and three of his reforms deserve particular mention.[21] First is the "fly-before-you-buy" approach that requires the military to know as much as they can about a product before they buy it in substantial quantities. Packard directed the military to modify the practice of concurrency, that is, not to begin substantial production until development is nearly completed. The more nearly finished a weapon is, the better one can predict the costs of its entire life cycle. Fly-before-you-buy also means that, where possible, prototype competitions are held to select the production contractor. Two firms will each actually produce a development model, and these will be tested against one another in order to determine which is the better.

The fly-before-you-buy approach of the early 1970s is thus a refinement of the contract-definition approach of the 1960s. The major difficulty with programs in the 1950s was their poor initial definition. Contract definition was supposed to remedy that by clearly specifying what was to be done before it was done. The basic idea behind the approach was sound, but it was poorly executed: companies spent too much of their time preparing paper studies and too little of it doing actual technical work. While paper piled up, actual development stagnated. The intent of fly-before-you-buy is to do more *hardware* development and testing, particularly of components and subsystems, and fewer paper studies. Contract definition is not bad *per se*, but paper prediction has its limits.

Packard's second reform was to upgrade the military management expertise by improving the quality of program managers and by increasing their authority. This will require, as Packard has testified, "a major change in the organizational structure of all three services" to insure that "the development and production of new weapon systems are managed by people who are experts in the business." Efforts are currently underway to increase the authority of the program manager, to give him better training before he goes on the job, to keep him there long enough to be effective, and to enhance the status of, and rewards for, good program management. This reform reflects the recognition that in the 1960s too much reliance was placed on incentive contracts to hold cost growth down. Such contracts are necessary, but without highly qualified governmental personnel to exercise continuous review, the incentives are rendered ineffective.

Third was the decision to control gold-plating. Packard stated that programs will not be put into development "until we are sure we need them." Once that decision is made, vigorous reviews will be conducted to eliminate "the many 'nice' or 'desirable' features which so often creep into these systems as they proceed through development and production." To monitor gold-plating before and during development, two controls have been devised. One is DSARC, the Defense Systems Acquisition Review Council, composed of those top civilian officials in the Office of the Secretary of Defense (OSD) who are responsible for weapons acquisition. The function of DSARC is to review a major program's progress at key points in order to retain control over it at the OSD level. The other device is to prohibit the military from authorizing a change order until after a ceiling price has been put on it.

Probable Results

Will these reforms work to reduce the costs of acquiring major new weapons systems? We will not know the definitive answers for four or five years. Based on past experience and practices, however, we can say a few things about the likelihood of their success.

First, these reforms are not sufficient to control costs completely. Certainly they are a step in the right direction, but more steps are needed. Two in particular should be adopted by the Defense Department. One, is to consider the capital investment that a contractor will make on a particular program when deciding whom to give the contract to and how large a profit he is entitled to. If defense firms know that the government is seriously comparing their relative efficiencies of operation in making award decisions, then they will be forced to become more efficient in order to stay in business. If they know, furthermore, that they can increase their profits (or at least not have them reduced) by making capital investments that improve efficiency, then the incentives to do so will be stronger. As Robert Anthony, former comptroller of the Pentagon, has said about considering contractors' capital investment in contract awards: "the possibility has been discussed in the Department of Defense at least since 1962. It is time to act."[22]

The other step is to make more extensive use of what are called "should cost" techniques—an approach to cost estimating that involves extensive and intensive analysis by a team of experts of a particular plant where a system is to be produced, rather than a statistical projection based upon past experience with similar systems. "Should cost" estimating can be used to determine whether a firm's proposed methods of operation for a particular contract are as efficient as they can be and hence whether the proposed costs are as reasonable as they should be. Because the government "marries" a particular firm once it signs the development contract, the "should cost" approach *should* put the government in a stronger bargaining position when it negotiates the production contract. By generating better cost data than the government has had available to it in the past, this technique will mitigate some of the undesirable consequences of the "lock-in effect."[23]

The second general point we can make is that all these reforms will take time to institutionalize, and none of them will work unless top civilian officials in the Pentagon continue to press them constantly. The military have "staying power." They are always there. They see civilians come and go. Now that Packard has gone, for example, will his reforms live after him?

In any event, the present reforms will be ephemeral unless the present and future civilian leadership dedicates itself continuously to cost control. Furthermore, without tight control, some of the present reforms will prove to be counterproductive. For example, Packard stressed—correctly—that "the most effective cost control of a development program is making practical trade-offs between operating requirements and engineering design" and "therefore, unless cost is continually kept in mind as an important factor in making [these] trade-offs or compromises, . . . cost never can be minimized."[24] The ability to make such tradeoffs requires a degree of flexibility in contractual arrangements. OSD must have the option not to push for a given increment in performance if its cost proves too great to justify it and to make such decisions without having to rewrite a large part of the original contract; for that is a time-consuming game that will reopen issues already settled.

The C-5A case illustrates how a wrongly-written contract can strait-jacket OSD. The contract signed in 1965 with Lockheed was the Total Package Procurement (TPP) type. Under its terms Lockheed was bound, not only to develop the C-5A, but also to produce a given number at a fixed per unit price *before* it had even begun development. TPP had been designed to make the lock-in effect work to the government's advantage—to make a virtue out of a necessary marriage—by preventing a contractor from buying-in on a development program and then getting well on the production contract. The rationale was that if he had to sign a contract stipulating both development and production costs at the outset, he could not inflate the production contract.[25] Unfortunately for Lockheed and ultimately for the government, the performance specifications for the C-5A required a much greater advance in the state of the art than anyone at the time realized. The technological solutions were quite expensive, but Lockheed was bound to provide them and initially, at least, to bear the cost. Had more flexibility existed in the contract, OSD could have made the tradeoffs Packard spoke of and not been faced with the subsequent choice of bailing Lockheed out or letting it go under.[26]

The point of the C-5A case is clear: flexibility is essential in programs requiring major technological advances. The danger in such flexibility, however, should be equally clear: unless OSD perseveres in vigorous, continuous supervision, the lower echelons will turn such flexibility to their own advantage to put the "kitchen sink" on every future major program. They have done so in the past; it is prudent to expect them to try to do so in the future.

Future difficulties aside, however, Packard's efforts have already encountered strong resistance from the military. Take the effort to tighten up and enhance the authority of the program manager. Here is what Packard said before the House Appropriations Committee in March, 1970:

With the long tradition of putting a general in charge of the battle, or putting an admiral in charge of a fleet, one would think it would be easy to get the Services to accept the proposition that you should have one man with authority in charge of a weapon development and acquisition program.

We have been able to get this done in a few isolated cases, *but it simply has not been fully accepted as a management must by any of the Services.* (italics added)[27]

Lest we think the world began with Packard's reforms, note these words by Secretary of Defense Robert S. McNamara in 1963 before a congressional committee:

I want to look to a point of central control and information in the form of a program manager for each major weapon system. . . . He shall be rewarded in his career for prompt and analytical disclosure of his problems as well as for his successes. *This is a key position in our military departments, demanding the best managerial talents on which I want to place full reliance for our future weapons inventories.* (italics added)[28]

McNamara found he could not do so. Because of service resistance, he was forced to centralize decision-making in his own office—to rely, as Packard put it, "almost solely on the analysis and recommendation of the OSD staff." Laird and Packard criticized the centralization of decision-making that occurred under McNamara and moved to reverse the process. Their key phrase is "participatory management"—the "decentralization and delegation of authority under specific guidance" that allots to "the military departments a larger role in making the decisions that affect them" and that gives "the military departments and the

Joint Chiefs of Staff the major responsibility for force planning and program development." Packard spoke proudly of the way this process worked on the FY 1971 defense budget: "This was the first time in over 10 years that the Defense program submitted to the Congress was one developed at the initiative of the Military Departments and the JCS rather than the initiative of the Secretary of Defense."[29] The budget process has worked basically the same way for this and next year's fiscal budgets.

This leads us to the third general point: "participatory management" is at war with Packard's stated procurement goal "we will buy only things that we need." The point is quite simple. Whenever each of the military services is permitted to allocate its funds in ways it sees fit, the overall outcome is usually duplication, gold-plating, and an unbalanced defense posture. What is good for the Army, Navy, and Air Force, separately, is not necessarily good for the Defense Department as a whole. Yet that is the way things are moving now, just as they did in the 1950s. For example, each of the three services is currently planning to buy a close-support aircraft designed to aid combat troops in the field. The Army, which—if we count helicopters—now has a larger air force than the Air Force, wants the Cheyenne helicopter gunship. The Air Force is asking for the AX; the Marines, for the British-built Harrier that can take off and land almost like a helicopter. Gold-plating is back again (indeed, did it ever go away?). The Air Force is requesting funds for the B-1 bomber, a plane that is to have a high Mach capability, even though all independent analyses have shown that the speed of the aircraft is not crucial to the success of its mission. Rather, what counts for a bomber, is the electronic gear that it carries to jam enemy radar and the air-to-ground missiles it can launch far from the reach of enemy ground-to-air missiles. Indeed, the present design of the B-1 looks much like the B-70, the program McNamara cancelled over 10 years ago. When duplication and gold-plating occur, can an unbalanced military posture be far behind?

None of the reforms that Packard has instituted will mean anything unless better decisions are made on what major systems to buy and unless more control is exercised over how the military allocate their funds. If we reduce the costs of acquiring a weapon, but decide to buy one ill-designed for a specific mission, or one well-designed for a superfluous mission, or if we buy three different weapons where one may suffice, we have wasted money.

Guidelines for the 1970s

A significant improvement in the weapons acquisition process is now within our grasp. We have two decades of experience to draw upon. We can learn from our past mistakes. The 1950s demonstrated the disadvantages of crash programs and widespread use of CPFF contracts. The 1960s have shown that incentive contracts and paper contract definitions are not sufficient to hold cost growth down. The 1950s were characterized by an almost exclusive reliance on government monitoring of contractor operations as the way to control cost increases. The 1960s were marked by an overconfidence in, and hence over-reliance on, the powers of incentive contracts to force defense firms to do the same job. The 1950s illustrated that close government oversight of contractor operations will not work without the proper contractual safeguards. The 1960s have shown that proper contractual incentives will not be effective unless the government improves its monitoring capability.

The management lessons of the past two decades for controlling cost growth in the 1970s are thus clear. First, crash programs should be used only in those few instances where the interests of national security are overriding. Second, a contractor's capital investment in a project should be an important criterion for awarding contracts. Third, incentive contracts are generally preferable to CPFF contracts; but they will have limited effect unless supplemented with tight controls on contract change orders. Fourth, the concept of contract definition is sound; but greater emphasis should be put on hardware development and testing before a commitment is made to advanced engineering development and to full-scale production. Fifth, total package procurement can be used on programs in which little or no technological advance is sought; but in programs that demand major advances, TPP should be avoided. Sixth, parametric costing is useful for yielding rough estimates of a program's cost; but "should cost" techniques should be used when negotiating development and production contracts. Seventh, top-level OSD managers must preserve their ability to make meaningful decisions at the various stages of a program; but they will not be completely free to do so unless the expertise of middle-level service personnel is improved and their perspectives altered.

The first six principles can be implemented by executive fiat and easily monitored. Improving expertise and altering outlooks, however, can be ordered but not thereby achieved. In the past the military have shown themselves to be remarkably resistant both to compromising on quality and to trading an improvement in quality for a reduction in quantity. Too often in the past, therefore, the management choices for OSD have been an either/or affair—either become deeply involved in the daily details of programs and become over-burdened, or delegate the details and be presented with faits accomplis. Neither of these alternatives is desirable.

The Laird-Packard approach attempted to steer between these two extremes. The approach—the delegation of daily management to the middle level and the retention of key decisions for the top level—is sound in theory, but prob-lematical in practice. Its success hangs heavily on service cooperation. If the past is a reasonable guide to the future, we should not expect too much too soon from the military services, and perhaps nothing at all. Should service coopera-tion not be forthcoming in a reasonable period, OSD must devise alternative ways of obtaining what it wants from middle-level personnel. One way might be the creation of a civilian corps of weapons acquisition managers—men who would work closely with military personnel, but who would retain the powers of decision-making. Contingency planning on such an alternative now might even be a good stimulus for obtaining future service cooperation.

But let us assume that the services do cooperate and that all the other reforms are fully implemented and work well, what then should we expect? How much improvement should we look for? Because our measure of success depends so heavily upon our expectations, two additional caveats are necessary. First, we should not expect to reduce the overall average cost overrun below 20 percent. In other words, expect the actual cost of a system to be at best 20 percent more than the originally estimated cost. We should not expect to reduce overruns any lower than this because of the inherent inefficiencies built into such large-scale enterprises, because of the limits on accuracy inherent in any cost estimating technique, and because of the desirability of some cost growth for program flexibility.

Second, we should not assume that a reduction in cost overruns means significantly less-expensive weapons systems. We must not fall into the trap of thinking that merely because we have reduced cost overruns, we are thereby spending money efficiently. We must distinguish between the management of an on-going program and the initial decision on which program to procure. As long as technological virtuosity continues to dominate these initial decisions, we will still be buying very expensive systems, *even though each one of them has a significantly reduced cost overrun.* Too many of our programs have been technologically muscle-bound: they have become so sophisticated that their reliability and maintainability have been severely degraded. The analogy with the fancy sports car that needs to be in the shop every three days is appropriate here. When it runs, it is unsurpassed. But it does not run very often.

More consideration, therefore, must be given to upgrading existing systems as an alternative to building completely new ones; and more effort should be put into developing simple, reliable systems. Controlling the cost growth of an on-going program is only the first step in achieving efficiency in defense procurement. A reduction in cost overruns is necessary in order to choose intelligently among alternative systems, but it cannot guarantee that the best available alternatives have been presented. Improving the procedures through which we develop and produce major weapons systems should be no substitute for intelligent decisions on which systems to procure.

Notes

*Reprinted with permission from FOREIGN POLICY, Number 6, Spring, 1972; Copyright 1972 by National Affairs, Inc. I have made some revisions and additions to the original paper for the present volume.

1. POLICY CHANGES IN WEAPON SYSTEM PROCUREMENT, Hearings before the Military Operations Subcommittee of the Committee on Government Operations, House, 91st Congress, 2nd Session, pp. 322-24; Senate Armed Services Committee, REPORT NO. 92-359, September 7, 1971, pp. 16-22; House Appropriations Committee, HOUSE REPORT NO. 91-1570, October 6, 1970, p. 5; CONGRESSIONAL RECORD, 92nd Congress, 1st Session, 15 April 1971, S4935.

2. See A.W. Marshall and W.H. Meckling, PREDICTABILITY OF THE COSTS, TIME AND SUCCESS OF DEVELOPMENT, RAND, P-1821, December 1959; and Merton J. Peck and Frederic M. Scherer, THE WEAPONS ACQUISITION PROCESS: AN ECONOMIC ANALYSIS. (Boston: Harvard Business School, 1962).

3. See Frederic M. Scherer, THE WEAPONS ACQUISITION PROCESS: ECONOMIC INCENTIVES (Boston: Harvard Business School, 1964), Chapters 6-10; and Office of the Secretary of Defense, INCENTIVE CONTRACTING GUIDE (Washington, D.C.: Department of Defense, 1965), for a thorough discussion of incentive contracting.

4. See R.L. Perry et al., SYSTEM ACQUISITION EXPERIENCE, RAND RM-6072-PR, November 1969; and A.J. Harmon and S. Henrichsen, A METHODOLOGY FOR COST FACTOR COMPARISON AND PREDICTION, RAND RM-6269-ARPA, August, 1970.

5. Cost overruns can be viewed as either a difference or a ratio. Strictly speaking, an overrun is the difference between an estimate and a final incurred cost. An estimate of $100.00 and an incurred cost of $200.00 gives an overrun of $100.00 or 100 percent. Expressed as a ratio, the overrun is twice the estimated cost. ($\frac{\$200.00}{\$100.00} = 2$). A ratio of 2 yields a difference of 100 percent; a ratio of 3, a difference of 200 percent; and so forth. Since a cost overrun can be expressed either as a ratio or a difference, I have used the term to cover both cases.

6. Adam Yarmolinsky, THE MILITARY ESTABLISHMENT (New York: Harper and Row, 1971), pp. 270-71.

7. See R.L. Perry, and Harmon and Henrichsen.

8. See, for example, I.N. Fisher, A REAPPRAISAL OF INCENTIVE CONTRACTING EXPERIENCE, RAND, RM-5700-PR, July, 1968.

9. There is no *a priori* answer to the first question. See, for example, Morton H. Halperin, "The Good, the Bad, and the Wasteful," FOREIGN POLICY, No. 6 (Spring, 1972), pp. 69-83.

10. There is a third choice: scrap the program entirely. Given the hold that the military services exercise over weapons procurement, this option is usually exercised only when development has proved the system to be unattainable technologically.

11. Quoted in Robert J. Art, THE TFX DECISION: MCNAMARA AND THE MILITARY (Boston: Little, Brown, 1968), p. 126.

12. PREPARED STATEMENT OF DEPUTY SECRETARY OF DEFENSE DAVID PACKARD ON SELECTED ASPECTS OF THE FY 1972-76 DEFENSE PROGRAM (hereinafter referred to as Packard's Statement), in DOD Appropriations for FY 1972, Hearings before House Committee on Appropriations, 92nd Congress, 1st Session, Part 2, p. 16; Statement of Deputy Secretary of Defense David Packard to the Press, 9 June 1970, in POLICY CHANGES IN WEAPON SYSTEM PROCUREMENT, p. 317.

13. See United States Department of Defense, Office of the Secretary of Defense, MILITARY PRIME CONTRACT AWARDS AND SUBCONTRACT PAYMENTS, Fiscal Years 1962-1972.

14. See George R. Hall and Robert E. Johnson, A REVIEW OF AIR FORCE PROCUREMENT, 1962-1964, RAND, RM-4500-PP, May, 1965, especially pp. 77-98; and Hall and Johnson, AIRCRAFT CO-PRODUCTION AND PROCUREMENT STRATEGY, RAND, R-450-PR, May, 1967.

15. See Planning Research Corporation, METHODS OF ESTIMATING FIXED-WING AIRFRAME COSTS, Vol. 1, PRC R-547A, April, 1967.

16. See the testimony of Frederic M. Scherer in COMPETITION IN DEFENSE PROCUREMENT, Hearings before the Subcommittee on Antitrust and Monopoly of the Committee on the Judiciary, Senate, 90th Congress, 2nd Session, pp. 125-36.

17. Four of the most recent studies on defense profits are: Murray Weidenbaum, "Arms and the American Economy: A Domestic Convergence Hypothesis," AMERICAN ECONOMIC REVIEW (May, 1968), pp. 428-37; William Baldwin, THE STRUCTURE OF THE DEFENSE MARKET, 1955-1964 (Durham: Duke University Press, 1967); Logistics Management Institute, DEFENSE INDUSTRY PROFIT REVIEW, 1967; and General Accounting Office, Report to the Congress, DEFENSE INDUSTRY PROFIT STUDY, 17 March 1971.

Weidenbaum found that in the 1962-1965 period, defense firms had a profit-to-net-worth return (the P/W ratio) of 17.5 percent, compared to 10.6 percent for an average sample of comparable nondefense industrial firms. Baldwin found a similar, albeit smaller, disparity in the P/W ratio between defense and commercial firms—in 1962, about 12.5 percent to 9.8 percent. The Logistics Management Institute found a secular decline in the profits-to-total-capital-investments ratio (where total capital investment = equity + long-term debt), from 10.2 percent in 1958 to 6.9 percent in 1966. The General Accounting Office study, analyzing firms doing both defense and commercial work for the years 1966-1969, concluded that the profits-to-total-capital-investment ratio was less on defense work than on commercial work (11.2 to 14.0 percent) and that the profits-to-equity-capital ratio was about the same for defense and commercial work (21.1 to 22.9 percent).

The disparities in the findings of the above studies are due partly to the differences in sample size (for example, Weidenbaum surveyed 6 firms; the General Accounting Office, 74 firms), differences in the years in which profits were analyzed, and differences in the data base (for example, Weidenbaum used public published data; the Logistics Management Institute used data furnished by contractors on request).

All four studies concluded that for defense work, the profits-as-a-percentage-of-sales ratio never went higher than 6 percent and usually hovered closer to 3-4 percent.

18. See the testimony of Robert N. Anthony in THE ACQUISITION OF WEAPONS SYSTEMS, Hearings before the Subcommittee on Economy in Government of the Joint Economic Committee, 91st Congress, 2nd Session, Part 2, pp. 440-46; and GAO DEFENSE INDUSTRY PROFIT STUDY, pp. 34-50.

19. See the testimony of A.E. Fitzgerald in THE MILITARY BUDGET AND NATIONAL ECONOMIC PRIORITIES, Hearings before the Subcommittee on Economy in Government of the Joint Economic Committee, 91st Congress, 1st Session, Part 2, pp. 595-607.

20. Testimony of Gordon Rule, Director, Procurement Control and Clearance, Navy Material Command Headquarters, in THE ACQUISITION OF WEAPONS SYSTEMS, Part 1, p. 191.

21. See Packard's Statement for a full description of his reforms.

22. Testimony of Robert N. Anthony in THE ACQUISITION OF WEAPONS SYSTEMS, Part 2, p. 444. A Defense-Industry Advisory Committee, chaired by Dr. J. Ronald Fox, former Assistant Secretary of the Army for Installations and Logistics, had recommended to former Deputy Secretary Packard that contractor capital investment be considered in award decisions. The indications are that the recommendation will be implemented.

23. See General Accounting Office Report to the Congress, FEASIBILITY OF USING "SHOULD COST" CONCEPTS IN GOVERNMENT PROCUREMENT AND AUDITING, in THE ACQUISITION OF WEAPONS SYSTEMS, Part 2, pp. 405-38.

24. See Packard's Statement and "Memorandum of Deputy Secretary of Defense David Packard, 28 May 1970, RE Policy Guidance on Major Weapon System Acquisition," in POLICY CHANGES IN WEAPON SYSTEM PROCUREMENT, pp. 313-15.

25. For a defense of TPP, see Robert H. Charles, "The Short, Misunderstood Life of Total Package Procurement," INNOVATION, April, 1971. For a critique, see Albert J. Gravallese, "An Evaluation of the Total Package Procurement Concept," Master's Thesis, M.I.T., June, 1968; and Logistics Management Institute, TOTAL PACKAGE PROCUREMENT CONCEPT; SYNTHESIS OF FINDINGS, June 1967.

26. Other factors were responsible for the C-5A's difficulties, including Lockheed's bad management and its highly optimistic bid (even in spite of TPP). The fact still remains, however, that everyone initially thought that the C-5A was an "off-the-shelf" item and therefore did not anticipate the technological effort subsequently required. See Berkeley Rice, THE C-5A SCANDAL (Boston: Houghton Mifflin, 1971).

27. See Packard's Statement, p. 15.

28. Quoted in POLICY CHANGES IN WEAPON SYSTEM PROCURE-MENT, 42nd Report by the House Committee on Government Operations, December 10, 1970, p. 7.

29. See Packard's Statement, pp. 28-29.

11 Multinational Corporations and Military-Industrial Linkages

Jonathan F. Galloway

The top defense contractors have significant assets in foreign countries. The top U.S. based multinational corporations are also among the top defense contractors. These corporations are generally in oligopolistic industries. Corporations in oligopolistic industries feel a necessity to expand their investments and sales, either in order to guard against relative losses in position to other enterprises in the industry, or to gain relative to these competitors. It thus may be postulated that there are relationships between being a firm in an oligopolistic industry, seeking to expand sales and direct investments abroad, and seeking to expand sales to the U.S. government. For those interested in reordering the priorities between America's military overinvolvement abroad and her underinvolvement at home,[1] it becomes necessary to understand the obstacles to choice which vested interests in certain industries present.

Of the top one hundred Department of Defense (DOD) contractors in FY 1971, thirty-nine were also multinational corporations; this means that they held equity interests in manufacturing enterprises located in six or more foreign countries at the end of 1963, such equity in each case amounting to 25 percent or more of total equity (Vaupel and Curhan: 3).[2] More significantly, among the top twenty-five contractors, which accounted for 51 percent of prime contracts in 1971 and were by and large the same firms that were in the top twenty-five category in the late 1950s (Yarmolinsky, 1971: 251), thirteen were multinational enterprises in the above sense. These thirteen accounted for twenty-five percent of all prime contracts. The top multinational DOD contractors— Lockheed, General Dynamics, and General Electric—had over 13 percent of the contracts amounting to over $4 billion in sales. If complete information on the international operations—sales, profits, investments, etc.—of the one hundred top defense contractors were available, one would have a clear picture of their dependency on foreign economic involvements. Then, with the data on their dependence on the governmental market at hand, one could determine what the interests of these firms were and are. Whether their economic interests determined or in some ways influenced the course of American foreign policy would then be the succeeding question. Unfortunately, although there is much data on the operations of the top defense contractors, especially in light of the studies by the Joint Economic Committee and the General Accounting Office (U.S. Congress, 1968 and 1969), there is no comprehensive data on the international

267

operations of American-based multinational firms. However, with the selective data that is now available, one can begin to make some interesting observations and speculative propositions concerning military industrial linkages with American-based multinational corporations.

Before plunging into this labyrinth, one must briefly consider what is meant by the military-industrial complex, for the explicit linkage of the international operations of the nation's largest corporations with prime military contracts may evoke the image of a pervasive economic and/or military elite controlling American foreign policy. The concept of the military-industrial complex has been subjected to diverse definitions and interpretations of its essence, origins, and solutions to the problems its existence creates. Scholars have argued about the validity of power elite, ruling class, pluralist, bureaucratic, and other models of military-industrial relationships. Rather than dismissing some models and seeking one correct theory of the military-industrial complex, as has been recently attempted (Lieberson, 1971; Slater and Nardin, 1971), this author prefers to view the military-industrial complex as an overarching concept like power, the state, or war. It is a general phenomenon which is composed of pluralist, elitist, and other elements *depending on the issue area.* All the views proposed seriously may be describing part of the beast we call the military-industrial complex, and they may be partially valid depending on the issue areas involved—foreign aid, arms sales, the strategic arms race, cost overruns, violence, genocidal wars, etc. It is true that the subtheories of a general theory need to be tightened up, but they do not need to be discarded. However, such a general theory will not be attempted here, for our interest lies in examining economic and political data concerning multinational corporate aspects of the military-industrial complex, rather than all the data of a political, economic, sociological, and psychological nature.[3]

Therefore, let us now return to the analysis of the extent of the convergence between DOD contractors and the American-based multinational enterprise. After this examination, there will be an analysis of the consequences of the linkages that exist for several issue areas. Specifically, we shall suggest and assess the validity of several hypotheses relating the operations of multinational firms in certain industries to (1) the incidence of war and the threat of force; (2) the growth of military aid and sales programs; (3) arms races; (4) a common defense market in the North Atlantic area; and (5) the energy crisis. These hypotheses are speculative and are deduced from the macro-data assembled below rather than induced from decision-making studies, etc.

With the selective information that is now available, it can be said that there are four types of defense contractors evaluated from the perspective of their sales abroad[4] to their sales to the government and the domestic commercial market (see Table 11-1). There are those firms such as General Electric and ITT which are significantly dependent on sales abroad and military sales. On the other hand, there are those firms like Lockheed and McDonnell-Douglas which

Table 11-1

Military Sales and Foreign Sales as Percent of Total Sales of Selected U.S. Firms

Firm	Fortune Rank, 1971	Military Sales[a]	Foreign Sales[b]
General Motors	1	2	14[c]
Standard Oil (N.J.)	2	2	68
Standard Oil (Calif.)	12	N.A.	35[f]
Ford Motor	3	3	36
Chrysler	7	4	21[cd]
IBM	5	7	30[d]
ITT	9	19	47
General Electric	4	19	18
RCA	18	16	6[g]
Lockheed	31	88	N.A.
AT&T (Western Electric)	10	9	N.A.
Goodyear Tire & Rubber	19	0[e]	30[d]
General Tire	128	37	N.A.
McDonnell-Douglas	45	75	N.A.
TRW	75	11[e]	22[e]
North American-Rockwell	39	57	N.A.

[a]1960-67 Department of Defense, as quoted in Melman (1970:77-78).

[b]1967 as found in Rose (1968:100).

[c]Excludes Canada.

[d]Includes export sales from the U.S.

[e]Data compiled from Department of Defense 100 companies list for FY 1970 and 1970 company reports.

[f]Excludes western hemisphere.

[g]1965 as found in Weisskopf (1972:433).

N.A. Not available. In all cases author estimates less than 5 percent.

are more dependent on the government than GE and ITT but less dependent on international operations. Thirdly, there are those firms which, although they are large defense contractors, depend very little on their sales to the government or abroad. AT&T, for instance, was the third largest contractor in FY 1971, having $1.2 billion in sales, but this amounted to only 5½ percent of Bell's total sales. Internationally, one may get an idea of AT&T's relative interests by pointing to the fact that the company has several hundred million in assets abroad and $54 billion at home. Fourthly, there are those firms like Standard Oil of N.J., Ford, and Goodyear which have significant sales abroad but whose sales to the government are less than 5 percent. From this breakdown into four types of DOD contractors, one can see that there is no one-to-one relationship between dependence on the governmental market and the international market.

In line with this observation, Murray Weidenbaum, Assistant Secretary of the Treasury, reminds us that we must avoid thinking of the top military contractors as a group possessing similar characteristics and behavior (1969: Ch.2). He contends that the giants of American industry do not dominate the governmental market. Rather, it is the medium-sized firms which receive the largest share of orders. Thus, it is not GM, Ford, Standard Oil of N.J., which are the core of the military-industrial complex, but Boeing, Lockheed, Hughes Aircraft, and North American-Rockwell, for the former have assets over $1 billion each but receive 25 percent of the DOD contracts, while the latter have assets of $250-$999 million and receive 50 percent of the contracts.

It can be argued that this aggregate comparison ignores the question of what percent of sales and profits are due to defense contracts. While Lockheed may be 90 percent dependent on government sales, if GE, ITT, and RCA, are approximately 15-20 percent dependent on sales to the government, presumably they could not lightly afford to lose approximately one-fifth of their business. Also, it may be that these firms are even more dependent on governmental policy, for if they are significantly dependent on three marekts—governmental, foreign, and domestic civilian—it stands to reason that their managements or "technostructures" will be interested in preserving the dynamic equilibrium between these markets. If policies which keep the equilibrium between these markets are upset, then the consequences for the firm may become so imponderable that they are unacceptable.

Radical analysts of U.S. foreign policy (Magdoff, 1969; Tanzer, 1971) have developed this proposition. They point out that the conventional wisdom that the U.S. trade accounts for only about 7 percent of GNP overlooks the fact that the GNP measures goods and services, while the services part of the economy is dependent on the goods production sector. Magdoff (1969) and Tanzer (1971) argue that military expenditures and exports have exceptionally large ramifications on the capital goods industry, "which historically has been the crucial transmission mechanism for boom and bust in the U.S. economy. Thus, while military expenditures plus exports amount to only 15 percent of the GNP, together they account for a share of the total output of most capital goods firms which ranges between 20 and 90 percent" (Tanzer, 1971:71). Furthermore, the overlay of 20 to 50 percent of demand from military purchases and exports probably accounts for the major share of profits in many crucial industries (Magdoff, 1969:190-191). The argument is then made that the economy requires increasing amounts of raw materials which must be imported, e.g., oil, chrome, cobalt, and bauxite. It is pointed out that the U.S. is becoming increasingly dependent on the rest of the world for these and other raw materials and fuels, for the prospects of technological substitutes for essential raw materials themselves depend on other raw materials. For instance, if aluminum and steel are interchangeable for some purposes, one can substitute bauxite and iron for each other, but if the supplies of each are located abroad, an economy is not self-sufficient.[5]

Another tendency which points to a close interconnection between firms and both the governmental and international markets, concerns the dynamics of particular sectors of the economy, rather than the size of firms or their relative assets and profits in different markets. That is, particular industries may be more dependent and become increasingly more tied to international financing and centralization of capital. It has been widely postulated that the advanced sectors of the economies of the world, i.e., computers, electronics in general, and chemicals, are becoming increasingly multinational in character..If multinational corporations dominate in growth sectors of the economy concerned with increasingly sophisticated technologies, then in the era of the qualitative arms race it will be the multinational firms and the multinational consortiums of government and business that will supply the defense needs of states. It may be postulated that to the extent that multinational corporations, which are either under the influence of foreign nations or are not under the control of nations at all, are supplying some of the defense needs of a state, then military defense in that state is being multinationalized. In fact, while it is often said that multinationalization of production is least apt to occur in military areas because no country wishes to be dependent on foreign interests for its defense, it is actually the case that cooperative projects in Europe have occurred more in the military than the civilian sphere (Behrman, 4). Examples of this can be seen in the Multi-Role Combat Aircraft (MCRA), the Anglo-French Jaguar, the Franco-German Alpha Jet, the Hawk ground-to-air missile, the NATO air defense ground environment, etc. And these ad hoc programs for single weapons systems may be replaced by a more thoroughly integrated defense market in Europe. Francois Duchene, for instance, predicts that "the aerospace industry, which accounts for almost 40 percent of arms spending, looks like it is being reduced to perhaps three major European consortia in a couple of years' time" (1971:80). Furthermore, the European defense market is partially controlled by American companies, as can be seen from Table 11-2. In addition, if one examines the licensing stage of the movement towards multinationalization rather than the ownership stage, one also sees a high degree of linkage (Harlow, 1967).

Multinational and Defense Industry Linkages

The above information indicates that the phenomenon of close military-industrial relationships is not only an American phenomenon but a European and Japanese one as well. The consequences of this growing penetrated system of international military production will be analyzed below, but before turning to this task let us examine the American situation more closely. We can discover by relating the top defense industries to the top multinational enterprises that the following industries are found in each category: transportation (including automobiles and aerospace) rubber, oil, electronics, and chemicals (see Table 11-3).

Table 11-2

U.S. Ownership in Selected European Defense Firms

Country	Firm	U.S. Interest (Percent)
Belgium	Bell Telephone Manufacturing Co.	ITT 100[a]
France	Bull General Electric	GE 50[a]
	Societe Nationale d'Etude et de Construction de Moteurs d'Aviation (SNECMA)	Pratt & Whitney 10[b]
Germany	Messerschmitt-Bokon-Blohm (MBB)	Boeing 8.9
German-Dutch	Vereinigte Flugtechnische Werke-Fokker (VFW-Fokker)	United Aircraft 13.5[c] Northrop 10[c]
Italy	Aernautica Macchi	Lockheed 20[b]
	Selenia	Raytheon 45[a]
Spain	Construcciones Aeronauticas	Northrop 24[b]

[a]Harlow (1967:11, 6, 38, 67).

[b]Veron (1971a:26).

[c]Aviation Week & Space Technology (1972:34, 41).

Aerospace is America's largest manufacturing industry, but it is the least multinational of the industries that coincide as being both multinational and defense contractors. Only four of the 187 multinational enterprises in the Harvard study (Vernon, 1971b:14) are aerospace firms, whereas in any given year approximately 20 of the top DOD contractors are in the aircraft industry and about 15 in the missile business. However, as Horst demonstrates, the largest firms in any industry are apt to be multinational (1972:8) and the top aerospace DOD contractors are all in the Fortune list, most being ranked in the first hundred. Nevertheless, there are several reasons why aerospace firms do not have many production facilities abroad: the cost of transporting finished products is low; very few foreign governments produce their own aircraft so there are usually no tax or quota obstacles; and the U.S. government's subsidies in R&D and capital expenditures make the U.S. an ideal place to do business. However, recently the rise of competition in the world aerospace market and the decline in sales to the domestic military market have affected the weight of these factors. The industry is becoming increasingly dependent on exports, which went from $1,726 million in 1960 to $3,400 million in 1970 and accounted for approximately 14 percent of total sales of $24.8 billion (Aerospace Industries Association of America, 1971:2). In addition, as Table 11-2 indicates, several top aerospace firms have considerable direct ownership in some of the top European defense industries. The industry thus is considerably more multinational than it was in 1963, the year on which the Harvard study bases its definition. However,

Table 11-3
A Rank Order Comparison of Defense Linked and Multinational Industries

DOD[a] (SIC No.[b])	Total Contracts[c]	Multinational[d] (SIC No.[b])	Sales Abroad[e]
Transportation Equipment[f] (37 & 1925)	16.2	Petroleum refining (29)	20.0
Electrical Machinery (36)	7.3	Transportation equipment (37)	14.5
Ordnance, Except Guided Missiles (19)	4.7	Chemicals and allied products (28)	10.2
Nonelectrical Machinery (35)	1.3	Nonelectric machinery (35)	8.2
Instruments and Related Products (38)	1.1	Food products (20)	5.4
Primary and Fabricated Metals (33 & 34)	0.9	Electrical machinery (36)	5.3
		Primary and fabricated metals (33 & 34)	4.7
Petroleum Refining (2911)	0.6		
Chemicals and Allied Products (28)	0.4	Paper and allied products (26)	2.5
Fabricated Rubber Products (3069)	0.2	Rubber products (30)	2.1

[a]1968 data on shipments to DOD (Department of Commerce, 1970: 8-10).

[b]SIC No. is Standard Industrial Classification number used by Department of Commerce.

[c]Prime contracts and subcontracts for 1968 in rounded billions of dollars. Total of this sample is $32.6 billion as compared to $33.4 billion for all U.S. industries.

[d]1968 data on sales of foreign manufacturing facilities of industries included in this study compared with manufacturing sales of all U.S. foreign direct investors (Department of Commerce, 1972a: II, 3).

[e]1968 sales of foreign subsidiaries in billions of dollars. Total of this sample is $72.9 billion as compared to $79.7 billion for all U.S. foreign direct investors.

[f]This category includes the following industries: aircraft ($7.1 billion), aircraft engines and parts ($2.9 billion), aircraft propellers and parts ($2.2 billion), ship building and repairing ($1 billion), trucks (over $100 million), and complete guided missiles ($2.9 billion). Note: SIC No. 1925 is complete guided missiles which is not included in multinational category.

there is no inevitability in this movement. The industry favors increased support from and participation by the government so that it will not have to form consortia with foreign interests, but if this is not forthcoming, greater denationalization of the aerospace industry will probably occur (Harr, 1972:270). In any case, while the almost total dependence of the aerospace industry on governmental sales is perfectly apparent, it may be said that dependence on foreign sales has been increasing and there exists an infrastructure for further movement towards multinationalization of production.

Another industry which ranks quite high on the Department of Defense prime contract list (Department of Defense, 1971), the Harvard Multinational Enterprise list (Vernon, 1971b:13-14), and the Fortune 500 list (1971) is the

Table 11-4

A Comparison of Government (DOD) Sales, Foreign Sales, and Domestic Sales in Six Industries (Billions of Dollars)

Industry	Government $	(DOD) %	Foreign[a] $	%	Domestic[b] $	%	Total $	%
Aerospace[c]	17.5	(14.6)	71	3.4	14	3.9	15	24.8	100
Electronic[d]	11.5[e]	(11.1)	46	3.6	15	9.7	39	24.8	100
Automobile[f]	1.3[e]	(1.1)	1	18.6	20	72.1	79	92.0	100
Oil[g]	0.9[e]	(0.8)	2	20.0	43	25.5	55	46.4	100
Rubber[h]	0.4[e]	(0.3)	4	2.5	26	6.7	70	9.5	100
Chemicals[i]	1.1	(0.3)	2	14.0	31	30.0	67	45.1	100

[a]The data in this column do not necessarily distinguish between foreign subsidiaries sales and export sales. Thus, there are no exact data for industries at large on their stages of multinationalization.

[b]Arrived at by subtracting foreign sales and government sales from total sales.

[c]1970 data from Aerospace Industries Association of America (1971-72).

[d]1970 data from Standard & Poor's Industry Surveys (May 20, 1971:E11-E29).

[e]Exact figures are available for DOD sales, FY 1971 (with the exception of oil, FY 1967). It is assumed that military sales account for 85 percent of all government sales.

[f]1969 data from Automobile Manufacturers Association (1971). DOD sales calculated on the basis of the top four auto companies. Foreign calculated on the basis that export sales were 4.1 billion and subsidiary sales 14.5 billion in 1968.

[g]1966-68 data. Sales to DOD are the FY 1967 combined sales of seven oil companies on DOD list. Foreign sales are the 1968 sales of foreign manufacturing facilities as estimated by Department of Commerce (1972:II, 3). Total sales are for 1966 (Vernon, 1971b:14).

[h]1970 data from Standard & Poor's Industry Surveys (August 12, 1971:R191) for six rubber companies. The foreign sales are estimated on the basis that foreign sales of affiliates of Firestone, Goodyear, and Uniroyal have been 25, 30, and 75 percent, respectively.

[i]1970 data on total sales and exports from Standard & Poor's Industry Surveys (August 19, 1971:C23). 1970 data on government sales from Department of Commerce (1972b:8-9). 1968 data on sales of foreign subsidiaries from Department of Commerce (1972a: II,3). Of foreign sales $3.8 billion were exports; $10.2 billion those of foreign subsidiaries.

automobile industry. This industry ranks number one on the multinational list, number three on the defense list, (see Table 11-4) and the companies in this industry number at the top of the Fortune list.

For the industry as a whole in 1969, total sales were $92 billion, divided between $73.4 billion in the domestic market and $18.6 billion in the foreign market (see Table 11-4). But the top firms were nore dependent on the international market and productive system than was the industry at large. In 1970, 19 percent of General Motors' net earnings came from abroad, while 32.4 percent of its manufacturing was abroad. (The usual earnings abroad are approximately 8 percent, but strikes caused a dramatic upsurge in 1970. This fact may show the reliance of this company on the international market as a safety valve.) In the same year, Ford derived 24 percent of its total income from outside the U.S. and Canada, while 30.6 percent of its manufacturing was abroad. Turning to the DOD list (1971), of the top four automobile firms, three were in the top twenty-five list of Department of Defense contractors—GM 17, American Motors 20, and Ford 24 for Fiscal Year 1971—while Chrysler was 33. From this information and Table 11-1 we can see that, while the Big Four automobile corporations are in the DOD top 100 list and thus tied into the governmental market to some degree, they are more dependent on the international market. (However, this does not tell us about profits in the two markets, as profit figures are amalgamated and are often questionable.)

Closely tied to the successes and failures of the automobile industry is the rubber industry. Of the largest four rubber companies, B.F. Goodrich, Firestone, Goodyear and Uniroyal, two are on the DOD top 100 list—Goodyear 52 and Uniroyal 66.[6] Uniroyal is also dependent on the international market, for in 1970 75 percent of its earnings came from foreign operations. Goodyear is expanding its foreign operations, which account for about 30 percent of its sales and income. An estimated 25 percent of the consolidated sales of Firestone is derived from abroad. B.F. Goodrich, the smallest of the Big Four, is also expanding its operations abroad (Standard & Poor's Industry Surveys, 1971:R-185-R186).

In the case of the oil companies, we find that four of the largest five are on the DOD top 100 list, but all four number below twenty-five. Standard Oil of N.J. is 27, Standard Oil of California is 38, Mobil is 55, and Texaco is 44, while Gulf is not listed and sells only about 1 percent of its total products to the government. Thus, as with the automobile and rubber industries, we may conclude that the oil industry is more dependent on the international market than the governmental market.

The electronics industry, on the other hand, is more equally dependent on the governmental and international markets. Almost half of all electronic business has been with the government during the last seven years. In 1970, the industry made total shipments of $24,290 millions, and $11,687 millions went to the government (Standard & Poor's Industry Surveys, 1971:E3). The principal electronics companies—GE, ITT, Litton, RCA, Sperry Rand, Texas Instruments, and Westinghouse Electric—are all top defense contractors, all but Texas Instruments being in the top twenty-five. Several of these companies do substantial business abroad, too, and are expanding their operations. For instance, GE does about 19 percent of its business with the government and 18 percent abroad.

The chemical industry is similar to oil, rubber, and automobiles in being slightly defense linked but significantly multinational. In 1970 total sales were $45.1 billion (Standard & Poor's Industry Surveys, 1971: C23). Of this amount, only $1.1 billion was sold to the Federal government, over half going to the AEC and $274.1 million to the DOD. (Department of Commerce, 1972b: 8-9). On the other hand, exports were three times as much as sales to the government, amounting to $3,826 millions (Standard & Poor's Industry Surveys, 1971: C23), and sales of foreign subsidiaries were even greater amounting to $10.2 billion in 1968 (Department of Commerce, 1972a: II, 3). Looking at the top eleven chemical firms in terms of 1970 sales, however, we find that five of them were also prime defense contractors for FY 1971, these being Olin 30, FMC 37, Hercules 40, Thiokol (W.R. Grace) 43, and Du Pont 46. Furthermore, each of these five is a multinational enterprise according to the Harvard definition (Vaupel and Curhan, 1969: 6-8). Therefore, while the linkage of the whole chemistry industry to the DOD is slight, some top firms in the industry are somewhat dependent on defense contracts. But these five firms are not in the top 25 on the DOD list, as is the case with three of the top four auto companies.

Having briefly surveyed the above six industries, let us further clarify the relations between the governmental/military, foreign and defense markets. For this purpose, Table 11-4 indicates the relative dependence of each industry on sales (not profits) in the three markets. We see that the electronics industry fits into the first category of those developed from the data in Table 11-1, i.e., the industry is significantly dependent on foreign and military sales, bearing in mind that it is the top firms in terms of the Fortune list that are most apt to be in each category. The aerospace industry appears to be moving from the second classification of large governmental dependence, small foreign to the first. The automobile industry is in the fourth category being a top defense industry from the point of view of the DOD list but not from its own sales perspective, while at the same time being considerably dependent on foreign markets for sales. Also, the oil refining, rubber and chemical industries are in the fourth category of small government dependence, large international.

Issue Areas and Multinational-Military Linkages

In this brief survey we have treated these six industries as separate entities. This is only a first step in beginning to understand the dynamics of the governmental and international markets in our advanced technological society. While in earlier days one could distinguish industries and neatly identify firms within each economic grouping, in postindustrial society industries tend to merge, aerospace with electronics, oil with coal, computers with everything. Furthermore, corporations become conglomerates and joint ventures increase. In 1969, according to the Federal Trade Commission (1970), 4,550 firms disappeared through acquisition and the number of new domestic and foreign joint ventures rose to 204, a 21 percent increase from 1968. Correspondingly, there is a rising tide of concentration in the economy. The share of assets held by the 100 largest corporations of 1968 exceeded that held by the 200 largest in 1950. Not surprisingly, in spite of the antitrust laws, interlocking management between corporations has also increased. This concentration can work to lessen competition and increase oligopolistic pricing and buying practices. The dynamics of technological change may require that industries become increasingly interdependent, although they do not necessarily require an increasing concentration of capital and management. However, both processes have occurred, and they have significant impacts on policy at home and abroad.

Thus, we live in an era of complex and constant change and incoherent transitions. The firm has an interest in controlling the potentially disastrous consequences of unforeseen changes. The distinctions between war and peace, public and private, domestic and foreign policy, economics and politics, are breaking down. The center will not hold; but the firm involved in the sinews of these transformations wishes to survive and prosper. Thus, it is going to be more active in attempting to influence policy. Consequently, it is not appropriate to overlook the connections between the multinational corporation, which tends to be a giant of American industry, and the military or governmental market. The interconnection between the two spheres may have important consequences on such issues as: the incidence of war, foreign aid, arms sales abroad, the arms race, the prospects for a common defense market in the Western world, apartheid, government subsidization of research and development, the administration of the antitrust laws, pollution control, unemployment policies, campaign spending, balance of payments, the future structure of the international monetary system, and policies for the energy crisis. As Nathaniel Samuels, the Deputy Undersecretary of State for Economic Affairs, has said, "It becomes difficult to know where business ends and foreign policy, political and economic, begins" (1970).

Let us briefly examine several of the above policy areas to see how firms and industries which have high stakes in both the governmental market and the international economy may influence and benefit from policy decisions. George Modelski (1971) states that the evidence at hand "does not support the case for the existence of strong links between multinational business and war and military activities." To support this proposition, he demonstrates that in the 65 major armed conflicts for the period 1945-1970 there were relatively few instances of direct participation by multinational business. Secondly, the evidence confirms the conventional wisdom that multinational business avoids areas of political instability for the numbers of subsidiaries of worldwide firms is much greater in areas of low conflict. Thirdly, Modelski demonstrates that there is no one-to-one relationship between being a multinational firm and being a top defense contractor. The data at hand, however, may force us to make conclusions which are not entirely warranted. Since World War II, there have been at least eleven nonmajor armed conflicts which have been associated with the activities of multinational firms—the CIA-sponsored coups in Iran in 1953, in Guatemala in 1954 and 1963, and in Bolivia in 1971, in addition to the major instances which Modelski mentions: Indonesia, Malaya, Algeria, Katanga, the

Suez crisis, the Nigerian civil war, and the policies of the United States towards Castro's Cuba. In addition, the interests of multinational firms have been involved in trouble areas where the threat of force has affected the policies of foreign governments, e.g., the ITT/CIA/Chile case (Johnson, Pollock, and Sweeney, 1972). But by its very nature the role of subversion in the overthrow or maintenance of governments unfriendly or friendly to the interests of "private enterprise" cannot be thoroughly documented. These operations can theoretically be operationalized, but unless there are more Ellsbergs, Andersons, and Rosses and Wises, we shall only see some trees and not the forest, assuming that there is a forest.

The issue of whether overt military force or the threat of force has been brought to bear on foreign governments in the direct interests of multinational corporations is only part of the problem, however. In what economic areas, e.g., tax policy, antitrust legislation, compensation for nationalization, etc., have the interests of multinational firms been served even if we lack complete data on the policy process during which particular decisions were made? Further, how have multinational enterprises influenced international organizations like the World Bank, the International Monetary Fund, and the Organization for Economic Cooperation and Development? One might hazard to make the proposition that while the multinational firm favors corporatism at home—("socialism for the rich, free enterprise for the poor" (Mitchell, Chap. 4)—they often favor free enterprise abroad because of the structure of the market, i.e., they are more equal than their competitors.

While it is true that the attention of multinational firms has shifted in terms of the numbers of subsidiaries and the value of investments from the poorer countries to the developed world, this does not mean that worldwide firms are not just as dependent on less developed countries as previously; perhaps more so. One has to analyze the situation qualitatively as well as quantitatively. What matters for determining interdependence is not the ratio of direct investment abroad to direct investment at home, GNP/trade ratios, etc., but as Richard Cooper (1972:179) points out, "the *sensitivity* of economic transactions between two or more nations to economic developments within these nations." Thus, if the investments in Europe of U.S. firms depend on the supply of raw materials or agricultural products from less developed countries, then, even if the stakes in Europe are greater, the stakes in the poorer countries are crucial. For instance, approximately 25 percent of U.S. direct private investments in Europe are in oil. These operations depend on oil imports from the developing world. Consequently, it is not very enlightening to separate the two areas of investment if there are such essential linkages between them.

Modelski's third argument carries weight and is the subject of the analysis at the beginning of the paper. Not all multinational industries are top defense industries. One thinks of chemicals and food products. Not all top defense industries are multinational industries. One thinks of the construction and ship-building industries. Furthermore, some major industries are neither top defense industries nor multinational in character. One thinks of the steel industry. However, there is enough overlap between the two categories in the aircraft, oil, electronics, rubber, and automobile industries to make the question of multinational corporate involvement in the military-industrial complex interesting, challenging, and heuristic. In addition, as Modelski points out, the giant firms of the economy are apt to be both major defense contractors and worldwide companies. This fact reminds us of the necessity of analyzing the increasing concentration of corporate power mentioned above.

Military Aid and Sales

Let us now briefly consider the interconnections between foreign aid, defense business, and multinational enterprise. The defeats on October 29, 1971 and July 24, 1972 of foreign aid in the Senate were not just short-term losses for the enlightened long-range interests of the United States, but for the short-term interests of certain military contractors. The aid program provides about $1 billion in sales annually for U.S. manufacturers and gives shipping companies about one-fourth of their total revenue for exports. The 1971 rejection of foreign aid eliminated, for a time, DOD plans to award the following contracts: $175 million to McDonnell-Douglas for aircraft, $116 million to GE for aircraft engines, $61 million to Lockheed for aircraft and maintenance services, $89 million to Bell Helicopter for helicopters, and $10 million to Chrysler for vehicles. (Wall Street Journal, 1971). Furthermore, the Joint Economic Committee found that while the military assistance program allotted for FY 1970 totaled $409 *million*, the real total military assistance grants were at least $2.9 *billion*. And Senator Fulbright (D.-Ark.) has introduced a table showing more than $6.9 billion in military sales and assistance for FY 1971, while the estimated total since 1945 comes to about $175 billion (U.S. Congress, 1971:4-5, 50). What explains this huge program which is increasing, and should increase more, given the presuppositions of the Nixon Doctrine? Conventional amoralistic theorizing about world politics has resulted in such normative-empirical propositions as "every country must (in the present international system) be accorded the right to define its national security needs as it thinks fit" (Gray, 1972:155). This type of reasoning determines supposedly correct conclusions which consider arms sales and aid a necessary evil because of the competitive dynamics of the international system. But, while emphasizing political explanations which explain everything in general and nothing in particular, these commentators see a certain part of this competition as economic, involving beneficial multiplier effects upon the national economy, contributions to the balance of payments, dependence upon foreign sales for economic-scale production runs, and increased employment and profits (Gray,

1972:168; Stanley and Pearton, 1971:7, 71-72). Therefore, a complete explanation for arms sales and aid abroad involves political economy and the dynamics of political, oligopolistic, and technological imperatives. While such an explanation cannot be offered here, some data and explanations relating to the linkage of multinational corporations with prime military contractors will be presented.

The most common explanation from the government has been about the need to offset the adverse balance of payments situation. Also, the administration reasons that if the United States does not sell arms, other countries will. But the Senate Foreign Relations Committee posits another explanation:

If the United States were to lose its entire arms market in the underdeveloped world the impact on our overall balance-of-payments accounts would be small. Therefore, our justification for such sales must be based on the other considerations, such as influencing the development of local military elites or helping a country resist the threat of external aggressions. (Melman, 1970:94)

If one relates this justification for the arms sales policy to the stated objectives of the aid program in assisting the establishment of private enterprise economies in the underdeveloped countries, one can reasonably conclude that there is a self-reinforcing relationship between military contractors and American-based multinational corporations. The relationship is even closer, of course, if the two roles converge in the same company. Table 11-5 gives us some indication of the corporations involved in arms sales overseas, and eight of these sixteen firms are on the Harvard list of multinational enterprises. Furthermore, 20 of the top 25 DOD contractors for FY 1971 were also on the list of major U.S. suppliers of weapons and equipment for the military assistance grant aid and sales program, and 11 of these 20 were on the Harvard multinational enterprise list (U.S. Congress, 1971:57). Taking the total population of arms manufacturers, it has been found that the DOD has encouraged 1,480 out of some 1,500 total to sell abroad (Stanley and Pearton, 1971:89).[7]

In addition, there is a close relationship between these sectors of the American economy and the ruling elites in many less developed states. These elites are tied into an international division of labor which by and large promotes the unbalanced economic "growth" of their countries at the expense of dynamically stable political and social modernization (Galloway, 1971:15-18). The imperative of this relationship is profits. As the profits in the defense market, figured on the basis of equity, are enormous, so are the profits on investments abroad—at least in the Third World. Between 1950 and 1965, U.S. firms invested $23.9 billion abroad, while income amounted to $37 billion. Nine billion dollars of the 23.9 billion was invested in the Third World, but $25.6 billion of the $37 billion in profits came from the less developed countries, where the profit rate by regions in the 1965-68 period was: Africa, 21 percent; Asia and the Middle East, 31 percent; and Latin America, 13 percent. This is to be contrasted with a 7-percent return in Canada and Europe (DuBoff, 1971:119). This data on profits should be related to Magdoff's analysis

Table 11-5

The Leading American Manufacturers in Arms Sales Overseas 1962-66[a] (In Millions of Dollars)

Manufacturer	Weapons	Sales (July 1962-66)
General Dynamics Corp.[b]	F-111A aircraft	$1,072.0
	Tartar missiles	34.4
Total		1,106.4
Lockheed Aircraft Corp.[b]	P-3A aircraft	23.5
	F-104 aircraft	527.1
	C-130 aircraft	409.3
Total		959.9
McDonnell Aircraft Corp.	F-4 aircraft	703.0
Lockheed-General Dynamics (joint venture)	Polaris missile system	427.0
Northrop Corp.	F-5 aircraft	355.0
Bath Iron Works-Defoe Shipbuilding Co. (joint venture)	Guided missile destroyers	277.0
Martin Marietta Corp.[b]	Pershing missile	253.0
Raytheon Co.[b]	Hawk missile	231.8
FMC Corp.[b]	M-113 personnel carrier	166.8
Chrysler Corp.[b]	M-60 tank	154.2
Sperry Rand Corp.[b]	Sergeant missile	149.7
Ling-Temco-Vought, Inc.	F-8E aircraft	66.0
General Motors Corp.[b]	155-millimeter howitzer	56.5
Boeing Co.	C-135F aircraft	53.0
Pacific Car & Foundry Co.	175-mm gun	38.7
Grumman Aircraft Engineering Corp.	8-2E aircraft	23.3
Total		$5,020.9

Source: Defense Department data.

[a]Reproduced from BUSINESS WEEK, 3 December 1966 (Stanley and Pearton, 1971:71).
[b]On Harvard list of multinational enterprises (Vaupel and Curham, 1969:6-8).

(1969:191), which posits that the major share of profits for certain American industries comes from the demand for military goods plus exports.

Arms Race

Related to the question of arms sales abroad is the arms race, at the nuclear level, with the Soviet Union[8] and now China, and at the conventional level, both with these two states and even our own allies, in the context of using arms sales and aid abroad to preserve regional balances of power. The Vietnam War, costing $30 billion a year at its peak, used only $2 billion of this for advanced weapons. With the decline in the Vietnam budget to around $8 billion for FY 1972 and in spite of SALT I, a great part of the excess has been used on new weapons systems—ABM, MIRV, Trident, B-1, etc. The research, development, and deployment of these weapons systems is justified by the need to preserve peace from a position of strength. It appears that the arms race is being fueled by the necessity to negotiate from strength at SALT II. This maxim—negotiate from strength—obviously cannot be followed by both sides. Its application has led cynics to conclude that we should abandon multilateral or bilateral attempts at arms control. Then we would not need to negotiate from strength, and thus could cease the deployment of new weapons systems. This is just logic, however, and to be sane in a world of madmen is a kind of insanity, as Rousseau suggested. Perhaps I.F. Stone is closer to the truth when he says, "Arms spending is a form of welfare for the rich; it may be a poor creator of jobs, but it is a major producer of profits" (Stone, 1971). In fact, while defense contractors have often pointed to low profits for military hardware when figuring profits as a percent of sales, the General Accounting Office has found in a study of 146 such companies that pretax profits as a return on equity capital have been 56.1 percent (Time, 1971:70). Thus, while war, or at least general war, itself is antithetical to the interests of multinational enterprise as it was to high finance in the 19th century, the perpetuation of various arms races seems quite functional.

Common Defense Market

Another issue area related to the linkage between the multinational corporation and the defense contractors concerns the possibility of a common defense market for the western world. As this author has argued elsewhere (1971:13-15), the North Atlantic region may be integrated into a pluralistic security community but this may be characterized by what Lowi calls "interest group liberalism," a mixture of capitalism, statism, and pluralism leading to a corporate state (1969:29, 84). In relation to the internationalization of defense production within NATO, the Senate Foreign Relations Committee has seen "the defense common market as little more than an arena for arms competition between resentful pygmies and an affable giant" (U.S. Congress, 1971:19). However, this political image of the NATO market was more true in the late 1950s than the 1960s or early 1970s; and, furthermore, related to arms sales abroad rather than the multinationalization of war materials production. By the late 1960s the image of U.S. hegemony had blurred with the waning of bipolarity. The decline in arms sales for the U.S. in the markets of its own developed allies has been replaced by an increase in joint procurement arrangements, especially among the less wealthy states—Belgium, The Netherlands, and Italy (Harlow, 1967:I, 26).

In addition, the declining power of the U.S. was witnessed, insofar as the multinational firm is concerned, by increased European competition, not only in Europe but in Latin America and the Middle East (Hymer and Rowthorn, 1970).

From today's perspective, the seeds of a truly international defense productive process are seen in the multinational ownership of different European defense contractors (see Table 11-2). These firms and consortia may be the base of a supranational corporatism with all the movements towards a westernized global culture that have been posited (Osterberg and Ajami, 1971), but including, in addition, certain military aspects of western culture that are not so civilized—institutionalized, structural violence, technological warfare, etc. If this development occurs, one arena of conflict in the world will not be between developed states and multinational corporations, since the personnel and value frameworks in each will be interchangeable, but between Western culture and the excluded—the wretched of the earth.

The Energy Crisis

The relationship between the military and foreign markets of certain multinational industries and companies also affects U.S. policies for the energy crisis and pollution. An oil company beset with pressures abroad for nationalization and greater profit sharing, and problems at home involving the energy crisis and pollution, will have to pay greater attention to the interlocking relationships between these problems. Oil, which now provides 45 percent of U.S. energy requirements, will be a commodity increasingly imported from abroad as domestic supplies decline and energy demands soar. Natural gas provides 31 percent of U.S. energy needs but the domestic reserves are approaching depletion. Coal, which at present provides 20 percent of energy demands, can last 650 years, but coal is linked to the pollution problem and is itself becoming increasingly involved in foreign trade. Nearly $1 billion was derived from coal exports in 1970 (U.S. News & World Report). It is clear that the future growth and composition of the nation's energy requirements will severely affect the prospects of important industries, among them the oil, automobile, and aerospace industries. As these sectors are at present so dependent on commodities which are increasingly being imported, it stands to reason that firms in these industries will have an interest in trying to affect foreign policies involving these commodities. Furthermore, the defense of the country is intimately connected with these industries. It would seem, therefore, that one could posit a growing link between defense, energy, pollution, and foreign policy issue areas.

Conclusions

Having briefly examined several of the issue areas that will be influenced by a convergence of the multinational enterprise with the military-industrial establishment, let us now conclude this article by focusing and summarizing the arguments and then considering the options available for restructuring U.S. national priorities. It has been postulated that certain—but not all—major industries and the large corporations in these industries are dependent on the equilibrium between the defense market, foreign markets, and the civilian market at home. To the extent that one market declines or is saturated, these firms and industries have an interest in expanding into the other markets. Furthermore, oligopolistic industries have a vested interest in seeing all markets grow. Currently, companies in the advanced defense sector of the economy are seemingly pressed to the wall by three factors: severe dependence on unpredictable technological innovations, extensive working capital requirements, and the leveling off of orders in the domestic defense market. (This last factor has become less important, given the FY 1973 DOD appropriations increase.) Military-oriented firms are thus impelled to seek out other markets; some of these will be abroad. These firms are required to search for more sources of capital; some of these will be abroad. And these industries are prone to search for increased governmental backing for technological breakthroughs, which will in some cases lead to the multinationalization of the research and development process.

Under what conditions might these pressures for further ties between multinational corporations and industries and military-oriented firms and industries become weaker, both in the United States and the North Atlantic area? The answer to this question depends on the view one has of the structure of power in these areas. Is it elitist, a system of oligopolistic pluralism? A detailed description of the structure of power in each issue area and the relation of one issue area to another cannot be offered in this essay. Therefore, let us be more general than precise. Nationalism may counter the tendencies towards the internationalization of capital, production, and research and development, especially insofar as the defense functions of sovereign states are concerned. On the other hand, huge capital requirements for advancements in military technology may encourage states to forego ideas of national self-sufficiency in arms in the era of the qualitative arms race. Furthermore, the internationalization of production in certain civilian areas, e.g., commercial airplanes, computers, nuclear energy, will have inevitable military side effects. Thus, these two considerations may cause one to foresee a partial multinationalization of the defense infrastructures of certain countries, especially those in the North Atlantic area. The market for the products of this new productive center will not be restricted to this area; many less developed states will continue their conventional arms races with the leftover inventories of the great powers.

Through which conscious policies might the United States affect these economic and military developments? The ways to control for the increasing interdependence of the multinational enterprise and the military-industrial establishment depend on one's perception of the increasing internationalization of the productive process and the nature of military industrial linkages. At the beginning of this essay, it was argued that all views of the military-industrial complex are probably at least partially correct, depending on the issue area. There may be a convergence of causes—economic, political, psychological and social, pluralist and elitist—leading to fighting among powers and the perversion of priorities the United States now faces. Consequently, a solution to the problem of the military-industrial complex may involve attacking it on all fronts and in all issue areas. However, the arguments in this essay have drawn attention to the multinational political/economic aspects of military-industrial relationships because of the inherent tendencies of oligopolistic corporations, the mad momentum of technology product cycles, and the concerns of vested interests. Let us therefore restrict our examination to several solutions, liberal, radical, and conservative, to the problems resulting from the intermeshing of military-industrial concerns with the multinational corporation.

Liberals might posit at least five ways to control the disadvantageous consequences of this new convergence. In the first place, there might be increased public control over the corporation through requiring federal incorporation, as suggested by Ralph Nader (1971). Secondly, one might nationalize the defense industries as suggested by John Kenneth Galbraith (1969). Thirdly, a renewed emphasis on conversion might be undertaken. Fourthly, one might suggest that there be an international code for multinational enterprise and perhaps an international charter for firms (Reisman, 1971; Ball, 1968). And lastly, liberals and conservatives might put their hopes on further sessions of SALT as well as conventional arms limitations negotiations. What is the likelihood that any or all of these policies will be adopted? It does not seem that corporations will be required to receive federal charters. What chance is there that Congress will change incorporation laws against the intensive lobbying efforts of corporate lobbyists? Secondly, nationalization of defense industries seems too much like socialism and communism to be politically feasible. Thirdly, conversion has by and large failed in the past. It does not meet the requirements and habits of those businesses dependent on the defense market (Weidenbaum, 1969; DuBoff, 1972). The fourth suggestion—an international code for business—is too legalistic an approach to regulation. As with the Corrupt Practices Act domestically, it may be predicted that there will be many loopholes and too little enforcement. The last approach seems to present the greatest hope for controlling arms sales and races, given the success of SALT I. On the other hand, these talks have slowed down part of the strategic arms race; they have not ended it, and ironically, the gambit of negotiating from strength means that arms control negotiations are being used to fuel the arms race.

It thus appears that liberal solutions for the control of the military-industrial linkages of the multinational corporation will not be adopted, or, if they are, they will not have any systematic impact on the direction of American policies. The domestic corporation is often superior to the power of states in the U.S.

federal system, and, in a world of states, the multinational corporation may act likewise, pursuing its equivalent of policies of divide and rule, balance of power, and containment and expansion towards at least the majority of the 135 states in the world. The nation state, especially the superpowers, will not be replaced, but the dynamics of the oligopolistic, technological, and profit imperatives could very well make multinational enterprises their coterminous and contiguous partners. It is thus incorrect to stress a conflict between states and corporations or economics and politics, for what we are viewing is a penetrated system of symbiotic relationships where the important boundaries are increasingly functional rather than territorial. Liberal politics may only be able to tinker with the machinery of this emerging world order, unless a series of incremental changes can eventually create a systematic transformation of the priorities towards more socially useful programs in transportation, housing, health, etc.

What can be said of the radical solutions to the disorders and incoherence of our times? Radical solutions may work, but we shall never know, for it is even less likely that there will be revolution in the United States than there will be a federal chartering of corporations. Thus, we and the world may be stuck with a system of priorities which emphasizes arms races, arms sales, energy crises, pollution, etc., for the rest of the century. Political scientists should criticize these developments and not succumb to individual relativism on moral questions or to the amoralistic theorizing which characterizes much of the discipline. To the extent that this normative position and its empirical supports are correct, then scholars could have some small, hopefully cumulative impact on the future priorities of American politics.

Notes

Author's Note: This article was originally presented as a paper at the International Studies Association Annual Convention in Dallas, Texas, March 14-18, 1972. I wish to thank Robert Dixon, Samuel P. Huntington, Edward P. Levine, George Modelski, Steven Rosen, and Wesley B. Truitt for their comments and criticisms on this paper. I alone remain responsible for the analysis in the final version.

1. I believe it is the function of social scientists to make objective value judgments as well as describe, explain, and predict behavior. Thus, I reject the following ethical theories: positivism and cultural relativism, an extreme form of which, individual relativism, seems very popular today. I also reject Fundamentalist ethics and accept a type of contextual ethics.

2. This definition is useful in that the Harvard Business School has identified and done extensive research on 187 such firms. However, the definition is static and does not give a developmental, process-oriented view of the evolution of the multinational firm evolving through the following stages:

(1) exporting to foreign countries, (2) establishing sales organizations abroad, (3) licensing patents to foreign firms, (4) establishing foreign manufacturing facilities, (5) multinationalizing management, and (6) multinationalizing ownership (Jacoby, 1970:38).

3. For a brief introduction to a general theory, see (Galloway, 1972). I am working on another version of this paper, focusing more on a general theory of the military-industrial complex.

4. Data on sales abroad by firms do not necessarily distinguish between export sales and sales by foreign subsidiaries. Export sales may be a stage on the way to establishing subsidiaries abroad but this is not necessarily the case.

5. The American economy each year consumes $100 million worth of 26 types of raw materials of which there are inadequate domestic supplies, and the list continues to grow (Harr, 1972:268). The argument can be made that the United States will have to become increasingly involved in the states in which such raw materials are found.

6. General Tire & Rubber, the smallest of the rubber companies, is the largest DOD contractor, 32, due to the contracts of its subsidiary, Aerojet General Corp.

7. While after World War II, 70 percent of arms sales abroad were handled by the government rather than privately, this distinction breaks down if there is interpenetration of personnel and attitudes in the two roles (Stanley and Pearton, 1971:85, 92).

8. As the Senator Beveridge of the 1970s, Senator Tower (R.-Tex.) has argued that we need to develop every weapon on the horizon. Otherwise, "an aggressive Soviet diplomatic and economic program backed by nuclear superiority could rob the United States of access to foreign markets and raw materials" (1972:43).

References

Aerospace Industries Association of America, Inc. (1971) AEROSPACE FACTS AND FIGURES 1971/72 (New York).

Automobile Manufacturers Association, Inc. 1971 AUTOMOBILE FACTS AND FIGURES (Washington, 1971).

Aviation Week & Space Technology. April 24, 1972.

Ball, G.W. "Making World Corporations into World Citizens." WAR-PEACE REPORT (October, 1968).

Behrman, J.N. "Multinational Production Consortia: Lessons from NATO Experience." Washington: Department of State Publication 8593 (August 1971).

Cooper, R. (1972) "Economic Interdependence and Foreign Policy in the Seventies." WORLD POLITICS 24, No. 2 (pp. 159-81).

Department of Defense. "Top 100 Defense Contractors." (Washington, 1970, 1971).

DuBoff, R.B. "Transferring Wealth from Underdeveloped to Developed Countries via Direct Foreign Investment: Comment." THE SOUTHERN ECONOMIC JOURNAL 38, No. 1 (1971), pp. 118-21.

_____. "Converting Military Spending to Social Welfare: The Real Obstacles." THE QUARTERLY REVIEW OF ECONOMICS AND BUSINESS 12 (Spring 1972), pp. 7-22.

Duchene, F. "A New European Defense Community." FOREIGN AFFAIRS 50 (October 1971), pp. 69-82.

Federal Trade Commission. News Release. May 13, 1970.

Fortune "The Fortune Directory of the 500 Largest Industrial Corporations." (May 1972), pp. 188f.

Galbraith, J.K. "The Big Defense Firms are Really Public Firms." FORTUNE 50 (November 16, 1969), pp. 162-76.

Galloway, J.F. "Multinational Enterprises as Worldwide Interest Groups." POLITICS AND SOCIETY 2 (November 1971), pp. 1-20.

_____. "Multinational Corporations and the Military-Industrial Complex." A paper presented at the International Studies Association Annual Convention in Dallas, Texas. March, 1972.

Gray, C.S. "Traffic Control for the Arms Trade." FOREIGN POLICY 6 (Spring 1972), pp. 153-69.

Harlow, C.J.E. "The European Armaments Base: A Survey." London: The Institute for Strategic Studies. 2 parts (June, July, 1967).

Harr, K.G., Jr. "Technology and Trade." VITAL SPEECHES OF THE DAY. (February 15, 1972), pp. 267-70.

Horst, T. "Firm and Industry Determinants of the Decision to Invest Abroad: An Empirical Study." Cambridge. Harvard Institute of Economic Research Discussion Paper Number 231. March, 1972.

Hymer, S. and R. Rowthorn "Multinational Corporations and International Oligopoly: The Non-American Challenge." Pages 57-91 in C. Kindleberger (editor) The International Corporation. Cambridge: M.I.T. Press, 1970.

Jacoby, H.H. "The Multinational Corporation." THE CENTER MAGAZINE 3 (May 1970), pp. 37-55.

Johnson, D.L., J. Pollock and J. Sweeney "ITT and the CIA: The Making of a Foreign Policy." THE PROGRESSIVE. (May 1972), pp. 15-17.

Lieberson, S. "An Empirical Study of Military-Industrial Linkages." AMERICAN JOURNAL OF SOCIOLOGY 76. (January 1971), 562-84.

Lowi, T.J. THE END OF LIBERALISM. New York: W.W. Norton, 1969.

Magdoff, H. THE AGE OF IMPERIALISM. New York: Monthly Review Press, 1969.

Melman, S. PENTAGON CAPITALISM. New York: McGraw-Hill, 1970.

Mitchell, W.C. PUBLIC CHOICE IN AMERICA. Chicago: Markham, 1971.

Modelski, G. "Multinational Business: A Global Perspective." A paper delivered at the American Association for the Advancement of Science, 139th Meeting. Philadelphia, 1971.

Nader, R. NEW YORK TIMES. (January 24, 1971): Sec. 3, pp. 1, 9.

Osterberg, D. and F. Aami "The Multinational Corporation: Expanding the Frontiers of World Politics" THE JOURNAL OF CONFLICT RESOLUTION 15, No. 4 (December 1971), pp. 457-70.

Reisman, M. "Polaroid Power." FOREIGN POLICY 4 (1971), pp. 101-110.

Rose, S. "The Rewarding Strategies of Multinationalism." FORTUNE (September 15, 1968).

Samuels, N. "American Business and International Investment Flows." DEPARTMENT OF STATE BULLETIN. (January 12, 1970).

Slater, J. and T. Nardin "The Concept of a Military-Industrial Complex." A paper presented at the 67th Annual Meeting of the American Political Science Association, Chicago. September, 1971.

Standard & Poor's Industry Surveys (1971).

Stanley, J. and M. Pearton THE INTERNATIONAL TRADE IN ARMS. New York: Praeger, 1971.

Stone, I.F. BI-WEEKLY. October 4, 1971.

Tanzer, M. THE SICK SOCIETY. New York: Holt, Rinehart and Winston. Chapter 3.

Time. March 8, 1972. "Shipments of Defense-Oriented Industries, 1968." Series: MA-175(68)-2. November 20, 1970.

Tower, J.G. "The Danger of Complacency." The New York Times, June 28, 1972.

U.S. Department of Commerce. THE MULTINATIONAL COPRORATION. Washington: Government Printing Office, 1972a.

_____. "Shipments of Defense-Oriented Industries, 1968." Series: MA-175 (68)-2. November 20, 1970.

_____. "Shipments of Defense-Oriented Industries, 1970." Series: MA-175 (70)-1. June 1972b.

U.S. Congress Joint Economic Committee. Subcommittee on Economy in Government. Hearings and Report, Economics of Military Procurement. 90th Congress, 2nd Session, and 91st Congress, 1st Session.

_____. Joint Economic Committee. Subcommittee on Economy in Government. Hearings, Economic Issues in Military Assistance. 92nd Congress, 1st Session, 1971.

U.S. News & World Report (August 24, 1970; November 9, 1970; February 1, 1971; March 29, 1971).

Vaupel, J.W. and J.P. Curhan THE MAKING OF MULTINATIONAL ENTERPRISE. Boston: Harvard Graduate School of Business Administration.

Vernon, R. "Multinational Enterprise and National Security." London: The Institute for Strategic Studies Adelphi Papers Number 74, 1971a.

_____. Sovereignty at Bay. New York: Basic Books, 1971b.

Wall Street Journal November 3, 1971.

Weidenbaum, M. "The Transferability of Defense Industry Resources to Civilian Use." Pages 101-113 in R.E. Bolton (editor) DEFENSE AND DISARMAMENT. Englewood Cliffs: Prentice-Hall, 1966.

_____. THE MODERN PUBLIC SECTOR. New York: Basic Books, 1969.

Weisskopf, T.E. "United States Foreign Private Investment: An Empirical Survey." 426-35 in R.C. Edwards and others (editors) THE CAPITALIST SYSTEM: A RADICAL ANALYSIS OF AMERICAN SOCIETY. Englewood Cliffs, New Jersey: Prentice-Hall, 1972.

Yarmolinsky, A. THE MILITARY ESTABLISHMENT. New York: Harper & Row, 1971.

12

Methodological Problems in Research on the Military-Industrial Complex

Edward P. Levine

Investigation of the military-industrial complex and of alternative models of defense policy formation is passing from a stage of polemical exposition to one of more rigorous empirical research. As is common in a field newly subjected to systematic inquiry, initial research efforts have been characterized by difficulties and disagreements over the proper questions to ask, the means by which hypotheses are to be tested, and the validity of indicators that are often improvised for the occasion. Jerome Slater and Terry Nardin detail elsewhere in this volume the confusion and imprecision that have typified much of the MIC debate. The present essay will suggest that unnecessary adoption of such early MIC formulations by empirical researchers has hindered the development of a logical and coordinated program of studies. We then will examine some questions of research design and measurement raised by recent MIC studies and suggest some paths for future research.

The Problem of Research Orientation

How does one determine the manner in which to research a question? Very often the answer is that one has been inspired or challenged by a particular theory—in this case by a particular vision of the military-industrial complex. This approach is useful if the theory is sufficiently well developed to provide explicit guidance regarding questions to ask, quantities to measure, and results to expect. Thomas Kuhn's description of "normal science" emphasizes the necessity of highly developed theories as paradigms influencing almost all empirical research (1962, pp. 29-34). But if we are still in a pre-paradigmatic stage—if such theories as "the power elite" or "pluralism" do not tell us how to conduct our research, but rather how to interpret whatever results we obtain—then we would be wise to seek other guides for our investigation of defense policy formation.

Current would-be paradigms have led to little more than quibbling over interpretations. Witness, for example, the different conclusions drawn by Stanley Lieberson in this volume and by Adam Yarmolinsky (1971, pp. 60-65) from the same information about industrial hiring of retired military officers. While the former author accepts the data as a sign of increased military-industrial ties, the latter emphasizes the larger proportion of retirees employed in other

291

fields and attributes the rise in military hiring mainly to an idiosyncratic occurrence: the retirement, for the first time in significant numbers, of Air Force and Navy officers familiar with guided missiles.

The continuing debate over how to investigate the role of Congress, and the paucity of well designed research in this field, suggests a lack of the research guidance commonly associated with successful, and even many *un*successful paradigms. *The* ideological guidance provided by current MIC theories is evident in Stephen Cobb's original conjecture that congressional support for defense appropriations was due to log-rolling in the absence of a countervailing "peace lobby" (1969, p. 368). One who doubted MIC theories could instead contend that congressmen's ideological predispositions or perceived public opinion were the crucial factors.

Current research on the military-industrial complex may be viewed as an imperfect attempt at *black-box* analysis. If we treat the process that results in defense policy as a *system*, then it is an imperfectly understood system whose outputs are more accessible than are its internal workings. As researchers we are nearly in the classic black-boxing situation, in which, "the system already exists (in reality) but nothing is known about it and its structure cannot be determined directly" (Klir and Valach, 1967, p. 29). Any version of the military-industrial complex is in turn an hypothesized *sub-system* which one may feel is crucial to the functioning of the larger defense policy system. MIC theories are in fact black-box hypotheses; this follows from the observation by Slater and Nardin that MIC researchers have tended to formulate their ideas by reasoning over the occurrence of diverse defense-related phenomena such as high defense budgets and the number of former military officers employed by industiral firms, rather than by analyzing information on policy formation processes.

We shall argue presently that this black-box hypothesizing is premature. In addition, it has tended to focus our attention upon a sub-system whose internal workings are even less accessible, and therefore probably less understood, than the workings of the overall defense policy system. Little wonder, then, that we find disagreement over what the military-industrial complex encompasses, or that researchers tend to study each peripheral (but more familiar) aspects of the hypothesized sub-system as congressional voting or stock market averages. Given our currently inadequate knowledge about defense and foreign policy making in general, we might be well advised to investigate this larger system, rather than trying to fathom an ill-defined sub-system whose relevance is not yet conclusively established.[1]

In formal black-box analysis, the investigation of the unknown system is based upon a definition of the system in terms of its *external quantities* (i.e., inputs and outputs) and their *level of resolution* (the precision and frequency of measurement).[2] Only when we have specified and analyzed these "observables" can we attempt to understand the structure and internal behavior of the system. Theories of the military-industrial complex, by contrast, define the defense policy system in terms of its *universe of discourse*: the system's elements and the couplings between those elements. Such an approach is wasteful; hypothesized MIC sub-systems are likely to be tested one at a time, while research based upon observable external quantities could test among a wide variety of possible MIC structures at one time. Moreover, an hypothesized sub-system may remain implicit in the research design, rather than being openly stated and tested. Conclusions supporting stated hypotheses regarding the sub-system may then be drawn despite the possibility that the sub-system itself is irrelevant to an understanding of defense or foreign policy formation. Thus studies focusing upon stock market averages assume—but may not demonstrate—that investors who buy common stock, or perhaps the business sector of the economy, can usefully be treated as an element in a defense or foreign policy system. Similar assumptions underlie any study of public opinion on defense issues. Definition of hypothesized systems or sub-systems in terms of their observed quantities, and attention to the need for each element of one's system to have some relationship to the system's output (Klir and Valach, 1967, p. 29), ought to reduce substantially the risk of focusing our research upon questions that fail to contribute to the identification of MIC behavior or structure.

Another major step in black-box analysis is to determine the range of values that each observed quantity can exhibit. This information, compiled for all the external quantities of a system at a given level of resolution, is known as the *activity* of the system (Klir, 1970, p. 41). We need to know the activity of a system because it forms our data base for determining the system's *behavior* (its set of *time-invariant relationships* between the various measurable quantities). In compiling a system's activity we make the multiple observations that are prerequisite to the discovery of even partially time-invariant relationships between stimuli and responses. But this operation also performs a more immediate function, in that it alerts us to quantities that do *not* vary (given our level of resolution and the period of time over which we make our observations). A quantity may fail to vary because it is in fact unrelated to the other quantities in the hypothetical system, or because the system is in a steady state in which other variables are also invariant. Or the behavior of the system may be so complex, perhaps due to time lags or threshold effects in relationships between quantities, that our choice of resolution level and time period yield insufficient data for a complete analysis of those relationships. Lieberson suggests that the peacetime defense budget as a proportion of gross national product has been rather invariant over substantial periods of time. A study confined to such a period—and this includes any study of the Eisenhower or Kennedy administrations—will be either at a severe disadvantage due to its inability to distinguish between competing explanations of this stability in a major variable, or else forced to use a more volatile variable such as the defense proportion of total government spending.

Studies of congressional voting on defense policy before 1968 have been especially hampered by the lack of variance in their main dependent variable. Cobb (1969, p. 360) and Russett (1970b, pp. 46-49) encountered this problem in their analyses of the 89th and 87th Congresses (1965-1966 and 1961-1962). Cobb's response was to concentrate upon general foreign policy issues instead of defense policy, constructing a "jingoism scale" as his dependent variable. This move raised serious questions as to the relevance of his study to any but the most extreme MIC hypotheses, for one could easily envisage a military-industrial complex that had great influence on defense matters without significantly affecting other aspects of foreign policy. Russett compiled a "general defense, east-west relations, and COMSAT" scale which contained very few defense issues. This was justified on the basis of a high rank-order correlation with a "general defense and east-west relations" scale for the 90th Congress (1967-1968) which contained many votes on the defense budget. Russett went on to defend Cobb's jingoism scale as one which "measured essentially the same phenomenon" that Russett had tapped (1970a, p. 288). This reasoning involves a dangerous inferential leap, for the systemic or environmental changes which produced variance in congressional voting on defense issues may also have caused congressmen for the first time to view defense and foreign policy issues as lying on a single dimension, resulting in a spurious correlation between the two scales. Indeed, it seems likely that the Vietnam War and subsequent domestic strife had such an effect upon Congress. The strength of Russett's study must rest upon his analysis of the 90th Congress. Neither he nor Cobb has found a way around the lack of variance in earlier votes on defense issues.

James Kurth's "follow-on imperative" described in this volume is limited by the lack of activity in a major external quantity, the amount of new technology necessary to develop each new weapons system. One would expect this quantity to be rather large at times—e.g., when guided missiles were introduced or when nuclear power was first used for naval vessels. Since Kurth looks only at cases of systems "structurally similar" to those they replace, the follow-on theory has been applied to only a sub-set of the possible states[3] that a weapons procurement system could assume. The findings of Peck and Scherer regarding competitive or non-competitive bidding on "new" versus "evolutionary" weapons systems suggest that the system may look very different under conditions of major innovation (1962, pp. 332-336). This limitation and those which Kurth himself notes indicate that the follow-on theory is an incomplete definition of a weapons procurement system. A full definition of a system in terms of its states must specify all the possible states and state-transitions. This will require a more systematic analysis of the external quantities that now are only implicit in the follow-on approach.

What are the hallmarks of a properly conceived study of the military-industrial complex? It should be an effort to discover the behavior or structure of that sub-system, or else to test explicit hypotheses concerning MIC behavior or structure. The study should define hypothesized systems in terms of external quantities; if sub-systems are to be hypothesized, they should be based upon previous analysis of external quantities and tied explicitly to system outputs. A study of influences upon congressional actions which in turn govern final defense budget figures, with changes in defense policy or budget allocations as our dependent variable, would be an example of research which focused on a sub-system but was properly related to observable system outputs.

Lieberson sticks closely to observed external quantities, examining data from various studies and asking what policy making processes would be consistent with that data. The inconclusive nature of his results serves as a commentary on the sad state of past studies, upon which Lieberson relies for most of his material. More positive success has come from the work of John P. Crecine on defense budget decisions (Crecine, 1971; Crecine and Fischer, 1971). Taking budget breakdowns as the basic data, and using interviews plus the timing of stages in budget formulation to gain insight into the internal behavior of their system, Crecine and his associates have developed a cybernetic model of defense budgeting which performs well for the years 1954-1969.[4] Interestingly, this model does not include a military-industrial complex as an element in the system, although we could see it as an important part of the environment producing inputs into the defense budgeting system. Crecine's budget system is separable from the decision systems concerning weapons programs or the letting of contracts, so there is still much room for MIC theorists—but only if we can demonstrate and analyze relationships between MIC inputs and defense policy outputs.

The Problem of Research Design

If we are to ensure the valid testing of our research hypotheses, three minimal requirements are that they be conditional, empirical, and testable (Isaak, 1969, pp. 80-85). A conditional statement, which takes the form, "if A, then B," is essential to any effort at hypothesis testing. Thus it is not sufficient to hypothesize the existence of a military-industrial complex; some input or output variables must be related to that sub-system. Possible hypotheses in conditional form include, "congressmen from states with major defense installations will support defense spending more strongly than will those from districts less dependent upon DOD money," or "major defense contractors with subsidiaries in foreign countries will obtain more help from the U.S. Government in protecting their overseas investments than will firms which do not have major defense contracts."

All the hypotheses in this volume appear to satisfy the requirement of conditionality. Jonathan Galloway tends to leave some of his hypotheses implicit, however, as in his discussion of arms sales and foreign aid. There the basic hypothesis might read, "if the continuation of military aid is threatened, multi-dimensional corporations interested in preserving their foreign interests will combine with U.S. arms manufacturers to oppose such threats to arms aid programs."

An empirical hypothesis deals with real-world relationships; a non-empirical hypothesis is rooted rather in its own definitions, and therefore cannot be tested empirically. Hypotheses relying upon such basically ideological concepts as "national interest," "aggression," or "imperialism" frequently turn out to be tautological once their authors' definitions of the concepts are inserted.

Michael Reich's argument that "Federal spending on socially useful needs . . . is not a feasible substitute" for defense spending in a capitalist system so long as defense spending opportunities persist rests upon non-empirical bases. Social spending is declared unfeasible because it challenges "the logic of a capitalist economy" or "the very necessity of private ownership and control over production," but these challenges depend upon our accepting Professor Reich's somewhat dogmatic version of capitalism. Moreover, Federal spending is always seen as direct investment, rather than purchasing programs that could involve the private sector of the economy; and Reich qualifies his examples of possible Federal programs with such undefined adjectives as "good," "large," "effective," and "adequate," which leave him the option of rejecting counter-examples on the grounds that they refer to inadequate or otherwise unacceptable programs.

To be testable, an hypothesis must be falsifiable; only a test which *could* reject the hypothesis can be trusted if it fails to do so. This means that we must be able to specify the criteria for rejection of our hypothesis, including the precise break-points in the quantities that would be measured in a test. The testability requirement also implies that concepts in an hypothesis must be independently defined. Otherwise the hypothesis may be tautological; at the least, it will be impossible to isolate the necessarily intercorrelated variables in order to observe the relationship between them.

Those authors in this volume who make an attempt to test their hypotheses are all dealing with propositions that are in fact testable—a welcome sign of the progress that is being made in the study of the military-industrial complex. But the continuing squabble over whether congressional voting is influenced "a little" or "not at all" by defense interests in members' districts suggests that researchers might pay a little more attention to the tradition of specifying one's break-points before the results are in. And although James Kurth's follow-on theory is testable, he is content merely to compare its predictive power to that of some alternative theories. This is an insufficient test, and an unfair one in that perfect prediction of events is an unrealistic expectation for a single-factor theory. A means of testing the follow-on theory will be proposed later in this section.

On the whole, the most recent studies of the military-industrial complex have met these minimal criteria of proper design. Black-box analysis is also consistent with these requirements. Black-box hypotheses are necessarily conditional and empirical, for they relate theorized MIC structure or behavior to observed input and output variables. Such hypotheses should also prove testable, unless the researcher neglects the need for independent definition of variables. And black-boxing does avoid a major source of such neglect, for it concentrates upon explaining observed behavior, rather than sustaining an ideologically-derived vision of the military-industrial complex. Black-boxing does not ensure valid testing in the strong sense that we shall discuss presently. But it does provide a means of avoiding some of the more basic pitfalls in research design, as well as leading us to more fruitful hypotheses in the first place.

In addition to using hypotheses which meet the three standards just discussed, the researcher should also design his investigations so as to obtain valid information on the variables whose relationship he is studying. This task is partly a matter of indicator selection, which will be considered in the next section. It also involves the isolation of research variables from outside influences, so that the *time-invariant* relationships between variables may be determined. This difficult step in black-boxing corresponds to the establishment of what Campbell and Stanley term *internal validity* in an experiment (1966, p. 5). (The *external validity*, or generalizability, of one's results is of less concern to us, although we will take note of it, for studies of the military-industrial complex frequently deal with the whole universe of actors to which we would apply our conclusions.)

True experimental designs ensure internal validity but are nearly impossible to achieve in studies of the military-industrial complex, for such designs demand random assignment of subjects to experimental and control groups. Perhaps one can occasionally achieve randomization—for example, in selecting congressional districts for a constituent letter-writing campaign. But as a rule, congressmen, defense contractors, and the Department of Defense are not open to such manipulation.

Unfortunately, researchers have tended to the opposite extreme, either eschewing any attempt at hypothesis testing or going ahead with what Campbell and Stanley call "pre-experimental" designs. Foremost among these are single case studies and ex post facto experiments. The single case study, even if it incorporates a pre-test, has almost no internal validity. Outside events may have been controlling factors, the subjects may have changed of their own accord due to the passage of time, and so on. Ex post facto experiments, in which the researcher conducts no pre-test but either tries to match his "experimental" and "control" group subjects regarding other possible explanatory variables or conducts a covariance analysis with those variables, fall down because of the probability that many more variables affect both selection into the experimental group and any later differences between that group and the control group. Conclusions in ex post facto research cannot be regarded as experimentally valid, even though one might feel that the researcher has controlled for the most obvious competing explanations of the phenomena under study. Both single case studies and ex post facto experiments also lack any external validity.

Interpretive journalism is usually pre-experimental, as in the case of a study of political pressures applied to senators in the ABM controversy (Miller, 1970). One can document the pressures, but not their effects; for one lacks a "pre-pressure" measurement of each senator's opinions on the issue or a means of eliminating such other variables as the SALT talks or peer group pressure. And the possible control group of un-pressured senators is clearly biased, as we must assume that pressure was applied where it was thought likely to be most effective: to presumed opponents of ABM or waverers, rather than to presumed supporters of the program.

The rival interpretations by Lieberson and Yarmolinsky of trends in industrial hiring of military retirees, which we noted earlier, are based upon similarly non-experimental analysis. Although Yarmolinsky does contrast the success of some firms hiring large numbers of retirees with that of others with contrasting policies, he fails to perform a systematic comparison of the groups or to use both a pre-test and a post-test—which would have resulted in a quasi-experimental design.

Campbell and Stanley propose greater use of several "quasi-experimental" designs which, while not as effective as pure experimental designs, do provide much more protection against the effects of extraneous variables than one finds in pre-experimental research (1966, pp. 34-64). None of these designs offer much hope for external validity, but four designs in particular would promote internal validity in MIC research: time series; multiple time series; the equivalent time samples design; and the non-equivalent control group design.[5]

Using a time series instead of the single pre-test and post-test provides a control over the effects of the selection and testing processes, and (so long as the experimental group remains constant) over those of maturation or mortality among subjects. The design is particularly powerful if one's hypothesis correctly predicts the shape of a curve over time. The major threat to internal validity which this design does not avert is "history," the influence of outside events at the time of the experiment. A control-group time series, used in a multiple time series design, enables us to control for the effect of history even if the control group is not equivalent to the experimental group. An alternative means of controlling for history is to observe the experimental group over time in alternating periods of presence and absence of the experimental variable, in what is called an equivalent time samples design. Thus one might observe congressional votes on similar bills at several times of high public awareness or of domestic apathy. The need for control over other variables and, ideally, randomization of the times at which observations are made makes this a difficult design to use.

The non-equivalent control group design is a useful approach when time series or equivalent time samples cannot be obtained. This use of a control group in an experiment involving only a pre-test and a post-test can control for history and other effects upon the experimental group only to the extent that such factors work equally on both groups. Such a condition is not assured, but care in the selection of a control group—*if* one also includes a pre-test in the design—can go a long way to eliminate major alternative explanations of one's results. The usefulness of even an imperfect control group argues strongly for adapting this design to all our research. The test proposed earlier as an extension of Yarmolinsky's argument would use a design of this type.

James Kurth's test of the follow-on theory, were it conducted more systematically (e.g., with precise breakpoints specified beforehand), would be a time series design in which the research hypothesis was that an impending phasing out of one contract (say, in two years) would produce a change in the dependent variable from "no new contract" to "new contract awarded." This design does not preclude the alternative theory that firms submit bids only when such an impending phase-out exists. We could control for this rival explanation by observing success rates given that the company does bid for a contract, rather than just looking at when contracts are received. If other variables appear stable over the period of our observations, we may construct an imperfect non-randomized version of the equivalent time samples design, in which a company's bidding success rate is observed in alternating periods of prosperity and phase-out. In any case, our test should achieve high internal validity; it would remain low in external validity until replicated for other weapons, types, companies, and time periods.

The Hanson and Russett study of the effect of Vietnam War events upon stock market prices appears to contain neither time series nor a control group. A time series approach would seem desirable in this study, for we know little about either the speed or the duration of the effects that we would expect outside events to have on the market. Control groups of days with similar stock prices (and price trends, if time series were used) would also enhance the internal validity of the research. If Vietnam War events were scaled, we could select days at random for a regression analysis, a study close to the equivalent time samples design. These procedures are difficult, so the reluctance of the authors to adopt them is understandable. Their study is seriously hampered, however, by the questions regarding internal validity which result from the design used. At the least, the study should be redesigned so as to take into account gross economic trends which may influence even short-term fluctuations in stock prices.

Studies of congressional voting patterns, such as those by Russett (1970b) and Cobb (1969), make use of essentially ex post facto designs. The correlations they obtain may be both interesting and insightful, and Russett does weed out some rival hypotheses. But researchers cannot counter all the rival interpretations of their results that an ex post facto approach leaves open. Thus one could argue that pre-Vietnam Congresses were fully under the thumbs of the arms makers, while more recent sessions were deviant due to the exceptional publicity generated by the war and the peace movement. Or one could maintain that congressmen's perceptions of constituent opinion were the controlling factor.

Since a control group for Congress is not readily available, a time series approach may be what is needed. A multivariate study which incorporated outside events as possible predictors of change in congressional support for defense spending would provide a surer test of the Russett and Cobb hypotheses. One logical format for such a study would be a computer simulation similar to that constructed by Crecine and Fischer (1971) with regard to DOD budget requests.

The Problem of Measurement

Our goal in measurement is to determine the value to assign to a particular variable at a particular point in time. There are four criteria by which we might evaluate an indicator used to measure a quantity: validity, reliability, accuracy, and level of resolution. The severity with which we apply these standards is governed by our needs for the purpose of testing a given hypothesis.

When we speak of the validity of an indicator, we refer to the question of whether the indicator is measuring what we want measured. Some variables, such as congressional perceptions of constituent opinion, may be difficult to measure directly. We might therefore knowingly use an indicator of lower validity, such as polling results published in a member's local newspaper. A more insidious problem arises when the researcher is unaware of an indicator's doubtful validity, perhaps because he has not given the matter careful consideration. This occurs most frequently when the researcher has only a sketchy theory, or is attempting only a quick heuristic test of his hypotheses. Then a poor indicator may be presented and accepted as a good one, thereby affecting the validity of later research.

As was noted earlier, there are serious validity questions regarding Bruce Russett's dependent variable for the 87th Congress (1970b). But even for the 90th Congress, in which defense issues do appear on his scale, one can question the validity of roll-call votes as a measure of a congressman's support for an issue. We have much anecdotal evidence that House whips release loyal supporters on some bills so that the members can "create a record" that will please their constituents (Ripley, 1964, p. 574). Moreover, support is a multidimensional phenomenon; the congressman who testifies at a committee hearing cannot be fully described with a voting measure. Voting figures are still less valid as indicators of total congressional support on an issue. In that case, we would be wiser to measure issue outcomes, such as differences between the White House budget for defense and the figure finally appropriated.

Arnold Kantor and Stuart Thorson raise substantial points regarding the validity of James Kurth's indicators for major weapons systems and for contractors. If Kurth were to treat cost as the major indicator of a weapons system's importance, then total contract cost or unit cost (e.g., per airframe) would appear to be valid measures. One way around the inconsistencies in his measure of major contractors would be to define as major contractors all those companies that bid for (and have previously received) a major weapons system contract. Such an indicator could also be used in the test of the follow-on theory which we proposed in the previous section.

A reliable indicator is one which gives us few worries about variability or dishonesty in the collecting or reporting of the information. Roll-call votes may not be valid indicators of overall congressional support for an issue, but they are fairly reliable. Congressional responses to newsmen's questions are probably less reliable measures, although they might be more valid ones. As researchers, we tend to shy away from unreliable indicators, probably because it seems easier to take into account the constant effect of an invalid indicator than to judge the varying effect of unreliability. The importance of reliability therefore lies in our willingness to sacrifice validity for its sake. Reliable indicators of the extent of military-industrial collusion are difficult to find, as Jonathan Galloway notes, because people engaged in such activity are rarely eager to publicize their efforts.

An indicator's accuracy refers to how nearly correct will be the value it assigns to a variable, given its level of resolution and assuming its reliability. Company earnings reports are probably accurate, although not always reliable; their estimates of the cost of producing new weapons systems are traditionally neither accurate nor reliable (Peck and Scherer, 1962, pp. 19-22). Grossly inaccurate indicators are as upsetting as unreliable ones. Slight inaccuracy is common, however, and indicators such as unemployment figures are used by researchers despite the fact that the Bureau of Labor Statistics occasionally has to issue corrections of its own reports.

Let us consider the task of designing an indicator of a company's need for a follow-on contract in James Kurth's theory. Perhaps the most valid indicator would be company executive perceptions of such a need. But political scientists rarely have access to company files, and executives' answers to the question, "Do you need a follow-on?"—or worse, "Did you need a follow-on in May of 1965?"—would probably be unreliable. Sacrificing validity for reliability, we can measure need in terms of the number of months remaining before the scheduled end of production on a current major defense contract which the company has. But if such schedules are frequently changed, as might be the case during war or budgetary retrenchment, then an indicator based upon these plans could be quite inaccurate. Should this potential inaccuracy appear too great, we can fall back on some ex post facto measures. One would be the number of months between the time of bidding for a new contract and the actual end of production on the old one. Another might be the current rate of production as compared to past periods, an indicator which would be valid only if there were characteristic curves in production over time (which would allow us to infer certain perceptions on the part of company executives). The importance of accuracy in production schedules looms large, due to the problems that all the alternative indicators present.

An indicator's level of resolution consists of its precision and the frequency of observation. Many indicators are reliable and accurate but imprecise because they are rounded off, or because they are only ordinal scale. This is especially true of simple scales such as some of those used in the interpretation of events data. Imprecision in an indicator is easily taken into account. Its effect is usually to make us adopt more conservative procedures, and hence to raise the likelihood of Type I error in our research. Some indicators are available in reliable or accurate form, only infrequently. Because our research designs usually specify the frequency of observation necessary to test our hypotheses, we tend to forego validity and precision in order to obtain the required frequency of measurement.

The use of stock market prices by Hanson and Russett is open to severe question on the grounds of validity. It would appear that long-term trends in stock prices are governed largely by the opinions of institutional investors (mutual funds, insurance companies, pension funds, etc.) regarding general economic trends and the future earnings of particular companies—matters often only indirectly related to the Vietnam War. Short-term reactions to world events, on the other hand, may be the result of odd-lot traders, while professionals stay out for a few hours or take the opportunity to reap speculative gains. If one wanted to measure the economic impact of the war, more logical sources would be figures on sales, profits, employment, plant expansion, and so on. But much of this information is available only on a yearly or quarterly basis, a frequency clearly insufficient for the tests that Hanson and Russett wish to run. At this stage of heuristic tests, their decision to adopt an imperfect measure for the concept of business community sentiment is defensible. But we must strive to find (or to invent) more useful indicators which will meet all our criteria rather than presenting us with Hobson's choices.

The data sources available to a student of a military-industrial complex are numerous, but they form a mixed bag. On the business side, they include company figures on profits, sales, stock prices, bond yields, capital investment, employment, the number of high-ranking ex-military officers employed, and the number of registered lobbyists in Washington. But profit and sales figures are rarely broken down into useful categories, the past duties of ex-officers are not listed, and only some congressional lobbyists are registered.

For Congress, we have roll-call and some teller votes, some committee votes, many speeches, and—if we are brave—thousands of bills whose progress we can trace and whose provisions we could codify. The material on committee votes is only for recent sessions, however, and only in incomplete form at that. The executive branch can offer us information on the defense budget and on eventual expenditures, the firms receiving prime contracts and the size of those contracts, weapons inventories, and official foreign and defense policy positions. But the budget information must be gleaned on an agency-by-agency basis if we want material regarding the preparation of departmental requests, the contract announcements rarely mention subcontractors and do not indicate particular plants that will be affected, and official policy statements may correspond only imperfectly to real policy. Finally, we also have domestic and international political events, which can be observed and analyzed. The sophistication of such analyses has been low in the past, with too many unreliable (e.g., overly crisis-oriented) information sources, but this situation appears to be improving markedly. On the whole, our indicators are reliable, accurate, and precise. They are not always frequent enough or really valid enough for use in hypothesis testing on the military-industrial complex.

The data sources that we desperately lack are more easily categorized. We lack process data: interactions between lobbyists and bureaucrats; arguments in congressional committees; the formation of understandings or mutual expectations on the part of diverse actors. We also lack elite perceptions data: congressional opinion; congressional perceptions of public opinion; businessmen's attitudes regarding the proper means of influencing Washington officials; military attitudes towards Congress; and so forth. From the standpoint of black-boxing, we still have little more than inputs and outputs to work with.

In this situation, it is time that we devoted some concentrated effort to the development of new information sources, more valid indicators, and means of manipulating indicators that are already available to us. One valuable source of information which we are just beginning to use systematically is interviews with policy-making actors. Crecine used interviews with Department of Defense officials to establish the sequence of events in formulating budget requests (1971). This enabled him to reject the program budgeting model as a descriptive theory of the defense budgetary process. Similar studies of the program decision process could provide us with information on when and where industrial interests would have to make their inputs in order to influence outcomes. A companion study of lobbying activities by defense businesses and interest groups, and of political processes within armed services committees in Congress, perhaps combining interviews with participant-observation, might then enable us to estimate the effectiveness of influence efforts. Interviews can also be used to enlarge our store of elite perceptions data regarding both particular issues and the political processes through which those issues are handled. Studies of this sort are becoming more common in the comparative politics field, and the work of Bauer, Pool, and Dexter on the politics of the Trade Expansion Act of 1962 (1963) suggests that studies of actor attitudes are feasible here as well. We might even go so far as to institute continuing panel studies to monitor actor attitudes over time.

While some indicators demand new sources of information, we can also create new indicators that would use present data sources. This seems particularly necessary in the area of output variables. Recent work has involved such "new" indicators as the White House budget and changes between that proposed budget and final congressional appropriations. We should codify and perhaps scale non-fiscal outputs as well. Examples would be adoption of aid, trade, or investment policies affecting particular defense contractors, and actions taken to affect procurement or force decisions by our military alliances. As better data sources are developed for events coding, an ambitious output coding project should become much more feasible than it has been in the past.

An important means of making fuller use of existing indicators would be the development of more longitudinal studies. Already in the budgetary field we have realized that predicting a single year's figures is neither as difficult nor as informative as predicting changes over time. The same observation may hold for such diverse dependent variables as congressional votes, program allocations within the Department of Defense, and the dollar value of contracts received by various companies. Insofar as an administration's policies are more clearly reflected in output changes than in output totals, an emphasis upon first differences in output variables would enable us to probe the question of whether military-industrial linkages affect the adoption of new policies or function primarily to support the continuation of current allocations.

Some Convergent Recommendations

The many particular criticisms and recommendations which dot this essay cluster largely around two foci: black-boxing and longitudinal studies. Our call for black-boxing is basically negativistic; it is a call for greater caution, for a retreat from heady hypotheses of particular MIC structures to an emphasis upon defense policy formation in general and especially upon input and output variables in the latter system. Black-boxing is advocated also as a means of restraining ourselves from gross errors in research design, although that danger seems less immediate than the danger of mis-directed research. One root of this methodological conservatism is our lack of information regarding political processes and the attitudes of various actors. These intra-systemic variables seem crucial to any understanding of sub-systems within the defense policy system; until we have developed valid indicators for such variables, it seems doubtful that reliable testing of hypotheses on sub-system behavior or structure will be possible. Hence the key step for those scholars who wish to test theories of specific MIC formulations should be to develop the data sources necessary to such testing. It may be possible at the same time to assemble a set of comparative pre-tested case studies covering a given time period, so that different cases could serve as non-equivalent control groups for the initial testing of particular hypotheses.

Longitudinal studies first drew our attention because of their greater likelihood of exhibiting variance in the quantities we measure. They assume special importance, however, because they are easily adapted to three of four quasi-experimental designs which appear applicable to studies of the military-industrial complex: time series, multiple time series, and equivalent time samples. Moreover, longitudinal studies, being concerned with changes in variables rather than just with values at a single point in time, should result in more powerful explanations of the political phenomena that interest us; values at a given point in time are too often correlated most highly with the previous year's value for the same variable. Studies over time would allow greater use of computer simulation as a mode of testing, and they also would make further use of currently available indicators by concentrating upon first differences in those indicators.

For scholars wishing to engage in hypothesis testing on the military-industrial complex, then, there appear to be two logical paths. One starts from the existing stock of input and output variables and proceeds to a black-box analysis of first differences in those variables, trying to specify (probably in simulations) the gross behavior of the defense policy system and thereby possibly to eliminate whole classes of MIC theories, while focusing attention upon those classes of theories which remain compatible with a growing body of information on budget, program, and contract decisions. The other approach is one of intensive micro-level research into influence processes and actor perceptions, so as to construct the indicators necessary to test more specific hypotheses regarding MIC structure and behavior. When this task of indicator development is completed, the paths may merge—one suspects eventually to the greater benefit of the systems simulators, who will incorporate the new data in more accurate sub-routines. Until that time, the black-box approach will be closer to our data, while the process students strive to create data that will move our hypothesis testing closer to the politics we claim to be studying.

Notes

1. The military-industrial complex is not the only sub-system to be focused upon prematurely. John P. Crecine (1970) raises analogous questions regarding a "politics of education" sub-system in the broader system producing educational outputs.

2. A testbook on systems theory lists the following steps in black-boxing:

1. The external quantities of the system are observed or measured in time at the respective resolution level and all the obtained results are arranged in the form of a single activity or a set of separate activities. Sometimes we can experiment with the external quantities, i.e., we can force some of the quantities to take on certain values and register the response of the other quantities.
2. The obtained activity is processed to discover the time-invariant relations between quantities.

3. The inside of the black-box is investigated (provided that this is possible) in order to obtain as much information about its organization as possible.
4. The permanent behavior is determined or a hypothesis is made about it on the basis of all the obtained results.
5. The organization is determined or a hypothesis is made about it on the basis of the permanent behavior and the other facts known about the system. (Klir, 1970, p. 243)

3. The state of a system is the set of values for all the external quantities of the system at a point in time, given the resolution levels at which the quantities are measured.

4. The Crecine and Fischer model does not handle wartime build-ups with great accuracy, but it performs impressively on peacetime fluctuations in allocations to the various services and budget categories.

5. Campbell and Stanley illustrate these designs as follows:

Time Series	O O O OXO O O O
Multiple Time Series	$\underline{\text{O O O OXO O O O}}$ O O O O O O O O
Equivalent Time Samples	$X_1 O X_0 O X_1 O X_0 O$
Non-equivalent Control Group	$\dfrac{\text{O X O}}{\text{O O}}$

where O denotes an observation and X (or X_1) is introduction of the experimental variable. X_0 denotes controlled absence of the experimental variable.

By contrast, the typical pre-experimental designs are:

Case Studies	X O or perhaps O X O
Ex Post Facto	$\dfrac{\text{X O}}{\text{O}}$

References

Raymond A. Bauer, Ithiel de Sola Pool, and Lewis Anthony Dexter, AMERICAN BUSINESS AND PUBLIC POLICY: THE POLITICS OF FOREIGN TRADE, 1963 (Atherton Press: New York).

Donald T. Campbell and Julian C. Stanley. EXPERIMENTAL AND QUASI-EXPERIMENTAL DESIGNS FOR RESEARCH, 1966 (Rand McNally: Chicago).

Stephen A. Cobb. "Defense Spending and Foreign Policy in the House of Representatives," JOURNAL OF CONFLICT RESOLUTION, 13:3 (September 1969), pp. 358-369.

John P. Crecine. "Defense Budgeting: Organizational Adaptation to Environmental Constraints," in Cornelius P. Cotter, ed., POLITICAL SCIENCE ANNUAL, IV, 1972 (Bobbs Merrill: Indianapolis).

_____. "The Politics of Education: Some Thoughts on Research Directions," Institute for Public Policy Studies Discussion Paper No. 25, 1970 (University of Michigan: Ann Arbor).

_____ and Gregory Fischer. "On Resource Allocation Processes in the U.S. Department of Defense," Institute for Public Policy Studies Discussion Paper No. 31, October 1971 (University of Michigan: Ann Arbor).

Alan C. Isaak. SCOPE AND METHODS OF POLITICAL SCIENCE: AN INTRODUCTION TO THE METHODOLOGY OF POLITICAL INQUIRY, 1969 (Dorsey Press: Homewood, Illinois).

George J. Klir. AN APPROACH TO GENERAL SYSTEMS THEORY, 1970 (Van Nostrand-Reinhold: New York).

Jiri Klir and Miroslav Valach. CYBERNETIC MODELLING (Translated by Pavel Dolan, translation edited by W.A. Ainsworth), 1967 (Iliffe: London).

Thomas S. Kuhn. THE STRUCTURE OF SCIENTIFIC REVOLUTIONS, 1962 (University of Chicago Press: Chicago).

Nathan Miller. "The Making of a Majority," Charles Peters and Timothy J. Adams, eds. INSIDE THE SYSTEM: A WASHINGTON MONTHLY READER, 1970 (Praeger: New York), pp. 158-182.

Merton J. Peck and Frederic M. Scherer. THE WEAPONS ACQUISITION PROCESS: AN ECONOMIC ANALYSIS, 1962 (Harvard University Graduate School of Business Administration: Boston).

Randall B. Ripley. "The Party Whip Organizations in the United States House of Representatives," AMERICAN POLITICAL SCIENCE REVIEW, 57:3 (September 1964), pp. 561-576.

Bruce M. Russett. "Communication," JOURNAL OF CONFLICT RESOLUTION, 14:2 (June 1970), pp. 287-290.

_____. WHAT PRICE VIGILANCE: THE BURDENS OF NATIONAL DEFENSE, 1970 (Yale University Press: New Haven).

Adam Yarmolinsky. THE MILITARY ESTABLISHMENT: ITS IMPACTS ON AMERICAN SOCIETY, 1971 (Harper & Row: New York).

About the Contributors

Robert J. Art is Associate Professor of Politics at Brandeis University. He is the author of *The TFX Decision* and coeditor of *The Use of Force*. His research interests center on international politics and American foreign policy.

Vernon V. Aspaturian is Research Professor of Political Science at the Pennsylvania State University and director of the Slavic and Soviet Language Area Center. His books include *The Soviet Union in the World Communist System, The Union Republics in Soviet Diplomacy*, and *Process and Power in Soviet Foreign Policy*.

Stephen Cobb is Assistant Professor of Sociology at Tennessee State University and director of the Program in Correctional Services. His publications include "Defense Spending and Foreign Policy in the House of Representatives" (Journal of Conflict Resolution, September 1969) and "The Military-Industrial Complex: Elite Domination or the Porkbarrel?" (forthcoming). His area of specialization is political sociology and social problems. He is active in Tennessee politics and was recently a candidate for the State Legislature.

Jonathan F. Galloway is Associate Professor of Politics at Lake Forest College, specializing in international relations. His publications include *The Politics and Technology of Satellite Communications* and "Multinational Enterprises as Worldwide Interest Groups" (Politics and Society, Fall 1971.)

Betty Crump Hanson is Research Associate with the World Data Analysis Program at Yale University, specializing in national security policy. She coauthored a critical introduction to Bruce Russett, ed., *Peace, War, and Numbers*, and is currently engaged in a study of businessmen's attitudes toward the economic consequences of war. Her dissertation (Columbia 1966) was on "American Diplomatic Representatives to the Soviet Union, 1933-1945: A Study of Political Reporting."

Arnold Kanter is Lecturer in Political Science at the University of Michigan and Research Associate in the Institute of Public Policy Studies, specializing in bureaucratic politics and foreign policy. He is coeditor of *Readings in American Foreign Policy: A Bureaucratic Perspective* and author of "Congress and the Defense Budget" (American Political Science Review, March 1972).

James R. Kurth is Associate Professor of Government at Harvard University, specializing in American foreign policy and international relations. He is the author of "A Widening Gyre: The Logic of American Weapons Procurement"

(Public Policy, Summer 1971) and is writing a book on American foreign policy with emphasis on relations with small states and less developed economies.

Edward P. Levine is Assistant Professor of Political Science at Rice University, specializing in international politics. His papers include "Mediation in International Politics" (Peace Research Society Papers, Vol. 18, 1971), which was based on his dissertation in international relations at Yale in 1971.

Stanley Lieberson is Professor of Sociology at the University of Chicago and Associate Director of the Population Research Center. His areas of specialization include race and ethnic relations, demography and ecology, and sociolinguistics. He is the author of *Language and Ethnic Relations in Canada, Explorations in Sociolinguistics*, and coauthor of *Metropolis and Region in Transition*.

Terry Nardin is Assistant Professor of Political Science at SUNY-Buffalo, specializing in international politics and political theory. His publications include *Violence and the State* and "Conflicting Conceptions of Political Violence" (Political Science Quarterly, 1973).

Michael Reich is Assistant Professor of Economics at Boston University, specializing in political economy, inequality, and the public sector. He was editor (1970-72) of the Review of Radical Political Economics. He is the author of "The Economics of Racism" in Gordon, editor, *Problems in Political Economy* and coauthor of *The Capitalist System* and "Capitalism and the Military-Industrial Complex" (Review of Radical Political Economics, Fall 1970).

Steven Rosen is Assistant Professor of Politics at Brandeis University, specializing in research on international political economy and conflict. He is coauthor of *International Relations: A Text* (Winthrop 1973); coeditor of *Alliance in International Politics* and *Testing the Theory of Economic Imperialism* (forthcoming); author of "War Power and the Willingness to Suffer" in Bruce Russett, ed., *Peace, War, and Numbers*, "The Tolerance of Human Life Costs for Foreign Policy Goals" (Peace Research Society Papers, 1971), and "Proliferation Treaty Controls and the IAEA (Journal of Conflict Resolution, 1967); and coauthor of "The Calculus of Cost-Tolerance" in Joseph Ben-Dak, editor, *The Future of Collective Violence*. From 1968-72, he was Assistant Professor of Political Science at the University of Pittsburgh.

Bruce M. Russett is Professor of Political Science at Yale University and director of the World Data Analysis Program. He has held appointments at MIT, Columbia, the University of Michigan, and the Universite Libre de Bruxelles. He is presently Editor of the Journal of Conflict Resolution. His most recent books in international relations and foreign policy include *What Price Vigilance? The Burdens of National Defense; No Clear and Present Danger: A Skeptical View of U.S. Entry Into World War II; Peace War and Numbers* (ed.); and *Military Force and American Society* (coeditor).

Jerome Slater is Associate Professor of Political Science at SUNY-Buffalo, specializing in American Foreign Policy. He is the author of *The OAS and American Foreign Policy* and *Intervention and Negotiation: The United States and the Dominican Revolution*. He was formerly associated with Ohio State University.

Stuart J. Thorson is on the faculty of the Department of Political Science at Ohio State University and is associated with the Polimetrics Laboratory.